D0560449

GOOD AS NEW:

A Radical Retelling
of the Scriptures

Copyright © 2004 O Books
46A West Street, Alresford, Hants SO24 9AU, U.K.
Tel: +44 (0) 1962 736880 Fax: +44 (0) 1962 736881
E-mail: office@johnhunt-publishing.com
www.o-books.net

U.S. office:
240 West 35th Street, Suite 500
New York, NY10001
E-mail: obooks@aol.com

Text: © 2004 John Henson

Design: Andrew Milne Design Limited

ISBN 1-903816-73-4

All rights reserved. Except for brief quotations in
critical articles or reviews, no part of this book may
be reproduced in any manner without prior written
permission from the publishers.

The rights of John Henson as author have been
asserted in accordance with the Copyright, Designs
and Patents Act 1988.

A CIP catalogue record for this book is available from
the British Library.

Printed by Maple-Vail Manufacturing Group, U.S.A.

GOOD
AS NEW:

A Radical Retelling
of the Scriptures

John Henson

A fresh and exciting version of the
Christian Scriptures from the ONE
Community for Christian Exploration

BOOKS

NEW YORK, USA
ALRESFORD, UK

This volume contains most of the books included in what is commonly called the "New Testament." See "Firing the Canon" for an explanation as to the selection of books. The terms Old and New Testament have been used by tradition to describe the first or second parts of the Bible. It's rude to those of the Jewish faith and the terms are misapplied, since in both Hebrew and Christian scriptures "New (Covenant)" refers to a new and radical relationship with God, not to a collection of texts.

Contents

Foreword

What would Christianity look like, what would Christian language sound like, if we really tried to screen out the stale, the technical, the unconsciously exclusive words and policies and to hear as if for the first time what the Christian scriptures were saying? John Henson has devoted much of his life to wrestling with this challenge, and has for many people made those scriptures speak as never before – indeed, as for the first time. Patiently and boldly, he has teased out implications, gone back to roots, linguistic and theological, and re-imagined the process in which a genuinely new language was brought to birth by those who had listened to Jesus because they knew they were in a genuinely new world.

Some of John's versions will startle; but only because we have forgotten what the impact might have been in the ancient world of a small library of books written in the dialect of the streets and shops, with many of the leading characters identified by slightly outlandish nicknames. And also, because we have not much living language left for authority figures, we fail to sense the impact of the images of royalty and so on in the pages of scripture; we need other terms to make them come alive.

John's presentation of the Christian gospel is of extraordinary power simply because it is so close to the prose and poetry of ordinary life. Instead of being taken into a specialized religious frame of reference – as happens even with the most conscientious of formal modern translations – and being given a gospel addressed to specialized concerns – as happens with even the most careful of modern "devotional" books – we have here a vehicle for thinking and worshiping that is fully earthed, recognizably about our humanity. Here are sensitive meditations, blunt and beautiful prayers, familiar hymns made fresh (polished and re-set as John likes to say). The Gospels tell us that Jesus' unprofessional and unreligious audiences heard him gladly: if they are to hear him gladly today, they will need something like John's renderings for this to be plausible. His work is for a large part of the "religious" reading public a well-kept secret; I hope that this book will help the secret to be shared, and to spread in epidemic profusion through religious and irreligious alike.

Rowan Williams, Archbishop of Canterbury

Introduction

Despite the fact that my shelves, and yours probably, are sagging beneath the weight of all the translations of the scriptures that have appeared in the past forty years or so, we still await a version that strikes as a genuinely contemporary version. Life and language move so quickly that it is a matter of running to stay on the same spot, and translators of the scriptures are characterized by care and caution rather than by the need to keep pace. Move on we must, however, if we believe the scriptures have abiding value for every age and culture as a unique record of humankind's adventure with God.

Two things need to be done. In the first place scholars must continue to study the original languages and explore the cultural situations they expressed. This work has been done very well in the past hundred years and there are commentaries full of sound scholastic argument for the probable meaning or meanings of every word of the received texts. Rarely, however, is there total agreement on the precise meaning of any particular passage, only a study of the options. The choice means that the translator can never avoid bias of a sort. An attempt at word-for-word translation of the Greek or Hebrew, even if possible, would not produce clarity but mystery and ambiguity. In order to clarify, the translator must opt, and this accounts for quite conflicting meanings in differing translations, which nevertheless claim to be true translations rather than paraphrases. Did Jesus say to Simon Peter, "Do you love me more than all else?" (*NEB*) or "... more than these others?" (*REV*)? Both are possible, but which you choose will strongly affect the total meaning of the incident recorded. It is of no help to take the line of the *NIV*, which translates "more than these." This allows us to make up our own minds but is of itself meaningless since we are given no clue as to the "these" referred to. Too much of this kind of ambiguity will confuse or bore especially the first-time reader who is seeking meaning not a puzzle. The common distinction made between a translation and a paraphrase is thus a false one. What usually passes for a paraphrase rather than a translation indicates the degree of venturesomeness in elucidating the meaning. This is what most readers want unless they are scholars, in which case they should be directed to the original languages. We need to warn people that no translation or paraphrase is any more than somebody's intelligent, scholarly, inspired, and, one hopes, honest guess. For those who prefer certainty to faith this is a hard pill to swallow. We should always advise the devotee to have at hand at least two translations in order to preserve choice in the matter of interpretation. The work of scholarship must go on in order to check avoidable inaccuracies and to open up the field of options.

The second thing needed is a combination of "human skills." The scriptures were written by real people for real people. We must assume a common humanity between the first writers and readers and ourselves, otherwise we may as well give up from the start. Nobody will communicate anything to anybody. However, within our common humanity people differ. Some people are held to be more "religious." Others are thought to be more down-to-earth. Some revel in wandering through the forests of scholarship and doctrinal dispute, others want to get to the point, otherwise they are not interested. The problem is that those who translate the scriptures have always been religious and scholarly and heavily committed in the matter of doctrine. To such people communicating with the rough and ready is difficult and for many of them it does not occur that they need to try. They translate in the language of an academic elite and assume this is the language that ought to be spoken by everybody else. I remember asking J. B. Phillips in a seminar what was the essential difference between the language of his translation and the language of the *New English Bible*, which had just appeared. He replied, "I read the *Daily Mirror*, the translators of the *New English Bible* read *The Times*." J. B. Phillips produced single-handed the best translation of the twentieth century simply because, at the time, it came nearer than anything else available to the language of the majority of ordinary people. It was thus downgraded in some quarters as a paraphrase, and indeed J. B. Phillips humbly claimed no more for it. Such a view suggested that the other translations were not paraphrases. But who translates more effectively – the one who translates in the language of an enclosed circle or the one who translates in a language understood by everybody?

According to the record of the Gospels, the genius of Jesus lay in his ability to put into language that could be grasped by ordinary folk things that the scribes obscured by their sophistication or pedantry. "He spoke as one having authority, and not as the scribes." The trouble is that Jesus' words and the words of his followers have been translated for us over and over again by those very scribes and Pharisees. "He spoke as one having authority" is ironically, a good example of a scribe-type translation. What someone in the crowds who heard Jesus for the first time would have said would have been something like, "That chap knows what he's talking about!" The question of authority is a scribal question ("By what authority do you do these things?"). Jesus was in the business of making God intelligible and lovable to ordinary people. So what is required to turn our scholarly paraphrases into lively translations is the spirit of the founder, the feeling for what makes contact with Ms. or Mr. Average – imagination and more imagination, based on a common and sympathetic humanity. Imagination is essential for translating and interpreting the scriptures. If you use your imagination you may get it wrong. If you don't use your imagination you are bound to get it wrong!

The *Good As New* version of the early Christian scriptures seeks to be an "inclusive translation" and this means in the first place of those who are neither Pharisees nor scribes. Ordinary people, even those with university degrees, rarely use correct grammar when they speak. The Gospel-writers used the simplest, most straightforward Greek. It is therefore bad translation to put the Gospels into sophisticated English. We avoid descriptions such as "Pharisee," which will require the novice to go to a Bible reference book for an explanation. Instead we seek descriptions which are immediate and require no explanation, such as "one of the strict set." Some words which started off as common, homely words in the original Greek have been allowed to become formal ecclesiastical terms by not being translated but left in Greek. Thus "baptize" for the Greek indicated "dip," but to us it has become exclusively the word for a religious rite, losing its common meaning on the way. When Jesus called Simon "Peter" it indicated something like our "Rocky." Previous translators simply fail to translate and Peter becomes a surname instead of an affectionate nickname. When we see a dove in the street we call it a pigeon! Numerous are the lay folk who when asked to read "the lesson" say, "Please don't give me a reading with lots of big words." Foreign personal names and names of places can be a block to instant comprehension. We have tried in the translations to produce shorter and more familiar names, either by the common practice of shortening, e.g. Nick for Nicodemus, or by choosing a name which reflects the meaning of the Greek or Hebrew name, e.g. Ray for Apollos (the sun God). (The first Christians shortened names in the same way, e.g. Priscilla into Prisca, our "Cilla.") We have also translated some biblical place names – Dategrove for Bethany, Fishtown for Bethsaida, etc. thus restoring the meaning they would have had for contemporaries.

More controversial is our principle of "cultural translation." We translate "demon possession" as "mental illness," which is what the instances in the Gospels would be called by most people nowadays. We can still relate to these stories provided we understand that the purpose of their telling is to illustrate the healing abilities of Jesus rather than to assert the existence of demons.

As the translation has progressed we have also become aware of the need for "contextual translation." The Greek can never be translated word for word. Neither should it be translated sentence by sentence, or even in some instances paragraph by paragraph. Sometimes the scripture writers developed what they wished to say over longer sections. For example, the words of Jesus about the "narrow way" have been taken in isolation to mean that the narrow way is the recommendation of Jesus for us. However, Matthew puts the saying in a context that begins with a warning about not judging others and the narrow-mindedness of those who go about looking for specks of sawdust in other people's eyes (Matthew 7). Looked at in context, the narrow/broad way picture is a favorite picture of the Pharisees, which Jesus quotes in order to refute it. We should no more go searching for the narrow way than we should go around looking for specks of dust. Similarly, Paul appears to advocate celibacy by saying, as in the KJV "touch not a woman" (1 Cor. 7). A reading of what he goes on to say shows he cannot be advocating any such thing, for he actually tells people not to go without sex for too long. Paul is quoting someone else's opinion in order to contradict it.

"Inclusive" also refers to the inclusion of the feminine experience. The custom of using male language to indicate everybody is no longer regarded as a valid way of translating into our culture. Sometimes it is argued that the culture in which the scriptures were written was male-dominated and that this should be reflected in translation. We are among those who would reply that the ministry of Jesus included a revolt against bad aspects of his culture. His radical inclusion of women among his disciples has been obscured by successive generations of male domination in the Church and the translation of the scriptures since the earliest days has reflected this bias.

We seek to include the experience of the feminine in our understanding of God. That aspect of God theologically understood as the "First Person" receives no sexual bias at all. "Father" is translated as "the Loving God." The "Second Person," Jesus, is male, and although maleness is part of his humanity, it is secondary to it. So titles of Jesus lose their exclusive masculine sense. The cryptic term "Son of Man" becomes "the Complete Person." "Son of God" is translated "God's Likeness." "The Third Person" is regarded as feminine. The Hebrew word for "spirit" (*ruach*) is feminine. The pigeon, the symbol of the Spirit at the dipping of Jesus is also feminine in Greek (*peristera*). It may be argued that feminine, masculine, and neuter categorization of nouns in a language do not necessarily denote anything other than a kind of convenience. To classify a pen as feminine means nothing in particular. However, when a word like "spirit," carrying with it the idea of personality and creativity is classified alongside other words, which are also words for persons, such as woman and mother, it is reasonable to suppose that the choice of classification is significant in terms of sexual understanding.

Other radical departures reflect the need to demythologize in order to translate adequately into our own culture. "Kingdom of God" thus becomes "God's New World," "Eternal Life" – "Life to the full," "Salvation" – "Healing" or "Completeness," "Heaven" – "The world beyond time and space" and so on.

ONE was largely responsible for introducing the concept of inclusive language to these islands in its pamphlet *Bad Language in Church* (1981) amidst some scorn. Our position is now accepted by all but the most change-resistant. We hope the *Good As New* translation will prove a fitting outcome of that first stand.

It is important to realize that the *Good As New* translation is unique as a community translation in which all interested Christians, not only members of ONE, have been invited to take part, whether assisting in first drafting, amending, revising the language, offering helpful suggestions, or simply pointing out howlers. The project was the brainchild of Michael (Meic) Phillips who also provided the first draft of James, and it was he who encouraged me to set aside other tasks in order to undertake the bulk of the work. I joyfully acknowledge the debt I owe to a small number of people whose contributions have provided some of the most inspired and sparkling touches to the translation, or who have painstakingly revised the text.

John Henson

Firing the Canon

was brought up an evangelical. An evangelical I still am because I believe in spreading "good news" which is what the word "evangelical" means. Since my childhood, an increasing number of self-styled evangelicals have turned good news into bad news. But that is no reason for me to drop the label.

An essential part of my evangelical upbringing was the singing of choruses. They were a form of brainwashing, but many of them put a strong emphasis on the love of God for us and still their words and bright tunes comfort me when I am feeling low. But some of them put me on the wrong track. Among these was "The best book to read... " We sang, over and over,

> *The best book to read is the Bible,*
> *The best book to read is the Bible;*
> *If you read it every day*
> *It will help you on your way,*
> *Oh, the best book to read... etc*

So my mind was conditioned to an untruth (not confined to evangelicals). Whether the Bible will help you on your way will depend on which part you read, but that's not the core untruth. The Bible is not the best book because it is not a book! The word, from the Greek *biblia*, means not "book" but "books." The Bible is a small library containing many different types of book – stories and legends, sometimes (not always) with a moral; historical records of varying degrees of accuracy;

poetry and songs; love stories; bold and revolutionary political comment; prophecies of the Old Moore type; erotica; incitements to racial hatred; biographies; letters; theological treatises; codes of ethics; and visions acquired in states of trance. Christians have a profound reverence for this collection of works. Contained within it is the story of God's affair with humankind as one section of humanity experienced and interpreted it over several thousand years. It is powerful in its witness to a God who impacts on the human psyche like a gigantic meteorite. It is also dotted throughout with canny insights into human nature. However, the books contained within the collection differ widely and wildly from one another, and such relationships as exist between them are a matter for scholarly reflection or religious piety. Some books don't seem to fit at all. Yet those who taught us to sing "The best book to read" believed that the whole corpus, bound together in black with gilt edges, was "The Word of God," every syllable infallible and speaking some message that would "help us on our way." Many who do not accept this extreme way of looking at the Bible, nevertheless hold it in superstitious awe and have a vague notion that the books we take a bite at each Sunday in a liturgical setting not at all suited to their comprehension, are somehow the essential diet for the nurture of our souls. The menu is lengthy but limited. It has a beginning and an end and nothing is to be added or taken away. There are no "offs" and there are no "specials." (See Rev. 22:8 – the words of a very insecure author!)

The canon (the selection of books we have in our Bibles) has been fixed for ever and ever! When? Where? By whom? Some would say, "The Holy Spirit." There's no answer to that, as Eric Morecombe would say. In fact, many Christians do not realize this – for five hundred years in western Christendom there has been schism over the contents of the canon. The dyke has already been breached. At the Reformation Martin Luther at a stroke expurgated from the Bible some fifteen books Catholics still have in theirs. The expurgated books are known by Protestants as "The Apocrypha" – their way of saying that the books are not quite kosher. Luther also had a mind to remove from the Bible several books written in the Christian era, especially Revelation and the letter of James, but decided it would be more than the punters would allow. However, he made his position clear in his 1522 preface to Revelation: "My spirit cannot accommodate myself to this book. There is one sufficient reason for the small esteem in which I hold it – that Christ is neither taught in it or recognized." What he meant was that the Jesus of the Gospels is unrecognizable in the triumphant Jesus of Revelation who leads his people in a war of cruel retribution. Luther's understanding was surely right. Most of the fundamentalist sects of the fringes of Protestantism, distinguished mainly by their lack of love, have gained their impetus, their twisted theology, their lunacy and fanaticism from too much reading of Revelation. If Luther had had his way we might have been spared Waco. But he was wrong to condemn the letter of James as "an epistle of straw." He was also wrong to put the Book of Wisdom in the Apocrypha. That's the problem, isn't it? Who decides? And because we cannot trust anyone to make the right decision, we must leave well alone.

Who decided in the first place? The surprising answer is that no one really knows. It just sort of happened. It would be of comfort to those of an ecclesiastical bent if it could be said that at some particular date in the first few centuries of the Christian Church the leading lights got together in a Council and agreed on the books of the canon in the same way they agreed on the creeds. How assuring if the bishops had examined the many sacred writings circulating among the Christian communities in those days and voted on them, one by one! It is perhaps significant that the first person to attempt to create an exclusive canon was Marcion in 150 C.E. He was proclaimed a heretic! By and large, the books we regard most highly today are those that were most highly regarded from the start, including our present Gospels and the letters of Paul. Thought by many in the early Church to be highly suspect were James, Hebrews, 2 and 3 John, Jude, 2 Peter and Revelation. The last four of these have remained under suspicion throughout the whole of the Church's subsequent history. Revelation squeaked into our Bibles because it was believed by some to be from the hand of John the Apostle. Had they known, as we do, that this was almost certainly not the case, it would now be unknown except to a few scholars. 2 Peter has always been rumbled by the discerning as fake Peter, as indeed we know it to be. Similarly Jude is fake Jude the brother of Jesus. Such books remain in the canon only because of the firm alliance between the fundamentalists who insist on the infallibility of the Bible in the form they have received it, and traditionalists who fear all change as unsettling and are loathe to admit that Holy Church is capable of getting it wrong. James and Hebrews have stood the test of time and have much to say that is relevant for us today. James is as likely from the brother of Jesus as not, and Hebrews is the best bet for a work written by a woman, Priscilla possibly.

The debate about the authenticity of Paul's letters continues, but the problem of "did he or didn't he" has largely been overridden by the realization that Paul rarely stated himself to be the sole author of a letter. He was the leader of a team, and much of the hard graft was done for him by friends familiar with his mind. We can imagine him agreeing with the theology of the disputed Colossians and Ephesians, even though he might have put it another way. 1 and 2 Timothy and Titus are a different matter. It is time to bite the bullet and declare these to be pious frauds on the lines of 2 Peter. Not only was the author not as stated but, more important, he did not speak the avowed author's mind. These "pastoral letters," as they are often called, got into the canon by incorporating snippets from letters of Paul in order to give verisimilitude to teaching which is not Pauline and which Paul would probably have been unhappy about. The letters represent the first signposts toward the Church's disgraceful history of heresy hunting. Paul gave up heresy hunting after his conversion. In his letters he strongly, but humbly argued his case. In the "pastorals," notions of orthodoxy take the place of Paul's understanding of faith as a journey not yet completed. The genuine quotes from Paul provide touches of warmth in letters whose style is chilly.

All in all, we must commend the choices made by those early Christians, whoever they were. By the time Athanasius in 200 C.E. listed the 27 accepted books of the Christian period of sacred writing, the choices had already been made, presumably on the basis of what the communities found helpful. What we today would call Mickey Mouse Gospels, and works of naïve and silly piety, were roundly rejected with a skepticism and maturity Christians today frequently lack in the face of the material presented to them. Their willingness to give the benefit of the doubt in a handful of cases has meant that some good stuff survived at the expense of the survival of more dubious material. If this were the work of the Holy Spirit, we are given an interesting insight into her way of operating (explains evolution?). And was it she who inspired those anonymous voters to put the Gospel of Thomas to one side and then arrange for it to be rediscovered in the twentieth century when we are more ready for it?

Where do we go from here? It's time we ditched our obsession with the hefty tome we have inherited, and recognized what a turn-off it is for those seeking enlightenment. Those who believe the Bible from "cover to cover" (especially the covers) make sure their novices are carefully guided so that they miss most of it. We need to revoke the redundancy notice given by the Church to the Holy Spirit the moment the last full stop was put to the Book of Revelation. We need the courage to say that some things in the Bible are no longer scripture for us, whereas the letters of Bonhoeffer and the sermons of Martin Luther King are, and the hymn/poems of Brian Wren and John Bell may one day be. We must say, if we find it to be true, that The Gospel of Thomas is closer to the Jesus we understand and appreciate than Revelation.

As a community we offer new and fresh versions of some of the earliest Christian writings. They include five "Gospels" (counting Thomas), Acts, the letters of Paul – to Rome, Corinth, Galatia, Ephesus, Philippi, Colossae, Thessalonika and Philemon; the letters of James, Peter, John the Elder and "To the Hebrews." These writings preserve truths and insights from the first Christians that continue to have value for us today. My own view is that the remaining books of the traditional canon do not have much to add and that Revelation in particular is contrary to the mind of Jesus. (There has not been a vote on this, but feedback suggests that the ONE community for the most part goes along with this. But it must always be stressed that the ONE community is a collection of individuals – very much so, and that none of our publications, including this one, is likely to reflect the standpoint of all our members.)

Our intention is not to create a new canon to replace the old, but to do away with the concept of a closed canon of scripture. The canon perpetuates some of what should not be there, and inhibits an enthusiastic appreciation of the treasure-store of Christian writing since biblical times to the present day (post-biblical scripture). The canon is an idol. We have fired the canon!!

John Henson

Good As New –
Order of Books

Mark's Good News

Thought-Provoking Sayings (*Thomas*)

From Sources Close to Jesus (*John*)

Good News From a Jewish Friend (*Matthew*)

Luke's Good News (*Part One*)

Luke's Good News (*Part Two – Acts*)

Paul's Letter to Rome

Paul's Letters to Corinth

Letters From Paul's Team

The Four Calls

Note: *The dating of the "Gospels" will always be a matter of conjecture. There is almost complete agreement among serious scholars that Mark came first. Thomas could be next. Most put John last, but others strongly argue for an early date, level with Mark or soon after. Matthew and Luke are usually thought to be about contemporary with each other except by those who think that Luke had Matthew to hand or, less commonly, but not impossible, the other way round. Some of Luke may be as early as Mark, but added to by additions from Mark and elsewhere after the writing of Acts. We place Luke last in this volume simply to encourage the reader to read Luke and*

Acts in sequence as Luke intended. The works can probably all be dated before 90 C.E., and the fragments and eyewitness accounts on which they are based before 50 C.E. for the main part. They are more reliable, even in the matter of detail, than they are often given credit for. The independent historian always welcomes a plurality of documents. It makes the quest for historical accuracy easier rather than otherwise – more exciting too. The Gospels are a good check on each other. Despite their differences, the story they present of Jesus is, in outline, the same.

With regard to authorship, majority opinion among scholars seems to be that Mark and Luke are as likely as not the authors of the works attributed to them. Matthew's Gospel comes from an author or group who direct the message to a mainly Jewish readership. Whether there was any input from Matthew the tax collector, it is impossible to tell, though tax collectors get a better press in the Gospel than the Pharisees, who get clobbered. The Gospel attributed to John is unlikely to have been penned by John the Galilean fisherman. For the most part the backdrop and the information provided comes from a different source from that of the Galilean disciples. Dategrove (Bethany), a suburb of Jerusalem, was obviously one fount of information. Lazarus is clearly identified as the "Beloved Disciple" in the text and given credit for at least some of the facts provided. For what reasons the Church decided at a very early stage to put people off the scent with regard to the identity of the special friend of Jesus is puzzling. The answer will probably escape us unless we are willing to accept the fact of the Church's frequent dishonesty throughout its history whenever it considered that the truth would not be helpful to its charges. Lazarus may have been disliked or the object of jealousy because of his close relationship with Jesus. Jealousy and rivalry among the disciples are well documented in all the Gospels. Or John's name may have been given to the Gospel because the author was a woman. Mary of Bethany must be a strong contender. Or it may have been attached to give it "apostolic" authority because the author(s), like the author(s) of Matthew, were not well known and appeared to carry no weight. We are unlikely to arrive at an agreed answer this side of heaven, but it is important to allow the genuine alternatives to have an airing and not to be afraid of the crusty old censor!

21

Glossary

Traditional to Good As New

Names of People

AARON	Ron
AENEAS	Aidan
AGABUS	Hopper (lit. meaning "locust")
AGRIPPA	Griff
ALPHAEUS	Alf
AMPLIATUS	Lee
ANANIAS	Nye (Acts 5); Ian (Acts 9); Ninus (Acts 23)
ANDRONICUS	Andy
ANNA	Anne
ANNAS	(The high-priest) Hank
APELLES	Les
APOLLOS	Ray (Greek "Apollos" = the sun god)
AQUILLA	William, Will (Cill and Will, wife and husband team)
ARCHELAUS	Archie
ARCHIPPUS	Captain Rider (Greek = Master of Cavalry. Possibly a converted soldier, later majordomo in Philemon's household.)
ARISTOBULUS	Bill
ASYNCRITUS	Chris
BARABBAS	Barry
BARNABAS	Cheery (from literal meaning of Aramaic)
BARTHOLOMEW	Bart
BARTIMAEUS	Barty
BLASTUS	Bud (Greek blastus = "bud," as of a flower)
CAIAPHAS	Guy
CLAUDIUS LYSIAS	Claude Lewis
CLEMENT	Clem
CLEOPAS/ CLOPAS	Clover
CORNELIUS	Neil
DAMARIS	Pet (Damaris = "heifer," "Pet" preserves the idea of a fond domestic animal.)
DEVIL, the	Evil, the power of evil
DORCAS (Tabitha)	Gazelle (lit. meaning of Greek Dorcas and Aramaic Tabitha)
DIONYSIUS	Dennis (English for Dionysius)
EPAENETUS	Wayne
EPAPHRAS/ EPAPHRODITUS	Charming (literal meaning of the Greek)
ERASTUS	Rastus

ELYMAS	Slippery Al (after the Hebrew "crafty")	*MARY OF MAGDALA*	Maggie
EUODIA and SYNTACHE	Edna and Cynthia	*MARY, wife of Zebedee*	Marion
EUTYCHUS	Explained in the text as meaning "lucky fall," probably his chosen baptismal name after his accident at Troy.	*MARY, mother of Joseph (of Arimathea?)*	Maria
		MARY, aunt of Jesus	Miriam
GAIUS	Gus	*MARY, mother of John Mark*	Marie
GALLIO	Leo		
GAMALIEL	Liam	**MANAEN**	Sturdy (lit. Greek)
HERMES	Mervyn	**MATTHIAS**	Matt
HERMAS	Massy	**MELCHIZEDEK**	"Righteous Ruler" (close to meaning of the name)
HERODIAN	Rod		
HERODIAS	Rose	**NAAMAN**	Norman
JAMES AND JOHN	(Mark's Gospel only) "Thunder and Lightning" (from Aramaic nickname of Jesus for them)	**NARCISSUS**	Cecil
		NATHANIEL	Nathan
		NEREUS	Neville
JAIRUS	Jay	**NICANOR**	Nicky
JOANNA	Joan	**NICODEMUS**	Nick
JOHN THE BAPTIST	John the Dipper (Greek baptizo = dip)	**NICOLAUS**	Colin
		NIGER	Blackie
JUDAS ISCARIOT	Judas from Kerioth	**NYMPHA**	Bridget (Greek – a bride)
ELIZABETH	Lisa		
LUCIUS	Lucien	**ONESIMUS**	Handy (literal meaning of the Greek)
LYSANIAS	Linus		
MARY	The number of Marys in the Gospels is bewildering and were confused by the first Christians. We attempt to distinguish them by using variants:	**PARMENAS**	Craig (Parmenas = enduring, rock-like = Craig – Celtic)
		PATROBUS	Paddy
		PERSIS	Percy
		PETER	Rocky (from literal meaning of the Greek)
THE MOTHER OF JESUS	Mary	**PHILOLOGOS**	Phil
MARY OF BETHANY	Mary (or Mary Dategrove)	**PHLEGON**	Sparky (close to meaning of the Greek)
		PRISCILLA	Cilla, Cill (Cill and Will, wife and husband team)

PROCHORUS	Russ
QUARTUS	Kurt
RAHAB	Barbara
SATAN	Evil, the power of evil
SERGIUS PAULUS	George Paul
SIMON THE ZEALOT	Simon the Hothead
SOSIPATER	Pat
STACHYS	Stan
TERTIUS	Terry
THADDAEUS	Ted
THEOPHILUS	Theo (Gk = "lover of God." The two parts of Luke's "Gospel" appear to have been addressed to a government official. His name may therefore be a meaningful pseudonym.)
THOMAS	Twin (literal meaning of the Aramaic and Greek equivalent)
TROPHIMUS	Tommy
TRYPHAENA and TRYPHOSA	those two ladies whose names mean "delicate" and "dainty"
TYCHICUS	Lucky (literal meaning of the Greek)
TYRANNUS	Tyrone
ZACCHAEUS	Keith
ZECHARIAH (father of John the Dipper)	Kerry (son of Barachiah) Gary

Names of Places

AENON NEAR SALIM	Peace Springs (combining "aenon" = springs and "salim" = peace)
ARIMATHEA	Ram (modern name for probable site)
BETHPHAGE	Figland (literal meaning, "house of figs")
BETHANY (Home of Martha)	Dategrove (literal meaning, "house of dates")
BETHANY (John the Dipper)	Dateford
BETHSAIDA	Fishtown (literal meaning)
CAPERNAUM	Nahum town (literal translation, after the Prophet Nahum)
CENCHREAE	Dockland district of Corinth
CHORAZIN	Dancetown (literal meaning)
COLOSSAE	Quaketown (Colossae was in an earthquake area and suffered many disasters. Greek "colasis" = punishment. Earthquakes were regarded as punishments from the gods.)
GERGAZA	Kursa (modern name)
HIERAPOLIS	Templetown (Greek = holy town, priest town)
LAODICEA	Banktown (situated on the banks of the Lycus, and a banking town)
LYDDA	Ludd (modern name)
LYSTRA	Lester
NEAPOLIS	Newtown (literal meaning)

PARADISE	God's Garden (from Hebrew "pardes" = garden)	**KINGDOM OF HEAVEN**	Bright New World
THESSALONIKA	Tessatown (modern Saloniki)	**THE LAW**	The Rule Book, "rules and regulations"
		LORD (of Jesus)	Leader
		MESSIAH (Christ)	God's Chosen, the Chosen One

Terms etc.

		PHARISEES	The strict set
ANGELS	God's agents, messengers, companions	**PARABLES**	Stories, pictures, riddles
		PRIESTS	God's representatives, links (between people and God); clergy (as a group with scribes and Pharisees, etc.); High Priest (as of Jesus) "the go-between", "the vital link"; High Priest (as of Caiaphas etc) Chief of the Clergy
APOSTLES	Special helpers, close friends of Jesus, Jesus' team		
BAPTIZE	Dip		
BELIEVE/BELIEF	Trust		
CHRIST (Messiah)	God's Chosen, the Chosen One		
CHIEF PRIEST/ HIGH PRIEST	Chief of the clergy	**PROPHET**	God's Speaker
		RABBI	Teacher, Sir
CHIEF PRIESTS, SCRIBES, etc (as a group)	The clergy	**SABBATH**	Rest Day
		SALVATION	Healing, completeness, full life and health
DISCIPLES	Friends, followers, team, gang		
		SCRIBES	Experts in the old books
ETERNAL LIFE	Life to the full, real life	**THE SCRIPTURE**	The old books
GALATIANS	Celtic Christians, Celts (living in Galatia, now central Turkey)	**TEMPLE**	Worship center, the central place of worship
		SADDUCEES	The easy-going set, the group who do not believe in the after-life
GLORY (of Jesus)	Special nature, beauty, splendor, brightness		
HEAVEN	World beyond time and space, God's world	**SIN**	Wrongdoing, faults
		SINNERS	Outcasts, those you call "bad"
HOLY SPIRIT/ SPIRIT	God's Spirit	**SON OF GOD**	God's True Likeness
JEWS	God's People	**SON OF MAN**	The Complete Person, "I" (for Jesus) "we" (for Jesus and his community or humanity)
JEWS (hostile elements among the Jews)	Temple clergy, Jewish authorities, religious leaders, etc.		
KING	Ruler, Leader, head of state, "the greatest"	**SYNAGOGUE**	Place of worship, Jewish place of worship
KINGDOM OF GOD	God's New World		

JESUS AND HIS FRIENDS

Introduction to the Gospels

Reg Bridle

Before this new translation is read, there are a few points about the Gospels that need to be borne in mind. Some of us were brought up as members of a Christian church and were made familiar with the Bible at an early age. We may not have been told in as many words, but we probably gained the impression that what we read was a factual record of what was said and done many years before. As we grew older we may have had some doubts about parts of it, especially the miraculous element, feeling that there may have been some exaggeration, but thinking that, for the rest, there was a fairly reliable account of the life of Jesus. That may be the position of many people today, but the truth is not so simple.

Just how the Gospels came to their present form cannot be stated with any degree of certainty. It is fairly safe to assume that the first disciples of Jesus, in the light of all that they had known about him and experienced after his death, came to believe that he was no ordinary person but that he was Someone Special, through whom God had done something unique for humankind, and they wanted everybody to know about it. So they began to talk about him. Just what they said there is no means of telling; each one probably had a different way of putting it, though the general sense would have been the same. Those who heard and were convinced would, in turn, have told others. In those days verbal memory was probably better than ours because there was so little writing, and so what was passed on would have been more accurately transmitted than it would be today. But even so, there would have been variations, partly because of what had first been heard, but also because they would each have emphasized the parts that appealed to them most. We can be fairly sure about this because of the variations in the written texts that eventually appeared.

Those who passed on the message were not concerned just to tell a tale; they wanted to convince others of the truth of what they said. (This intention is clearly stated at the end of the twentieth chapter of John's Gospel.) Moreover, in order to do that, the tellers of the tale may well have added to it and enlarged upon it to show how wonderful Jesus was. To us such a procedure may not seem honest, but evidently ideas were different then. The miraculous element may have been "high-lighted," but it must be remembered that the people of those days had no conception of what we call the "Laws of Nature" and readily believed in "supernatural" workings. Further, again, in all good faith, what they experienced later may well have affected what they said. For example, it is difficult to believe that Jesus would have foretold his resurrection or spoken about his "coming in glory." As time went on, a split developed, which led to strife between the orthodox Jews and those who had become Christians. Does that situation account for some of the sayings attributed to Jesus? The general picture of Jesus that emerges from the Gospels is surely that of one who is tender and compassionate, showing love to all around. It is difficult for some of us to imagine him calling the Jewish leaders "a generation of vipers," "whited sepulchers," and so on. Such phrases may owe their origin to the unhappy experience of the early Christians. Such a suggestion may seem strange, but it must be remembered that the writers of the Gospels were very different from ourselves. They wanted to promote the Christian cause by whatever means were available to them, and what they did seemed right to them. These considerations lead to another point. In the Gospels as we now have them, especially John's Gospel, we find many long speeches put into the mouth of Jesus. This is in line with the practice of the classical Greek and Roman historians, which in those days was accepted as normal and in no way unhistorical.

There is one final point. We do not know how many such "Gospels" came to be written. A number have survived in whole or in part, and some of them contain some strange material. For that reason, as time went on, Church leaders had to decide which ones were reliable and which not. Eventually what we know as our Four came to be regarded as reliable and have come down to us. This all took place before the invention of printing, so that all "books" had to be copied by hand. Although great care may have been taken to ensure that the copying was correct, mistakes were bound to occur and these, in turn, would have been copied. So, as time went on, there was a variation in what was handed down, and today scholars have to use all their skill to decide just what is the most likely reading, before attempting to translate it into language and thought-forms that will be understood today.

Reg Bridle, *an Anglican priest, was a long-standing member of ONE, and – by this time in his eighties – an enthusiast for the projected* Good as New *translation. He was involved in the first drafting of Mark's Gospel, where his hand may still be seen, despite many changes. It was for the publication of Mark that he wrote the above introduction, which was to serve as the introduction to all the Gospels. He was busy working on the early chapters of Romans when he passed on. We hope he will smile on this completed volume.*

Mark's Good News

1 If you want to know "The Good News," read this. It's about Jesus, God's true representative and faithful likeness. God's Speaker wrote,

> *"Watch, I'm sending my messenger ahead of you to get things ready."*

Then there was "The Voice," shouting in the desert,

> *"Repair the road for God; straighten out the bends!"*

John, nicknamed "the Dipper," was "The Voice." He was in the desert, inviting people to be dipped, to show they were determined to change their ways and wanted to be forgiven. People from the south of the country and the city of Jerusalem were attracted by the message, and responded by admitting their faults and being dipped by John in the River Jordan. John had a simple lifestyle, wearing only a camel skin with a leather belt and eating carob nuts and tree sap. He told people, "Someone is on the way who is so much more able than me. I'm not fit to untie his sandals. I've dipped you in the water, but he will drench you with God's Spirit."

(9) Then Jesus came from Nazareth to be dipped by John in the Jordan. As he was climbing up the bank again, the sun shone through a gap in the clouds. At the same time a pigeon flew down and perched on him. Jesus took this as a sign that God's Spirit was with him. A voice from overhead was heard saying, "That's my boy! You're doing fine!"

Straight away the Spirit sent Jesus into the desert. He stayed there for six weeks with wild animals all round him. God's helpers were there to look after him. This was a time of decision for Jesus between the ways of right and wrong.

After John was arrested, Jesus came to Galilee, passing on the Good News of God. He used these words, "Now is the time to turn your backs on wrongdoing and accept the Good News that God's New World has arrived."

(16) As Jesus walked along the edge of Lake Galilee, he saw the brothers Simon and Andrew casting a net into the water. They ran a fishing business. Jesus called out to them, "How would you like to be my friends and fish for people?" They left their nets and went with Jesus straightaway. A little further on he saw James and John, Zebedee's sons. They were busy mending their nets in the boat. Jesus called out to them, and they left their father Zebedee in the boat with his hired workers and became friends of Jesus.

They went to Nahum town, and on the Rest Day Jesus visited the local place of worship and taught there. People were amazed at his teaching, for he sounded as if he knew what he was talking about, unlike the usual run of teachers. There was a man there in a confused mental state, which people thought was caused by an evil spirit. He shouted out, "Why are you pestering me, Jesus of Nazareth? Are you going to kill me? I know who you are – God's Chosen!" Jesus quickly dealt with him. He said, "Calm down, and be yourself!" After rolling about on the floor and a lot of noise, the man calmed down. All the people there were stunned and kept asking one another, "What's going on? This is something new – a teaching that really works! He can even heal someone's mind with his words!" The fame of Jesus began to spread around the region of Galilee.

After worship they went home with Simon and Andrew. James and John went with them. Simon's mother-in-law was in bed with the 'flu, and as soon as they told Jesus about her, he went over to her, took her by the hand and lifted her up. She got over the 'flu and was able to look after her guests.

That evening after sunset, they brought to Jesus all who were unwell or mentally disturbed. The whole village tried to gather round the house. Jesus cured lots of people from various diseases, including people who were disturbed. He was able to quiet them down because they knew by instinct who he was.

(35) In the morning, before dawn, Jesus got up and went to a deserted spot to pray. Simon and his companions came looking for him. When they found him they said, "Everyone's looking for you." Jesus said, "Let's go on to the other villages round about so I can share the Good News with them as well. That's what I'm here for!" Jesus traveled all round Galilee, giving the message in the places of worship and dealing with people's anxiety problems.

A man who everybody kept at a distance, because he had a skin disease, came to Jesus and begged him, "I'm sure if you want, you can cure me of my complaint." Jesus put his arm round him and said, "Of course I want to help you. You're going to get better now!" Immediately the man felt well and his skin healed up. Then Jesus sent him away, asking him not to tell anyone, but to report to the health officer and observe the regulations to get the cure recognized by the community. But the former outcast went around telling everyone, so that Jesus could not enter any village openly, but stayed outside in the country. Even so, people flocked to him from everywhere.

2 After a few days, when Jesus had gone back to Nahum town, people heard he was at home. So many turned up, they blocked the doorway. While Jesus was presenting his message, four people came along carrying a paralyzed man. They could not get through the crowd, so they tore off part of the roof and lowered the man down through the hole on his stretcher. When Jesus saw their trust, he said to the man, "Friend, your wrongdoings are forgiven." Some of the experts in the old books who were sitting there thought to themselves, "Who does he think he is? Only God can forgive sins!" Jesus knew what they were thinking and said to them, "I know what's going on in your minds. You think, don't you, it's easier to say to someone who is paralyzed, 'Your wrongdoings are forgiven' than to say 'Get on your feet, pick up your stretcher and walk?' I'm going to show you we can forgive wrongs, here on earth!"[1] Jesus turned to the

---

[1] "We" = The Son of Man. The "Son of Man," which is most often rendered in this translation as "The Complete Person," seems sometimes to have been used by Jesus in its basic sense "humanity," and on other occasions to indicate a combination of himself and his community. It was the "trust" of the four friends that brought the comment from Jesus, "Your sins are forgiven," for their action in accepting the outcast was as crucial in the man's healing as the words and actions of Jesus himself. Humankind can forgive. Similarly, it was the friends of Jesus who made the choice to pick the ears of corn not Jesus, and it was thus they, together with their Leader, who taught the strict set how to use the Rest Day for its original purpose.

paralyzed man and said, "Get on your feet! Go home and take your stretcher with you!" The man stood up, picked up his stretcher, and with all eyes on him, walked off. Everyone was amazed and thanked God, saying, "We've never seen anything like this before!"

(13) Once again Jesus went to the lakeside and a large crowd gathered round for him to teach. As he walked along, Jesus saw Levi in his tax office, working for the Romans. Jesus said to him, "I want you to be my friend!" Levi got up and went with Jesus.

Levi held a party in Jesus' honor. Many traitors like Levi were there and others with doubtful reputations, and they shared the party food with Jesus and his friends. The house was packed, for the number of supporters was growing fast. When the strict set saw that Jesus was accepting the hospitality of these outcasts from society, they asked his friends, "Why does Jesus eat with such bad characters?" Jesus overheard and said, "It's those who are ill need a doctor, not those who are well. I don't ask people who think they've nothing wrong with them to be my friends, but people you label 'bad.'"

The followers of John the Dipper and those who belonged to the strict set were going without food for religious reasons. Some people came and asked Jesus, "Why aren't your followers going without food too?" Jesus said, "Wedding guests don't refuse to eat – it would be rude to the happy couple! One day the party will be over – that will be the time for going without!

"You don't sew a patch of unshrunk cloth on to an old coat; otherwise the patch comes off and takes a bit of the old coat with it. You end up with a bigger hole. You don't put new wine into dirty old bottles. That would ruin the wine. You put new wine into fresh bottles!"

(23) One Rest Day, Jesus and his friends were going for a walk through the cornfields. As they went along, they began to pluck the ears of corn. The strict set said to Jesus, "Look what your followers are doing! They're breaking the rules of the Rest Day!" Jesus said, "Haven't you ever read what David did when he and his companions were hungry? David went into the house of God and ate the special bread, which only the clergy are allowed to eat, and he gave some to his friends." Then Jesus said, "The Rest Day was meant to help people relax, not to be a burden. So you see, we even have to show you how to enjoy the Rest Day!"[2]

3 Another time when Jesus visited a place of worship there was a man there with a shriveled hand. Some were on the look out for a pretext to accuse Jesus of wrongdoing. So they watched eagerly to see if he would cure the man on the Rest Day. Jesus said to the man with the shriveled hand, "Come up here where everyone can see you!" Then Jesus said, "Is it right to do good or to do harm on the Rest Day, to save life or to kill?" There was a stony silence. Jesus, looking all round, was grieved and angered by their lack of feeling. He said to the man, "Put your arm out straight!" When he did, his hand came back to normal. The strict set went off at once to join with the supporters of Herod to plot the death of Jesus. Jesus and his friends left that town, and a large crowd from Galilee joined him. As the news of Jesus' work spread, their numbers grew. People came from as far afield as the lands south of Jerusalem, the east bank of the Jordan, and from Lebanon in the north. Jesus asked his friends to have a boat ready, to avoid being crushed by the crowd. Because he had cured so many people, all those who had illnesses kept pushing their way forward to touch him. Whenever those who were disturbed saw Jesus, they fell down in front of him and shouted, "You're God's Chosen." But Jesus sternly told them to keep it quiet.

Jesus climbed a mountain with a group of chosen friends. He picked out twelve for special tasks. They were to keep him company at all times, help present the Good News, and free those trapped by evil. The twelve picked were Simon, who Jesus nicknamed "Rocky"; Zebedee's sons James and John, who Jesus nicknamed "Thunder and Lightning"; Andrew, Philip, Bart, Matthew, Twin, James (Alf's son), Ted, Simon nicknamed "Hothead", and Judas from Kerioth (the traitor).

(20) Later Jesus went back to his lodgings, and the crowds gathered again. There was no chance to eat. When his family heard about it, they came to take him away and put him under lock and key. They thought he was out of his mind. Some of the experts who had come from Jerusalem to investigate said, "He knows how to deal with evil because he's evil himself!" Jesus asked them to gather round, and he used this picture to argue his case. "How can an evil force drive out evil? A nation divided against itself will fall

[2] See footnote 1.

35

apart. If the members of a family are fighting one another, it isn't a family any more. And if evil is turning on itself, its end is near. You can't rob a wrestler's house without tying up the wrestler first. Only then can a robber ransack the house. Believe me, every wicked act and every evil word can be forgiven; but those who call the work of God's Spirit evil can never experience forgiveness, for they've no sense of right or wrong." Jesus was referring to the accusation that he relied on evil powers. At that moment Jesus' family arrived. They waited outside and sent a message asking him to come out to meet them. A crowd was sitting around Jesus when the message was passed to him, "All your family are outside, asking for you." Jesus said, "Who are my family?" Turning to the circle of people around him he said, "This is my family. Those who do what God asks them to do are my family – mother, sister, and brother."

4 Jesus went on teaching by the lake. The crowds became so large, he had to get into the boat and use it as a seat, while the crowd listened from the beach. Jesus taught them many things by means of stories. This is a good example of his teaching:

"Listen, a farmer went out to sow his field. As he scattered the seed, some of it fell on the path and the birds swooped down and ate it up. Some seeds fell on rocky ground and the shoots sprang up quickly as there wasn't enough soil for the plants to take root. When the sun came up they withered away. Some seeds fell among the thistles. When the thistles grew, the plants were choked and didn't produce any grain. Other seeds fell into good soil and yielded a fine crop of grain, between thirty and a hundred times what the farmer sowed." Jesus added, "If you've got ears, use them!"

When the crowds had gone away, Jesus' friends asked him about his stories. Jesus told them, "You realize they are clues to the meaning of God's New World. But there are other people who haven't yet seen the point, and for them the stories are no more than stories. The old books talk about people who look without seeing and listen without hearing, because if they understood they would have to change their ways and be forgiven. I'm surprised you didn't grasp the meaning of the story about the seed. It's one of the easiest to understand!"

(Here is the meaning: The farmer represents someone who spreads the

Good News. The seed on the path means people who hear the words but straightaway evil thoughts wipe them clean from their minds. The seed on rocky ground refers to people who enjoy hearing the words, but don't allow the ideas to sink in. They only keep going for a while until they meet with hassle because of their beliefs, or other difficulties. Then they give up. The seed among the thistles stands for those who listen to the words, but the cares of daily life, greed for money and goods, or obsession with trivial things, crowd in and choke the words, and they have no effect. As for the seeds sown on good ground, they are like people who welcome the words, accept them, and act upon them, producing a bumper crop.)[3]

(21) Then Jesus said, "Do you bring in a lamp and hide it under a bucket or under a bed instead of putting it on a lamp stand? There's nothing hidden that won't be exposed, and no secret that won't come to light. If you've got ears, use them!

"Listen carefully. The more attention you pay, the more you'll learn, and you'll improve your ability to listen at the same time. Those who don't listen, forget how to, and lose what they used to know.

"This is how things are in God's New World. A farmer scatters some seeds in a field, goes to bed, gets up next day, goes to bed again and so on, many times. Although nothing appears to be happening, the seed is sprouting and growing under the soil. The first stalk appears, then the corn grows to its full height, and last of all the grain forms. When the grain's ripe, it's harvest time, and the farmer can start reaping.

"How can we describe God's New World? What picture can we use? It's like a mustard seed, which is very small when you sow it in the ground, but it grows to become the largest of shrubs, and its branches are wide enough to provide shade for the birds to build their nests in."

By using pictures like this Jesus put over his teaching, as far as those listening were able to understand it. In his public teaching he always used stories, explaining their meaning to his friends when they were alone together.

(35) In the evening Jesus said, "Let's go across the lake." They left the

---

[3] There are no inverted commas in the Greek text. Thus the "explanation" of the story may well be from the Gospel-writer rather than from Jesus. This is more likely, since Jesus preferred his hearers to think for themselves.

crowd behind and took the boat Jesus had been sitting in to speak to the people. He was very tired. They were followed by a number of other boats. Suddenly they were hit by a hurricane, and the waves leapt over the side of the boat, beginning to fill it with water. Jesus was asleep in the back of the boat with his head on a cushion. His friends woke him and shouted, "Teacher, don't you care if we drown?" Jesus woke up, looked at the wind and waves and said, "Quiet! Calm down!" The wind eased off and the lake became peaceful again. Then he said to his friends, "Why the panic? Where's your trust?" But they were still scared, and said to one another, "Who is this? Even the wind and the waves do what he says!"

5 Jesus and his friends landed on the other side of the lake near the town of Kursa. Just as Jesus was stepping out of the boat, a man who was mentally ill came to meet him. He lived among the graves because no one could control him, not even with chains. On previous occasions when he had been chained hand and foot, he tore the chains apart and broke the shackles on his feet, and no one was strong enough to hold him down. He spent the day and night shouting and cutting himself with stones. He saw Jesus from a distance and ran and fell down in front of him, shouting, "Why can't you leave me alone Jesus. You're God's Chosen. For God's sake, stop torturing me!" While the man was shouting like this Jesus started the treatment by saying, "Come on, let's have that filth out!" Then Jesus asked, "What's your name?" "My name's Legion," he said. "I'm so many people all in one. Please, please don't have me put away!"

On the hillside nearby a large herd of pigs was feeding. The confused voices from the man's mind begged Jesus, "Send us into the pigs; we'll plague the life out of them instead!" Jesus agreed, and he got the man to direct all his confusion toward the pigs. The herd of about two thousand rushed down the steep bank into the lake where they were drowned. Those tending the pigs ran off and told the people in the village and round about what had happened, and they came to see what was going on. They found Jesus with the one who had been ill. He was sitting quietly with his clothes on and clear in his mind, but the people were still afraid of him. Those who had seen everything told the rest what had happened to the man and the pigs. Then they asked Jesus to leave their district. As Jesus was getting into the boat, the man who had been cured begged to go with him. Jesus would not let him, but said, "Go home to your own people and tell them what God has done for you and the kindness you've been shown." He went around the whole area east of Lake Galilee, telling what Jesus had done for him. And everyone was amazed.

(21) When Jesus had returned by the boat to the other side of the lake, a large crowd gathered on the beach. One of the leaders of the local place of worship came by. His name was Jay. When he saw Jesus, he fell at his feet. Sobbing his heart out, he said, "My little girl is dying. Please come and touch her to make her better and be herself again." So Jesus left with Jay. A large crowd followed and pressed around Jesus.

There was a woman in the crowd who had been suffering from bleeding for twelve years. She had been through a bad time at the hands of many doctors and spent all her money, despite which she was no better, worse if anything. She had heard about Jesus, so she caught up with him in the crowd and touched his coat. She thought, "If I just touch his clothes I'll be better." Her bleeding stopped immediately and she sensed that she was cured. That moment Jesus suddenly felt weak. So he turned round in the crowd and asked. "Who touched my clothes?" His friends said. "You can see the size of the crowd pressing round you. What do you mean, 'Who touched me?'?" But Jesus kept looking round to see who had done it. The woman, aware of what had happened to her, in a highly nervous state, fell down in front of Jesus and told him the whole truth. Jesus said to her, "Friend, your trust in me has made you well again. Everything's alright. Your suffering's over."

Just as Jesus was saying this, some people came from Jay's house with the message, "Your daughter is dead. There's no point in troubling the teacher any further." Jesus overheard what was said and reassured Jay with the words, "Don't be afraid; trust me!" Jesus only allowed Rocky, Thunder, and Lightning to go with them. When they arrived at Jay's house they found a great commotion. There was loud weeping and wailing. Jesus stepped into the house and said, "What's all this noise for? The child isn't dead, only asleep." They burst out laughing. Jesus told them to get outside. Then he took the mother and father and his friends into the room where the child was lying. Jesus took hold of her hand and said, "Time to get up, little one!" Immediately the girl got up and began to walk about. She was twelve years old. They could hardly believe their eyes. Jesus asked them to keep the matter quiet and suggested they give the girl something to eat.

6 Jesus went from there to his hometown. His friends went with him. On the Rest Day he began to teach in the place of worship, and many who listened were amazed. They said, "What does all this clever talk amount to? You wouldn't believe the things he's been doing! He's only a carpenter, isn't he? He's Mary's boy. James, Joseph, Judas, and Simon are his brothers. We know his sisters too!" So they turned against him. Jesus said to them, "God's speakers are respected everywhere except the town they come from and the family at home." Jesus could not do anything remarkable there except touch a few sick people and heal them. He was surprised at their lack of trust and went to the other villages to teach.

Jesus called his twelve helpers together and sent them out in twos, teaching them how to calm those who were disturbed. He instructed them not to take anything with them except a walking stick for their journey – no food, no bag, no money belt. They could wear sandals but not take a change of clothes. He told them, "Wherever you go, if you are offered hospitality, stay there until you leave the district. As for any place not giving you a welcome and not allowing you to speak, you should leave with dignity and not go back there." So the friends went on tour, inviting everyone to turn their backs on wrongdoing. They brought peace to troubled minds and put ointment on many who were ill and cured them.

(14) Herod the ruler of Galilee heard about all this, and the reputation Jesus was getting. To explain his powers, some people were claiming Jesus was "John the Dipper" brought back to life. Some thought Jesus was Elijah and others said, "It's one of God's speakers, like those of long ago." But Herod came to his own conclusion when he heard the reports. "I cut John's head off and now he's come back again!"

Herod, on his own authority, had sent guards to arrest John, tie him up and put him in prison, because he was under the influence of his wife Rose. She was his brother Philip's wife, but Herod had married her. John had been telling Herod, "It's wrong for you to marry your brother's wife." Because of this, Rose had a grudge against John, and wanted to kill him. But she couldn't manage it because Herod respected John and protected him, knowing him to be a good man, especially close to God. Although John's message worried Herod, he still liked to listen to him. Rose had her opportunity at Herod's birthday party, to which all the courtiers, officers, and leading citizens were invited. When Rose's daughter came on and danced, she gave Herod and his guests so much pleasure, he said to the girl, "Ask me whatever you want and I'll give it you." He promised, "Anything you ask – even half the land I rule!" She consulted her mother. "What shall I ask for?" Her mother replied, "The head of John the Dipper." The girl rushed straight back to Herod with the request, "I want the head of John the Dipper on a plate." Herod was upset, but because of his public promise he felt unable to refuse. So he sent a guard with orders to bring John's head. The guard went to the prison and cut John's head off. Then he brought John's head on a plate and gave it to the girl, who then gave it to her mother. When the followers of John heard about it, they came and took the body and laid it to rest in a grave.

(30) The friends of Jesus met and reported back on what they had done and taught. Jesus said to them, "Let's go somewhere quiet and have a rest for a while." There were so many people coming and going, they didn't even have enough free time to eat. They went by boat to a deserted spot on their own. A lot of people noticed them going, recognized them, and hurried round the lake on foot, getting there first. As he got out of the boat, Jesus saw a big crowd and was deeply sorry for them. They looked lost. So Jesus spent a long time teaching them.

At the end of the day, Jesus' friends came to him and said, "This is an out-of-the-way place and it's getting late. Send the people away so they can buy something to eat." Jesus replied, "You give them something to eat!" They said, "Do you expect us to spend a whole year's wages on food and hand it over to them to eat?" Jesus asked, "How many loaves have you got? Go and find out!" They came across five loaves and two fish. Jesus told the people to sit down in groups on the grass, which was green at that time of the year. They sat down in groups of hundreds and fifties. Jesus took the five loaves and the two fish, and said "thank you" to God. Then he broke the loaves and the fish and gave them to his friends to hand round to the people. Everyone had enough to eat. The leftovers filled twelve baskets. Five thousand had shared the food!

Jesus insisted on his friends getting into the boat and going on ahead to Fishtown on the other side, while he said goodbye to the crowd. Then he went up the mountain to talk with God. By the time it was dark, the boat was way out on the lake, while Jesus was on his own on the land. In the early hours Jesus saw that his friends had trouble rowing against a strong wind. He came out to meet them, walking on the lake. Jesus looked as if he was going to pass by them, but when they saw him walking on the water, they thought it was a ghost and cried out in terror. They could all see him. Jesus shouted, "Don't worry, it's me! No need to panic!" Then Jesus got into the boat with them and the wind dropped. They were gobsmacked! They did not understand the meaning of the loaves. It just hadn't sunk in! At last they landed not far from home, and tied up the boat. Jesus was recognized getting out of the boat, and as usual whenever he turned up, there was a race with stretchers to bring him those who were ill. Everywhere Jesus went, into communities large or small, or out among the farms, people would bring the sick to some central spot, hoping to touch the edge of his clothes. All who did that were healed.

7 (with 8:1-10) Some of the strict set who had among them some experts in the old books, came from Jerusalem to see what Jesus was doing. They noticed some of Jesus' followers eating without going through the customary ceremony of hand washing. (It was the religious tradition not only with the strict set but with all the Jews to wash their hands frequently. They washed everything they bought in the market, not just the food, and they had a complicated way of washing crockery and kitchen utensils.) So they asked Jesus, "Why don't your followers do what other religious people do and wash their hands before meals?" Jesus replied, "God's speaker spoke the truth about you play-actors:

> 'These people name me with their lips,
> But their hearts are far away;
> They make their own rules sound like mine:
> I see the game they play!'

You've turned your backs on God's way to follow human traditions instead. I'll give you an example of how you reject God's way in order to keep your own tradition. Moses said, 'Respect your parents' and 'Those who speak evil of their parents are worthy of the death sentence.' But your idea is that someone can tell their father or mother, 'Whatever money you might have had from me to support you in your old age, has been offered to God. So it's no longer available for you.' You ignore God's wishes by that dodge. I could give you many examples of similar tricks you play." Then Jesus shouted across to the crowd, "Listen to me, all of you. I want you to understand. It's not the things that go into people that pollute them, but the things that come out. If you've got ears, use them!"

When Jesus left the crowd to go into the house, his friends asked him to explain what he meant. Jesus said, "Don't you see? The rules about eating have missed the point. Food is not what pollutes. Food just goes in one end and out the other!" (These words of Jesus abolished the food laws at a stroke!) Jesus went on, "It's what comes from someone's mind that pollutes – evil plans, abusing others to satisfy your lust, stealing, killing, disloyalty, greed, malice, deceit, rowdy behavior, envy, slander, pride, stupidity. It's these evil things coming from inside which pollute you."

(24) Jesus then moved on to the region of Tyre, and found lodgings there. He tried to escape notice, but, as usual, he was recognized. A woman with a little girl who was unwell, came to Jesus and fell at his feet. This woman was not Jewish but Syrian. She pleaded with Jesus to heal her daughter. Jesus said, "What about the proverb which says the children should be fed first? 'You don't take food from your children to give to your pet dogs.'" She said, "Sir, even the pet dogs eat the children's scraps when they fall under the table!" Jesus said, "What a good answer! You can go; your daughter is better!" When she got home she found her daughter had recovered and was lying peacefully on the bed.

Jesus returned to Lake Galilee by a roundabout route, first visiting Sidon, then the Ten Towns east of the River Jordan, all parts where people of other races lived. A group brought along a man who was unable to hear or speak clearly. They asked Jesus to touch him. Jesus took the man aside privately. First he put his fingers in the man's ears, then spat and touched his tongue. Then, looking up to the sky, Jesus took a deep breath and said,

"Open up!" Instantly the man could hear and speak plainly. Jesus told the group not to tell anybody. They ignored his request and enthusiastically spread the news. They just couldn't stop themselves. They told everybody, "Jesus is wonderful; he even gets the deaf to hear and the dumb to speak."

(8:1-10) It was during this visit to foreign parts that Jesus again found himself with a large crowd of hungry people. Jesus called his friends together and said, "I'm concerned about all these people who've been with me for three days and haven't eaten. If I send them away hungry some may collapse before they get home, because they've come a long way." The friends asked, "How can we get enough bread to feed everyone, out here in the country?" Jesus asked how many loaves there were and they told him "Seven." Jesus told the crowd to sit down and took the seven loaves. He said "thank you" to God, broke the loaves and gave them to his friends to pass among the crowd. They also had a few small fish. Jesus thanked God for these and handed them on to be passed around. The crowd had as much to eat as they wanted and seven baskets of leftovers were collected. About four thousand people were fed before being sent home. Then Jesus boarded a boat with his friends and made for the west side of the lake.[4]

8

(11) The strict set came to Jesus and started an argument. They wanted proof that he was qualified to speak for God. Jesus groaned and said, "Why do this lot want proof? They're not going to get any!" Jesus left them to it, got into the boat again, and went back across the lake.

Jesus' friends had forgotten to bring any bread; they only had one loaf in the boat. Jesus said, "Don't buy your bread from the strict set or from Herod's friends." They discussed with one another what Jesus had said, thinking that Jesus was talking about shopping. Jesus overheard them and said, "What's all this talk about bread? Don't you understand yet what I'm getting at? You're not using your eyes or ears! Think back! When I broke the loaves for the five thousand, how many baskets of leftovers did you collect?" They replied, "Twelve." "And what about the seven loaves for the four

---

[4] Mark 8:1-10 should be read with 7:24-37. It marks the concluding climax of an extended tour by Jesus of Gentile territory, as the geographical references make plain. Perhaps the whole section should be a chapter on its own – Chapter 7B!

thousand, how many baskets of leftovers that time?" They replied, "Seven." Jesus said, "You haven't made sense of the clues yet, have you?"

When they arrived at Fishtown, some people brought a blind man to Jesus and asked for his healing touch. Jesus led the blind man out of the village. After putting spit on his eyes and touching him, Jesus asked, "Can you see anything?" The blind man looked up and said, "I can see people, but they look like trees walking about!" Then Jesus touched his eyes again. The blind man stared hard and his sight came back so he could see everything clearly. Then Jesus sent him home, telling him to bypass the village.

(27) Jesus and his friends went on to the villages near Philiptown-Caesar. On the way he asked his friends, "Who do people say I am?" They replied, "John the Dipper, Elijah, or one of God's speakers from the old days." Then Jesus asked, "But who do you say I am?" Rocky answered, "You're God's Chosen." Jesus gave them strict instructions to keep it quiet. At this point Jesus started to teach that the Complete Person would have to go through great suffering, be rejected by the various religious groups, and be killed, then rise again from the dead after three days. Jesus was quite clear. Rocky took Jesus to one side and contradicted him crossly. Jesus turned round to face his other friends, saying to Rocky. "Get away from me! You're a bad influence. You get your ideas from people, not from God!"

Jesus called his friends and the crowd together and told them, "If you want to be my followers, forget about yourselves, shoulder your cross, and do things my way. Those who try to save their lives will lose them, but those who lose their lives for me while sharing the Good News, will make their lives complete. What's the use if you have everything, but aren't true to yourself? Can you put a price on being true to yourself? Those who are embarrassed by me and my ideas in this heartless and selfish world will feel sick when the Complete Person appears in the splendor of the Loving God, and all God's company gather together."

9 Jesus went on to say, "Believe me, some of you here will not die until you see the grand dawn of God's New World." A week later Jesus took Rocky, Thunder, and Lightning up a mountain on their own. They saw a great change in the way Jesus looked. His clothes became gleaming white, whiter than any washing powder

would make them. Elijah and Moses appeared to be there, talking with Jesus. Rocky said to Jesus. "Teacher, it's great up here! Let's make three shrines, one for you, one for Moses, and one for Elijah!" Rocky blurted this out without thinking, to cover his confusion. Then a cloud cast a shadow and a voice came from its direction. "This is the one I love, my own, listen to him." Suddenly when they looked round there was no one there except Jesus and themselves.

As they came down the mountain, Jesus told them not to tell anyone about their experience until he had come back to life from the dead. So they kept it to themselves, but were puzzled about the meaning of "life from the dead." Then they asked Jesus, "Why do the experts in the old books say Elijah has to return first?" Jesus replied, "Quite right! Elijah does have to come first to make sure everything is ready. But what do you make of the book that says the Complete Person will face a lot of suffering and meet with contempt? I'll have you know Elijah has come, and people treated him with abuse. That's in the old books too!"

When they joined their companions, they found them arguing with some experts in the old books. A big crowd was looking on. When the people saw Jesus coming, the tension increased and they ran to meet him. Jesus asked, "What's the argument about?" Someone in the crowd answered, "Sir, I brought you my son who suffers from fits and can't speak properly. Whenever a fit comes on he falls down, foams at the mouth, grinds his teeth, and goes stiff. I asked your assistants to help him, but they couldn't do a thing!" Jesus shouted at his friends, "What a useless bunch you are! How long do I have to put up with you? Let me have a look at him!" They brought the boy to Jesus. Straightaway he was seized with an attack. He rolled on the ground, shaking from head to toe. Jesus asked the father, "How long has this been going on?" He replied, "Since he was a child. The fits have often thrown him into the fire or the water. We're afraid he's going to kill himself. If you can do anything, please have pity and help us!" Jesus said, "What do you mean, If? Everything is possible for those who trust!" The father cried out, "I'm doing my best to trust; please help me make it!" When Jesus saw the crowd was getting out of hand, he said to the boy, "No more deaf and dumb!" After more screaming and shaking, the boy lay completely still. The crowd gasped, all together, "He's dead!" But Jesus took hold of his hand and pulled him to his feet. He was quite steady. When they got indoors, the friends asked Jesus, "Why couldn't we do that?" Jesus replied, "In cases like this, you must ask God to help."

(30) They continued their journey, passing through Galilee. Jesus tried to avoid being seen, because he wanted to spend the time teaching his friends. He told them, "The Complete Person will be betrayed and killed, but three days later come back to life." This was too much for them to grasp and they were afraid to ask questions.

Later, back in the house at Nahum town, Jesus asked his friends, "What were you arguing about on the way here?" There was an embarrassed silence because they had been arguing about which of them was the most important. Jesus sat down and asked the twelve of them to gather round. He began by saying, "Whoever wants to be first must go to the end of the queue and do the dirty jobs for everybody else." Then Jesus stood a little child in the middle of the circle, and taking her in his arms he said, "Whoever cares about a child like this cares about me, and whoever cares about me cares for the one who gave me my job."

Lightning said to Jesus, "Teacher, we saw someone healing people by using your name, and we tried to stop him because he's not a member of our team." But Jesus said, "Don't get in the way! No one who does something wonderful in my name is likely to give me a bad reputation! Anyone who's not against us is for us! Even someone who gives you a cup of water because you follow God's Chosen will be the better for it. But if you make difficulties for those simple people who trust me, you'd be better off being thrown into the sea with a big stone round your neck! If your hand gets in the way of you behaving yourself, you'd better cut it off! Better to be handicapped than miserable ever after. If your foot won't walk the right path, off with it! Better lame than a tortured personality! And if your eye gives you a crooked view of things, you may as well tear it out. Better far to be one-eyed in God's World than live in a world of horrible fantasies!"

Jesus said, "We can all be improved by suffering. Just as salt can blend together a variety of tastes (provided it hasn't lost its tang), so suffering can bring people together in closer understanding. I want you to be at ease with one another."

10 Jesus moved on, this time south to the Province of Judea and across to the other side of the River Jordan, where once again a large crowd gathered. Jesus taught them as usual. Some of the strict set came to him with a trick question, "Does our religion allow divorce?" Jesus answered, "What ruling did Moses give?" They replied, "Moses allowed the husband to divorce his wife by writing her a certificate of separation." Jesus said, "Moses made that provision because of your insensitive attitude to women. But God's creation included female as well as male. That's why, in our wedding ceremonies, it's the man who has to leave his parents to go and join his wife, and then the two are united. If God has brought them together, no one should separate them!" Back in the house, Jesus' followers brought up the topic again. Jesus explained, "Anyone who turns their back on their partner to go with someone else does a very wicked thing. It's wrong to destroy one relationship in order to have another. It makes no difference whether it's a woman or a man who is responsible."

(13) People were bringing young children for Jesus to hold, but his friends tried to shoo them off. This made Jesus very angry and he said, "Let the children come to me; never try to stop them. They already belong to God's New World. In fact, anyone who doesn't naturally accept God's New World in the way a child does, has no chance of being part of it." Then Jesus took the children in his arms, cuddled them, and made them laugh.

Just as Jesus was setting out on another journey, a man ran up and knelt before him. He asked, "Good Teacher, what must I do to have life to the full?" Jesus said, "You shouldn't be so free with your compliments. Only God is good! You know the rules – don't kill, don't take away someone else's partner, don't steal, don't lie or cheat, respect your parents." The man said, "Teacher, I've kept all the rules since I was a child." For Jesus it was love at first sight. So he said to the man, "There's only one thing missing. Go and sell everything you've got, give the money to those in need, and you'll find things of real value in God's New World. Then come and be my friend!" This advice was not what the man wanted. He went away very depressed, since he was very wealthy. Jesus turned to his friends and said, "It's exceedingly difficult for the well-off to become citizens of God's New World." This disturbed them. But Jesus pressed the point by saying, "Don't be so innocent! You've no idea how hard it is! It's easier for a camel to get through the eye of a needle than for the wealthy to get into God's New World!" This shocked them and they said to one another, "There's not much chance for anybody then!" Jesus looked at them and said, "It's impossible for people to make it without God's help, but with God everything's possible!"

Rocky said, "Do you realize we've given up everything to follow you?" Jesus said, "The fact is, all those who've left their homes, family, business, or property to help me spread the Good News are a hundred per cent better off here and now. You belong to many families and share their homes and their luxuries. Although you'll experience persecution, you have the prospect of life to the full in the new age now dawning. But many of those at the front of the queue will find themselves at the back, and those at the back will be in front."

(32) They now started to go in the direction of Jerusalem. Jesus was striding out in front. His friends and followers were amazed and frightened. Again, Jesus took the twelve to one side and told them what was going to happen to him. "You see we're on our way to Jerusalem. The Complete Person will be handed over to the religious authorities. They will pass the death sentence. Then the Romans will take charge. They will mock him and spit on him, flog him and kill him. After three days the Complete Person will come back to life."

Thunder and Lightning approached Jesus and said, "Teacher, we have a request." Jesus said. "What do you want?" They asked, "Can we book the best seats, either side of you, for when you rule the world?" Jesus said, "You don't know what you're asking! Can you drink the bitter cup I'm going to drink, or be dipped in the chilly waters I'm going to be dipped in?" "Count on us!" they said. Then Jesus said, "Yes, you'll drink my bitter cup and pass through the same waters, but I've no say as to who will get the best seats; they've already been reserved."

When the other ten got wind of this, they were angry at Thunder and Lightning. So Jesus drew them together and said, "You know that many countries have leaders who throw their weight around, and some of them are cruel dictators. You must never behave like them. Anyone wanting to make their mark must outdo the rest in being of help to others. And if you want to be number one, you must be at everybody's beck and call. The Complete Person isn't here to be waited upon, but to wait on those in need, giving up life itself to set people free."

(46) They next visited Jericho. On the way out of the town, Jesus and his friends were joined by a large crowd. Barty Timson was blind and begged for a living by the roadside. When he learnt that Jesus of Nazareth was walking by, Barty shouted out, "Jesus, New David, please help me!" Despite attempts from the crowd to keep him quiet, he shouted louder, "Jesus, New David, help me for pity's sake!" Jesus stopped and said, "Ask him to come over here!" Some of them went to fetch the blind man, encouraging him by saying, "It's going to be alright. Come along, he wants to meet you." Barty tossed aside his cloak, leapt to his feet, and came to Jesus. Jesus said, "What can I do for you?" The blind man said, "Sir, I want to see again." Jesus said, "On your way, then. Your trust has cured you." Immediately Barty could see and he joined the procession.

11 When they reached the suburbs of Jerusalem, between Figland and Dategrove near Olive Hill, Jesus gave these instructions to two of his friends, "Go into the next village, and at one of the first houses you come to, you'll find a young donkey tied up. She's not yet been broken in. Untie her and bring her to me. If anyone asks you what you are up to, you can say, 'The Leader needs her and will return her shortly.'" They went off and found a donkey tied near a door in the street. As they were untying her, some people standing by asked, "What do you think you're doing, untying that donkey?" The friends used the words Jesus had given them and were allowed to lead her away. They brought the donkey to Jesus, made their cloaks into a saddle, and Jesus got onto her. Many people spread their cloaks on the road and others used branches they cut down from the trees. Then those in front and those behind kept up a chant,

> "*Freedom now! Freedom now!*
> *God's on our side!*
> *New David! New World!*
> *Freedom for ever!*"

When he entered Jerusalem, Jesus went to the temple and had a good look round. But as it was getting late he went back to Dategrove with his friends.

The next day, on the way from Dategrove, Jesus was feeling hungry. He noticed, some way off, a fig tree in leaf and went over to see if there was any fruit on it. There was nothing but leaves since it was not the right time of the year. Jesus said to the fig tree, "No one will eat your fruit ever again!" The friends overheard what Jesus said.

They reached Jerusalem and Jesus went into the worship center and drove out the traders. He knocked over the moneychangers' stands and the stalls of the pigeon sellers, and stopped the use of the precinct as a short cut for those making deliveries. Jesus explained by saying, "The old books say, 'My house shall be known as a place where people of all races meet with God!' But you've made it into a thieves' den!" This provoked the clergy into trying to find a way to kill Jesus. He frightened them by his ability to win over all types of people. In the evening, Jesus and his friends left the city again.

In the morning, as they passed by, they saw the fig tree had withered down to its roots. Rocky remembered about it and said, "Teacher, look! The fig tree you spoke harshly to has withered." Jesus replied, "Put your trust in God. Believe me, if you say to this mountain, 'Jump into the sea,' without any doubts in your mind, really expecting it to happen, watch out for the splash! I tell you, if you bring any request to God, trusting it's already been granted, you won't have long to wait. Whenever you talk to God, forgive those who've wronged you. Then the Loving God can forgive your wrongdoing."

Jesus went back to Jerusalem. While he was walking in the precinct, the clergy came to him with the question, "What right have you to do these things? Where do you get your orders?" Jesus said, "I'll answer your question if you'll answer mine. Was John inspired by God to dip people, or did he get the idea from someone else? Well?" They talked among themselves and realized if they said "John was inspired by God," Jesus would say, "Why then didn't you accept his teaching?" But if they said, "He got his ideas from someone else," they were afraid it would upset the crowd, for the popular opinion was that John was a genuine messenger from God. So they answered, "We don't know." Jesus replied, "Then I'm not going to tell you where I get my orders."

12

Then Jesus told this story to the clergy who had been challenging him. "A landowner planted a vineyard, put a hedge round it, dug a pit for the winepress and built a watchtower. Then he leased it to tenants and went abroad. When it was time to harvest the grapes he sent an agent to the tenants to collect the landowner's share. But the tenants grabbed hold of the agent, beat him up, and sent him away with nothing. So the landowner sent another agent. They punched this one in the face and made fun of him. The next agent the landowner sent they killed. Many more agents they treated in the same way, killing some and assaulting others, until the only person left to act as agent was the landowner's son, the apple of his eye. He was sent in the hope that a member of the family would be respected. But the tenants said to one another, 'This is the heir; come on, let's kill him and the property will be ours.' So they seized him, murdered him, and threw the body out of the vineyard. What do you expect the landowner to do? Yes, he will come and put the tenants to death and find some new tenants for the vineyard. Haven't you read these words?

> 'The stone the builders thought was useless
> Is the stone that takes the stress.
> God gives us such a big surprise,
> We scarcely can believe our eyes.' "

When the clergy realized the story was about them, they wanted to arrest Jesus, but they were afraid of the crowd. So they slunk away.

Next they sent some of the strict set and some supporters of Herod with a trick question. They came to Jesus and said, "Teacher, we know you're sincere and not afraid to speak your mind. You don't worry what position people hold, you just speak God's truth to them as you see it. Is it right to pay taxes to the Roman emperor or no? Should we pay up or should we refuse to pay?" Jesus knew their motives were not honest, so he said to them, "Why are you trying to trip me up? Has anyone got a silver coin for me to have a look at?" They handed him one. Then Jesus asked, "Whose head is this, and whose name's above it?" They answered, "The emperor's!" Jesus said, "Give the emperor what belongs to the emperor, and give God what belongs to God!" They were lost for words!

A religious group who said there is no such thing as life after death came to Jesus with their question. "Teacher, Moses made this rule for us. If a man's brother dies, leaving a wife but no child, the man shall marry the widow and produce children for his brother. Just suppose there were seven brothers; the first married and, when he died, left no children; and the second one married her and died, leaving no children; the same with the third, and so on, none of the seven leaving children. Eventually the woman herself died. Whose wife will she be in the next life? All seven had married her." Jesus replied, "You've got it all wrong because you don't understand the old books, and you've no idea what God can do! In the next life there is no such thing as marriage. There will be a different form of existence. As to the question of whether the dead live again, haven't you read in the book about Moses, the part where God speaks from a bush and says, 'I am the God of Abraham, the God of Isaac, and the God of Jacob'? God isn't God of the dead, but God of the living. You really have got it all wrong!"

One of the experts in the old books overheard this conversation and was impressed by the answers Jesus gave. So he asked the question, "Which is the most important of all God's rules?" Jesus answered, "The most important rule is:

> *'Listen, people of Israel. There is only one God. Love God with everything you have – your feelings, your intelligence, your physical strength.'*

The next most important rule is.

> *'Love the person next to you as you love yourself.'*

These are the most important rules." Then the man said to Jesus, "Well said, Teacher! You are right in saying 'God is One' – no one else deserves our allegiance; and to love God with everything you've got, feelings, intelligence, physical strength, and to love the person next to you as you love yourself is more important than all our acts of worship." These comments led Jesus to remark, "One more step and you'll be in God's New

World." After that no one risked asking Jesus any questions.

Jesus went on teaching in the temple. He said, "I'm surprised the experts say God's Chosen One is to be a descendant of David, since David was inspired by God's Spirit to say,

> God said to my Leader: 'Sit by me.
> Then you'll have no enemy.'

If David calls God's Chosen his Leader, how can he be David's descendant?" This brought some chuckles from the crowd.[5]

Jesus said, "Don't trust your clergy. They like to parade in their expensive robes and have everyone make a fuss of them when they appear in public. They hog the best seats in the places of worship and sit at the top table when there is a banquet! They take advantage of widows and coax money out of them, and say long prayers in order to impress everybody. They'll pay for it one day!"

Then Jesus sat down opposite the offertory box and watched as people put their money in. Many of the well-to-do put in large amounts. Then a poor widow came and put in two small coins, barely enough to buy anything. Jesus called his friends over and said, "I'm telling you, this poor woman has contributed more than all the others who've put their money in the box. All these wealthy people can easily afford what they gave, but she has given all she had to live on."

13 As Jesus was leaving the temple, one of his friends remarked, "These really are magnificent buildings; just look at the size of those stones!" Jesus said, "You'd better take a good look. It's all due to be demolished!" Later Jesus was sitting with Rocky, Thunder and Lightning, and Andrew, on Olive Hill where they had a good view of the temple. As there was no one else around, they asked Jesus, "When will the temple be demolished and what events will lead up to it?"

Jesus said, "Don't let anyone fool you. There will be many who claim to be acting on my behalf or use God's name, and they will mislead lots of

---

[5] Jesus is not indulging in fundamentalist literalism, quite the opposite. Jesus is humorously caricaturing the Pharisees' literalistic approach to scripture, beating them at their own game!

people. There's no need to get excited when you hear about wars and rebellions. This is the natural course of events; it doesn't mean the end of the world has come. Countries will go to war with one another, and rulers will engage in power struggles. There'll be natural disasters in various places and severe food shortages. These things are painful, like the pain a woman has to go through when she has a baby. You'll have to watch your step, because you'll be arrested and taken to court; you'll be flogged in the places where God is worshiped and you'll find yourselves up in front of rulers and high officials because of your allegiance to me. It will be your chance to tell them the truth. Make sure the Good News gets to every country in the world. That's your first priority! When they take you to court, don't worry about what to say. Rely on God's Spirit; she will prompt you! Brothers and sisters will betray one another, parents will disown their children, and children will be responsible for seeing their parents killed. You'll attract hatred from all quarters because of your loyalty to me. But those who stay the course will come through to full life and health.

"When you see the 'Big Eyesore' where it shouldn't be (work that out for yourself), then the people who live near Jerusalem should take refuge in the mountains. They will have no time to go through the house to collect their belongings. Anyone out in the fields shouldn't go home to get a coat. It will be hard on those who are pregnant or nursing young children when the time comes! Just hope that it doesn't happen in the winter. It will be a time of great suffering, greater than ever before or ever again. Only because God intends to shorten the period will there be any chance of survivors. For the sake of God's people there'll be a limit to those days.

"Don't believe anyone who claims to be able to point out God's Chosen at that time. There will be impostors and pretenders who use tricks to convince people. They'll come close to deceiving God's best friends. So be on the lookout. I've warned you!"

Jesus also told them, "Sometime in the future, after a period of suffering, there will be a time when no one can see clearly what is going on. There will be great changes, and it will seem as if the whole universe is falling apart. Then the Complete Person will appear and scatter all the clouds. It will be a tremendous occasion! The Complete Person will send out God's messengers and gather God's family from every part of the world."

Jesus said, "You can learn a lesson from the fig tree. When a branch grows, it becomes tender, and its leaves come out. Then you know summer is on the way. When you see things turning out in the way I've described, you'll know what's going to happen next. Believe me, the world as you know it won't disappear until the events I've told you about have taken place. One civilization will give way to another, but my words will last forever.

"But no one knows when the final end of history will come, apart from the Loving God. Even I don't know that. Be careful, watch out; you're likely to be taken by surprise. Think of it like the manager of a business going on holiday. The deputies are put in charge and told to get on with their various duties. The porter has special instructions to keep a look out. Keep awake! You don't know when the boss will come back. It may be evening, it may be midnight, or it may be early in the morning. There won't be any warning. Don't be caught napping! I'm saying this to all my friends: Keep on your toes!"

14 Two days before the festival when the Jews celebrated their escape from Egypt, the clergy were trying to work out a plan to kidnap Jesus and kill him before people knew what was happening. They said, "It had better not be over the holiday. There would be riots!"

Jesus was being entertained at Dategrove in Simon's house. This Simon was an outcast because he had a skin disease. Jesus was lying on a couch near the table. A woman came in with a glass jar filled with very expensive perfume, pure oil of nard. She broke the jar and poured the ointment on Jesus' head. There were angry comments. Some said, "What a waste!" "That ointment was worth a year's wages. It could have been sold and the money given to charity!" And they gave her a telling-off. But Jesus said, "That's enough of that! Why must you be so rude? I think she's done something very wonderful for me. Your sort make sure there'll always be plenty of poor people to practice your charity on. But you're not going to have many more opportunities to show kindness to me! This woman has done what she felt able to do; she has embalmed my body ready for my burial. Believe me, wherever the Good News is told all over the world, her story will be included, and what she has done will be commended."

It was at this time that Judas from Kerioth, one of the twelve close friends of Jesus, went to the clergy and offered to give Jesus away. They were delighted and promised to pay him well. Judas began to look out for a good chance.

(12) On the first day of the festival in which only bread without yeast is eaten, a lamb was offered to God in worship. Jesus' friends said to him, "Where do you want us to get the food ready for the celebration?" Jesus told two of them, "Go into the city and look out for a man carrying a jar of water. Keep on his track and mark which house he goes into. Then speak to the owner of the house and say, 'We have a message from the Teacher. Where's the guest room for me to celebrate the festival meal with my friends?' You'll be shown to a large upstairs room, with couches set out, and everything you need. You can get the food ready there." The two went into the city and everything worked out as Jesus had said. So they set out the food for the celebration.[6]

Jesus arrived with his twelve friends in the evening. When they had settled down and started eating, Jesus said, "Believe me, one of you eating with me will give me away." They were distressed and each of them protested, "It can't be me!" Jesus persisted, "I'm talking about one of my twelve closest friends – someone dipping bread in the same bowl with me! The Complete Person is going to follow the pattern found in the old books, but shame on the one who betrays the Complete Person. That traitor will wish he'd never been born!"

During the meal, Jesus took a loaf of bread, and thanked God for it. Then he broke it and handed it on to them. He said, "Take this: it's my body." Then Jesus took a cup, said "thank you" to God, and passed it on to them. Everyone drank from it. Jesus said, "This is my blood; it brings people into friendship with God. It will flow for many! Believe me, I won't drink wine again until I drink it in God's New World!"

They sang a song to God, then made their way to Olive Hill. Jesus told them, "All of you will lose your nerve and run off. As our old books say,

> 'When the shepherd falls dead,
> The sheep run in dread.'

---

[6] See footnote 7.

But when I come back to life, I'll go ahead of you to Galilee." Rocky said, "The rest may desert you, but I won't!" Jesus replied, "Before dawn tomorrow, before the cock crows twice, you will disown me three times." Rocky was furious, and said, "Even if I have to die by your side, I'll never disown you." And they all said the same.

(32) They reached a secluded spot near an old olive press, and Jesus said to his friends, "Sit here while I talk with God." He took Rocky and Thunder and Lightning a little further. He became distressed and agitated, and told them, "My heart's breaking. I feel as if I'm being crushed to death. Please stay close to me and keep awake." Jesus went a bit further away and threw himself on the ground, asking if there was any way of getting out of the horrible things that were about to happen. He said, "Dear Loving God, you can do anything. Get me out of this! … No, what I want doesn't matter, only what you want." Jesus came back and found the three friends asleep. He said to Rocky, "Simon, you? Asleep? Couldn't you manage to keep awake for an hour? You must all keep your eyes open and ask God to spare you the test. You want to help me, but you haven't got the guts." Jesus went away again and talked with God, using the same words as before. Coming back he found them asleep again. They could not keep their eyes open. They were too embarrassed to say anything. The same thing happened a third time and Jesus said, "Still asleep? Still taking it easy? Enough is enough. The time has come. The Complete Person is about to be handed over by the traitor to evil people. Up you get! Time to go! Look, here comes the traitor!"

Then Judas, one of the twelve close friends of Jesus, appeared with a mob waving swords and clubs. They were sent by the clergy and the city councilors. The traitor had a signal, "The one I kiss is the man you want. Grab him and watch he doesn't escape." Judas came up to Jesus and without hesitating said, "Hello, Leader!" and kissed him. They grabbed hold of Jesus and held him tight. Someone struck out at a lad who worked for the High Priest and cut his ear off. Then Jesus said, "What are you doing with those clubs and knives? What do you think I am, a terrorist? You've seen me teaching in the temple every day. Why didn't you arrest me then? You're determined to do what the old books say." Then all Jesus' friends ran for their lives.

A young man was following Jesus, wearing only a bed sheet. The mob caught hold of him, but he struggled out of the sheet and ran off naked.[7]

(53) They took Jesus to Guy, Chief of the Clergy. He was joined by other members of the clergy. Rocky followed at a distance, as far as the courtyard of the Chief's house. He sat down with the guards, to keep warm by their fire. The council met to prepare evidence on which they could execute Jesus, but they failed to come up with anything convincing. Plenty of people came forward with false evidence, but they contradicted one another. Some of these took the stand and said, "We heard him say he'd destroy this temple, which our skilled workers have built, and build another in three days by superhuman means." But even on this their evidence conflicted. Then Guy broke in and spoke to Jesus, "What have you to say to all this? It's time for you to explain yourself!" But Jesus kept quiet. Then Guy asked, "Are you the Chosen One, God's own?" Jesus replied, "I am what I am. You're going to see my new humanity championed by God. The Complete Person will break the barrier between time and eternity."[8] Then Guy lost his temper and said, "We don't need any more witnesses; you've heard the insult to God! What's your verdict?" They all agreed on the death sentence. Some of them began to spit at Jesus, and some blindfolded him and took turns at punching him, shouting, "Guess who that was!" And the guards joined in, slapping Jesus in the face.

Meanwhile, Rocky was still hanging around in the courtyard when a woman who worked for the Chief came by. She noticed Rocky warming himself and stared hard at him. Then she said, "Haven't I seen you with Jesus of Nazareth?" Rocky shook his head and said, "I don't know what the hell you're talking about!" Then as he moved to the gateway, a cock crowed. But the girl kept her eye on him and pointed him out to the people

---

[7] Probably the author's anonymous inclusion of himself in the story. As a longer shot, this might also apply to 14:13 and 16:5.

[8] "I am what I am," literally "I am." Jesus quotes in answer to his questioners the reply given to Moses when Moses sought to learn God's name and identity. God's reply was not an answer but a divine dodging of the question. Those versed in the Hebrew scriptures would realize that Jesus was doing the same. "I am" in Hebrew understanding is not simply the first person of the verb "to be" but means, as Exodus 3:14 makes clear, something like "I am what I am" or "I will be what I will be." Jesus proceeds to link his current humanity with his future humanity (inclusive of the humanity of the community he is transforming). It was blasphemous to utter the divine name and resulted in the court's verdict of blasphemy. Jesus was again breaking barriers. For him blasphemy was not a matter of verbal taboo, but the spiritual blindness that fails to appreciate the good things of God (See Mark 3:28).

standing around. "He's one of them!" Again Rocky refused to admit it. After a little while, someone else challenged him. "You must be one of them; you're from Galilee!" Rocky lost control of himself and began to use foul language, "I'm telling you, I've never bloody set eyes on him!" At that precise moment the cock crowed again. Rocky remembered Jesus had warned him, "Before the cock crows twice, you will disown me three times." Rocky broke down and cried.

15 In the early morning, the full council met together again. They tied Jesus up and took him to Pilate, the Roman Governor. Pilate began to interrogate Jesus. "So you're the Leader of the Jews?" Jesus said, "That's *your* way of looking at things!" The council had drawn up a long charge sheet, so Pilate spoke to Jesus again, "See all these things they're accusing you of? I'd like to hear your side of the story." But to Pilate's great surprise, Jesus had no more to say.

Pilate had the custom of setting one prisoner free at the festival, whoever the people shouted for. There was a prisoner called Barry, one of a group of terrorists who had committed murder during a riot. So when the crowd came to ask Pilate to keep his custom, Pilate said, "How would you like me to set free the Leader of the Jews?" (Pilate realized that envy was the reason why the clergy had brought Jesus to trial.) But the clergy had agents in the crowd to get people to shout for Barry instead. Pilate spoke to them again. "In that case, what do you want me to do with the one you call the Leader of the Jews?" They screamed back, "Put him on a cross!" Pilate asked them, "Why? What's he done wrong?" But they roared, "Hang him high!" Pilate was anxious to please the crowd, so he released Barry. He had Jesus flogged, and made arrangements for him to be hung on a cross.

First the soldiers led Jesus back inside and called together the rest of their mates. They put a purple cloak over his shoulders and twisted some thorns into the shape of a crown and rammed it on his head. Then they began to salute him and shout, "Three cheers for the Leader of the Jews!" They hit Jesus about the head with a stick, spat in his face, and knelt down in front of him. When they had finished their fun, they stripped off the purple cloak and put his own clothes on him. Then they marched him off to the place of execution.

(21) The soldiers forced someone to help carry Jesus' cross. He was an African called Simon (the father of Alex and Rufus). He just happened to be passing that way, coming into the city from the country. They took Jesus as far as Skull Hill. They tried to get him to take a painkiller, but he refused it. Then they fastened Jesus to the cross and put it in place. They shared out his clothes, throwing dice for each item.

This was at nine o'clock in the morning. The poster with the charge on said, "The Leader of the Jews." Two thugs were hung either side of Jesus. The people who passed by shouted insults at him, falling about with laughter. Someone shouted, "Hey, you! Weren't you going to knock down the temple and build it in three days? How about jumping off the cross and saving yourself?" The clergy joked among themselves. "He was very good at helping other people. He's not much good at helping himself! Why doesn't God's Chosen, the Leader of the Jews, get off the cross now? If we see that, we'll support him!" Even the thugs hanging either side of Jesus shouted abuse.

At twelve o'clock it became very dark everywhere until three in the afternoon. At three o'clock Jesus shouted out in Hebrew, "My God, my God, why have you left me?" The Hebrew for "My God" sounds something like Elijah, so some of the onlookers said, "He's calling for Elijah!" Someone ran and filled a sponge with some cheap wine, put it on a stick and held it up for Jesus to drink, saying, "That's enough poking fun! We'd better watch out. Elijah might come and take him down." But Jesus gave a loud cry and died.

At that moment the curtain in the temple was ripped from top to bottom. When the Roman officer on duty saw the way Jesus died, he said, "He was truly God-like."

Some women were watching a little way off, including Maggie, Sally, and Maria (the mother of Joseph from Ram and James, his younger brother). These were loyal friends of Jesus who had helped him when he was in Galilee. Other friends of Jesus who had come as visitors to Jerusalem were also there.

(42) It was time to get ready for the Rest Day. In the evening Joseph from Ram, a respected member of the council, who was looking forward eagerly to God's New World, went with great courage to Pilate and asked for Jesus' body. Pilate was surprised to hear Jesus was already dead. He called for the officer on duty and asked if Jesus had been dead long. When the officer

certified that Jesus was dead, Pilate gave permission for Joseph to take the body. Joseph took the body down, wrapped it in a linen cloth he had brought with him, and laid it in a grave that had been dug out of solid rock. Then he rolled a stone against the entrance of the grave. Maggie and Maria (Joseph's mother) were at the burial.

16 When the Rest Day was over, Maggie, Maria, and Sally bought some spices to embalm Jesus' body. Very early on Sunday morning, as soon as it was light, they made their way to the grave. As they went along they said, "Who are we going to get to shift the stone?" But when they got there, they noticed the stone, a gigantic one, had already been moved. They went inside and got a fright when they found a well-dressed young man sitting on the right hand side.[9] He said to them, "There's no need to be frightened. You're looking for Jesus from Nazareth who was hung on a cross. He's come to life again: you won't find him here. Look, that's where they laid him out! Go and tell his friends, including Rocky, he plans to go ahead of you to Galilee, just as he said he would. You'll meet him there." They rushed out and ran away as fast as they could, frightened and confused. They said nothing about it to anyone, because they were in a state of shock …[10]

---

[9] See footnote 7.

[10] Mark's Gospel appears to be incomplete. Two endings were later added, neither satisfactory. In our two first drafts of Mark we produced translations of both these false endings. We now think it better to omit them.

Thought-Provoking Sayings of Jesus

As recalled by Twin

Introduction

The Gospel of Thomas was discovered in 1945 in Egypt among a collection of ancient documents found by accident in an old jar. The assessment of scholars is that the document, in Coptic, is a translation of an early Christian scripture in Greek, now lost, but known to the early Church, and a matter of controversy. It is mentioned by Hippolytus of Rome in the third century in the context of refuting heresy. Those who have studied the work in detail conclude that it is probably to be included among the earliest of Christian writings, possibly as early as the Gospels we use, or second century at the latest. It is not a Gospel in the sense that we understand it, but a collection of the sayings of Jesus on the lines of the Sermon on the Mount in Matthew and its equivalent in Luke, sharing some common material with both. Some of the sayings of Jesus are presented in a rougher and less polished form than their parallels in the other Gospels, and one way of explaining this would be to say that Thomas is closer to the original. Other sayings strike us as odd at first acquaintance, especially in the word-for-word translations that have been produced hitherto. Oddity may account in part for the decision of the Church councils not to include Thomas in their authorized collection of scriptures. The other reason was that Thomas was probably identified with the Gnostics. Grant and Freedman, who in the 1960s introduced Thomas to the English-speaking public, assume that Gnosticism is what Thomas is all about and interpret it accordingly, seeking illumination of Thomas's meaning from other Gnostic texts of the early centuries. By doing this they ensure a bizarre interpretation of sayings that might otherwise be interpreted in a more intelligible way.

A definition of Gnosticism is not easy. The word "gnosis" (knowledge) sometimes refers to the knowledge of an exclusive elite whose company one cannot join without accepting the codes and practices of the elite. That's a very good description of the Christian Church and also of each of its denominations and sub-cultures! As applied to Thomas, it is argued that its emphasis on the importance of understanding the teachings of Jesus, and making them the basis of individual practice, amounts to an intellectual path to salvation indicative of one type of Gnosticism. But Matthew and Luke also conclude their accounts of the teaching of Jesus with the parable of the house builder in which salvation depends on paying attention to the words of Jesus.

Like the other Gospel writers, Thomas frequently records the saying of Jesus, "If you've got ears, use them!" The teaching method of Jesus was based on the practice of inviting his listeners to reflect on, wrestle with, debate his stories and sayings, and to come up with the truth that makes sense to them. Thomas's collection includes some sayings which take considerable unraveling, possibly because we have not met them before. We would do better, however, to use our own ears rather than those of the Gnostics of the early Christian era.

As with the other Gospels, the question of authorship cannot ever be answered with any certainty. There is good reason to believe that Mark was responsible for Mark, and Luke for Luke and Acts, but not Matthew for Matthew or John the son of Zebedee for John. It is attribution to the very earliest members of the disciple group that is always suspect. Twin was a member of the very earliest group and on balance it is doubtful if he penned the work. As in the case of Matthew or John, a disciple or admirer may have done so. The fact that there is so much common material between Matthew, Luke and Thomas, and Mark and John for that matter, does not mean they all copied from documents that were circulating before them, but rather that the stories and sayings of Jesus were well known and recited by many of Jesus' first hearers. However, the writer who appears behind the selection of sayings and stories of Jesus in the Gospel of Thomas, with its emphasis on thinking things out, is consistent with the Thomas as portrayed in the Gospel of John. So it is not implausible that we have an authentic line to Jesus via Twin.

In updating Thomas we use the freedom we have employed in our approach to the other Christian writings, and have applied the concepts of cultural and contextual translation. We admit to gently helping the reader by pushing her or him in the direction of an intelligent meaning, but enough is left of puzzle for the challenge to remain valid, "If you've got ears, use them!"

1 Jesus is alive! Here is a collection of some of his most intriguing and challenging sayings, as passed on by one of his closest friends, whose real name was Jude, but better known by his nickname, Twin.

Anyone who unravels these sayings and takes their truth as guide, will not experience death.

Jesus said, "Make your life a quest and don't give up till you find what you're looking for. What you find may upset your prejudices, but you'll discover much to wonder at and get to grips with what the world is all about."

Jesus said, "If the leaders of your community tell you God's New World is in the sky, you'll know they've got it wrong. That's where the birds will discover the New World! To say the New World is in the sky is as silly as saying it's under the sea. That's where the fish will discover it! In fact, God's New World has no precise location. It's to be found inside you and all around you.

"Other people won't understand you until you understand yourself. When you understand yourself, you'll realize you have a family relationship to the Loving God, and recognize the life of God inside you. There's no greater poverty than not understanding who and what you are."

Jesus said, "Someone who is old will have the sense to ask someone much younger about what's going on in the world today, and that up-to-date knowledge will give them a new lease of life.

"People's ideas of who is important and who isn't must be turned right around. One day, everybody's experience will be valued and be part of a shared whole.

"Recognize what's staring you in the face and everything else will make sense."

The friends of Jesus asked him many questions, such as "Do you want us to do without food from time to time?" "How do we talk with God?" "What provision should we make for those in need?" "Is there any food or drink we ought to avoid?" In answer to these questions Jesus said, "If you have a feeling deep inside you that something is wrong, don't do it. Don't let your minds play tricks on you. God sees things as they really are. One day your behavior will be seen by all for what it is."

Jesus said, "Splendid are those born with the character of a wild animal who allow themselves to be tamed by tender human qualities. Disgraceful are those born with tender human qualities who choose to develop the behavior of a wild animal."

He went on to say, "Human beings throw their nets into the sea of life and come up with all manner of fish, mostly small and worthless. Experienced fisherfolk pick out the big tasty fish and throw the rest back. If you've got ears, use them!"

Here is a story Jesus told. "One day a farmer went out onto his land with some seeds and scattered them around. Some fell on the path and the birds pecked them up right away. Some fell among the rocks and either didn't take root, or didn't find enough soil to produce full-grown plants. Some fell among the weeds and were choked; others were eaten by pests. But some fell on good soil and produced a good crop, yielding sixty or a hundred times the seed sown."

Jesus said, "I've set the world on fire. I must keep fuelling it until there's a good blaze!"

He said, "Everything that now exists will change – what you can see, and what you can't see.

"Being alive or dead has nothing to do with breathing and nothing to do with corpses.

"Ideas come to life when you let them shape your personality.

"When you learn something which sheds new light on things, you can either act on it or ignore it. Which will you do?"

The friends of Jesus said to him, "We know you're going to leave us. What shall we do for a leader?" Jesus said, "If you have any problems, you can always go to my brother James for advice. He's honest and fair. I think the world of him!"

(13) Jesus said to his friends, "How would you describe me, as compared with other people?"

Rocky said, "You're like a reporter who gets the facts right."

Matthew said, "You're a deep thinker who makes good sense."

Twin said, "Teacher, I'm lost for words!"

Jesus said, "I'm not your teacher. I'm just somebody standing by the spring of knowledge, inviting people to drink. You've been over-drinking from the spring lately and getting confused." Then Jesus took Twin to one side and had a serious chat with him. When he joined the other friends again they said, "What did he say to you?" Twin said, "If I tried to tell you, you'd kill me, and then you'd be in right trouble!"

Jesus told his friends, "If you try to score points by going without food, you'll be making a big mistake. Your talk with God will be insincere and your help to those in need will be given grudgingly.

"When you visit other countries and travel around, if people invite you into their homes, eat whatever food they put in front of you. Heal any members of the household who are unwell. What goes into your mouth doesn't make you a bad person, only what comes out of it!"

Jesus said, "You shouldn't bow or curtsey to other human beings. They were all born as babies like you were. Your true parent, the one you should honor, was not born that way."

Jesus said, "Some people think I'll get the peoples of the world to live together in peace in no time at all. It's not as easy as that. What I have to say will lead to deep divisions, conflict, killings, and all-out war. Families will be torn apart, and individual members made to feel lonely and isolated. But I do have something good to give you. It has not yet been seen, heard, or touched; indeed it's beyond human imagination."

The friends of Jesus said to him, "What will happen to us in the end?" Jesus said, "Why do you want to know about the end when you've only just started? Every end depends on where you begin. If you're lucky enough to get the beginning right, you'll discover that life is all beginnings with no final end.

"It's good if, before you develop your personalities and ideas, you first realize how lucky you are just to be alive!

"If you adopt my attitude to life and take to heart what I have to say, you'll learn to use the material things around you for your benefit.

"A garden has been provided for you where the trees are always green. Learn to appreciate the lovely things around you, and then, like them, you'll last forever."

(20) The friends of Jesus said to him, "What's God's New World like?" Jesus said, "It's like a mustard seed. It begins as something very small and ends up as a large plant, big enough for the birds to roost in."

Maggie asked Jesus, "What sort of people do you want your friends to be?" Jesus told a story. "One day some children were innocently playing in a field. The farmer came along and said, 'This is my field, get out of it!' The children stripped in front of the farmer to show they had stolen nothing and said, 'You can have your field, we mean you no harm!' "[1]

"Wise home-owners who've been told there's a burglar about make sure their property is well protected. In the same way, you must take precautions against those who would do you harm. You need an inner strength to meet the troubles that are sure to come. It helps to have an understanding friend you can talk to.

"The moment a crop is ripe, the farmer gets on with harvesting it. If you've got ears, use them!"

One day Jesus saw some mothers feeding their babies at the breast. Jesus said to his friends, "Little babies are the perfect example for those who want to be citizens of God's New World." The friends said, "Surely we don't have to become babies in order to qualify for the New World?" Jesus replied, "When two people become one, like a mother feeding her child; when there's no difference between the way you behave and what's going on in your mind, or between your head and your heart; when you treat males and females equally, without any distinctions whatsoever, when you respond naturally to another's body language; when you accept people as they are – then you'll be ready for God's New World."

Jesus said, "I select my friends very carefully. I expect them to stand shoulder to shoulder with one another."

The friends said, "Tell us exactly how you are thinking and feeling. We want to model ourselves on you!" Jesus said, "Trust your senses! If you're honest at heart, your honesty will help you to understand everything in the world, in the way a strong light shows everything more clearly. If you're confused inside, then everything you see will be blurred."[2]

---

[1] Maggie – in the text "Mary," almost certainly Mary of Magdala rather than Mary, the mother of Jesus. The Gospel of Thomas reflects the honor given to Maggie in the earliest days of the Christian communities, some of which was transferred to Mary the mother in succeeding generations when the Gospel characters were no longer remembered from personal contact. There are clear indications in the Gnostic writings that Maggie rivalled Rocky in authority, a competition she was bound, because of the culture of the time, to lose.

[2] "Trust your senses" i.e. "if you've got ears, use them!"

Jesus said, "Love other people as you love yourselves. Protect their interests as keenly as you protect your own eyes."

Jesus said, "You're very good at seeing the bit of sawdust in someone else's eye, but somehow manage to miss the plank in your own eye. Only when you've dealt with your own weaknesses will you be qualified to attend to the weaknesses of others."

"Until you free yourselves from your attachment to material things, you won't be ready for God's New World. If you don't make the Rest Day a day free from life's stress, you won't be in the right frame of mind to meet with the Loving God."

2 (28) Jesus said, "I've mixed with all sorts of people and always let them see my human side. But their minds were too full of their own concerns to have any interest in what I had to say. My heart went out to them because they just couldn't understand. They lacked any special advantages when they came into the world and seemed determined to end their days with none. It's as if they'd been drugged. One day they'll come to their senses. Then they'll see things differently."

Jesus said, "It's very wonderful how God's Spirit brought our bodies to life. It's even more wonderful how God's Spirit can use our bodies to express herself. The world is such a wonderful place – so much of value amongst so much poverty!"

Jesus said, "Some people have many gods. Their gods mark the presence of the true God.

"Where two people meet together, I'm there with them. I'm also the companion of those who are on their own."

Jesus said, "God's speakers aren't appreciated where they come from. It's difficult for a doctor to be the doctor to family or close friends."

Jesus said, "A town on the top of a steep bill can be seen from all around, and it's well protected from attack. So any truth whispered in your ear you must use every means to make public knowledge. You don't light a lamp and put it under a basket or in a cupboard. You put a lamp on a stand so that everyone coming in and going out can benefit from its light."

Jesus said, "If someone who doesn't know the district offers to show someone else the way, they'll probably both get lost!"

Jesus said, "A robber can't take possession of the house of someone strong until he's tied the strong person up. Then he can take his pick of the house's contents.

"Don't get yourself worked up about what you're going to wear to town this morning, or to a party this evening."

The friends of Jesus said to him, "We never know when we're going to see you next!"

Jesus said, "When you learn to be like little children who, without feeling the least bit shy, take off all their clothes and leave them in an untidy heap on the floor, then you'll relate to God's True Likeness without embarrassment."

Jesus said, "You've enjoyed listening to the many things I've had to say to you. I've told you what no one else can tell you. Make the most of the opportunities you have to get my advice. There will be times when you won't be able to get hold of me."

Jesus said, "The members of the strict set have taken away the keys of knowledge and hidden them. They're not interested in the truth themselves and do their best to make sure no one else has access to it either. You can only outwit them by being as crafty as snakes and harmless as pigeons."

Jesus said, "A form of religion has grown up which has nothing to do with the Loving God. Such a pathetic faith will have to be pulled up by the roots and allowed to die."

Jesus said, "If you offer what you have to others, you'll find you have more to offer, If you have nothing to offer, you'll end up with nothing,"

Jesus said, "Keep on the move."

The friends of Jesus said to him, "We'd like to know who you really are. Where have you got your ideas from?" Jesus said, "It seems you've not yet recognized me by what I say to you. Some of you are like people who claim loyalty to God without being interested in what God says, and some of you are like those who discuss what God says without being interested in God."

Jesus said, "You'll be forgiven for being an atheist, and you'll be forgiven for failing to recognize my relationship with God, but if you despise the good things that come from God's Spirit you'll become so twisted that no one will be able to put you right, in this world or in any other."

Jesus said, "You're no more likely to have a good time with prickly people than you are to find your favorite fruit in a bed of thistles. It's as if we each have a cupboard inside us. Good people bring out good things from their cupboard, but bad people have only nasty things to offer from theirs. You can spot a bad person from the way they talk about others."

Jesus said, "From the dawn of humanity until now, there has not been a better example of how we are meant to be than John the Dipper. He's someone we can all look up to. But, as I've told you before, anyone who becomes a citizen of God's New World by becoming as innocent as a child, will be of even greater value to humankind than John."

Jesus said, "You can't ride two horses at once or aim for two different targets at the same time. You must make up your mind where your loyalty lies. Anyone used to drinking vintage wine will not be enthusiastic about cheap table wine. You don't put new wine into dirty old bottles. You'd ruin the wine that way! You don't patch a new shirt with a piece of rag taken from an old shirt. It wouldn't look right!"

"If two people in a family or a community re-direct the energy they've been wasting on fighting each other into working together in harmony, there's no limit to what they'll be able to achieve."

Jesus said, "If anyone asks you, 'Where do you come from? Where do you get your ideas?' you should reply, 'We come from the light which appeared at the beginning of all things. That same light has made us what we are.' If they ask you, 'Are you the light itself?' you must say, 'No, we're only children of the light, people who know the living God as our parent.' And if they ask you, 'What evidence can you give us of your family likeness to God,' say, 'Like God we're always on the move and always at rest.'"

The friends of Jesus asked him, "When will those who have died be at peace, and when will God's New World come?" Jesus said, "It's all happened already; you just can't see it!"

The friends said, "We've counted over two dozen of God's speakers who spoke about you in times past." Jesus said, "They are no longer relevant. I don't know why you bother with them when you have among you someone who's right up to date!"

The friends of Jesus asked him, "Should males have their foreskins cut to conform with our tradition?" Jesus said, "If it were so important, boys would be born without their foreskins. There's more to be gained by removing restrictions of the mind and heart."

Jesus said, "The poorest people count most in God's eyes. They're already citizens of God's New World."

Jesus said, "Unless you escape from the patterns of thought and conduct given to you by your parents; unless you develop your own personality, distinct from your brothers and sisters; unless you become truly adult and take full responsibility for your actions, as I've done, you won't be fit to be a member of my team."

Jesus said, "You must get to know all about the world in order to discover how empty it is. Anyone who has experienced that emptiness is ready to be a first-class citizen!"

Jesus said, "Here is a picture of the Loving God's New World. A farmer sowed his seed, but during the night, someone who didn't like the farmer very much sowed weeds among the seed. The farmer didn't let his workers pull the weeds up, but said, 'If you try to pull up the weeds, you'll pull up the wheat with them. When the crop is ready to harvest, it will be easy to spot the weeds. They can be sorted out then and put on the compost heap.'"

Jesus said, "People who've had a hard life are the ones who count in God's eyes. They know what life's all about."

Jesus said, "Now is the time to learn how to live. Keep in touch with the one who lives forever. Don't wait until you die to experience life. It will be too late then to develop the art of living or to recognize God as the source of life."

Jesus drew the attention of his friends to someone from another country who was on the road to Jerusalem and carrying a lamb. Jesus asked them, "Why has he got the lamb tied up?" They said. "Probably because he means to kill it and have it to eat." Jesus said, "He won't get any food from the lamb until he's killed it." "That's obvious!" they said. Jesus said, "If you have no wish to give yourselves for the life of others, like a lamb, then you'd better find yourselves a secure hide-out. There's no security in making yourself comfortable with a friend on a sofa. At any moment one of you will be taken out for execution and the other spared."[3]

---

[3] The nearest equivalent to this advice from Jesus is to be found in the words he spoke to his friends in the garden, according to Luke. Either they should stand by him or make good their escape. The worst course was to dither. See Luke 22:35-38 and the accompanying footnote.

Sally said, "Who are you, Sir? You've shared a sofa with me and eaten from my table as if you were used to moving among the ruling classes!" Jesus said, "I come from a place where there are no distinctions of any kind. My parent taught me how to mix with everybody." Sally said, "You can count me as one of your friends!" Jesus said, "You and I can be friends because, like me, you have no prejudices. Prejudices make a person blind. To see clearly you must be ready to embrace all types."[4]

Jesus said, "To understand the things I say, you need to use your imagination."

Jesus said, "Don't disclose secrets of a personal nature to those you can't trust."[5]

Here are some stories Jesus told.

(i) *"There was once a man who came into a large amount of money. He decided to buy a farm. He planned to equip it with the latest machinery, buy the best seed for planting and build some new barns to store the crops. He thought, 'It will be a good investment and I'll be able to look forward to a comfortable old age.' The very night after he'd made this decision, he died." Jesus said, "If you've got ears, use them."*

(ii) *"A business woman was planning a dinner party. When she had fixed a date and made all the preparations, she sent a member of her office staff to the business premises of each of her colleagues, with a personal invitation. The first one he called on said, 'I'm having trouble at the moment getting money back from some of my debtors. I've arranged to meet them the day of the dinner party.*

---

[4] Sally – in the text "Salome." Obviously, like others among Jesus' female disciples, Sally was from the upper classes, and may, like Joan (Joanna), have been a member of the court of Herod Antipas. She may even be identified as Rose's dancing daughter, as suggested in John Henson's imaginative biographies, *Or was it like this?*

[5] Literally, "Do not let your left hand know what your right hand is doing," as in Matthew 6:3. In Matthew it is used in the context of giving, but the absence of such a clear indication of meaning here suggests the more basic meaning of circumspection.

I'm sorry, I won't be able to come.' The next one said, 'I've bought a new house and we're moving the furniture in that day. I'm sorry I won't have time for the party.' The third one to get the invitation said, 'My friend is getting married that day. I'm the best man and I've got to arrange the wedding breakfast and the dance afterwards. No chance of my getting to your dinner, I'm afraid!' The last one the messenger called on said, 'Your boss has chosen an inconvenient date. That's the day I always collect the rents from my tenants. Thanks for the invitation all the same.' When the man got back to the office, he said to his boss, 'None of them are coming. They're all too busy and send their apologies.' She said, 'Let's have some fun. Go out on the streets and invite some interesting characters to share my meal. It will be good to talk about something other than work for a change!' " Jesus said, "People who devote their whole lives to possessions or making money don't appreciate the good things my parent has to offer."

(111) *"A landowner let out his property to tenant farmers who agreed to supply him with a proportion of the produce as rent. When he sent his agent to collect what was due to him, they grabbed hold of him, beat him up and very nearly killed him. When he reported to the landowner what had happened, the landowner said, 'Perhaps they didn't know who you were.' When he tried again with another agent, the same thing happened. The next time, the landowner sent his son. He said, 'Perhaps they'll show a bit of respect for my son.' But the farmers, realizing they had the heir to the estates in their hands, beat him to death." Jesus said, "If you've got ears, use them!"*

Jesus said, "That stone the builders couldn't get to fit anywhere – put it where it's going to get noticed. It's the keystone. It will hold the whole building together!"

Jesus said. "Those who are highly educated but haven't learnt to understand themselves don't know very much at all."

Jesus said, "Think yourselves lucky when you're hated and persecuted. You'll find a secret place of peace where nothing can touch you. Those whose persecution comes in the form of anxiety are lucky too. They'll come close to the mind and heart of the Loving God."

Jesus said, "Well done those who go without food in order to provide food for those whose stomachs are empty!"

Jesus said, "If you use your natural gifts and talents to the full, you'll lead a worthwhile life. If you don't have that urge to make the very best of yourself, you'll shrivel up and die."

Jesus said, "I'm going to bring about a revolution which no one can reverse!"[6]

3 (72) A man said to Jesus, "My brothers have stolen my share of the family property. Tell them to give it to me." Jesus said, "I'm sorry friend, I don't know anything about property rights." Then Jesus turned to his followers and said, "I'm not a lawyer, am I? I work out in the fields, bringing in the harvest. I'm looking at a bumper crop, but I need more help. Ask the owner of the estate to hire some more workers. It's a matter of urgency!" The man said, "It seems to me there are many standing round the bar waiting for a drink, but the tap's run dry!" Jesus said, "I'd put it another way. At a party there are always some who nervously huddle together near the door, but only those who take that lonely step and walk right in enjoy the fun!"[7]

---

[6] Literally, "I'm going to knock the whole house down, and no one will be able to rebuild it." There are different versions of this saying of Jesus, quoted against him at his trial. Unlike the other Gospel writers, Twin does not soften its radicalism by seeking to explain it or put it in context. Perhaps, therefore, he gives us the saying in its original form, advocating the total destruction of that which has served it purpose.

[7] Jesus enjoyed this kind of banter where one person throws a proverb or witty saying at the other. He did not aim to win the game, but to establish the truth by means of dialogue. (His dialogue with the Syrian woman is a good example of his cheerfully losing the contest! See Mark 7:24-30.) Socrates had used a similar method, as Jesus would probably have been aware.

Jesus said, "The New World of the Loving God is like someone who kept a well-stocked jeweler's shop. One day she came across a very fine pearl. She had a keen eye to the value of things, so she sold up all her stock to become the owner of the pearl. You should be like her and go for the things of highest value which stand the test of time."

Jesus said, "I'm the light, shining everywhere. I'm the sum total of everything. Everything started with me and everything is coming home to me. Split a piece of wood and you'll see me there; lift up a stone and you'll find me there."

Jesus said, "Why have you chosen the country for your day out? Who do you expect to see? A politician who sways with the popular mood? Someone wearing the latest court fashions? Your rulers may be well dressed, but they're not very bright!"

A woman who was listening to all this said, "I bet your mother's proud of you. I'd be, if I were your mother!" Jesus said, "Save your kind remarks for those who do what the Loving God asks them to do! The time's coming when it will be better to be without children."

Jesus said, "When someone comes to grips with what life is all about, they will also understand the part their own bodies have to play in the scheme of things. People who are at ease with life and at ease with their bodies are very rare and should be highly valued."

Jesus said, "People get to positions of power by means of their wealth. But real power is being able to cast wealth and position aside. In God's New World, those who sit by me have places near the fire, but those who keep their distance from me are out in the cold."

Jesus said, "You can see what someone looks like on the outside, but their relationship to God is hidden and mysterious. It's impossible to know what God looks like. The sight is too bright for our eyes. But God's character can shine through human beings.

"You like looking at your faces in a mirror. But when you get a picture of God's pattern and purpose for you, you see how much room there is for improvement! God has given humanity great resources and ability, but the results have been disappointing. We're only worth a short life."

Jesus said, "Foxes have holes they can bolt to and birds can fly up to their nests, but humanity has no place of rest. It's part of being a human being to feel frustrated because we're limited by what our bodies can do, but some people allow their personalities to be completely taken over by their physical needs, and that's really tragic."[8]

Jesus said, "Be grateful to those who bring the good things God has intended for you. You should do your best for them in return. Indeed, you should say, 'When are they going to come this way again so we can reward them as they deserve?'"

Jesus said, "I notice some of you religious people washing the outside of your cups. It's obvious you're only interested in outward appearances. It's time you realized that God, our maker, is concerned about what goes on inside us as much as how things look on the outside."

Jesus said, "If you let me be your friend, I'll teach you to relax. I'm a carpenter by trade. The yokes I make for oxen are smooth and light. I'm a teacher too and I don't bully my pupils. You'll be at ease with me."

The people listening said, "Who are you exactly? How can we trust you when we don't know anything about you?"

Jesus said, "You're very sharp in your observation of the world of nature, but you've not observed me very closely. You're not even aware of the challenge I'm giving you this very moment. If you have open and inquisitive minds, you'll get the answers you're looking for. It's true that in the past I sometimes dodged your questions. Now that I'm offering you the answers, you've lost your curiosity. You're fond of saying, 'You can't preach to a dog or teach a pig its lessons.' Make sure those words don't apply to you! Those who explore discover; those who knock get invited in."

4 (95) Jesus said, "If you've got money to spare, don't lend it at an interest. It's better to give your money freely to someone you don't expect to give it back."

Jesus said, "The New World of the Loving God is like someone making bread. They take a little yeast and put it in the dough and it produces many large loaves of bread. If you've got ears, use them!

"God's New World is like someone walking from the shop with a bag of

---

[8] "Humanity," literally "Son of Man," which we generally translate "The Complete Person." In the context Twin gives it here, it seems to have its more basic meaning, humankind in general. See Matthew 8:20 and Luke 9:58 for the differing slants the Gospel writers give to the words of Jesus.

flour. They haven't noticed there's a big hole in the bottom of the bag, and they leave a long trail of wasted flour behind them. Imagine how they feel when they get home.

"God's New World is like someone preparing to run the Marathon. First they put themselves to the test on practice runs. Then when the day of the big race comes, they'll be able to complete the course."[9]

The friends of Jesus said to him, "Your brothers and your mother are waiting for you outside." Jesus said, "Those here who are doing what the Loving God wants are my true family. They will be citizens of God's New World. Like me, my followers must grow up and break free from the ideas they got from their parents. They must learn to love their true mother, God's Spirit. She is the one who gave me life."[10]

Somebody showed Jesus a large coin and said. "The Emperor's agents make us pay our taxes." Jesus said, "Give the Emperor what belongs to the Emperor, give God what belongs to God, and give me what belongs to me!"

Jesus said this about the strict set, "I wish those Holy Joes would get lost! They're like the dog in the manger. They don't eat what's there and don't let the cows eat! You're lucky if you realize the strict set are out to rob you of the good things you're enjoying. Be ready to defeat their arguments."[11]

Once some members of the strict set said to Jesus. "We're having a day of prayer and fasting, will you join us?" Jesus said, "Why? What have I done wrong? What have your spies caught me at? There's no need to stop eating until the party's over. That will be the time to go without food and to ask for God's help."

---

[9] More literally, "The New World is like an assassin planning to kill a well-known public figure. First of all he practices with his weapon and puts his skill to the test, then he goes out and does the deed." Our translation makes the same point, but in our culture an assassin is not acceptable as a role model. (Jesus had within his circle of friends at least one who would have understood his metaphor.)

[10] We have amended the order of the verses, postponing the well-known response of Jesus to the question of taxes to the Romans, since it interrupts the flow. The text at this point is incomplete, so we hope we have conveyed the most likely meaning. The language of the original is extreme, like the language of the equivalent texts in Matthew and Luke. This example of Hebrew hyperbole requires softening in translation.

[11] Jesus quotes directly from one of Aesop's fables. Aesop lived from 620-560 B.C.E., and his stories were popular throughout the world of Jesus' day.

Jesus said, "If, like me, you know your Mum and Dad, then, like me, they'll call you a bastard!"[12]

Jesus said, "You'll be truly human when you learn to live in harmony. Then you'll overcome all obstacles."

Jesus said, "God's New World is like a shepherd who owned a hundred sheep. The fattest of them wandered off, so the shepherd left the other ninety-nine and searched for the fat one until he found it. Because he'd gone to all that trouble, he said to the sheep he'd rescued, 'I love you more than all the others put together!'"

Jesus said. "Those who show me affection will share my character and I'll identify myself completely with them. They'll get to know the secrets of my heart."[13]

Jesus said, "God's New World is like a farmer who didn't know that one of the fields belonging to the farm had treasure buried in it. When the farmer died, the property went to the next of kin. The treasure still remained undiscovered. Then the heir sold the field. The new owner plowed the field, discovered the treasure and was able to finance the projects of others." (So those who've made good use of their time in the world to make valuable discoveries, should share them.)[14]

Jesus said, "Our universe may suddenly come to an end and you may see it happening, but those who have God's life within them won't die." (Remember Jesus said that those who've honestly come to terms with themselves are worth more than all the world!)

Jesus said, "It's sad when people cannot relax their bodies because their minds are full of hang-ups, and it's sad when people cannot think straight because of the demands of their bodies."

Jesus' friends asked him, "When will God's New World come?" Jesus

---

[12] Jesus had to face gossip concerning his biological parents. Some believed him to be a Samaritan, i.e. of mixed race (John 8:48). Origen records the tradition that some believed him to be the illegitimate child of Mary and a soldier called Panthera. A gravestone marks a Sidonian archer of that name who was stationed in Palestine around the time of the birth of Jesus. It is interesting that, according to both John and Twin, Jesus did not directly contradict the rumors.

[13] "Those who show me affection," literally, "whoever drinks from my mouth" (i.e. "kisses me").

[14] As in the other Gospels, the explanation of a parable is the Gospel-writer's idea of what Jesus had in mind. The method of Jesus was to allow his hearers to work out the meaning for themselves. This parable is rich in possible interpretations.

said, "It won't come if you spend all your time looking for it! No one can say, 'I've got it!' or 'Look, there it is.' The New World of the Loving God is spread all over the world today, but people can't see it."

Simon, otherwise known as "Rocky," said to the others, "Maggie should leave us. 'Life to the full' is not for women!" Jesus said, "I intend to train women like Maggie to do all the things that men can do and to give them the same freedoms you have. Every woman who insists on equality with men is fit to be a citizen in God's New World."[15]

---

[15] Literally, Jesus promises to make Maggie (Mary of Magdala) "male," and encourages other women to seek this step. Jesus was talking about roles, since it was Maggie's already established place in the group of leaders that Rocky objected to. A power struggle in the early church is reflected here, with women leaders as one of the issues. It seems that Twin was on opposite sides from Rocky and claimed the authority of Jesus for his position. Rocky won and women lost out for two thousand years. Twin's witness is making slow but sure headway at last.

Good News From Sources Close to Jesus

Attributed to "John." The main source probably the
"Dategrove Set"

1 In the beginning God spoke. This is just like God – part of the way God is. Everything there is comes from God speaking; otherwise there would be nothing at all. God speaking brought into being the life and intelligence we all share. These have kept on shining like light in the darkness and have never been defeated by the darkness. There was a messenger from God called John. John, known as "the Dipper," played his part in keeping the light shining, encouraging people to trust the light, although he was not the light himself. The full light that makes things clear to everybody was then coming into the world. The one who made the world appeared in the world, but the world paid no attention. Those specially prepared, God's chosen people, turned their backs. Nevertheless there were many who opened their arms in trust, and these are the rightful children of God. They are not children in the human sense, the result of family planning or physical passion, but in the sense of sharing God's nature. God spoke by means of a human being living among us. We have seen the beauty of the only complete physical expression of the Loving God, wonderful to look at and to know. John the Dipper showed his support by shouting out, "This is the one I was telling you about, 'The one who arrives after me is more important than me, because he existed before me.' " From his superstore we have received one good gift after another. Moses gave us rules and regulations; Jesus, God's representative, gave us true love. No one has ever seen God, but the one faithful likeness who shares God's nature has shown us what God is like.

(19) This is how John answered when the Jewish authorities sent a deputation of religious leaders from Jerusalem to ask him. "Who are you?"

John did not mince his words but said quite plainly, "I'm not the Chosen One." So they asked, "Who are you, then? Are you Elijah?" He said. "No, I'm not." "Are you the special speaker from God we've been promised?" Again John said. "No." Then they said, "We need to know who you are so we can make our report. What do you say about yourself?" John replied, using words from one of God's speakers, "I'm 'The Voice' crying out in the desert. 'Build a straight road for God to travel on.'"

Some messengers who had been sent by the strict set asked John, "Why do you dip people if you're not the Chosen One, nor Elijah, nor the promised speaker?" He answered. "I only dip people in the water. Among you there's someone you don't know who is going to take over from me. I'm not fit to do up his shoe laces!" This all happened in Dateford across the Jordan where John was dipping. The next day, John saw Jesus coming toward him and shouted, "Here's God's Lamb who'll take away everything wrong in the world! This is the one I told you about when I said, 'After me, someone will come who is more important than me, because he was around before me.' Even I didn't realize who he was, although my job is to introduce him to God's People. That's what my dipping in water is all about." Then John explained why he was so sure. "I saw the Spirit coming out of the sky like a pigeon, and she perched on him. I didn't realize who he was until then, but the one who sent me to dip people in the water said to me, 'The one you see the Spirit land on is the one who will drench you with God's Spirit.' I've seen the evidence, and I'm stating publicly that this is God's Chosen One."

(35) Next day John the Dipper was talking with two of his followers. Seeing Jesus walking by, John pointed to him and said, "Look, there's God's Lamb!" This caught their interest and they went after Jesus. When Jesus turned and saw them following him he said, "What do you want?" They answered, "Teacher, where are your lodgings?" Jesus said to them, "Come and see." So they went to see where Jesus was lodging and spent the day with him. It was about four o'clock in the afternoon. One of the two who heard what John said was Andrew. The first thing Andrew did was to find his brother Simon and tell him, "We've found God's Chosen." He brought Simon to Jesus who looked him in the eye and said, "So you're Simon Johnson! I'm going to call you 'Rocky.'"

The next day, Jesus decided to go to Galilee. He met Philip and said to him, "Join my team." Philip, like Andrew and Rocky, was from Fishtown. Philip went to find his friend Nathan and told him, "We've found the one Moses wrote about in our book of rules, the one God's speakers wrote about too. His name is Jesus Josephson, and he comes from Nazareth." "Nazareth!?" Nathan sneered, "Can anything good come from that dump?" Philip said, "Come and see." When Jesus saw Nathan walking toward him he said, "Here's a descendant of Jacob without any deceit in him – and that's the truth!" Nathan asked Jesus, "How do you know me?" Jesus answered, "I saw what you were doing under the fig tree before Philip called you." Nathan said, "Teacher, you're God's Chosen One! You're the right leader for God's People!" Jesus said, "Do you trust me because I told you I saw you under the fig tree? You'll see greater things than that." Then Jesus said to him, "Believe me, you'll go right to the heart of things. You'll recognize the Complete Person as the link between this world and God."

2 Two days later there was a wedding at Cana. The mother of Jesus was there, and Jesus and his friends were guests as well. When all the wine had been drunk, Jesus' mother said to him, "They've run out of wine." Jesus said to her, "Stop interfering, woman! Our ideas are worlds apart. I'm not seeking to attract attention." Jesus' mother said to the waiters, "Do whatever he tells you." Nearby there were six big stone jars, the kind used by Jewish people for ceremonial washing. Jesus said to the waiters, "Fill the jars with water." And they filled them right up to the top. Then he said, "Now go back to the well and take what you draw from it to whoever is in charge of the catering." So they did. The supervisor, tasting the water, which had now become wine, did not know where it had come from (though the waiters knew). He called across to the bridegroom and said, "Everyone else serves the top quality wine first and the poorer quality after the guests have got drunk. But you've kept the best wine till now." By showing his special qualities like this in Cana of Galilee, Jesus gave the first clue as to who he was. His friends learned to trust him. After this, Jesus went on to Nahum town with his mother and the rest of his family and friends. They stayed there a few days.

(13) As it was near the time of the Jewish festival called the Passover,

Jesus went up to Jerusalem. In the temple he found people selling cattle, sheep, and pigeons, and others sitting at stalls changing money. He made a whip out of some cords and drove all the sheep and cattle out of the temple. He knocked over the tables of the moneychangers and the coins flew all over the place. Then he turned on the pigeon sellers. "Get out of here," he said, "Stop making my Parent's house a market place!" His friends were reminded of the words in the old writings, "Enthusiasm for your house will set me on fire." The temple clergy asked Jesus, "What miracle can you perform for us to prove you have the right to do this?" Jesus answered, "Knock this temple down and I'll build it again in three days." They said, "This temple has been under construction for forty-six years, and you're going to build it in three days?" (Jesus was talking about his body as a temple. After his return to life, the friends of Jesus remembered what he had said, and they trusted the old books and the words Jesus had spoken.)[1]

While Jesus was in Jerusalem for the festival, many put their trust in him. They saw the remarkable things he was doing. But Jesus did not trust the crowds. He knew how unreliable they could be. Jesus didn't need others to tell him what people were like. He could read their thoughts.

3 Nick was one of the strict set and a member of the Supreme Council. He called on Jesus after dark. He began by saying, "Sir, you're obviously a teacher sent by God. Your splendid record of good work proves that God is with you." Jesus said, "Believe me, no one can recognize God's New World without starting life all over again." Nick asked, "How can someone make a new start when they are as old as I am? You may as well ask me to get back into my mother's womb and come out again." Jesus answered, "Believe me, no one can be a citizen of God's New World without being born of water and the Spirit. The waters of birth deliver a physical body, but the Spirit makes you a person. Don't be so surprised at me saying 'You must start life all over again.' Like the wind, the Spirit blows where she chooses, and like the wind, you hear the sound she makes, but you don't know where she's coming from or where she's going. That's what

---

[1] 2:21. As a possible alternative rendering, for "body" read "body of followers." In John's Gospel, as in the other Gospels, Jesus and his community are virtually inseparable. See comments on "The Complete Person"/"Son of Man."

it's like when the Spirit takes your life in a new direction." Nick said, "I don't follow." Jesus said, "You call yourself a teacher of God's people, and you don't understand what I'm talking about? Believe me, I'm speaking from experience, but you religious people won't take me seriously. So far I've only mentioned things to do with this life. What if I were to talk to you about things outside the realm of time and space?"

(13) (No one has had experience of that world except the one who came from there, the Complete Person. Just as Moses set up the bronze snake on a pole in the desert, the Complete Person must be exposed to view, so that everyone has a chance to trust him and experience life to the full.

If you want to know how much God loves, trust the unique self-portrait God has given the world. Then you won't shrink to nothing but always be full of life. God's Likeness was not sent into the world to show the world in a bad light, but to bring healing to the world. Those who trust are not shown up; but those who don't trust have ensured their own disgrace in advance, because they haven't trusted God's only faithful likeness. This is the heart of the matter: light has come into the world, but people prefer darkness to light because they do such wicked things. Those who do wrong hate the light and avoid it. They are afraid their conduct will be exposed. Honest people step into the light to show everybody that what they do has God's approval.)[2]

(22) After this, Jesus and his followers went south to the province of Judea and spent a while together out in the country. They also dipped some people. At the same time, John was dipping at Peace Springs because the water was deep there. People kept coming to be dipped. This was before John was put in prison.

There was a discussion between John's followers and some other religious people about the use of water in religious ceremonies. They brought this question to John. "Teacher, you had a companion when you were on the other side of the Jordan. You spoke highly of him. Now he is dipping people, and everyone is flocking to *him*." John replied, "We all get

---

[2] 3:13-21; 31-36. There is no punctuation in the Greek text and no quotation marks. It is often difficult to tell where the words of Jesus end and the comments of the Gospel writer begin. Also the Gospel writer puts his/her own words into the mouth of Jesus or translates the speech patterns of Jesus as we are familiar with them from elsewhere into his/her own speech patterns. It seems fairly clear, however, that the words we bracket in this chapter are intended to be read as comment.

our jobs from God. Remember what I said, 'I'm not the Chosen One. I'm the one who goes in front to announce him.' It's the bridegroom who gets the bride. The best man, who stands by the bridegroom at the wedding ceremony and hears him singing, is happy at the bridegroom's good fortune. Jesus must have center stage, and I must step aside."

(31) (The one coming from beyond time and space is more important than anyone else. Anyone who comes from our world can only speak about things of here and now. The one from beyond has a total view of everything and can give us information no one else possesses. But people don't want to know this! To accept the authority of the one who has come, is to accept the truth of God, because the one sent by God speaks God's words, inspired by God's Spirit. Love flows from the Loving God to God's Likeness who is entrusted with responsibility for everything. Those who accept God's Likeness will experience life to the full; those who turn their backs will not know the meaning of life. They will have a bad time.)[3]

4 Jesus heard that the strict set were saying, "Jesus is winning more followers than John and dipping them," although it was not Jesus but his friends who were doing the dipping. So Jesus left Judea and made his way back north to Galilee. He decided to go through Samaria. He came to a village called Jacob's Well, near the plot of ground Jacob had given his son, Joseph. The well was still there. Jesus was feeling tired after the hard walk, so he sat down by the well.

A Samaritan woman came to get some water, and Jesus said to her. "Give me a drink." (His friends had gone to the village to buy food.) The Samaritan woman said to Jesus. "How can you, a Jew, ask me for a drink? I'm a woman and a Samaritan!" (Jews do not eat or drink with Samaritans.) Jesus said, "If only you knew what God has on offer and who is saying to you, 'Give me a drink,' *you* would be the one to ask, and I would provide you with a constant supply of water." The woman said to Jesus, "Sir, it's a deep well and you haven't even got a bucket. How are you going to get the constant supply of water you're talking about? Are you greater than Jacob, our ancestor, who gave us this well and drank from it himself, and his

---

[3] See footnote 2.

family and animals?" Jesus said, "Everyone who drinks water from this well will be thirsty again, but those who drink the water I give them will never be thirsty. The water I give them will turn into a spring of water deep inside them and give life to the full." The woman said, "Sir, give me this water. Then I'll never get thirsty or have to keep coming here to fetch water." Jesus said to her, "Go and get your husband!" The woman answered, "I haven't got a husband." Jesus said, "Quite right you haven't! You've got through five husbands, and the one you're living with now isn't your husband! You never spoke a truer word!" The woman said to Jesus, "Sir, I can tell you're one of God's speakers. Our ancestors worshiped on this mountain, but you Jews say that Jerusalem is the right place to worship." Jesus said, "Friend, believe me, the time is coming when you won't worship the Loving God on this mountain or in Jerusalem. You Samaritans don't really know what you're worshiping; we Jews have a better idea, since we're the ones whose job is to bring healing to the world. But the time's coming, has come in fact, when people seeking to worship the Loving God will worship with sincerity of heart and mind. That's the sort of worshipers God wants. God's Spirit is like the wind, open and free. God's worshipers must be the same." The woman said to Jesus, "I know that God's Chosen is coming. On that day all our questions will be answered.' Jesus said, "I am answering your questions *now!*"

Just then Jesus' friends came back and were surprised to find him chatting with a woman, but they did not like to ask "What's the problem?" or "Why are you talking to *her*?" Then the woman left her water jar and went back to the village. She said to the people there, "Come and meet someone who told me my life-story! Do you think it could be the Chosen One?" They came out from the village and made their way to Jesus.

Meanwhile Jesus' friends tried to get him to eat something. But Jesus said, "I've got food to eat you don't know anything about. So they said to one another, "Could somebody else have brought him some food, perhaps?" Jesus said to them, "My food is to please the one who sent me and to finish the job I've been given. You have a saying, 'It takes four months for harvest to come.' But I say, look around you. The fields are ready to harvest. Some workers are already getting their wages and bringing in a healthy crop. Those who sowed the seed and those who harvested the corn are going to have a great barn dance together! The saying is true, 'One sows and another reaps.' I've sent you to reap where you haven't had to do anything. Others have done the hard work, and you're getting the results."

Many Samaritans from that village trusted Jesus because of what the woman said, "He told me my life-story!" When the Samaritan people met Jesus, they asked him to stay with them. So Jesus stayed there two days. Many more trusted Jesus when they heard what he had to say. They told the woman, "Now we don't have to rely on what you told us. We've heard for ourselves, and we know this is the one the world's been waiting for."

(43) Then Jesus continued his journey to Galilee. He did not expect Galilee to give him the warm welcome he got from the Samaritans. Jesus often said, "Nowhere is God's messenger less popular than on home ground." But when Jesus arrived in Galilee, the people there opened their arms. They had seen everything he had done in Jerusalem at the festival because they had been there on holiday.

Jesus visited the village of Cana again, where he had brought happiness at a wedding. In Nahum town, the government officer's boy was ill. When the officer heard that Jesus had come from Judea to Galilee, he went to Jesus and asked him to come and heal his boy who was dying. Jesus said, "As long as you don't expect magic tricks. Just trust me!" The officer said, "Please hurry, Sir, before my boy dies." Jesus said, "Off you go! Your boy will live!" Trusting the words of Jesus, the officer started for home. On the way, some of his staff met him with the news that his boy was going to live. He asked them when they had noticed a change for the better, and they told him, "He got over the fever yesterday, at one in the afternoon. The officer realized this was the time when Jesus said, "Your boy will live." He trusted Jesus and so did his family and friends. This is the second clue Jesus gave as to who he was. It was straight after he had come from Judea to Galilee.[4]

---

[4] 4:46. "Boy" = Greek *paidion*, an affectionate diminutive of *pais*. Possible meanings, "child," "boy," "mate," "boy-friend." "Officer" = Greek *pater*, someone in authority or care over, "father," "guardian," "officer." Though whether this is the same incident as in Matthew 8 and Luke 7 is a matter of dispute, the similarities are too close for it not to be, including the intriguing uncertainty as to the nature of the relationship.

5 Jesus went to Jerusalem for one of the festivals. In Jerusalem, by the Sheep Gate, there is a pool known as "The Five Arches." The pool is indeed surrounded by five arches, and in these a large number of disabled people used to lie around, including blind, lame, and paralyzed people. A man was lying there who had been ill for thirty-eight years. Jesus spotted him, and realizing he had been there a long time, asked him, "Do you want to get better?" The man said, "Sir, I've got no one to help me into the pool when the waters bubble; and while I'm trying to get down there, someone else pushes in front of me." Jesus said, "Stand on your feet, pick up your mat, and get moving!" The man recovered instantly, picked up his mat and walked off.

It was the Rest Day, so the clergy said to the man who had previously been disabled, "It's Saturday; you are forbidden to carry your mat!" But he said, "The person who cured me told me to pick up my mat and be on my way." They asked him, "Who was it told you to do that?" The man did not know who Jesus was, and Jesus had disappeared among the crowd before he had time to ask. Later Jesus came across him in the temple and said to him, "Look here, you've been healed, so stop misbehaving, otherwise you're going to be in worse trouble!" The man went off and told the clergy that Jesus was the one who had cured him. The clergy began to make trouble for Jesus, accusing him of working on the Rest Day. But Jesus defended his actions by saying, "My Parent is working today as usual and I'm doing the same." This made the clergy even more determined to kill Jesus, not just for ignoring the Saturday restrictions, but for claiming that God was his parent, and talking as if he was equal with God.

(19) Jesus said, "Believe me, a child relies on its parent and imitates its parent's behavior. Parents love their children and teach them their skills. So expect to be surprised – there's more to come! The ability to raise the dead and give them life is passed on from one member of the family to another. The Loving God does not judge anybody, but the True Likeness can make decisions on God's behalf. That's why God and the True Likeness should receive the same respect as each other from everybody. To respect one is to respect the other, and to despise one is to despise the other. Believe me, those who accept what I have to say, and trust the one who sent me, have nothing to worry about. Death will be no threat for them, and they will

have life to the full.

"Believe me, the time is coming, in fact it's already come, when those who are dead will hear the voice of God's True Likeness, and come alive again. For just as the Loving God is the source of life, so too the True Likeness has the key to life and can decide what's best for each person's future. I hope this doesn't confuse you. Very soon, all those who are in their graves will hear the voice of the Complete Person and step out – those who have done good, to life that is new and full; and those who have done evil, to shame. I can't do anything on my own. My decisions are based on what I hear. Those decisions are fair because I have no motives of my own. I aim simply to carry out the wishes of the one who sent me. If I argue my own case, it won't stand up. But there is someone to argue on my behalf, someone whose words cannot be doubted. You sent messengers to find out John's views and he gave you an honest opinion. Not that one person's opinion counts for much. I mention it in order to help you. John was a lamp shining all around, and for a while you enjoyed his light. But the witness I'm talking about is greater than John's. The things the Loving God has given me to do, which I'm doing at this very moment, are the proof that the Loving God has sent me. The God who sent me argues my case. You are not tuned to hearing or seeing God because God's ideas have no place in your thinking and you don't trust God's representative.

"You bury your heads in the old books because you think you can find real life there. It's strange that the old books recommend me, yet you refuse to come to me for life. I'm not interested in being popular. But I know why you think so little of me. It's because you don't have the love of God in your hearts. I'm like my Parent, the Loving God. That's why you don't warm to me! You prefer famous celebrities. How can you trust me, the one who has the approval of the only true God, when you're only interested in cheap popularity? Don't imagine that I will bring evidence against you to God. The prosecution will be led by your hero Moses. You think he's on your side. But if you really trusted Moses, you would trust me, since Moses wrote about me. If you don't accept what he wrote, it's not surprising you don't accept what *I* say!"

6 Jesus went to the other side of Lake Galilee. He was followed by a lot of people attracted by his success in healing. Jesus went up the mountain and found a place to sit with his friends. It was springtime. When Jesus looked up and saw the size of the crowd making its way toward him, he asked Philip, "Where can we buy enough food for all these people?" (This was a test for Philip. Jesus had already made his plans.) Philip replied, "Six months' wages wouldn't buy one mouthful each!" Another friend, Andrew, Rocky's brother, told Jesus, "There's a youngster here with five loaves of barley bread and two fish. But they won't go very far!" Jesus said, "Get everybody to sit down." There was plenty of grass to sit on, and about five thousand sat down. Then Jesus took the loaves, said "thank you" to God and passed them round to the people sitting down. He did the same with the fish, and everyone had as much as they wanted. When they had all finished eating, Jesus told his friends, "Go round and pick up the leftovers. We can't have any waste!" So they went round and collected twelve baskets full of scraps from what was left of the five barley loaves. What Jesus had done impressed the people so much, they started to say, "This is the messenger the world has been waiting for!" As soon as Jesus realized the people were going to force him to become their political leader, he went back up the mountain alone.

(16) In the evening the friends went down to the beach, got into a boat and started across the lake in the direction of Nahum town. Although it was dark, Jesus had not yet got back. A strong wind made the lake choppy. When they had rowed quite a long way, they saw Jesus walking over the water and getting near to the boat. They began to panic, but Jesus shouted out, "Don't worry! It's only me!" They were just about to help Jesus on board when they found they had already reached land.

Next day, the crowd, which had stayed on the other side of the lake, realized there had only been one boat there. They also saw that Jesus had not got into the boat. His friends had left without him. Then some boats from Tiberius came to shore near where the crowd had shared a meal. When they realized that neither Jesus nor his friends were there, they got back into the boats and made for Nahum town, keeping an eye out for Jesus. When they found Jesus on the other side of the lake, they asked, "When did you get here, Teacher?"

(26) Jesus answered, "The truth of the matter is that you're looking for me because you had a good meal, and not because you saw signs of God at work. Don't waste your energy on food that goes off. Look for the food that keeps fresh and gives you life to the full. The Complete Person can give it to you, because the Complete Person has the approval of the Loving God."

Then they asked Jesus, "What do we have to do to please God?" Jesus said, "You can please God by trusting God's representative." Then they said, "What proof can you give to convince us? Our ancestors ate the mystery food in the desert. It says in the old books, 'They had bread from the sky to eat.' " Jesus said, "You're mistaken in thinking it was Moses who gave you bread from the sky. It's the Loving God who provides you with food. The food which comes from God is the source of life for the whole world." They said to Jesus, "Please Sir, give us that food, over and over again."

Jesus said, "I'm the food which gives life. Anyone who comes to me will never be hungry, and whoever trusts me will never be thirsty. But I repeat what I've said before – you've seen me and yet don't trust me. I have on offer what the Loving God has given me. I'll never turn away anyone who comes to me. I haven't come from the world beyond to please myself, but to carry out the wishes of the one who sent me. I must not lose any of those entrusted to my care. I will give them a worthy place at the end of time. All who see the True Likeness of the Loving God and trust me, will have life to the full and a place at the end of time."

The words of Jesus, "I'm the food from God," brought some unfriendly comments, such as, "Isn't this Jesus Josephson? We know both his parents well. How can he possibly say, 'I'm from God'?" Jesus said, "Stop looking for faults! Those who respond to me are attracted by the Loving God who gave me my job. I'll acknowledge them at the end of time. God's servants wrote, 'Everyone will be taught by God.' Everyone who has paid attention to the Loving God responds to me. No one has seen God, except the one who has come from God and has experienced God's loving character first hand. Believe me, whoever trusts me has life to the full. I'm the food that gives life. Your ancestors ate the mystery food in the desert, but they died just the same. The food I'm talking about comes from God. If you eat it, you won't die. I come with living food from God. Whoever eats this food will live forever. I'm going to give my own flesh for the life of the world."

When they heard these words, people said to one another, "How can we eat this man's flesh?" So Jesus said, "Believe me, unless you share in the life of the Complete Person, you've no real life at all. Those who take life from me into themselves have life to the full, and I'll acknowledge them at the end of time. My life keeps others alive. Those who share my life are part of me and I'm part of them. The Loving God has sent me. That means I'm alive with God's life. So anyone who takes life from me is bound to live. This is the food from God. It's not the same as the food your ancestors ate, which didn't stop them dying. Those who eat my food will live forever." (This is a summary of Jesus' teaching in the synagogue at Nahum town.)

(60) Many of Jesus' followers said, "This teaching is difficult. It goes too far!" Jesus was aware of their problem and said, "Are you put off so easily? What if you were to see the Complete Person returning to God? Life is a gift from the Spirit; human effort can't achieve it. The words I've spoken to you are exciting; they promise a new life. But some of you don't trust me. I've told you, no one can respond to me unless moved by the Loving God." (Jesus knew from the start the people who were not with him, and he knew who would be the traitor.)

From this point on, many of the followers of Jesus changed their minds and broke away from him. So Jesus asked his twelve closest friends, "Would you like to leave me, too?" Rocky answered, "Leader, who can we go to? We only feel alive when we're listening to you! We've learnt to trust you, and we know you're God's Chosen!" Jesus said, "I chose all twelve of you, didn't I? Yet one of you is evil." (Jesus was referring to Judas Simson from Kerioth. Although one of the twelve closest friends of Jesus, he was going to be the traitor.)

7 Jesus went on a tour of Galilee. He avoided Judea because he had enemies there who were out to kill him. It was nearly the time of the festival where people camped out in tents. Jesus' brothers said to him, "Wouldn't it be a good idea if you left here and went to Judea to show your followers what you can do? You'll never be famous unless you show your face. If your achievements are genuine, you should let more people know about them." Really his brothers had no confidence in him. Jesus said, "You can do what you want any time you want. I have to keep to

a timetable. You don't have to face unpopularity, whereas I'm unpopular for pointing out what is evil. You go to the festival. I'm not going; it's not the right time." So Jesus stayed behind in Galilee.

But after Jesus' brothers had gone to the festival, Jesus followed them, being careful not to let anybody see him. The religious leaders were looking out for Jesus at the festival and tried hard to find out where he was by asking anyone who might know. His name was on everybody's lips among the crowds of visitors. Some said, "He's a good man," and others said, "No, he's going to get us all into trouble." But people were careful not to speak too loudly, because they were afraid of the authorities.

(14) Only when the festival was already half way through did Jesus go into the temple and start teaching. The temple clergy were very impressed and said, "How can anyone know as much as this without any special training?" Jesus answered them by saying, "My learning isn't my own. I got it from the one I represent. Anyone who sets their heart on pleasing God will know at once whether what I say comes from God or whether I make up my own ideas. Those who offer their own ideas are out for themselves. But those who give credit to their teacher are genuine and not just out to impress. Wasn't it Moses who gave you the ten basic rules? Yet none of you keep them! Why, for example, are you planning to murder me?"

A shout came from the crowd, "You're out of your mind. Who would want to murder you?" Jesus replied, "I did one act of kindness and you are all excited about it. But look at it like this. Because Moses gave you the rule about cutting the foreskin (though the idea did not start with Moses, but his ancestors), you do that on the Rest Day. If a small part of the body can be treated on a Saturday to ensure that the rules of Moses are kept, why are you so upset because I healed someone's whole body on a Saturday? Stop being so petty and try to think straight!"

This led some of the people who lived in Jerusalem to ask, "Isn't this the one our leaders want to kill? Why do they let him speak like this in public without challenging him? Perhaps they've decided he really is God's Chosen! On the other hand, we all know where he comes from, whereas when the Chosen One comes, no one will know where he's from." So as he was teaching in the temple Jesus shouted for everybody to hear, "Yes, of course you know me, and you know where I come from. But it wasn't my decision to come; the one who is true has sent me, someone I know but you don't!" Some of them tried to make a grab at Jesus but couldn't get hold of him. It was not the right moment. Many people in the crowd stood up for Jesus and said. "When the Chosen One comes, will he be more impressive than this man?"

(32) The strict set heard the things being whispered about Jesus in the crowd, and together with the temple clergy they called in the police to arrest him. Jesus said, "I won't be with you much longer. I'll be going back to the one who sent me. You'll try and hunt me down, but you won't find me, because you can't go where I'm going." The police said to one another, "Where's he thinking of going so we can't find him? Will he go to foreign parts, to Greece perhaps, where some of our people live? Will he teach people who aren't Jews? What was he hinting at when he said, 'You won't be able to find me,' and 'You can't go where I'm going'?"

On the last and most important day of the festival, Jesus stood in the temple and shouted out, "Anyone who is thirsty can come to me for a drink. The old books say, 'Whoever trusts me will have a supply of fresh water inside them.'" (Jesus was talking about the experience of the Spirit. This experience was not available until Jesus had completed his work.)

Some of the people in the crowd who heard Jesus speaking said, "This is the great speaker God promised." Others said, "This is God's Chosen One." Others were not so sure and argued, "God's Chosen can't possibly come from Galilee. Don't our old books say the Chosen One is descended from David and comes from Bethlehem, the same town David came from?" So opinion in the crowd was divided. Some wanted to have him arrested, but no one laid a hand on him.

When the police reported to the clergy, the clergy asked them, "Why didn't you arrest him?" The police said, "He's a great speaker – the best ever!" The strict set replied, "He's certainly got *you* fooled, hasn't he? We experts know better – he doesn't fool any of us! As for that lawless rabble, they're beyond help!"

But one of the strict set, Nick, the one who had once visited Jesus, interrupted them, and said, "According to our rules we should not condemn people without giving them a hearing and making sure of the facts." The others said, "You're sounding just like one of the mob from

Galilee. If you took the trouble to read the old books you would realize that none of God's speakers come from Galilee!"

(8:1) Then everybody went home. Jesus went to Olive Hill.

8 **(8:2)** Early next morning Jesus went back to the temple. Everybody gathered round him and he sat down and began his teaching. Some of the strict set, experts in the old books, brought in a woman who had been caught having unlawful sex, and they made her stand in front of the group. They said to Jesus, "Sir, we were eyewitnesses to this woman's immoral behavior. According to the rules Moses gave us, a woman like this should be stoned to death. What do you think?" They were trying to trap Jesus, so they could accuse him of breaking the rules. But Jesus ignored them and started doodling on the ground with his finger. But when they persisted with their questions, Jesus sat up straight and said, "Anyone here who has never done anything wrong can throw the first stone!" Then Jesus ignored them again and went back to doodling on the ground. When they had thought about what Jesus said, they all slunk off one by one, the oldest first. Jesus was left alone with the woman who was still standing there. Jesus sat up straight again and said to her, "Where have they all gone? Hasn't anybody said you're guilty?" "Nobody, Sir," she replied. Jesus said, "You're not guilty in my eyes, either! You're free to go. Put your days as an outcast behind you!"

(12) The next time Jesus spoke to the people he said, "I'm like a beam of light for the world. Those who keep close to me will see where their lives are leading and never have to grope in the darkness." The strict set said to Jesus, "You are arguing on your own behalf – we don't accept the views of anyone who does that!" Jesus replied, "Even if you're right that I'm arguing on my own behalf, I'm telling the truth because I know where I come from and where I'm going. Your understanding of people is based on prejudice, whereas I don't condemn anybody. If I do form an opinion it's fair, because the Loving God and I have the same point of view. Your book of rules says that when two witnesses agree in court, that settles the matter. I count as one witness, and my Parent who sent me here counts as the other!" They asked Jesus, "Where is this parent you keep talking about?" Jesus replied, "You don't know me or my Parent. If you knew me, you'd know my

Parent too."

(Jesus said all this while he was teaching in the place where the money was collected for the upkeep of the temple. Nobody arrested him, because it was not yet the right time.)

Jesus continued, "I'm going away and you'll try to find me. You're determined to be nasty people till the day you die. That means you can't go where I'm going." So the clergy said, "He says we can't go where he's going. Is he thinking of committing suicide?" Jesus said, "You belong to your world and I belong to mine. That's why I say you'll be nasty till the day you die. There's no possibility of change unless you recognize who I am." "And just who are you?" they asked. Jesus said, "I don't know why I bother to say anything to you at all! There's a lot I could say, especially about your faults. But the one who sent me is positive, and I want the whole world to hear the positive message I've been given." They did not understand that Jesus was talking about the Loving God. So Jesus said, "When you give the Complete Person a special place for all to see, then you'll recognize me. I'm not acting on my own. I say what my Parent has taught me to say. I always seek to please the one I represent. I'm never on my own. The one I represent is always with me." These words led many to put their trust in Jesus.

(31) Jesus said to those who had been inclined to trust him for a time, "If you base your lives on my teaching, you will be my true followers. You will discover the truth and be free." They replied, "We are Abraham's descendants, we have never been slaves to anybody! What do you mean by saying we shall be *free*?" Jesus answered, "Believe me, everyone who does wrong is a slave to wrongdoing. A slave cannot be a permanent member of a family. Only children are in that position. If a member of the family gives you your freedom, then you can belong to the family as a free person. I accept that you are descendants of Abraham, but you would like to kill me because you don't follow my teaching. I tell you what my Parent has shown me, and you do what your parent tells you." They shouted, "Abraham is our parent!" "Then why can't you behave like Abraham?" Jesus said. "You'd like to kill me because I've told you the true things I learnt from God. That's not the way Abraham behaved! You're behaving like your real parent!" They shouted back, "How dare you suggest that we are bastards! God is our one and only parent!" Jesus replied, "If God were your parent you'd love me,

because I came from God and now stand in front of you. My coming here isn't my own doing; God sent me. Why do you find that so difficult to grasp? Is it because it's not what you want to hear? You started out evil, and you're determined to carry on as you began. The character that has been bred in you is that of a murderer and a liar. The language you've been brought up in is the language of lies! Because I tell you the truth, you don't trust me. Can one of you point to anything I've done wrong? If I tell the truth, why don't you trust me? Those who belong to God listen to what God says. You don't belong to God, and that's why you won't listen."

(48) This led some of them to say, "You're a Samaritan really, aren't you? Out of your mind as well!" Jesus replied, "My mind is sound. I simply have respect for my Parent. You have no respect for me. I'm not after any special position for myself. There's someone else seeing to that, the one who is in a position to judge. Believe me, anyone who follows my teaching will never die." They said, "Now we know you're out of your mind! Abraham and all the prophets died, and yet you say, 'Anyone who follows my teaching won't die.' Are you greater than our ancestor Abraham, and greater than all God's speakers? They are dead, every one! Who do you think you are?" Jesus replied, "If I drew attention to myself, you'd be right to think nothing of me. It's my Parent, the one you claim as your God, who puts the spotlight on me. You don't know God, but I do. I would be a liar if I said I didn't. I follow God's instructions. Your ancestor Abraham looked forward to my coming and celebrated when I came." They said, "You aren't fifty yet, and you're telling us that you've seen Abraham?" Jesus said, "Believe me, I existed before Abraham – I am who I am."

They picked up stones to throw at Jesus, but he slipped away, out of the temple.

9 One day Jesus was out walking and saw a man who had been born blind. His friends asked, "When this man was born blind, whose fault was it, his own or his parents'?" Jesus answered, "It's not his fault, nor his parents' fault that he's blind. His blindness is best seen as a challenge to God's healing power. As long as daylight lasts, we must get on with the work of the one I represent. When night comes, no one will be able to work. While I'm here, I supply enough light for everybody to see." As if

to demonstrate what he was saying, Jesus spat on the ground and made a paste with the spit. Then he put it on the man's eyes. Jesus told him to go and wash it off in the Public Baths. The man went to the Embassy Baths and washed, and when he got back home, he could see. The neighbors, and other people who had seen him begging before, were puzzled, saying things like, "Isn't this the man who used to sit and beg?" Some said, "It's him!" others, "No, its not; he just looks like him." But the man said, "It's me alright!" Then they asked, "So how is it you can see?" He explained, "Someone called Jesus made some paste and rubbed it on my eyes and told me to go to the Public Baths to wash. So I went and had a good wash, and afterwards I could see." They asked. "Where is this person?" He answered, "I've no idea."

They took the man who had been blind to the strict set. The day Jesus gave the man his sight by making a paste happened to be a Rest Day. So when they asked the man how he had got his sight, he told them, "He put a paste on my eyes, I washed, and then I could see." Some of them said, "Whoever he is, he's ungodly, because he doesn't keep the Rest Day." Others said, "How can someone bad do such wonderful things?" So they fell out amongst themselves. They questioned the man again and said, "We'd like to know *your* opinion, since you're the one who's got your sight back." The man replied, "He's one of God's speakers." The clergy were not willing to believe the man had been blind and had got his sight until they interviewed his parents. They asked them, "Is this your son? Was he born blind? How is it he can see now?" The parents replied, "This is our son, and he was born blind, but we don't know how he can see now or who's responsible. You'd better ask *him*. He's old enough to speak for himself." His parents were on their guard, afraid of getting into trouble. The clergy had gone as far as ruling that anyone who suggested Jesus was the Chosen One should be banned from the places of worship. It was a wise move on the parents' part to say, "He's old enough to speak for himself." So the man who had been born blind was called back in. "Come on," they said, "Let's have the truth! We know this man's reputation – he's not straight!" "I don't know anything about his reputation," the man replied. "The only thing I know is I used to be blind and now I can see!" They kept up the questioning, "What did he do to you, then? How did he get you to see?" He answered, "I've already told you. You can't have been listening. Why have I got to go all over it again? Are you interested in becoming his followers too?" "Aha!" they shouted, "Now we've got you, you low-down scum! You admit to being a follower of his. We are followers of Moses! We know God spoke to Moses. As for this fellow, we don't even know his racial background." The man answered, "I find this difficult to believe. How can you be so ignorant? I'm telling you – HE OPENED MY EYES!! We know God doesn't co-operate with evil people, but only with people who put God first and try to do the right thing. This is the first time anyone has given sight to somebody born blind. If Jesus didn't come from God, he wouldn't be able to do anything!" "How dare you try to tell us what is right and what is wrong!" they shouted. "You come from a bad home!" And they banned him from the places of worship.

When Jesus heard that the man had been made an outcast from the community in this way, he found him and asked him, "Do you trust the Complete Person?" The man answered, "Who are you talking about, Sir? Tell me who I have to trust." Jesus said, "It's someone you've seen – the one you're talking to now!" The man said, "I trust you, Sir," and gave Jesus a hug.

Jesus said. "My coming here has had the effect of turning things round. The blind can see, and those who see have become blind." Some of the strict set overheard Jesus saying this and said, "You're not suggesting we're blind, are you?" Jesus said, "If you were earnestly groping for better understanding, that would be okay. But because you think you see it all, you're still getting it all wrong."

10 Jesus continued, "If anyone tries to get into a sheep pen any other way than through the entrance, you can be sure it's either a thief or a vandal. The shepherd responsible for looking after the sheep goes in through the entrance. The gatekeeper opens the gate for the shepherd and the sheep recognize the shepherd's voice. Each sheep responds to a name and the shepherd calls them one by one to come out. When they are all collected together, the shepherd walks in front of them and they follow on, recognizing the familiar voice. They won't follow someone they don't know, but run away. They don't respond to a strange voice."

There was a hidden meaning in the words of Jesus, but those listening did not grasp it. So Jesus said, "Believe me, I'm the entrance to the sheep pen. The sheep didn't respond to previous leaders because they were all thieves and vandals. I'm the way in; I'll shepherd you safely into the pen and give you freedom to go in and out to graze. A thief is only out to steal and kill and vandalize. I want you to have a life packed with good things. I'm the best sort of shepherd, ready to lose my life for the sheep. Someone just hired for the day to look after the sheep doesn't have the same feelings as the shepherd who owns them, but will run away when a wolf appears and leave the flock open to attack and panic. The one who is hired runs away because it's just a job and there's no real care for the sheep. I'm the best sort of shepherd. I know the people in my care and they know me, just as the Loving God and I know one another. I'm ready to die for the sheep. I also own other sheep, who don't belong to this sheep pen. I must collect them too. They'll recognize my voice. There's going to be one flock, with one shepherd. The Loving God loves me because I'm willing to die so as to come to life again. Nobody can take my life away from me; I choose to give it. I'm free to give my life away and free to take it back again. I'm doing what my Parent has asked me to do."

These words of Jesus led to more argument. Many people said, "He's a raving lunatic! There's no point in listening to him!" Others said, "Someone who's mentally unbalanced couldn't speak so clearly, or give blind people their sight."

(22) It was winter. In Jerusalem they were celebrating the festival in which the temple was recognized as God's house. As Jesus was walking through Solomon's Arches in the temple, the people gathered round him and asked, "How long are you going to keep us guessing? If you're the Chosen One, tell us straight!" Jesus replied, "I've told you, but you don't trust my words. The things I've done on my Parent's behalf should be enough proof. But because you're not my sheep you don't trust me. My sheep recognize my voice. I know them and they follow me. I'm giving them real life and they'll never die. No one can snatch them away from me. My Parent who has entrusted them to me is greater than anyone. Nothing can take them out of the care of the Loving God. The Loving God and I are in complete agreement." Again people picked up stones to throw at Jesus. But Jesus said, "You've seen me do a lot of good things with the help of the

Loving God. Which one of those good things are you throwing stones at me for?" They answered, "We're not throwing stones at you for any of the good things you've done, but for your outrageous way of talking. You're pretending to be God when you're only human." Jesus answered, "Doesn't your Rule Book record that God said: 'You are gods'? If those who passed on God's messages were called 'gods' in this way (and the old books must not be ignored), why do you regard it as offensive for me to say, 'I'm God's Likeness,' since it was the Loving God who chose me and sent me into the world? If I'm not doing as my Parent would wish, then you've got grounds to mistrust me. But if I'm carrying out my Parent's wishes, although you may still find it difficult to trust me as a person, you ought at least to be able to appreciate my achievements. Perhaps then you will understand how the Loving God and I work together." Once again they tried to grab hold of Jesus, but he managed to escape.

Jesus crossed back over the Jordan to the spot where John had once been dipping people, and stayed there for a while. Many people came to see him. Some said, "John was not one for doing miracles, but he was right in his opinion of Jesus." Many people came to trust him there.

11 Larry was taken ill. He lived in Dategrove with his sisters, Mary and Martha. (Mary is best known as the one who gave Jesus a foot massage with scented oil and used her hair as a towel.) The sisters sent a message to Jesus, "Dear Leader, the friend you love is very ill."[5] When Jesus got the message he said, "This illness isn't fatal. It's another opportunity for us to see how wonderful God is. It will be a good advert for God's Likeness too." So, although Jesus loved Martha and her sister, and Larry, he seemed to take no notice of the news that Larry was ill, and stayed put for another two days. Only then did Jesus say to his friends, "Let's go back to Judea!" They said, "Teacher, last time we were there, people wanted to throw stones at you. Surely you can't risk going back again?" Jesus said, "There are only so many hours of daylight. People who walk

---

[5] In 11:3 and 11:36 the Gospel author clearly and unambiguously identifies the "beloved disciple" as Lazarus (Larry). The appellation only appears after this point, which the author intends to be our introduction to him. To suggest any other candidate is thus tantamount to suggesting that the author is deliberately misleading!

during the day don't bump into anything, because the light from the sun shows them where they're going. Those who walk at night bump into things, because there's not enough light for them to see the way clearly. Our friend Larry has gone to sleep, but I'm going to wake him up!" The friends said, "Leader, a good sleep will do him good!" They thought Jesus meant natural sleep, not that Larry had died. So Jesus put it clearly, "Larry is dead. I'm pleased I wasn't there, for your sake. It will teach you to trust me. It's time we paid Larry a visit!" Twin said to the others, "Come on, let's go. We'll probably end up dead, like Larry!"

(17) When Jesus arrived, he found that Larry had been buried four days before. Since Dategrove was only two miles away from Jerusalem, many people had come out to visit Mary and Martha to offer sympathy on the loss of their brother. When Martha heard that Jesus was on the way, she went out to meet him, but Mary stayed at home. Martha said to Jesus, "Leader, if you'd been here, my brother wouldn't have died! Even now I know that God will do whatever you ask." Jesus said, "Your brother will live again." Martha replied, "I know he'll come to life when everyone else does, at the end of time." Jesus said, "I'm in charge of bringing people to life. Anyone who trusts me will live, even if they have to die first. Those who are living now, and put their trust in me, will never really die. Do you trust me?" Martha said, "Yes, dear Leader, I trust you. You are God's Likeness, the one the world's been waiting for."

Then Martha went back to have a quiet chat with her sister Mary. Martha said, "The Teacher's here and wants to see you." When Mary heard that, she got up quickly and hurried out to meet Jesus. He was still where Martha had left him, outside the village. The friends from nearby who were in the house, looking after Mary, saw her jump up and rush out. They went after her, thinking she was going to the grave to cry. When Mary came face to face with Jesus, she hugged him and said, "Leader, if you'd been here, my brother wouldn't have died." Jesus saw that Mary was crying. So were the people who were with her. The sight of their grief disturbed and upset him. Jesus said, "Where have you laid him to rest?" They said, "This way, Sir." Jesus broke into tears. So some said, "It's obvious Jesus loved him very much!"[6] But others said, "It's a pity the one who gave the blind man his sight didn't use his skill to keep his friend from dying!" Jesus was still in a state of distress when he saw the grave. It was a cave with a stone up against it. Jesus said, "Take the stone away." Martha, the dead man's sister, said to Jesus, "Leader, think about the smell – the body's been there four days!" Jesus said, "Didn't I tell you that if you trusted, you'd see what God can do?" So they took the stone away. Jesus looked up and said, "Loving God, thank you for listening to me. I know you always do, but I want these people to know, so they will accept me as the one you've sent." Then Jesus shouted in a loud voice, "Larry, come on out!" Larry came out, with his hands and feet still tied by the grave clothes and a cloth over his face. Jesus said to them, "Untie him so he can move."

(45) Many of the people who had come to visit Mary and saw what Jesus did, put their trust in him. But others went to the strict set and told them what he had done. These met together with the leading clergy. They said, "What can we do? This man's actions are very impressive. If we just let him carry on, everyone will put their trust in him and the Roman armies will destroy our place of worship and our nation." But Guy, their chief for that year, said, "You're getting confused. It should be obvious that it's better for one person to die for the people than for the whole race to be wiped out." Guy was thought to be God's official mouthpiece. On this occasion he didn't realize the full meaning of what he was saying. God was saying through him that Jesus was going to die for the Jewish people, and not just for the Jewish people, but to bring together a new community of God's people from all over the world. The clergy started to make plans to kill Jesus from that day on. So Jesus avoided being seen in public and laid low in a village on the edge of the desert with his close friends.[7]

It was nearly time for the festival that celebrates the escape of the Jewish people from Egypt. Lots of people from all over the country were on the way to Jerusalem to get ready to worship. Those who met in the tmple were looking out for Jesus. The sort of thing they said to one another was, "What do you think is going to happen? He won't dare show his face at the festival, will he?" The leaders and the strict set had given orders for anyone who knew where Jesus was to report it, so they could arrest him.

---

[6] See footnote 5.

[7] 11:54. The Greek text identifies this village as "Emphraim."

12

About a week before the festival, Jesus went back to Dategrove where Larry lived. To celebrate Larry's recovery, the family held a party for Jesus, with Martha in charge of the refreshments. Jesus and Larry, and the other guests, relaxed on couches round the table. Then Mary brought a pound of very expensive perfume, pure oil of nard, smeared Jesus' feet with it and used her hair as a towel. The beautiful scent spread all through the house. But Judas from Kerioth, the follower of Jesus who was going turn traitor, said, "That perfume was worth a fortune! Why wasn't it sold, and the money given to charity?" (Really Judas didn't care much about people in need. He was thinking how he could have helped himself, as he usually did when he looked after the group's money.) But Jesus said, "That's enough of that! Mary's used the oil now instead of waiting for my funeral. There are always people needing charity, thanks to you! But you won't always have me to do things for."

When it was known publicly that Jesus was in Dategrove, people turned up in large numbers, not just to see Jesus, but to get a look at Larry, back from the dead. The clergy decided they would have to kill Larry as well as Jesus, since Larry was the reason so many were rejecting their leadership and going over to Jesus.

(12) By next day, the news that Jesus was on his way to Jerusalem reached the crowds of people who had come to celebrate the festival. So they went out to meet him, waving branches they had cut down from the palm-trees. They shouted:

> "Freedom now! Welcome God's Chosen! A big cheer for our
> Leader!"

Jesus found a young donkey and sat on it, just as it says in the old books,

> "People of Jerusalem, have no fear;
> On a little donkey, your leader draws near."

At first, Jesus' friends did not understand what all these things meant; but when Jesus received the full recognition he deserved, they realized how events in his life tied up with what had been written about him. Those who had been there when Jesus called Larry out of the grave carried on spreading the news. The report of this remarkable happening was largely responsible for the great numbers turning out to give Jesus a welcome. The strict set said among themselves, "It's hopeless! Everybody's gone crazy over him!"

(20) Among those who had come to worship at the festival were some Greeks. They came to Philip, the friend from Fishtown in Galilee, and said, "Sir, we'd like to meet Jesus." Philip spoke to Andrew about it and they both went and told Jesus. Jesus responded by saying, "It's time for the Complete Person to become world-famous. Believe me, a grain of wheat stays a single grain unless it's sown in the ground and rots; but if it rots it produces a new plant covered in grain. Those who hang on to life, lose it; those who are willing to lose the life they have now will experience life to the full. Anyone who wants to help me must go the way I'm going, and keep close to me. The Loving God will have a special regard for anyone who helps me. I'm feeling rather anxious now. What should I be saying? Should I say, 'Loving God, get me out of this'? No – this is how things were meant to be. Loving God, show everybody how wonderful you are!"

Then a voice was heard above their heads. "I have shown myself and I'll show myself again." The people crowding round heard the voice. Some thought it was thunder and others said, "A messenger from God spoke to him." Jesus said, "The voice wasn't speaking to me, but to you! The world is facing its greatest moment of crisis; the forces of evil are going to be defeated once and for all. When I'm strung up for all to see, I'll attract everyone to me from all over the world." (Jesus was hinting at the way he was going to die.)

Some of the people shouted back, "Our Rule Book tells us that the Chosen One will live for ever. What do you mean when you say the Complete Person will be strung up? Who is this Complete Person?" Jesus replied, "Daylight is shining round you for just a little longer. Use the light to complete your journey, so you don't get lost in the darkness. If you choose to walk in the dark, you won't know where you're going. Dare to step out boldly, while the light is shining, and you'll be guides to others."

When Jesus had said this he left them and went into hiding. Although they had seen Jesus do so many wonderful things, they still refused to trust him. God's speaker spoke the truth about these people:

> "*Though we spread the news abroad,*
> *No one sees what you're doing, God.*"

They found the truth impossible to accept, because, to quote the same speaker again,

> "*The sight of God dazzled them;*
> *Their minds were inward turned;*
> *Though clear as day the better way,*
> *God's gift of life they spurned.*"

God's speaker said this because he caught sight of God's beauty and was disappointed by the response when he tried to share the experience with others. It was the same in the case of Jesus. Even so, many people in influential positions trusted Jesus, though they kept quiet about it, because they were afraid the strict set would have them thrown out of the places of worship. The approval of other people was more important to them than the approval of God.

Jesus made sure that everyone got this message. "Anyone who trusts me is really trusting the one who sent me. Anyone who sees me, sees the one who sent me. I've come like a light into the world, so anyone who trusts me doesn't need to stay in the darkness. I don't condemn anyone who hears what I have to say and takes no notice. It's not my purpose to condemn but to bring healing to the world. Anyone who turns me down and ignores what I say will one day have to face up to the words they heard me speak, and that will be judgment enough. I haven't pushed my own ideas, but the Loving God who sent me has told me what to say and how to put things. I know God's words will bring life to the full. That's why I stick closely to what the Loving God tells me to say."

13

By the evening before the festival, Jesus had realized the time had come for him to go beyond the world of time and space into the presence of the Loving God. He loved the friends he had made in the world and never stopped loving them. Evil, treacherous thoughts had taken over the mind of Judas Simson from Kerioth. While they were eating, Jesus, knowing the Loving God had given him control over everything and that he had come from God and was going back to God, left the table, took off his coat and tied a towel round his waist. Then he poured some water into a bowl and started washing his friends' feet, using the towel round his waist to dry them. When it was Rocky's turn, he said to Jesus, "What makes you think you're going to wash *my* feet, Leader?" Jesus said, "You may not understand what I'm doing at the moment, but one day you'll see the point." Rocky said, "You'll never get to wash my feet!" Jesus replied, "Unless you let me wash you, you're not really my friend." "In that case," Rocky said, "wash all of me, hands, face, the lot!" Jesus said, "Since you've just come from the public baths, it's only your feet need washing. Every other part should be clean. Everyone of you is clean – almost." By saying "almost," Jesus was hinting he knew who the traitor was.

After Jesus had washed their feet and put his coat on again, he went back to the table and began to explain. "Do you understand what I was doing for you? You call me 'Teacher' and 'Leader,' and they're good names for me. If I'm your teacher and leader, you should wash one another's feet in the same way I've washed yours. I've set you an example. Try and behave like me! You know that workers aren't more important than the manager or a messenger more important than the one who sends the message. Now you've got the point, put it into practice, and you'll be happy! I'm not including all of you. I know all about the people I've picked. Those words in the old books will come true – 'Someone shared my food, then kicked me.' I'm telling you this now so that when it happens you'll know for sure who I am. Believe me, anyone who accepts one of my people is really accepting me, and anyone who accepts me is accepting the one I represent."

(21) Jesus was clearly upset as he said all this. He went on, "It's just as well I tell you – one of you is going to help my enemies to capture me." The disciples looked anxiously at one another, not sure who Jesus meant. One of his friends, the one Jesus had a special love for, was snuggling close to him. Rocky caught his attention and got him to ask Jesus who he was talking about. He leant back and whispered, "Who is it, Leader?" Jesus said, "It's the one I give this piece of bread to when I've dipped it in the sauce." Then Jesus took a piece of bread, dipped it in the sauce and handed it to Judas Simson. As soon as he had taken the bread, Judas allowed his evil thoughts to take over completely. Jesus said, "Don't waste time, get on with it!" No one at the table understood this remark. Some thought, since Judas was in charge of the group's money, Jesus was telling him to get something for the festival, or to give something to someone in need. So Judas, the one who had been given the piece of bread, rushed off. It was pitch black outside.

When Judas had gone, Jesus said, "Now the special nature of the Complete Person is going to be seen. Watch, and you'll see God's character shining through. The brightness that shone from God on the Complete Person, will now shine out from the Complete Person. My friends, I'm not going to be with you much longer. You'll try and find me, but as I said publicly, no one can go where I'm going. That includes you. Your priority from now on should be to love one another. Copy my love for you. If you love one another, people will recognize you as my followers."

Rocky asked, "Where are you going, Leader?" Jesus said, "Somewhere you can't join me for the time being. But one day you'll be able to join me there." Rocky said, "Leader, why can't I come with you now? I would die for you!" Jesus said, "Are you sure you'd die for me? Believe me, before the cock crows in the morning, you will have said three times you don't know me."

14

Jesus said, "Don't be upset. Trust God, and trust me. There's plenty of room in my Parent's house. I would have warned you otherwise. I'm going to make things ready for you. That means I'll come back to fetch you later. Then we shall all be together. You know where I'm going and how to get there, don't you?"

Twin said, "Leader, we've no idea where you're going, so how can we know how to get there?" Jesus said, "I'm the road to the Loving God. I supply the directions and the strength you need. You'll only get there by trusting me. If you know me well, you won't have any difficulty in recognizing my Parent, indeed you've already done that."

Philip said, "Leader, just show us the Loving God and we'll be satisfied." Jesus said, "Have we been together all this time without you getting to know me, Philip? Anyone who's seen me has seen the Loving God, so there's no need to say, 'Show us the Loving God.' Don't you realize that the Loving God and I are closely linked? The Loving God is responsible for the words I say and the things I do. The Loving God and I are united together as one. That's something you can trust. If you have any difficulty, just think about what I've been able to do. I assure you, anyone who trusts me will do the same things as me, and even more amazing things, because I'm on my way to the Loving God. Anything you ask in line with my character I'll do for you. You'll see the Loving God shining through me. Provided it matches my character, I'll do it. If you love me, do the things I ask you. I'll ask the Loving God to give you someone else to help you, someone who'll always be with you. She's the Spirit, who makes you aware of the truth. Most people don't accept her because they don't recognize or even notice her. But you recognize her, because she keeps you company all the time and will become part of you. I won't leave you all alone. I'm coming back to you. Soon people won't be able to see me any more. But you'll be seeing me. Because I'm always alive, you'll always be alive. The day will come when you realize that you, my Parent, and I, cannot be thought of apart! Those who remember my teaching and follow it show their love for me and will experience my Parent's love. I'll show my love for them by showing myself to them."

Judas (not the one from Kerioth) said, "Leader, how are you going to show yourself to us but not to everybody?" Jesus replied, "Those who love me will remember what I've said, and my Parent will love them and we'll both come and live with them. Those who don't love me will forget my words. But you've realized I speak the words of the Loving God who I represent. I've told you all this while I'm still with you. But your special helper, the one who's going to be sent to you by the Loving God on my behalf, she will teach you everything and remind you of all I've been saying to you.

"Before I go, I'm going to give my peace to you. It's a special kind of peace, much deeper than anything the world can give you. Don't be upset or afraid. I've given you my word. Although I'm going away, I'll come back to you. If you loved me you'd be pleased I'm going to the Loving God, because the Loving God has a higher form of being. I've told you about events before they happen, so that when they happen you'll still trust me. I haven't much more time to talk to you, because the enemy is on the way. The enemy can't touch me, but I'm going to do what the Loving God has told me to do. Then my love for the Loving God will be clear for all to see. Let's finish our meal, it's time we got going!"

15 Jesus said, "I'm like a healthy grapevine in my Parent's vineyard. My Parent chops off any of my branches that don't produce grapes, but prunes the branches that produce grapes, to make them grow more grapes. You've just been pruned by the things I've said to you. We need to stay attached to one another. Just as a branch doesn't have any grapes unless it's attached to the vine, you can't do anything useful unless you're attached to me. I'm the grapevine, you're the branches. If we stay attached to one another there'll be a good crop. You'll never achieve anything on your own. Anyone who doesn't stick to me gets thrown away like a withered branch and ends up being burnt in the fire. If you stick to me and remember what I've told you, then you can ask whatever you want and you'll get it. My Parent's reputation will be increased if you're successful as my followers. I've loved you in the same way the Loving God has loved me. Hold on to your loving relationship with me. If you follow my teaching, our relationship will keep strong. I have a strong relationship with my Parent because I carry out my Parent's wishes. I've spoken to you like this because I want to share my happiness with you. I want you to be completely happy!

"I want you to love one another like I've loved you. Those prepared to die for their friends show the highest form of love. You're my friends when you put into practice what I've taught you. I don't think of you as my staff any more. Members of staff don't have access to the private files of the boss. I think of you as my friends, because I've let you have the full data entrusted to me by my Parent. You didn't pick me to be your friend, I picked you. I've trained you to get results that will bear the test of time. My Parent will answer your requests for anything you need to do my work effectively. Everything depends on your loving one another.

"If you're unpopular, don't forget I was unpopular too. If you went with the fashion, you'd be popular and accepted. Because I've taught you to be different, you'll be hated. Don't forget what I said earlier, 'Workers are not more important than the manager.' The people who've made life difficult for me will make life difficult for you. On the other hand, those who listened to what I had to say will listen to you as well. Being linked with me will make life hard for you. It's because people don't know the one who gave me my job. Those I've never met or spoken to are not to be blamed. But those I've spoken to haven't any excuse for their hostility. Their hatred of me amounts to hatred of my Parent. They wouldn't be to blame if I hadn't done anything exceptional in front of them. But they've seen it all, and still hate me, and my Parent too. There's a good description of them in their own Book of Rules:

> 'Unreasonably
> They hated me.'

"When you get the helper I'm going to pass on to you from the Loving God, the Spirit who makes people aware of the truth, she will back me up. I expect you to back me up too, because you've been with me every step of the way."

16 Jesus went on. "I've said all this so you won't get confused. You'll be banned from places of worship, and the time will come when those who kill you think they're doing God a good turn. People behave like this because they haven't got to know the Loving God or me. I'm warning you in advance. I didn't say anything to you at the start, because I was here to protect you. I'm on my way to the one who gave me my job, yet you still haven't worked out where I'm going. What I've said has made you miserable. You should realize I'm going away for your good. If I don't go away, the helper won't come to you; but if I do go, I can send her to you. When she comes, she'll show how mistaken people are in their ideas of right and wrong and justice. Wrongdoing stems from lack of trust in me. When you can't see me any more, I'll be with the Loving God, and that means right is on my side. As for justice, the powerful

in the world are already on their way out! I've still got a lot to say to you, but you can't take it at the moment. But when the Spirit comes, she'll make you aware of many different types of truth. She won't push her own ideas. She'll open your minds and teach you how to listen. She'll make you aware of possibilities in the future. The Spirit will ensure my reputation by explaining my teaching to you. She'll continue to pass on to you the truths my Parent and I share. Soon you'll miss me; then it won't be long before you see me again."

(17) Some of Jesus' friends found this last remark puzzling. They also wondered what he meant by "going to the Loving God." Jesus knew they wanted him to make it clearer, so he said, "Believe me, you will sob your hearts out while other people are celebrating. Your spirits will be very low, but then suddenly you'll cheer up. When she is having a baby, a woman suffers pain up to the moment she gives birth. Then she forgets all about the pain; she is so happy at seeing her baby! It's painful for you at the moment, but when we next meet you'll be jumping up and down for joy, and you'll never be miserable again. Then you won't need to ask me anything. Don't forget, the Loving God will give you anything you ask for, so long as it's in keeping with my character. You haven't tried it out yet! You only have to ask, and you'll get what you need. Then you'll know the meaning of happiness. I know that up to now I've been speaking in riddles. But soon I'll be able to speak plainly to you about the Loving God. Then you'll ask God for the things I want you to ask for. I won't need to ask for you. The Loving God has a special love for you, because you've loved me and trusted I come from God. I came here from the Loving God, and now I'm on my way back again."

Jesus' friends said, "That's better. We can understand you now you're speaking plainly, instead of in riddles. Now we know beyond question you're the one who knows what's what! We're sure you've come from God." Jesus said, "Sure, are you? Any moment now, this group is going to break up. You'll all run off home, leaving me on my own. Of course, I'm not on my own, because the Loving God is with me. I've told you all this, so you can share my peace of mind. The world will try to cause you pain. Cheer up! The world's mine now!"

17

When Jesus had finished what he had to say to his friends, he began to talk to God.

"Loving God, the time has come; let your brightness shine through me, so I can show how wonderful you are. You've given your Likeness a special place among all the people on earth, to give real life to those you've put in my care. Real life means knowing you, the only true God, and me, Jesus, the one you've chosen to represent you. I've increased your reputation here by finishing the job you gave me to do. So now, Loving God, give me that great time I enjoyed with you before the world came into being. I've shown what you are like to those you've entrusted to me here. They already belonged to you, and you asked me to look after them. They've responded to your message. They realize now that my gifts come from you, and that I've been passing on your words to them. They've accepted your words because they've seen the link between us. I'm asking you to help them. I'm stressing their needs in particular, because you put them in my care, and because they belong to you. We share responsibility for them, and they've been a credit to me. The time of parting has come. I'm coming to you, but they're staying behind.

"Good and loving God, look after my friends, for your sake and mine, and keep them together, just as we are always together. While I was with them, I looked after them for you. I kept them safe, and none of them has been lost, except the one mentioned in the old books. That was unavoidable. Because I'm coming to you, I'm saying these things out loud, so they can share my happiness completely. I've passed your message on to them. They're already unpopular because they're different just as I'm different. I don't want them to be killjoys, I simply ask you to keep them from evil. They're different, just as I'm different. Keep them honest and open, loyal to the truth of your teaching. In the same way as you gave me a job to do, I've given them a job. I'm determined to do my best for them, so they'll do their best in the cause of truth.

"But I'm not asking your help just for my friends here, but also for those who will come to trust me through what my friends tell them. I want them to stick together. Just as you and I, Loving God, cannot be separated, so may they be part of us. Then people will know for sure I stand for you. The nature you've given me, I've given them, to keep them close, as we are close

– I with them, you with me, all together as one. Then people will know I stand for you, and that you have the same love for my friends as you have for me. Loving God, I want those you've put in my care to join me, so they can see the splendor of your love, which has surrounded me from before the world began. Good and loving God, although people don't know you, I know you, and my friends know I belong to you. I've told them what you're like, and I'll carry on telling them. Your love for me will help them to love one another and to keep me in their hearts."

18 After talking with God, Jesus took his friends across the Cedar brook into a garden. Judas, the traitor, knew the spot, because Jesus often met his friends there. So Judas led a group of soldiers to the garden, including some of the temple police provided by the clergy. They were armed and carrying lanterns and torches. Jesus knew exactly what was going to happen, so he stepped forward and asked, "Who are you out to get?" They answered, "Jesus from Nazareth." Jesus said, "That's me!" Judas the traitor was standing there with them. When Jesus said, "That's me," they jumped back and fell over one another. So Jesus asked again, "Who are you out to get?" They said, "Jesus from Nazareth." Jesus said, "I've told you, I'm the one you want. You can let these people go." Jesus was keeping to what he said to God, "I haven't lost any of those you put in my care." Then Rocky pulled out the knife he had on him and attacked Malcolm, one of the boys who worked for Guy, the religious chief. Jesus said, "Put that sword away! The Loving God's way means suffering, and I'm going to take it!" On the command of the officer in charge, the soldiers and the temple police grabbed hold of Jesus and tied him up. First they took him to Hank, Guy's father-in-law. (Remember, Guy had advised that it was better for one person to die than for everybody to suffer.)

Rocky and another friend followed Jesus. This friend knew the Chief, so was able to gain access to where Jesus was, in the yard in front of the Chief's house. Rocky was left standing outside by the gate. So the friend had a word with the woman in charge of the gate and was able to get Rocky in. The woman said to Rocky, "Are you one of that man's followers, too?" Rocky said, "No, I'm not!" It was very cold, so the police and those who worked for the Chief got together to make a charcoal fire. They were huddled round it, trying to keep warm. Rocky joined them.

Hank began to question Jesus about his followers and his teaching. Jesus said, "I've always spoken in public. I've taught in our places of worship and here in the temple, meeting-points for all our people. I've said nothing behind anyone's back. Why do you need to ask me? Ask the people who listened to me; they're sure to remember what I said." At that, one of the police standing there slapped Jesus across the face and said, "How dare you talk to the chief like that!" Jesus said, "If I'm lying, you're free to give evidence to that effect. But if I'm telling the truth, why hit me?" Then Hank sent Jesus, with his hands tied, to Guy.

Rocky was still warming himself, standing near the fire. Some of the group asked him, "You're one of his friends too, aren't you?" Rocky shook his head and said, "No, I'm not." A boy who worked for the Chief, a relative of the one Rocky cut off the ear from, said. "Didn't I see you in the garden with him?" **(27)** Again Rocky said, "No!" At that very moment they heard the cock crowing.

(28) Early in the morning, Jesus was taken from Guy's house to the house of the Roman governor. The clergy did not go inside. They wanted to feel decent and respectable, so they could share the festival meal. So Pilate went outside to meet them. He asked, "What have you got against this man?" They answered, "We wouldn't have brought him to you unless he were a trouble-maker!" Pilate said. "You had better deal with him yourselves, according to your own rules!" The clergy replied, "We're not allowed to carry out the death penalty!" (Jesus had hinted at the way he was going to die. Now they were proving Jesus right.) Pilate went back inside and ordered Jesus to be put in front of him. He asked Jesus, "Are you the rightful Leader of the Jewish people?" Jesus replied, "Was it your idea to ask me that question, or have other people been talking to you about me?" Pilate said, "Not being a Jew, I can't understand what all this is about! Your own people, your appointed leaders have brought you to me. What have you been up to?" Jesus said, "I have responsibility for a different sort of world from the one you hold power in. Otherwise my followers would put up a fight to save me from the hands of our leaders. No, I'm not after your sort of power." Pilate said, "But you're some kind of leader, aren't you?"

Jesus said, "That's your way of putting it. My life's work has been to make people aware of the truth. People who are interested in the truth listen to me." Pilate said to Jesus, "Truth? What on earth is that?"

Then Pilate went outside again and told the people, "There's nothing wrong with him, as far as I can tell! Would you like me to keep my custom of releasing someone to you at festival time by releasing the Leader of the Jews?" They shouted back, "We don't want this man. Let's have Barry!" (Barry was a thug.)

19 Then Pilate sent Jesus to be flogged. The soldiers made a crown from the twigs of a thorn bush and put it on his head. Then they put a purple cloak on him and started coming up to him one by one and saying things like, "Why, if it isn't the greatest Jew that ever was!" and they slapped his face each time.

Pilate went outside again and said to the people, "Listen, I'm going to bring him out again to make it clear to you I can't find anything wrong with him." So Jesus came out, wearing the thorny crown and the purple cloak. Pilate said, "This is the man!" As soon as the clergy and the temple police saw him, they yelled out, "Stick him on a cross! Hang him high!" Pilate said to them, "Do your own dirty work. He's innocent as far as I'm concerned." They shouted back, "According to our rule book he deserves to die for claiming to be God's Likeness." Hearing this made Pilate even more nervous. He went back inside again and asked Jesus, "Where do you come from?" But Jesus kept quiet. So Pilate said, "Haven't you anything to say? Don't you realize I'm in a position to set you free or to hang you?" Jesus said, "You only have power over me because it's been entrusted to you by God. The one who handed me over to you is supposed to represent God, and so is more to blame."

From that point on Pilate did his best to set Jesus free, but the people shouted, "If you let this man off, you're not the emperor's friend. Anyone making a bid to be leader is a rival to the emperor." When Pilate heard them say this, he brought Jesus outside and sat him down on "The Stone Slab," which was the judge's seat. It was the day before the festival, the time of getting ready, about twelve o'clock mid-day. Pilate said to the people, "Here's your leader!" They shouted back, "Take him away! Take him away!

Stick him on a cross!" Pilate asked, "Do you want me to hang your leader?" The religious chiefs replied, "The emperor is our leader." Then Pilate let them have their way and made arrangements for Jesus to be executed.

(17) They took Jesus to Skull Hill. He had to carry the cross himself. Then the soldiers hung Jesus on the cross. Two others were also hung and placed either side of Jesus. Pilate had a poster put on top of the cross. It said, "Jesus from Nazareth, Leader of the Jews." A lot of people got to read this because the place of execution was only just outside the city, and it was written in the three main languages. The religious leaders complained to Pilate and asked him to change the wording to "This person *claimed* to be Leader of the Jews." Pilate said, "The words will stay just as I've written them!" After the soldiers had hung Jesus on the cross, they divided the clothes they had taken from him between the four of them equally. His vest was left over, and since it was made from a single piece of cloth, they said, "It would be a shame to tear this. Let's throw dice for it." As the old books say,

> *"On a couple of throws*
> *I lost my clothes!"*

While the soldiers were doing this, Jesus' mother, with her sister Miriam (Clover's wife) and Maggie, were standing near the cross. When Jesus saw his mother and the friend he had a special love for standing next to her, he said to his mother, "*He's* your son now!" Then Jesus said to his friend, "She's your mother." From then on the friend took her into his home.

(28) By this time Jesus realized he was dying. He said, "I need a drink." This too reminds us of words in the old books. The soldiers went to their jar of cheap wine, soaked a sponge in it, put it on a stick and lifted it to his mouth. As soon as Jesus had drunk the wine, he said, "It's all over!" His head fell and he stopped breathing. The clergy were getting ready for the special Rest Day, so they did not want bodies hanging on crosses. So they asked Pilate to have the legs of the victims broken and the bodies taken out of the way. The soldiers broke the legs of the two who had been hung with Jesus. But realizing that Jesus was dead already, they did not bother with him, except that one of them stabbed his side with a sword, causing a gush of blood and urine. (There is a reliable eyewitness to this. You can be sure

it is the truth.) The old books say, "None of his bones will be broken" and "They will look at the one they stabbed."

Then Joseph from Ram asked Pilate if he could have Jesus' body. Joseph was a friend of Jesus, but not openly because he was afraid of the authorities. Pilate agreed, so Joseph came and took the body away. He was joined by Nick, the one who visited Jesus at night. Nick brought a large supply of perfumes and spices, which they used for the laying out. They sprinkled the spices between the linen wrappings round the body, as was the custom. Near the place of execution there was a garden with a new grave, which had not been used. Since it was time to get ready for the special day, and the grave was handy, they buried Jesus there.

20 Early on Sunday morning, while it was still dark, Mary from Magdala (Maggie) went to the grave and found the stone had been moved from the opening. She ran off to find Rocky and the friend Jesus had a special love for, and told them, "Someone has moved our leader out of the grave and there's nothing to tell us where he's been taken." The two friends hurried off to the grave. At first they ran side by side, but Rocky could not keep up and the other friend got to the grave before him. He put his head just inside so he could see where the linen cloths were lying, but did not go in. Then Rocky joined him and he went right inside the grave. He saw Jesus' head cloth folded up neatly apart from the other pieces of cloth. Then the other friend who had got there first went inside and had a good look to make quite sure. They still did not realize that Jesus would return to life, although the old books make it clear. So the two went back home again.

(11) But Maggie stayed on beside the grave, her eyes filled with tears. While she was crying she looked in through the opening, and saw two of God's messengers with bright clothes on, sitting at either end of the slab where Jesus' body had been lying. They said, "Why are you crying?" Maggie said, "Somebody has taken away the one who made my life worthwhile, and I don't know what's happened to him!" Then she turned round and saw Jesus standing there but did not recognize him. Jesus said to her, "What are you crying for? Are you looking for somebody?" Maggie thought he might be the gardener, so she said to him, "Sir, if you have moved him somewhere

else, tell me where and I'll take charge of him." Jesus spoke her name, "Mary!" She looked up and said, "My Dear!" Jesus said, "Don't try and hold on to me, because I must first go home to the Loving God. You must go to my friends and give them this message, 'I'm going home to the one who is my Parent and your Parent, my God and your God.' Mary went straight to Jesus' friends and said, "I've seen the Leader!" and she passed on his message.[8]

(19) On Sunday evening, when the friends of Jesus met, they locked the doors of the house, because they were afraid of the police. Jesus joined them and said, "Keep calm everybody!" Then Jesus showed them his hands and his side. The friends went wild with joy when they realized their Leader was alive. Jesus had to say again, "Keep calm! The Loving God gave me a job to do, and now I'm going to give *you* something to do." They felt the breath of Jesus on them as he said, "Let God's Spirit in! From now on it's your job to free people from their guilt. Otherwise they will remain prisoners of their past mistakes."

Twin was not there when Jesus came. The other friends told him, "We've seen the Leader!" Twin said, "I won't believe that until I see the holes made by the nails in his wrists and put my finger into them. And I'll have to examine his side too!"

Next week Twin was there when the friends met again in the house. The doors were locked, but Jesus joined them and said. "Keep calm!" Then he spoke to Twin. "Come on, Twin, have a good look at my hands and my side. It's okay if you want to touch! It's time for you to get over your doubts and start trusting." Twin said, "My God, it's the Leader!" Jesus said, "It's easy for you to trust me now you've seen me. Those who trust me without seeing me deserve their happiness more."

The friends saw Jesus do many other remarkable things, but there is not enough space to tell you about them in this book. What you have just read has been written to convince you that Jesus is the Chosen One, God's Likeness. If you put your trust in Jesus, you will have life to the full.

---

[8] 20:16. An editor here anxiously explains that the word Maggie uses to address Jesus, "rabbouni" means "teacher." The editor probably knows that it does not. "Rabbi" is the word for teacher. "Rabbouni" is an affectionate diminutive, almost impossible to translate, but meaning something like "dear teacher," or even "husband" or "dear friend." We choose, in this translation, to restore the affectionate aspect of the greeting, which fits the context more naturally than the respectful aspect.

21

Some time later Jesus met his friends again by the lake in Galilee. This is how it happened. Rocky, Twin, Nathan from nearby Cana, Zebedee's boys, James and John, and two other friends met together. Rocky said, "I'm going fishing." The others said, "A good idea!" So they took the boat out onto the lake. But although they worked hard all night, they didn't catch anything.

Early in the morning Jesus came down to the beach, but the friends did not recognize him. Jesus called out, "Have you caught any fish, boys?" They called back, "Not a thing!" Jesus shouted, "You'll catch something if you cast your nets over there to the right!" They threw the net where Jesus was pointing and they could not pull it back in again – it was so full of fish. The friend Jesus had a special love for said to Rocky, "It's the Leader!" Rocky had no clothes on, so when he realized Jesus was there he grabbed his cloak and dived into the water. The other friends came on in the boat, pulling the net full of fish behind them. They were not far from the beach, within easy shouting distance.

When they came on to the beach, they saw a barbecue fire with some fish being cooked, and some bread beside it. Jesus said, "We could do with some of the fish you've just caught as well." So Rocky went back into the boat and dragged the net onto the beach. It was full of large fish, a hundred and fifty-three. Although there were so many, the net was not torn. Jesus said, "Time for breakfast!" None of the friends needed to ask Jesus, "What's your name?" They knew it was their Leader. Jesus came close to them, took the bread and gave it to them. Then he handed round the fish. This makes the third time Jesus had met with his friends after he had come back to life.

(15) After breakfast Jesus had a talk with Rocky. "Simon Johnson, do you have a strong love for me – more than these other friends of mine?" Rocky said, "You must know, Leader, how strong my feelings are for you!" Jesus said, "Look after the weak people I care about." Jesus asked Rocky again, "Simon Johnson, do you love me?" Rocky said, "Of course, Leader, you know I'm your friend!" Jesus said, "I want you to look after my tough people too!" The third time Jesus said, "So you're my friend, are you?" Rocky was hurt because Jesus asked him three times about his feelings for him. Rocky said, "Leader, you know everything about me. You know I love you as a friend!" Jesus said to him, "You've got to have enough love to meet

the needs of all my people! The problem is that up to now you've lived just like a teenage delinquent, doing up your belt and going off wherever you fancied. When you're old, you'll have to stretch out your hands and someone else will tie a belt around you and force you to go where you don't want to." (Jesus was giving Rocky a clue as to how he would die in the cause of God.) Then Jesus said, "You'd better stay close to me!"[9]

Rocky looked round and saw the friend Jesus had a special love for, just behind them. (This was the friend who snuggled up close to Jesus when they were having a meal and asked Jesus who the traitor was.) When Rocky saw him, he said to Jesus, "What about him, Leader?" Jesus said. "I may want him to hang around till I come for him, but that's none of your business. You stay close to me!" (These words led to a misunderstanding among the early Christians. They thought this friend of Jesus would not die. But Jesus did not say he would not die. He simply said, "I may want him to hang around till I come for him." It was this friend of Jesus who gave us all this information, putting it down in writing. We know he can be relied on.)

Jesus did much more, but it cannot all be written down. There simply is not room in the world for all the books that could be written about him.

---

[9] 21:15-19. In this interchange, Jesus and Rocky use two different Greek words for love. Rocky uses "philos" = "friendship love," whereas Jesus uses "agape" which is much stronger and denotes complete commitment. Jesus uses the word "sheep" or "lambs" for those on whom he wishes Rocky to practice this love.

Good News From a Jewish Friend

Attributed to Matthew

1 Jesus, God's Chosen, has an impressive pedigree. His ancestors include Abraham, Isaac, Jacob, Judah and Tamar (Judah's daughter-in-law), Barbara (the Palestinian prostitute), Ruth and Boaz, King David and Bathsheba, the wife he stole from Uriah, King Solomon, and many other kings, priests, and leaders. Jesus came from this line through Joseph, husband of Mary. They were the parents of Jesus, God's Chosen. In all there were fourteen generations from Abraham to David, fourteen from David to the time of the exile in Babylon, and fourteen from then to Jesus.

(18) This is how Jesus, God's Chosen, was born. His mother Mary was engaged to Joseph. She was pregnant before they were married. This was the work of God's Spirit. Joseph, her fiancé, was a good man. He did not want to expose Mary to a public scandal, so he thought to break off the engagement without making any fuss. When he had almost made up his mind to do this, he had a message from God in a dream.

"Joseph, remember you're a descendant of David. There's no need to have any worries about marrying Mary. This baby has been planned by God's Spirit. It's going to be a boy and you must call him Jesus. He will be a healer and cure people of their wrongdoing."

The birth of Jesus reminds us of words spoken by one of God's speakers in times past: "A young woman will become pregnant and give birth to a son. He will be the sign that God is with us."

When Joseph woke up, he took God's advice and got married to Mary. They did without sex until the baby boy was born. Joseph called him Jesus.

2 Jesus was born in Bethlehem during the reign of Herod the Great. Some magicians from Persia traveled to Jerusalem. They asked, "Where's the new baby who will lead God's people when he grows up? We've seen a new star that tells us he's been born. We want to pay our respects to him." This news put Herod into a state of panic, which frightened the people of Jerusalem. Herod called together the religious leaders and experts in the old books and asked them where God's Chosen was likely to be born. They turned his attention to Bethlehem, quoting words from one of God's speakers:

> *"Bethlehem, there's no reason for you to think you are not*
> *important.*
> *You are going to be the birthplace of someone who will lead*
> *my people like a shepherd."*

Herod had a private meeting with the magicians, and found out from them the precise time the star appeared. Then he gave them directions for Bethlehem and said, "Do your best to find the little boy. I would like to pay him my respects too." When they had heard what Herod had to say, they continued their journey. They spotted the new star again. It seemed to move on in front of them and stop over the house where the boy lived. They got very excited by this. They went inside the house and met Jesus and his mother and expressed their pleasure at the honor they felt. They took out from their luggage the presents they had brought with them including money, medicine, and perfume. They had a hunch it would be a mistake to go back to Herod, so they took a different route back home.

When the magicians had gone, someone sent by God came to Joseph during the night with the message, "You had better get your wife and little boy out of Bethlehem right away. Egypt would be the best place to make for. Don't come back until I get word to you that it's safe. Herod is sending out a search party. He's bent on murder!" So Joseph that very night fled with his family and sought asylum in Egypt. They lived there until Herod's death. This calls to mind God's words in the old books,

> *"I brought my people out of Egypt."*

When Herod realized the magicians had given him the slip, he went berserk. He sent his soldiers to Bethlehem and the villages nearby to kill all the children who were two years old or less. He used the information he had from the magicians to work out about how old the child would be. The people of Bethlehem experienced what Jeremy had spoken about in years gone by:

> "In ancient Ram a noise is heard,
> Wailing, loud and wild;
> Rachel has lost her little ones
> And will not be consoled."

After Herod had died, Joseph had another message from God. "It's safe now for you to go back to your own land. Those who wanted to kill your little boy have died." So Joseph took his family back to Palestine. But when he found out that Herod's son (Archie) had succeeded his father as ruler in the south of the country, Joseph was afraid to go back to Bethlehem. He was guided instead to Galilee in the north. The family set up home in the town of Nazareth. That's why Jesus is sometimes called "The Nazarene."

3 It was the time when John the Dipper started speaking in the desert. "Change your ways," John shouted. "The Bright New World will be here any day now!" One of God's speakers talked about John the Dipper.

> "Listen for the 'Voice' in the desert, shouting,
> 'Clear the road for God; put up the bunting!' "

John had a simple lifestyle, wearing only a camel skin with a leather belt and eating carob nuts and tree sap. People from the south of the country and the city of Jerusalem were attracted by the message and responded by admitting their faults and being dipped by John in the River Jordan. But when John saw many from the strict set and their rivals from the wealthy free and easy set coming to be dipped, he said, "You poisonous snakes! I see you're wriggling out of the cornfield now harvesting is about to start! Let's see a change in your behavior! Don't rely on the fact that Abraham is your ancestor to save you from trouble. God can make new children for Abraham out of people you've no more regard for than these stones! The chopper is ready; it will strike at the very roots of your religion and society. Every institution that has outlived its usefulness will be pulled down and disposed of, like rotten wood on a bonfire. I'm dipping you in the water, inviting you to change. But someone is coming more able than me. I'm not fit to carry his sandals. He will drench you with God's Spirit and that will be like fire. When corn has been harvested the grain has to be separated from the useless husks. That's going to happen to you. The one who is coming will do the job thoroughly. He'll store the grain in his barn and the rubbish left over he'll put on the fire until it's burnt to nothing."

Jesus came from Galilee to the Jordan to see John. He asked to be dipped by him. John tried to put him off. He said, "It doesn't make sense. You should be dipping me!" But Jesus said, "Please do it! It's best we stick to the rules for the time being." So John gave way.

After Jesus had been dipped in the river and was climbing up the bank, there was a sudden gap in the clouds and he experienced the coming of God's Spirit. She was like a pigeon flying down and perching on him. A voice from overhead was heard to say, "This is the one I love. I'm delighted with him."

4 Jesus felt he needed to spend some time in the desert to be clear in his mind which direction his life should take. He went without food for about six weeks. By then he was near to starvation. The thought came to him, "If I am God's Chosen One, all I need to do is to order these stones to become bread." Then he remembered some words from the old books, "People cannot live just on bread. They need God's words as well." Then he had another idea. He saw in his mind's eye the temple in Jerusalem. "Perhaps if I were to jump off the highest point I could prove I come from God? It should work like the song,

> 'God has friends who only wait
> To catch you as you fall;
> Your feet will gently touch the ground

Without a scratch at all.' "

But then Jesus thought again of some other words from the old books, "You must not push God too far." Then his mind formed another picture. This time he seemed to be looking down from a very high mountain on all the countries of the world. Jesus thought, "All this could easily be mine. All I have to do is to be cunning and gain the support of the right people." Jesus quickly dismissed these ideas. He thought, "These are the ways of evil. The old books tell us the only one we should try to please is God."

Then Jesus felt at peace. Some of God's helpers arrived to look after him.

(12) News came to Jesus that John the Dipper had been put in prison. So Jesus went back to Galilee. He left his home in Nazareth and took up lodgings in Nahum town, close to the border with Syria. It's as if the words of God's speaker were coming true:

> *"Country of the northern tribes,*
> *High road by the Sea,*
> *Astride the Jordan River,*
> *Heathen Galilee;*
> *Though you sat in darkness,*
> *Great is now your light;*
> *God will change death's shadows*
> *Into dawning bright."*

Then Jesus started to say to people, "Turn your backs on wrongdoing. The Bright New World is on its way!"

(18) One day Jesus was walking along the edge of Lake Galilee. He saw two brothers, Simon (nicknamed Rocky) and Andrew, casting a net into the sea. They ran a fishing business. Jesus called out to them, "How would you like to be my friends and fish for people?" They left their nets and went with Jesus straightaway. A little further on he saw another pair of brothers, James and John, Zebedee's sons. They were with Zebedee in the boat, mending their nets. At once, they said goodbye to their father and became friends of Jesus.

(23) Jesus went on a tour of Galilee, teaching in the places of worship and telling everyone the Good News about the New World. He cured all kinds of illnesses among the people he met. He became famous in Syria and people from that country brought their sick people across the border to him. He cured people with infections, muscle pains, mental disorders, and those who had lost the use of their limbs. Great crowds of people flocked to him from every part of Palestine, north, south, east, and west.

5 Jesus went up a mountain to escape from the crowds. He sat down the way a teacher does, and his friends formed a circle round him. This is a summary of his teaching that day:

"Splendid are those who take sides with the poor:
They are citizens of the Bright New World.
Splendid are those who grieve deeply over misfortunes:
The more deeply they grieve, the stronger they become.
Splendid are the gentle:
The world will be safe in their hands.
Splendid are those who have a passion for justice:
They will get things done.
Splendid are those who make allowances for others:
Allowances will be made for them.
Splendid are those who seek the best for others and not themselves:
They will have God for company.
Splendid are those who help enemies to be friends:
They will be recognized as God's true children.
Splendid are those who have a rough time of it because they stand up for what is right:
They too are citizens of the Bright New World.

(13) "You are like a rich flavoring for adding to the world. So don't be like the packet that goes past its sell-by date and has to be thrown out. Enthusiasm once lost is difficult to get back.

"You are like a lighthouse built to make travel safer in a dark world. Just like the big city whose lights can be seen miles away because it is on high ground, you must be in the right position for your light to be directed to best effect. Don't be secretive. Only if people can see the good things you're doing will they learn to appreciate the Loving God who inspires you.

(17) "You may have the impression that I want to do away with all rules and regulations. If so you've got me wrong. My object is to bring about the society the rules were made for. Only when we adopt the style of life the rules were designed to produce will we be able to do without the rules themselves. That time is a long way off. Those who adopt a careless attitude to the rules, and influence others to ignore them, will not be thought much of in the Bright New World. Whereas those who keep the rules and explain what they are meant to achieve, will be greatly respected there. On the other hand, don't make the mistake of thinking you can become a citizen of the Bright New World just by keeping rules. The experts in the old books who belong to the strict set keep all the rules. But if you don't behave any better than them you'll never make it!

(21) "Take for example the rule given to our ancestors, 'Do not kill.' 'Anyone taking the life of another will have to pay for it.' I would rather you deal with your anger against another human being, because that's what leads you to kill. It's your feelings that need to be corrected! Other human beings are your brothers and sisters, and if you use insulting language toward them you deserve to be taken to court. People who call others by rude names are only good for the city rubbish dump. So when you are on your way to your place of worship, if you remember that you've been the cause of grief or harm to someone else, don't go through the pretence of honoring God. Go and put matters right with the brother or sister you are on bad terms with, and then you can perform your act of worship. It makes sense to come to an agreement with someone who is taking you to court before you get into the courtroom. The prosecutor may win the case, the judge send you down, and the police officer take you to prison. Then you will have to serve out your full sentence, unless you can pay adequate compensation to the person you've wronged.

(27) "Here's another example from the same set of rules: 'Don't take away someone else's partner.' I want you to think about where such bad behavior begins. It begins in the mind when your imagination fixes on someone you have no right to. You must learn to exercise control over where you put your eyes and your hands, otherwise it's the rubbish dump for you – hands, eyes, the lot.

(31) "What about the old rule which protects the rights of women? It provides that if your relationship with your wife has broken down you must not keep her as a plaything but give her a note to certify her freedom. I say that to withdraw your loving care from your wife, certificate or no certificate, is to treat her like a plaything, unless perhaps she has formed a relationship with someone else.

(33) "Then there is the old rule about making promises. 'Don't make any promise you do not intend to keep. Fulfill all the promises you make in the presence of God.' But I say it's better not to make promises or to use things associated with God to make a promise sound more serious. It's also foolish to stake your life on a promise. You're not in control of your own destiny. You can't even stop yourself going bald! Just be someone whose word can be trusted. Then 'Yes' or 'No' will be good enough. Elaborate vows foster deceit.

(38) "Another rule seeks to put a limit to vengeance. 'One eye only may be removed as punishment for blinding someone in one eye, and one tooth only removed for knocking out one tooth.' But I would go further and say it's time to put a stop to the game of paying back wrongs. Instead of putting your fists up when someone picks a fight with you, lower your guard. If someone demands compensation from you, pay them a sum above what they were expecting. If a soldier asks you to carry his pack for a mile, help him on a second mile. Respond readily to everyone who asks a favor of you, and don't go shirking your responsibility if someone with a hard-luck story wants to borrow some money.

(43) " 'Love your friends and hate your enemies,' is the rule you've got from times past. What I say is, Love your enemies and ask God to help those you feel to be against you. Then you will bear a family likeness to the Loving God. It makes no difference whether we are good or bad, we all get God's gifts of sun and rain. What's so very special about loving those who love you? Even those you despise as traitors for collecting taxes are great mates to one another. If you only give the time of day to close family and friends, what's special about that? The foreigners you look down your noses at do just as well. God's love includes everybody. You should be the same.

6 "Don't be a holy Joe. You may impress some people, but you won't impress God. Whenever you give money to a good cause, don't advertise the fact. Don't be like those phonies who make sure everyone notices how much they put on the offering plate or in a street collecting box. I'm telling you they get the pat on the back they're looking for. Keep your generosity private. The Loving God will see what you're doing and pat you on the back.

"When you talk with God, don't show off. Some people put on an act in their place of worship or in public for the benefit of the onlookers. It gives them a buzz! When you talk with God, do it somewhere on your own, quietly. God will be there and you'll get a buzz. And when you talk to God don't use high-faluting language or spin it out like someone who fancies they've a way with words. There's no need to go on and on. God knows what's on your mind before you open your mouth. Here is a simple pattern to hold in mind when you talk with God:

> Loving God, here and everywhere,
> help us proclaim your values and bring in your New World.
> Supply us our day-to-day needs.
> Forgive us for wounding you, while we forgive those who
> wound us.
> Give us courage to meet life's trials and deal with evil's power.

If you forgive the people who cause you pain, God will forgive you when you're a cause of pain. When you go without something for God, don't be like those people who show what a hard time they're giving themselves by the look on their faces. They enjoy being miserable! Freshen yourself up with a good wash and a squirt of your favorite deodorant. That will please God more than a permanent frown.

(19) "Don't go in for expensive luxuries. They attract thieves, or else go wrong. Go for things that don't fall apart after a time or need a burglar alarm. You can tell what people are like by what they value.

"We see with our eyes. If you've got good eyesight your whole body can move around freely. If you've got bad eyesight, you bump into things. Some people think they can see when they can't. They are a danger to themselves and others!

"You can't hold two conflicting sets of values at the same time. Whichever you choose, you'll have to reject the other. You cannot be God's friend and live a life of luxury!

"Stop fretting about things of no importance. What does it matter what you eat or drink or whether your clothes are in fashion? A good life doesn't depend on going to posh restaurants or having a full wardrobe. Take a tip from the birds. They don't go to work every day or put their money in the bank when they get paid, but the Loving God makes sure they have something to eat. You rate yourselves more highly than the birds, don't you?

"You won't make your life last any longer by worrying about it. And why all this fuss about clothes? Be like the wild flowers. They don't earn their living, yet they're better dressed than Solomon with all his beads and bangles! Since God cares so much about the looks of the grass which ends up as straw in a matter of days, God is bound to see to your clothes. It's more trust you need! It's time to stop vexing yourselves with questions like, 'Where shall we eat tonight?' or 'Have we ordered the right wine to go with the meal?' or 'Is this dress suitable for the occasion?' People who are bothered by such questions don't yet know God. God loves you and knows what's best for you. Center your minds on God's New World. Use your energy to create a just and fair society. Then you can live it up!

"Don't fret about the future. It's pointless to worry about things before they happen. Live one day at a time.

7 "Don't think the worst of other people, or other people will think the worst of you! You'll suffer the rejection you think fit for others. If you make allowances for others, allowances will be made for you. How do you manage to see a speck of sawdust in someone else's eye when you're walking around with a great plank in your own? You've got a cheek to say, 'Would you like me to take that bit of dirt out of your eye?' with that plank blocking your view! You humbug! You're not qualified to help someone else with their problem until you've owned up to your own!

(6) "You're fond of those sayings, 'Don't try to have a conversation with a rabid dog' and 'You can't teach pork.' Make sure you are not the ones who fail to appreciate the good things offered you![1]

"If you have an open and inquisitive mind you'll get the answers you're looking for. Those who ask questions learn; those who explore discover; those who knock the door get invited in.

"Some of you have children. Would you give your little girl or boy a stone if they asked for a sweet? Or poison if they asked for fruit juice? You're a rotten lot, but you look after your children and give them the right things. God is the very best of parents and always provides what's good for us when we ask.

"Treat others as you would like them to treat you. Then you'll do what God wants without needing to think about the rules.

"You think the right way ahead is through a narrow gap in the wall rather than along one of the new Roman roads which make travel easy for everybody. Your gap in the wall is hard to find, and it's a tight squeeze.[2] You should be careful about accepting everything you're told. Some religious people have false motives and only want to make life difficult for you. You'll get to know them. They're not nice people. You're no more likely to have pleasant experiences with prickly people than find your favorite fruit in a bed of thistles! Just as good trees produce tasty fruit and bad trees diseased fruit, so good people are nice to know and bad people give you the creeps. Farmers don't waste time on trees that don't fruit well. They cut them down and burn them. Save yourselves trouble by spotting a humbug.

"It's not those who try to flatter me with high-sounding names who'll be citizens of the Bright New World, but those who carry out the wishes of my Parent, the Loving God. A day will come when lots of people will say to me, 'Dear Leader, we've been working very hard for your cause, fighting evil and telling other people what's good for them. We've got so many success stories to report.' Then I'll say, 'You're not my friends; you're trouble-makers; get out of my sight!'

"Everyone who listens to what I say and puts it into practice is like someone who chooses to live in a well-sheltered spot on a piece of high

---

[1] The Gospel's first readers would have realized that Jesus was quoting well-worn sayings, not to confirm but to refute or give a twist to them, as is made clear by the context. These passages are good examples of the need to translate contextually rather than word for word. Verses 7:6 and 7:13 must be understood in the light of 7:1.

[2] See footnote 1.

ground. When heavy wind and rain cause flooding down below, their home is safe. Those who hear what I say but think they know better are like those who choose to live on the bank of a river which overflows from time to time. When the bad weather comes their home is destroyed by the floods and they've nowhere to go!"

8 Jesus came down from the mountain and was met by large crowds. A man who was an outcast because he had a skin disease came to Jesus and begged him on his knees, "Sir, I'm sure, if you want, you can cure me of my complaint." Jesus put his arm round him and said, "Of course I want to help you. You're cured this very moment!" Immediately his skin healed up. Then Jesus sent the man away, urging him not to tell anyone, but to report to the health officer and observe the proper regulations to get the cure recognized by the community.

(5) When Jesus returned to base in Nahum town, an officer in the Roman army came to see him. He was in distress and said, "Sir, my house boy is very ill. He's in bed at home. He can't move and he's in a lot of pain." Jesus said, "I'll come and put him right." The officer said, "Sir, I'm not a fit person to invite you home. I'm sure if you say the right words here and now, my boy will get better. You and I have this much in common. We've both been given control over others. The soldiers in my unit have to obey my orders. The people who look after my house have to obey me too. I find that one word is enough." Jesus was very impressed by the officer's way of putting things. He said to the friends who were with him, "Isn't it amazing? I haven't come across any of our people with so much confidence in me! Believe me, great numbers of people from all over the world will be guests at a banquet with our ancestors, Abraham, Isaac, and Jacob in the New World, whereas there'll be people here from religious homes who won't get a look in. They'll be so upset!" Then Jesus turned to the officer and said, "You can go home now. You'll find your trust has been well-founded." The officer's friend got better from that moment on.[3]

---

[3] 8:6. "House boy ... friend" (Greek *pais*, ambiguous boy/servant; usual word for servant, *doulos*, not used) likely junior officer doubling as same-sex partner, common practice in the Roman army. The day will come when this interpretation causes Christians no problems. It explains the officer's reluctance to invite Jesus to his home. He mistakenly assumed that Jesus would disapprove of his style of life, as would strict orthodox Jews.

(14) One day Jesus visited Rocky's home and found Rocky's mother-in-law in bed with the 'flu. Jesus held her hand and she got better. She was able to get up and cook Jesus a meal. That same evening the townsfolk brought to Jesus many who were sick or mentally disturbed. Jesus cured them all. This reminds us of the words,

> *"He eased our woes*
> *And took our blows."*

(18) When the crowds got too much for Jesus, he asked his friends to take him across to the other side of the lake. Just as they were about to get into the boat, an expert in the old books came up to him and said, "Sir, I'd like to come with you, wherever it is you're going." Jesus said, "Foxes have holes they can bolt to and birds can fly up to their nests. Is there nowhere a man can escape for a bit of peace and quiet?"[4]

One of Jesus' friends said, "Please can I be excused this trip? I have to make arrangements for my father's funeral." Jesus said, "Leave that to someone with nothing better to do. My business is life. I want you with me!" Then Jesus jumped into the boat and his friends got in after him.

(24) While they were sailing across the lake they were hit by a hurricane. The waves leapt over the side of the boat and it began to take in water. Jesus was asleep. They woke him up and said, "Leader, give us some help. We're sinking!" Jesus said, "Why the panic? Where's your trust?" Then he stood up, faced the wind and waves, and soon all was calm. The friends were amazed and said, "Who is this? Even the wind and the waves respond to him!"

(28) They landed on the eastern side of the lake where people of a different culture lived. A couple mentally ill came out of a graveyard and stood in his way. They looked so threatening, it didn't seem safe to go past. Suddenly they started screaming, "Go away, God's Boy! We don't need you to make life worse for us!" A large herd of pigs was feeding in the next field. They said, "Why don't you worry the pigs instead of us?" "Right!" said Jesus. The pigs quickly became agitated and stampeded down the bank into the

---

[4] Here the term "Son of Man" may carry its basic sense, "a man." (Also 16:13 and elsewhere.)

lake. They were all drowned. The farmhands rushed off to the village nearby and reported the incident. All the villagers came out to protest. They had a meeting with Jesus and asked him to move on.

9 Jesus went back by boat to his base in Nahum town. Some people brought a paralyzed man to Jesus on a stretcher. When Jesus saw their trust, he said to the sick man, "Cheer up, friend, your wrongdoings are forgiven." Some experts in the old books overheard Jesus say this and thought, "This can't be right. The man's talking as if he were God!" But Jesus knew what they were thinking. He said, "Why do you have such a bad opinion of me? You think it's easier to say, 'I forgive you,' than to say, 'Get up and walk'? All right then, I'll show you the Complete Person can forgive, here, on earth!" Jesus turned to the sick man and said, "Get on your feet! Go home and take your stretcher with you!" The man got up and walked home. Lots of people were there and they were all very excited. They thanked God because Jesus showed how people can free one another from their feelings of guilt.

(9) One day Jesus walked by the tax office and saw Matthew at his desk. Jesus said to him, "Come and be my friend!" Matthew got up and went with Jesus.

One day when Jesus was at home having dinner he had with him a rum bunch of people including tax collectors, thought of as traitors. This came to the notice of the strict set and they asked some friends of Jesus, "Why does your teacher entertain such bad characters?" When Jesus got to hear about it he told his critics, "It's those who are ill who need a doctor, not those who are well. It's time you learnt the meaning of God's words, 'I want kindness, not religious observance.' I don't ask people who think they've got nothing wrong with them to be my friends, but people you label 'bad.'"

Another time some friends of John the Dipper came to see Jesus. They asked him, "Why are we and the strict set expected to go without food from time to time, whereas your followers eat whenever they want to?" Jesus said, "At a wedding the guests don't refuse to eat – it would be rude to the happy couple! One day the party will be over – that will be the time for going without!

"You don't sew a patch of unshrunk cloth on to an old coat; otherwise the patch comes off and takes a bit of the old coat with it. You end up with a bigger hole. And you don't put new wine into dirty old bottles. You'd ruin the wine that way. You need fresh, clean bottles for new wine!"

(18) While Jesus was speaking, a leader of the community rushed into the house and grabbed Jesus by the arm. "My little girl has gone into a coma," he said, "but if you come and touch her, she'll pull through." Jesus left the table and went with him. His friends went too.

On the way a woman who had been suffering from bleeding for twelve years came up behind Jesus and touched the edge of his coat. She thought, "If I just touch his clothes I'll be better." Jesus turned round and when he saw who it was he said, "Don't worry, friend; your trust has made you well again!"

By the time Jesus got to the councilor's house, there was a band outside playing funeral music and a very noisy crowd. Jesus said, "Go away, all of you! The little girl isn't dead, only asleep!" There were howls of laughter. But when Jesus had got rid of them, he went inside, took hold of the little girl's hand and she sat up. This added to his fame in that district.

(27) On his way back home, Jesus was followed by two blind people. They were shouting, "New David, please help us!" They followed him into the house and Jesus said to them, "Do you really think I can help you?" They said, "Yes Sir, of course!" Then Jesus put his hands on their eyes and said, "Your trust will make it happen!" And that is how they got their sight back. Jesus told them on no account to talk about it to anyone else. But they went off and told all the neighbors.

Not long after this Jesus was asked to help someone who was autistic. Jesus brought the person to the point where they could hold a normal conversation. Everyone was very impressed and said, "We've not seen anything like this in our part of the world before." But the opinion of the strict set was, "He knows how to handle evil because he's evil himself!"

(35) Then Jesus went on tour, visiting all the towns and villages in the district. He taught in the places of worship and passed on the Good News about the New World. He had great success as a healer, bringing relief to sufferers of every kind. It gave him great pain to see so many people with problems and no one to turn to. They were in need of a leader to give purpose to their lives. Jesus was moved to say to his friends, "There's a bumper harvest out there but we're short of workers. We must ask the

farmer to take on some more."

10 Jesus had a dozen full-time helpers. He called these together and trained them to deal with all the common illnesses, including mental disorders. They worked in pairs: Simon (nicknamed Rocky) and his brother Andrew; James and John (Zebedee's sons); Philip and Bart; Matthew (the tax collector) and Twin; James (Alf's son) and Ted; Simon (nicknamed "Hothead") and Judas from Kerioth, the traitor. Jesus sent these on tour with this advice: "Stick to the areas you know best. Target our own people in special need. Everywhere you go, pass on the Good News, 'The Bright New World is on its way!' Heal the sick, including those on their deathbeds; help outcasts back into the community and give peace of mind to the disturbed. You haven't had to pay for what I've done for you, so don't expect anyone to pay for what you do. You won't need money – not even small change, nor a travel-bag. You don't need a change of clothes and you can manage without shoes or a walking stick. Good workers will find their needs are met. When you go into a village or town, find out where you're most likely to be welcome and stay there until it's time to leave. When you're at the door of a house, give a friendly greeting. If you're made welcome, do your best for all who live there. If you're not welcome, leave with dignity. As for those who are rude to you or won't give you a hearing, when you've gone on your way don't let it play on your mind. Ancient Sodom and Gomorrah offended against the customs of hospitality, but they'll get higher ratings than places which reject you.

"You're going to find yourselves in some tricky situations with nothing to protect you except your sensitivity and good intentions. So be wary. You're likely to be arrested and brutally punished, and religious people will be your accusers. You'll be brought before the highest courts in the land, just because you're working for me. This will be your opportunity to get the message across to our own people and to people of other races. When you find yourselves in the dock, don't worry what you're going to say. The words will come. It won't be you speaking, but the Spirit of God, the one who looks after you. Families will be divided and relatives give evidence against one another, even when it means the death penalty. You'll be hated. But stay on track and you'll come through it all. When things become too hot in one town, get out quickly and move on to the next. Remember you're working to a tight schedule. You'll have to get on with it if you're to get round every town in the land before my target date.

"Students don't look for greater respect than their tutors, and employees shouldn't expect better working conditions than the manager. A successful student may become a tutor and a keen member of the workforce get to be manager. I'm a manager who's been accused of running a shady company, so don't be surprised if you, the workers, are thought of as crooks!

"Don't be put off by criticism. You've nothing to hide, nothing to fear from questions. The things we've discussed in private you're free to make public. We're not a secret society. Tell everybody everything! Don't be afraid of those who can kill you but can't change the way you are. To have your character end up on the rubbish tip – that's what you should be afraid of!

"God is grieved every time a pair of sparrows is sold for next to nothing, then killed as an act of worship. God cares about you too – even notices when your hair starts falling out. Relax! God holds no life cheap, not even sparrows. Don't undervalue yourselves!

"I promise those who stand up for me, I'll stand up for them when I speak with God, my Parent. I won't remember those who disown me.

"My coming to the world doesn't guarantee an easy time for anybody. What I have to say is controversial. It will lead to family quarrels. Best friends will become bitter enemies. You may have to choose between your love for your parents or children and your love for me. All my true friends shoulder the responsibilities I give them. Those who pursue their own interests will feel life slip from their grasp, but those who set aside their ambitions for me will find fulfillment. Anyone who proves to be your friend is a friend of mine and God's friend too.

"But I warn you, anyone who recognizes God's helpers and shows them friendship will be liable to receive the rough treatment God's helpers get. The same is true if you befriend someone whose cause is just.

"Sometimes a simple act of kindness to someone in need will mark you off as my friend. It won't go unrecognized."

11

When Jesus had finished briefing his trusted helpers, he went on tour of the largest towns in Galilee, introducing his message and teaching. John the Dipper was in prison. When he heard what God's Chosen was doing, he sent some of his followers to him with this message, "Are you the one we've been expecting, or do we have to wait for someone else?" Jesus said, "Go back to John and give him a full account of everything you've heard and seen. Tell him that blind people are getting their sight back, disabled people are able to get about again, outcasts are being restored to the community, deaf people can hear, many are getting a whole new life, and those who don't count for much in our society have had Good News for the first time in their lives. Some object to what I'm doing, but you should be thrilled to bits!"

When the messengers had gone, Jesus spoke about John the Dipper to the crowd around him. "When you went out into the desert, what were you expecting to see? Herod? – a bent reed, like the symbol on his coins? No?[5] What, then? Were you hoping to see someone dressed in the latest court fashion? You won't catch the upper classes on parade in the desert. The palace is the place for that! Why did you choose such a drab place for your day out? Did you go to hear one of God's speakers, the kind not seen since the old days? Yes, that's why you made that hard trek. But John was more than one of the old time religion, wasn't he? You'll find him mentioned in the old books.

'Watch out! My envoy's on the way
To set the stage for that great day!!'

I believe John is the most important person who ever lived. But you will all be important in the Bright New World, even more important than John. Since the time John made his stand, many have tried to bring about that world by force. They should have listened to John and the rest of God's speakers before him. It should be obvious that John is the Elijah of our day. If you've got ears, use them!

"Do you remember the games we used to play in the street when we

---

[5] The pattern here suggests a humorous repartee between Jesus and the crowd. To the first two questions the crowd would have laughingly shouted out "No!" and to the third "Yes."

were children – weddings and funerals? When our team played music, the others had to dance, but if we sang funeral songs, they had to cry. Some children got the sulks and wouldn't play. Then we would sing:

> *'To dance the tune you wouldn't try*
> *And when we wailed you wouldn't cry!'*

There are people like that today. John the Dipper ate and drank so little, they called him mad. Because I'm human and enjoy my food with a jug of wine, they say, 'Look at him! Spending all his time at parties, mixing with the lowest of the low!' If they were as bright as they think they are, they'd make the right response on the right occasion!"

(20) Jesus had harsh words for those places where he had worked hard but got no response. "Shame on you, Dancetown! Shame on you, Fishtown! If towns in Lebanon, like Tyre and Sidon, had seen me at work as you have done, they would have changed their ways at once. God will excuse Tyre and Sidon, but there's no excuse for you! And don't look so smug, Nahum town. You expect to be top of the class, don't you? Bottom more likely! If Sodom had seen the wonderful things you've seen, it would still be standing! The people who live near where Sodom used to be will have a higher rating than you!"

Then Jesus talked with God. He said, "I thank you, loving God, ruler of time and space, that your truth cannot be grasped by the clever, but only by the simple and straightforward. Yes, loving God, that was a good idea of yours! You've put me in charge, just as a parent would a trusted child. You know me better than anybody, and I'm the only one who knows you, except those I talk to about you."

Then Jesus said, "I offer my friendship to all who are finding life hard or struggling with problems. I'll teach you to relax. I'm a carpenter by trade. I can recommend the yokes I make for oxen. They're well known for being smooth and light. I'm a teacher too; my methods are gentle and I don't bully my pupils. Rest assured, you'll be at ease with me."

12 One Rest Day, Jesus and his friends were going for a walk through the cornfields. They were feeling hungry and some of them started plucking the corn and eating it. Some members of the strict set caught them at it and said to Jesus, "Look what your followers are doing. They're breaking the rules of the Rest Day!" Jesus said, "Haven't you ever read what David did when he and his friends were hungry? David went into the house of God and ate the special bread, which was taboo for himself and his friends. Only the religious leaders were allowed to eat it. Or perhaps you're not aware that the rules about doing no work on the Rest Day don't apply to those working in the place of worship? This is a better place of worship than the temple in Jerusalem! You've made a mistake in condemning my friends for doing nothing wrong because you don't know the meaning of God's words, 'Kindness is what I'm looking for, not religious observance.' The Complete Person knows how to use the Rest Day."

(9) The very next time Jesus attended the local place of worship, one of the worshipers present had lost the use of his hand. The strict set tried to trap Jesus by asking him, "Do the rules allow you to heal someone on the Rest Day?" Jesus said, "Just suppose one of you loses your only sheep because it has fallen down a hole on the Rest Day. Are you just going to leave it there or help it out? Surely people mean more to you than sheep? The Rest Day is a good day for helping those in need." Then Jesus spoke to the man, "Try stretching your hand out, like this." He did what Jesus said and the feeling came back into his hand, as good as the other one. The strict set walked out in protest and made plans to kill Jesus. Jesus found out about the plans and moved on to another district. Large numbers of supporters followed him and he dealt with all their health problems. Jesus asked them not to give him away. The words found in the old book give a very good description of Jesus at this time.

> *"Here is my helper, the man I chose;*
> *He is the one for whom my heart glows;*
> *He will share my mind divine*
> *And justice to the world proclaim.*

He will not shout to raise the rabble
Or vex the neighbors with his babble;
He will not kick those who are down
Or send them packing with a frown;

The rule of justice is his aim,
The hope of every race, his name."

(22) One man brought to Jesus was severely disabled, confused in mind and unable to see or speak. Jesus restored his sight and speech. Everyone was amazed and said, "Is this the new David we're looking for?" The answer of the strict set was, "He knows how to deal with evil because he's evil himself!"

Jesus saw into their minds and said, "A nation divided will fall apart. The same applies to a town or a family. Evil forces set against one another will bring about their own destruction. You say I use evil to combat evil? I could just as easily say the same about you. You're not making sense. The obvious explanation is that I'm defeating evil by means of God's Spirit. It shows that God's New World is in sight. You can't rob the home of a wrestler without tying him up first. That's why those who don't support me are doing their best to tie my hands. Those who won't join me in my work do nothing but cause trouble. I'm warning you, people can be forgiven for all sorts of wrong things, even for atheism, but to call God's Spirit evil displays a moral blindness not open to being put right. You can call me what you like. But don't pick a quarrel with God's Spirit. Turn a blind eye to reality and you may lose sight of it forever.

"Plant a good tree and you'll get good fruit; plant a bad tree and the fruit will be bad. Nothing is more certain. You religious people are full of poison, like snakes. You've got nothing good to say about anybody! What your mouths come out with shows how rotten you are inside. Good people treasure pleasant thoughts to share with others. Bad people think up nasty things to say. I warn you, one day you'll be asked to explain all your unkind remarks. The things you say show what sort of people you are."

(38) A group from the strict set said to Jesus, "Teacher, show us something to prove you're qualified to speak on behalf of God." Jesus said,

"Only wicked people who don't trust God need proof. Wait till you see something that reminds you of the story of Jonah. Just as Jonah was a prisoner for three days under the sea, so the Complete Person will be a prisoner underground. The people of Nineveh will be your judges one day because they changed their ways when Jonah told them about God. Today you have a better chance to learn about God than they had. The African Queen will judge you because she made a long journey to seek advice from Solomon. There's better advice to be had here today!

"Once a dirty old tramp was thrown out of an empty house where he had been squatting. He looked all round the town for somewhere suitable to sleep but couldn't find anywhere. Then he thought he would try his old place again. It was still empty so he broke in. He saw that someone had cleaned up his mess while he had been away. Then he had an idea. He invited seven other tramps even more dirty than himself to share the squat. The mess they all made together was much worse than when he had lived there on his own. That's a lesson for these bad times!"

(46) One day when Jesus was talking to a lot of people in a house, his mother and his brothers came to the door. They wanted to see him. Someone brought the message to Jesus, "Your people are at the door. They want a word with you." Jesus said, "My people? Who are they?" Then he pointed to his followers and said, "My people are here! Those who do what God, my Parent, asks them to do are my people, all the brothers, sisters, or mother I need!"

13 Later on in the day Jesus left his lodgings and went to sit on the beach. He was mobbed by so many admirers, the only way he could get space for himself was to get into a boat. Then from the boat he spoke to the crowd on the beach. Jesus taught them many things by means of stories. This is how he began: "Listen, a farmer went out to sow his field. As he scattered the seed, some of it fell on the path and the birds swooped down and ate it up. Some seed fell on rocky ground and the shoots sprang up quickly as there wasn't enough soil for the plants to take root. When the sun came up they withered away. Some seed fell among the thistles. When the thistles grew the plants were choked. Other seeds fell into good soil and yielded a fine crop of grain, thirty, sixty, and even a hundred times what the farmer sowed. If you've got ears, use them!"

Later Jesus' friends asked him, "Why do you speak to the people in riddles?" Jesus said, "My stories may sound like riddles to them, but you should realize they're clues to the meaning of the Bright New World. Those who use their imagination will open up to wider experience, whereas those who don't exercise their minds will become more and more ignorant. I use stories as a test. Some people, it's true, don't get the point. They're like the people in the old book who look without seeing and listen without hearing. They refuse to put their senses and their imagination to good use in case they have a change of heart and let God make them better people. You're lucky. You've had a grandstand view! Many of God's speakers and other good people in the past would have given anything to have your advantages."

(Here is the solution to the riddle of the farmer sowing seed. The seed scattered on the path is when someone hears about the New World and decides it's not for them. Evil makes quick work of the idea before it stands a chance. The seed on rocky ground refers to people who enjoy listening to a good talk, but don't take anything in. The moment they meet with hassle because of their beliefs or other difficulties, they give up. The seed sown among the thistles represents people who do at first take the message seriously. But they're distracted by anxiety to get on in the world and by greed, and their good intentions get crowded out. The seed sown on good ground stands for those who grasp what is said and really take it to heart. Their lives become worthwhile.)[6]

(24) Here are some more stories Jesus told about the Bright New World. "A farmer sowed his field with good seed. But while everybody was in bed, someone with a grudge against the farmer sowed weeds among the wheat and got away without being seen. So as the wheat grew up with plenty of corn on it, the weeds grew in between. The farmhands called on the farmer and said, 'Boss, that batch of seed wasn't as good as you thought. There were lots of weeds with it!' The farmer said, 'Someone's been up to no

---

[6] The explanation of the parable of the Sower is probably the work of the first Gospel-writer, Mark. His explanation was subsequently included in the work of Matthew and Luke. The explanations of the other parables in this section of Matthew seem to be those of the friends of Jesus in response to his question, "Have you worked out the riddles?" to which they reply, "Yes." The standard bidding of Jesus in respect of his parables was, "If you've got ears, use them." It is unlikely that he was willing to do the work for the disciples. We have slightly altered the order of the verses to make this more obvious.

good!' The farmhands said, 'Do you want us to try and pull the weeds out?' The farmer said, 'Better not; as you pull the weeds you'll disturb the wheat. Leave it all to grow together till harvest. Then I'll tell the workers to collect the weeds first and put them in heaps for compost and then collect up the wheat for my stores.'

"The Bright New World is like a mustard seed which a farmer plants in his field. A mustard seed is very small to look at, but it can grow into a large shrub. It becomes tall enough for birds to make their nests in. The Bright New World is like the bit of yeast a baker puts in a much larger amount of flour. The yeast works its way all through the dough."

Jesus always used stories in his public teaching. He was never without a story. This reminds us of the words of one of God's speakers:

> *"I'll speak to you in a riddle-me-re,*
> *So you can know what none can see."*

When Jesus had taken leave of the crowds and gone back to his lodgings, his friends asked him to explain the story about the weeds. Jesus said, "If you've got ears, use them!"

(Here is the explanation. The farmer who sows the seed is Jesus, the Complete Person; the high quality seed are members of the New World; the weeds are evil people, out to cause harm; harvest is the end of time and the workers who harvest the crop are God's agents. Just as the weeds are raked together for compost, so at the end of time the Complete Person will instruct agents to deal with every form of evil and those responsible for it. There will be a big compost heap and many people will be very upset to find themselves on it! This will be the time when good people get the recognition they deserve in the New World of the Loving God.)[7]

Then Jesus gave them some more riddles to think about. "The Bright New World is like a field with buried treasure in it. Someone discovered it and buried it again. Then he sold everything he had and bought the field.

"The Bright New World is like a jeweler with a special line in pearls. One day she came across a very valuable pearl. She mortgaged her business

---

[7] See footnote 6.

in order to buy it.

"The Bright New World is like a large net dragged through the sea so that every kind of fish is caught. When the net's full, the fishers bring it to land and put the fish that can be eaten into buckets. Fish which are no good are thrown back."

Jesus asked his friends, "Have you worked out the riddles?" They said, "Yes. That riddle is about the end of time when God's agents sort out the good people from the bad. The bad will be very upset when they find themselves rejected."[8]

Jesus said, "Every teacher who has been trained to teach in the Bright New World is like someone showing a visitor round their house. They point out their oldest and most treasured possession and the very latest thing they've bought."

(53) After this course of teaching, Jesus left his lodgings and returned to his hometown. He taught in the local place of worship and those who heard him were surprised. They said, "Where's he picked up all this knowledge and skill?" "He's the carpenter's boy. We know his mother – Mary; and his brothers James and Joseph and Simon and Jude. And we know his sisters too!" "Where's he got all his airs and graces from?" So they gave Jesus a cold reception. But Jesus said to them, "It's strange how God's speakers are appreciated everywhere except where they come from and by their families!"

Jesus did not achieve much in his hometown because the people there didn't trust him.

14 At the time Jesus was teaching in Galilee, Herod was the ruler there. He heard about Jesus and said to his advisors, "It's John the Dipper all over again. He's acting in just the same way!" Herod had arrested John, tied him up, and put him in prison. He did this to please his wife Rose, who was really his brother Philip's wife. John had told Herod "Your marriage is illegal!" Herod would have liked to kill John, but he was afraid of losing his popularity. People thought John was one of God's speakers. On Herod's birthday, Rose's daughter danced in front of

---

[8] See footnote 6.

the guests. Herod was so pleased with her dancing, he promised to give her whatever she asked for. Her mother put her up to asking for the head of John the Dipper on a plate. Herod was not happy about this, but because he had promised in front of his guests, he agreed to give her what she asked for. He gave the order for John to be beheaded in the prison. John's head was brought in on a plate and given to the girl, who handed it to her mother. John's friends came for the body and buried him. Then they told Jesus about it.

(13) When Jesus learned what had happened to John, he left in a boat for a quiet spot where he could be alone. But people worked out where he was going and made their way round the shore of the lake. By the time Jesus landed, a big crowd was waiting for him. He felt deeply for them and healed the sick people they had brought along. At the end of the day, Jesus' friends came to him and said, "This is an out-of-the-way place and it's getting late. Send the people away so they can go to the villages and buy something to eat." Jesus said, "There's no need for them to go away. You give them something to eat!" They said, "All we've got is five loaves and two fish." Jesus said, "Let me have them." Then he asked everybody to sit down on the grass. He took the five loaves and the two fish and thanked God for them. Then he broke the loaves and gave them to his friends to hand round to the people. Everybody got something to eat and nobody felt hungry afterwards. The leftovers filled twelve baskets. About five thousand joined in the meal. The women and children had their share too.

Hurrying his friends into the boat, Jesus told them to sail back across the lake where he would join them later. Then he told the people to go home. When they had gone he went up the mountain to talk alone with God. He was still there on his own when it got dark. By this time the boat was well across the lake, but making slow progress because the wind was against it and the waves giving it a strong battering. Very early in the morning Jesus came walking toward them through the water. When his friends saw him they were scared stiff and said, "It's a ghost!" and they started screaming. But straightaway Jesus shouted to them, "Relax, it's me! Nothing to get worked up about!" Rocky shouted back, "Leader, if it's really you, let me come and fetch you." Jesus said, "Come on then!" So Rocky got out of the boat and started walking through the water toward Jesus. Then suddenly aware of the strong wind he panicked and lost his footing. "Help, Leader!" he screamed. Jesus quickly reached out and caught hold of him and said, "What happened to your nerve? You need to have more trust!" When they got into the boat the wind calmed down. All the friends in the boat were greatly impressed. They hugged and kissed Jesus and said, "You must be God's Chosen!"

They at last landed at Gennesar. Jesus was soon recognized by the townsfolk. They spread the news around and everyone in the area who was ill was brought to him. Some just wanted to touch his clothes, and that was enough to make them better.

15

A group of experts in the old books, members of the strict set, came from Jerusalem to see Jesus. They asked him, "Why do you let your followers break the cherished customs of our people? For example, they don't go through the correct hand-washing routine before eating." Jesus said, "I would like to ask you why you break God's rules to keep your customs? God said, 'Look up to your father and mother' and 'Anyone who willfully harms either of their parents does not deserve to live.' But you have a custom, which saves you from having to help your parents in their old age by saying you've set aside your money for religious purposes. Your custom allows you to neglect your parents! So much for customs if they go against what God wants! You people turn religion into a game! You remind me of what God's speaker said,

> 'These people have me on their lips,
> But their hearts are far away;
> They make their own rules sound like mine:
> I see the game they play!' "

Then Jesus spoke to the people who were standing around listening. He said, "Let's get this clear. You don't need to watch what goes into your mouth so much as what comes out of it. That's where the filth comes from!"

Jesus' friends had a quiet word with him. They said, "Do you realize what you said upset the strict set?" Jesus said, "There are only flowers in my Parent's garden; weeds are not allowed to take hold! Let the strict set go their own way. They're like people who can't see, trying to show others the way to go. Anyone who goes along with them will land up in the same hole." Rocky said, "What was that you said about our mouths? I didn't understand it." Jesus said, "Surely you can't be that dull? The food that goes into your mouth goes down to your guts and you get rid of it when you go to the toilet. But the words you speak with your mouth are the product of your mind. It's a dirty mind that makes a dirty mouth! It's the mind that produces the evil plans which lead to killing, taking another's partner from them, using people for your lusts, stealing, lying, and gossip. These are the things that make you dirty. It's nothing to do with washing your hands the strict set way!"

(21) Then Jesus traveled north into Syria. A woman came out of her house and shouted at Jesus, "New David, please help me. My daughter suffers from depression. She's very low at the moment." Jesus appeared not to notice. After a while his friends said, "Tell her to go away; she's making a nuisance of herself!" Jesus said, "I've enough to do to care for those in need from my own race." But she begged him on her knees, "Sir, please help me!" Jesus said, "Is it fair to take food from your children and throw it to your pet dogs?" She said, "You're right, Sir, but even the little dogs eat the scraps that fall from their owner's table." Jesus said, "What wonderful trust you have! You deserve to have your wish granted!" The woman's daughter was a new person from that day on.

Then Jesus went up a mountain overlooking Lake Galilee and found a suitable spot to teach. People flocked to him, bringing their sick and disabled with them. They put them in a semi-circle round him and he healed them. Everyone was amazed to see withdrawn people chatting, some recovering the use of their limbs and walking about, others getting their sight back. These people were from different races, so they formed a good impression of the God worshiped by the Jews.[9]

Then Jesus had a word with his friends. "I'm getting anxious about all these people. They've been with me for three days now without anything to

---

[9] The Gospel-writer's remark, "They praised the God of Israel," made it clear to first-century readers that this crowd was largely composed of non-Jews. It would not be necessary to say this of Jews. They would not have praised any other God! Since the point does not make itself so obvious to us, we need to highlight it in translation. It is crucial to the understanding of the passage and marks the logical outcome of the previous story, vs. 21-28.

eat. I don't want to send them away hungry. Some of them may not be strong enough to make it." The friends said, "Where do you expect us to get enough food to feed so many people? There are no shops out here in the desert!" Jesus said, "How many loaves of bread have you got?" They said, "Seven and a few small fish." Jesus asked the people to find places to sit. Then he took the seven loaves and the fish and said "thank you" to God. He broke the food into little portions and handed it to his friends to take to the people. Everyone got something to eat and no one felt hungry afterwards. There were seven baskets of leftovers. About four thousand joined in the meal. Women and children had their share too. After Jesus had said goodbye to all these people, he went by boat to another lakeside district.

16

Members of the main religious groups got together and sent a deputation to find out more about Jesus. They asked him to give some proof he was qualified to speak on behalf of God. Jesus said, "You know the old rhyme about the weather,

> *'Red sky at night, shepherd's delight;*
> *Red sky in the morning, shepherd's warning.'*

It's odd you know how to forecast the weather, but don't understand what's happening in the world today. Only people who aren't open and honest need proof. Think about what happened to Jonah!" Then Jesus walked away from them. The next time the friends of Jesus took a trip across the lake they forgot to take any bread with them. Jesus said, "It's best not to buy bread from any of those cranks. It may not be safe to eat." The friends misunderstood Jesus and thought he was criticizing their shopping. Jesus overheard them talking and said, "You've got no imagination, have you? Fancy thinking I meant ordinary bread! When are you going to learn to think about more important things? Remember the five loaves that fed five thousand, and how much was left over? Remember the seven loaves that fed four thousand, and how much was left over then? How could you possibly think I was concerned about bread? I'll say it again. Don't get your bread from those who make religion a matter of party faction." Then Jesus' friends realized he was warning them against the teaching of the religious groups.

(13) When Jesus was in the district of Philiptown-Caesar, he said to his friends, "I'm human. I call myself the Complete Person. What do other people think about me?"[10] They said, "You remind them of John the Dipper; others think you're like Elijah or Jeremy; others that you're one or other of God's greatest speakers." Then Jesus said, "But what do you think about me?" Simon known as "Rocky" said, "You're God's Chosen, God's True Likeness." Jesus said, "Well done, Simon Johnson. No one told you that. My Parent, the Loving God, has put the idea in your mind. 'Rocky' is a good name for you. You'll be like a rock for my people. The barriers set up by the wicked will fall down when you're hurled against them! You'll be able to open the New World to others and lead them to the new freedoms God wants for them." Then Jesus told them on no account to tell anyone he was God's Chosen.

From that moment on Jesus changed the tone of his teaching. He told his friends he would have to go to Jerusalem and be tortured on the orders of the religious leaders, and then he would be executed. But three days later he would return to life. Rocky had a private word with Jesus and told him he was making a big mistake. "In God's name, Leader, keep out of trouble!" But Jesus looked him in the eye and said, "Don't try to put me off course, Rocky. You're a bad influence. Your ideas are human, not God's!"

Then Jesus told his friends, "If you want to be my friends, you must put your safety at risk, look death in the face, and stick close to me. Those who think only of themselves will get nowhere, but those who risk their lives for me will end up with a better life than they ever dreamed of. What sort of bargain is it, if you have everything the world has to offer and are empty inside? There's no price tag you can put on the life I'm offering!

"One day the Complete Person will be surrounded by those who have fulfilled their tasks. They will stand in the brightness of the Loving God and be thanked for what they have done. Believe me, some of you will see what I look like in the New World, while you're still in this world."

---

[10] Here again the term "Son of Man" may carry its basic sense, "a man."

17 A week after Jesus had said that some of his friends would see what he would look like in the New World, he went walking high up in the mountains with Rocky, James, and his brother John for company. Against the clear sky he looked different, with his sunburned face and white clothes reflecting the bright light. Then they saw him talking to two people. The friends saw these as Moses and Elijah. Then Rocky said, "Leader, being up here has given me a good idea! Why don't we make three holy shrines, one for you and one each for your two friends?" At that moment a cloud came over, catching the sun's rays, and they heard someone say, "*This* is the one I love, my very own. He's doing a good job, so listen to what he says!" The friends were so frightened they dived for cover. Jesus came over to them and said, "Get up and stop being so panicky." When they looked up they saw that only Jesus was there.

As they came down from the mountain, Jesus told them, "Don't tell anyone what you saw today until the Complete Person has come back to life after dying."

Jesus' friends asked him, "Why do the experts say that Elijah has to come before God's Chosen?" Jesus said, "They're right about that. Elijah's job is to set the scene. The truth is that Elijah came and the experts didn't recognize him; in fact they treated him badly. So the Complete Person can't expect any better from them." The friends understood that by "Elijah" Jesus meant John the Dipper.

(14) There were lots of people waiting for Jesus. One man paid his respects to him, then said, "Sir, please do something to help my son. He suffers very badly from epilepsy. He often falls into the fire or into a stream. I tried your friends but they couldn't do anything for him." Jesus shouted across to them, "What a useless bunch you are! How long do I have to put up with you? Let's have a look at him!" Jesus said something to the boy, and he was cured on the spot. When next Jesus was on his own, his friends asked him, "Why couldn't we make the boy better?" Jesus said, "Because you lack confidence. You don't need a lot – the size of a grain of mustard seed will do. Then, however large the obstacle in your way, you'll find some means of coping with it."

On another occasion when they'd got together in Galilee, Jesus told his friends, "The Complete Person will be betrayed and killed, but three days later come back to life." They were very upset when they heard this.

(24) When they reached Nahum town, the people who collected dues for the upkeep of the temple visited Rocky and said, "I don't suppose your tutor pays his dues?" Rocky said, "Oh yes he does!" When Jesus came in he brought the matter up. "Look at it like this, Simon. Where do rulers get their money from – from members of their own families or by raising taxes?" Rocky said, "By raising taxes, of course." Jesus said, "That means members of the ruler's family don't have to pay! But there's no need to make life difficult for those who are only doing their duty. Take your boat out. One catch of fish should be enough to pay your tax and mine."

18 One day Jesus' friends came to him with the question, "Who will be head of state in the Bright New World?" Jesus called a little child, stood her up in front of them and said, "Believe me, unless you change your attitude and look at life the way children do, you won't even be ordinary citizens in the Bright New World. Someone who doesn't care about their status, like this child, will be head of state. In my community you must always fully include children. That way you will include me!

"Anyone who makes religion an obstacle course for those taking their first steps toward God would do better to jump off a cliff into the sea with a brick round their neck and see how they like it! The world has enough people in it who make life difficult for others! Life is a bumpy ride as it is and we can do without those who put extra humps in the road.

"As for you people who aim to be perfect, why don't you cut your hands or feet off if they're causing you so much trouble? You can't get your fingers burnt if you haven't any to burn. If you think you can only keep out of trouble by not seeing anything unpleasant, why not pull your eyes out? You would be a sorry sight, all hobbling around legless and eyeless. You're thinking to escape the rubbish dump by living half a life? What a silly idea![11]

"Don't look down your noses at simple-minded people. They have special lines of contact with my Parent, the Loving God."

For the Complete Person, people in need are the first priority. This is

---

[11] This passage represents a typical piece of Hebrew humor. It cannot be translated adequately without taking into account the author's tongue-in-cheek.

how Jesus made it clear:

Jesus said, "How's this for good farming practice? A shepherd who owned a hundred sheep one day noticed one was missing. And would you believe, he left ninety-nine sheep unprotected on the mountain and went off looking for the one he missed? When he found it the shepherd went wild with joy and made it his pet. He thought more of it than the ninety-nine which had not wandered off."

This was Jesus' way of saying that it is those who need special care who are valued most by the Loving God. So if a friend from your community does something to upset you, have a quiet word together in private. If you talk it out reasonably, you'll be the best of friends again. But if the one who has upset you proves difficult, invite two other friends to be there so they can hear the arguments on either side. If they can't bring about an agreement, then the matter must be taken to the community as a whole. If he or she is unwilling to accept the advice of the community, they must then become the prime target of the community's care and concern.[12]

Jesus said, "Your task is to bring lasting happiness to others and lead them to the new freedoms God wants for them. Believe me, if two of you come to a common mind about something which needs to be done, my Parent, the Loving God, will give you all the help you need. Whenever a group of my friends get together, I'll be there too."

(21) On one occasion, Rocky asked Jesus, "Leader, if a friend causes me pain over and over again, how many times must I let it go? Seven?" Jesus said, "Not seven times. Seventy times seven would be nearer the mark!"

Then Jesus said, "Let me tell you another story to show how things work in the Bright New World. There was once the head of a large business who decided to call in her debts from her associates. She looked at the books and found that one was up to his neck in debt, more than would take several lifetimes to repay. She made an appointment to see him and threatened to send in the bailiffs and deprive his wife and children of house and home. The man, with tears in his eyes, pleaded for more time. 'Give me a chance,' he said, 'and I'll pay it all back!' The woman's heart melted. She released her

---

[12] A "contextual translation." It is unlikely to be accidental that vs. 15-17 are set adjacent to 11-14 and close to 21-22. Verses 14-17 are probably those of the Gospel-writer who is telling Christians in the early Church how to apply the teaching of Jesus.

associate from his debts and told him not to worry about it any more. But that very lucky man, as he was on his way out, bumped into a member of his club who owed him a small sum, no more than a few weeks' wages. He grabbed him by the throat and said, 'Where's my money?' The man, shaking all over, said, 'Please don't be hard on me. You'll get your money back. Just give me time!' But he wouldn't hear of it. He took him to court on a charge of theft, and the poor man ended up in prison. He was also ordered to repay the money. The other club members knew about what had happened and were disgusted. They made sure the company boss got to hear the story. She sent again for her associate. She said, 'You nasty piece of work! I released you from your debt because of the tears in your eyes. Wasn't that the cue for you to go easy on your friend?' In anger she severed all business connections with him, ensured that he was completely ruined and called for his debts to be paid in full from his assets. That's how my Parent will treat you if you don't in love pass over the wrongs others do you."

19

Jesus left Galilee and went down south to the area the other side of the River Jordan. He was met by large crowds, and he gave new health and strength to everybody.

Some members of the strict set asked Jesus, "Is it right for a man to divorce his wife whenever he feels like it?" Jesus said, "Haven't you read the old books? They say sex was invented when God made the first humans. That's why people lessen their ties with their parents to make new ties with a partner. The new couple are meant to live as one. No one should mess up God's good idea." They said, "Can you explain then, why Moses said if a man gave his wife a certificate of divorce, that would make it alright?" Jesus said, "It's because you're so difficult to live with that Moses let you give your wives their freedom back. But that was not what marriage was meant to be like. Only something very serious, like a breakdown caused by another partner, should be grounds for each to go their own way. Otherwise, you're stepping out of line as far as God is concerned."

Jesus' friends said to him, "You're making marriage sound very difficult. Perhaps it would be better not to get married." Jesus said, "It is difficult for some people. Marriage is a special relationship for those suited to it. Marriage is not right for certain types. It may be just the way they are, or something to do with how they've been brought up. Sometimes people choose to avoid close personal attachments so they can give their full time to help bring in the Bright New World. We must be understanding of one another."

(13) Once some people brought their babies to Jesus. They wanted him to hold the babies in his arms and speak with God on their behalf. The friends of Jesus were quite rude to them. But Jesus said, "Let the children come to me; never try to stop them, for they already belong to the Bright New World." Jesus took time to give each baby a kiss and cuddle before returning to his program for the day.

(16) A man came to Jesus and asked him, "Is there something special I could do to make my life worthwhile?" Jesus said, "Why are you asking me how to live your life? Only God knows what's good for us because God is all goodness. You can have a worthwhile life by keeping the rules." The man said, "What rules?" Jesus said, "The rules about not killing, not destroying others' relationships, not stealing, not lying, being good to your parents, and loving whoever you happen to meet as you love yourself." The young man said, "I've done all that, but I still don't feel right somehow!" Jesus said, "If you really want to complete the job, sell all your property, give the money to charity, and you'll be happy ever after!" This advice was not what the young man wanted. He went away very depressed, since he owned a lot of property.

Then Jesus turned to his friends and said, "It's exceedingly difficult for the well-off to become citizens of the Bright New World. In fact it's easier for a camel to go through the eye of a needle than for the wealthy to get there!" This shocked them, and they said, "There's not much chance for anybody then!" Jesus looked at them and said, "It's impossible for people to make it without God's help. But with God's help everything is possible."

Rocky said, "We've given up everything to follow you. What's in it for us?" Jesus said, "I foresee a time when things will be very different. The Complete Person will be honored, and my friends will have positions of trust among their own people. All those who've left home, family, or business for me will be a hundred times better off, enjoying life to the full. But many of those at the front of the queue will find themselves at the back, and those at the back will be in front."

20

Jesus told a story about those at the back of the queue getting a surprise by suddenly finding themselves at the front. He said, "This is what it's like in the Bright New World. A farmer went out early one day to find casual labor to harvest the grape crop. A group of workers agreed to be taken on for the regular daily wage, and the farmer set them to work in the vineyard. Walking past the Job Center in Market Square at about nine o'clock, the farmer noticed a few more people looking for work. 'Join the others in my vineyard,' the farmer shouted to them, 'I'll pay you a fair wage!' So they went along. The farmer made several trips to Market Square that day, at midday, at three o'clock, and five o'clock. Each time the farmer said to the people standing around, 'Haven't you anything better to do than loll around all day?' When they said, 'We're unemployed,' the farmer said, 'You can join the rest in my fields.' In the evening the farmer instructed the pay-clerk to give the workers who had come in last their pay first, and to place those who had come at the beginning of the day at the back of the queue. When those who had started work after five o'clock were paid, they got the full wage for the day. Those who had started early expected to get a bonus when it was their turn. But they just got the normal rate. So they complained to the farmer, 'Some of these people have only worked an hour and you've paid them the same as us. We've been sweating our guts out all day with the sun on our backs.' But the farmer said, 'Comrade, I haven't treated you unfairly. Remember what we agreed? The regular daily wage? Be content and go home. If I chose to help the unemployed, isn't that my right? You're surely not resentful because I have a social conscience?'"

(17) On the way to Jerusalem, Jesus took his closest friends to one side and said, "As you see, we're heading for Jerusalem. The Complete Person will be at the mercy of the religious leaders. He will get the death sentence. It will be the turn of the Romans to make fun of him, to beat him and hang him. Three days later he will return to life."

Then Marion (Zebedee's wife) came to Jesus with her sons, James and John. She greeted Jesus respectfully and asked him to do her a favor. Jesus said, "What can I do for you?" She said, "I'd like you to give my two sons the very best positions in the New World you talk about." Jesus said, "You don't know what you're saying. Can you share the horrible experience I'm about to have?" "Yes," they said. Jesus said, "You will indeed be affected by what happens to me, but the top jobs are not mine to hand out. They have already been allotted by my Parent."

The other friends of Jesus were angry when they got to hear about the two brothers and their mother. This was the cue for Jesus to call them all together for a chat. Jesus said, "You know that many countries have leaders who throw their weight around and some of them are cruel dictators. You must never behave like them. Anyone wishing to make their mark must outdo the rest in being helpful to others. And anyone who fancies being number one, must be ready to do the chores. The Complete Person isn't here to be waited on, but to look after those in need. There are countless numbers of people waiting to be set free!"

(29) As they left Jericho they picked up a large crowd of supporters. Two blind people were sitting beside the road. When they heard that Jesus was passing by, they shouted, "Hey, New David, help us!" People in the crowd told them angrily to shut up. This made them shout louder, "Sir, … New David, help us!" Jesus stopped and shouted back, "What can I do for you?" They said, "Sir, we wish we could see you!" Jesus, choking with emotion, put his hands on their eyes. At once they got their sight back. Then they became friends of Jesus.

21

When they reached Figland, a suburb of Jerusalem, near Olive Hill, Jesus gave these instructions to two of his friends, "Go into the village over there, and at one of the first houses you come to, you'll find a donkey tied up with a young untrained donkey beside her. Untie them and bring them both to me. If anyone challenges you, just say, 'The Leader needs them.' You'll have no trouble." This reminds us of the words of one of God's speakers in the old books,

> "Celebrate this happy day;
> The people's Leader makes his way;
> He doesn't brag or strut about;
> A little donkey is his mount."

The friends carried out their instructions. They brought the donkeys to

Jesus, and used one of them to carry their cloaks, while Jesus sat on the other. Lots of people put their cloaks in front of Jesus on the road and others did the same with branches they had torn down from the trees. The people in front and the people behind formed two choirs, and they sang at the top of their voices.[13]

> *"Freedom now, freedom now!*
> *Welcome, New David!*
> *Welcome, God's Chosen!*
> *Freedom for ever!"*

The arrival of Jesus in Jerusalem threw everything into confusion. Some people had never heard of Jesus before. Others recognized him as the famous speaker from Nazareth in the north. Then Jesus went into the temple and expelled all the tradespeople. He knocked over the stands of the moneychangers and the stalls of those selling pigeons. Jesus told them, "The old books say, 'My house shall be known as a place where people meet with God.' But you're just here to rip people off."

Blind people and lame people made their way to Jesus in the temple and he healed them. The success Jesus was having annoyed the religious leaders and teachers there. They were especially upset when the children started chanting, "Freedom now! New David for Leader!" They said to Jesus, "Do you realize what they're saying?" Jesus said, "Of course. Don't you know the old song?

> *'For children in their earliest days,*
> *God has composed a song of praise.'* "

Jesus said goodbye to them, then left the city. He spent the night at Dategrove.

(18) In the morning, on his way back to the city, Jesus felt hungry. He saw a fig tree on the side of the road. He stopped to have a look and found there were only leaves on it. Jesus said, "You've had your last chance to produce

---

[13] This is a description of responsive (antiphonal) chanting after the manner of psalm singing. Hosanna (meaning "save now") was a political exclamation, later cauterized by liturgical usage, but clearly holding its political meaning for the pilgrims on the first Palm Sunday.

fruit!" The fig tree looked unhealthy. Jesus' friends were intrigued. They said, "The fig tree seems to be withering in front of our eyes!" Jesus said, "Believe me, it has to do with attitude of mind. Fig trees or mountains, it's all the same. Any problem too great for you can be overcome if you have the confidence. Ask God for help in a spirit of trust and you'll get whatever help you need."

(23) Jesus went into the temple again and taught the people there. Those in charge of the temple and some city councilors interrupted him and said, "What right do you have to take over like this? Who gave you permission?" Jesus said, "Let me ask you a question. Then I'll answer yours. Was John inspired by God to dip people or did he get the idea from someone else?" They talked among themselves and realized that if they said "John was inspired by God," Jesus would say, "Why then didn't you accept his teaching?" But if they said, "His ideas were human," they were afraid it would upset the crowd, because most of the ordinary people believed that John was a true messenger from God. So they answered, "We don't know." Jesus said, "In that case I'm not going to tell you who gave me the right to do what I'm doing."

"Here's a strange story for you to think about. There was a man with two children. One day he asked one of them to do some tidying up in the garden. She said, 'No way!' But later on she thought better of it and got on with the job. In the meantime the father had spoken to his other child and asked him to do the work. 'Of course I'll do it for you, Daddy,' he said. But then he forgot all about it. Which of those two children pleased their father most that day, do you think?" They said, "The first one." "Believe me," said Jesus, "traitors and prostitutes are going into God's New World in front of you. John told you what to do and you did the opposite. But the traitors who collect taxes for the Romans, and their prostitute friends, followed John's advice. Even when you saw what a difference it made to their lives, you still didn't accept that John was genuine.

"Here's another story for you. There was once a wealthy farmer who planted a vineyard, put a hedge round it, dug a pit for the winepress and set a lookout post. Then the farmer let the vineyard to tenants and went abroad. At harvest time the farmer sent his agents to collect the produce required as rent. But the tenants attacked them, beating one, killing another, and pelting another with stones. The farmer tried again with more agents this time, but they got the same treatment. As a last resort, the farmer sent his son. He thought, 'They're sure to respect my son.' But when the tenants caught sight of him they said to one another, 'This is the heir; come on, let's kill him and the property will be ours.' So they seized him, dragged him out of the vineyard and killed him. What do you think the farmer will do to the tenants when he comes?" They said, "The thugs will pay for it with their lives. The farmer will lease out his property to more responsible tenants who will pay up when the rents are due." Jesus said to them, "You haven't studied the old books very well, have you? Remember these words?

> 'The stone the builders thought was useless
> Is the stone that takes the stress;
> God gives us such a big surprise;
> We scarcely can believe our eyes.'

"So, I'm telling you, you'll lose your chance of being citizens in God's New World. The honor will be given to others who show themselves more worthy of it."

When the temple clergy and members of the strict set realized these stories were about them, they wanted to arrest Jesus, but were afraid of the crowd who looked on Jesus as one of God's speakers.

22 Here are some more stories Jesus told at this time.

"This is what it's like in the Bright New World. There was once a head of state whose son was getting married. The head of state was making plans for the wedding reception and sent details of the time and place to those on the invitation list. But nobody replied to say they were coming. So the head of state sent another set of messengers with a note saying, 'Everything is ready. The food has been prepared and the table decorations have been made. Please let us know if you intend to come to the wedding reception.' But nobody could be bothered to reply. One booked a holiday for the same date, another went off to a cottage in the country, and another arranged a business trip. Some gave the messengers a hostile reception. The head of state was very put out. Those who had treated the invitation with contempt were deprived of their offices of state and all their privileges. The head of state said to the messengers, 'It will all go ahead as planned, but those on the official invitation list don't deserve to be there. Go into the street and invite everybody you meet to the wedding reception.' The messengers went up and down the high street and invited everybody, good and bad. As you can imagine, the place was heaving. But when the head of state came in to chat with the guests he noticed someone wearing a disapproving frown. The head of state said, 'Friend, how did you get in here with a face like that?' The person with the angry look couldn't think of an answer. So the bouncers were called to do their duty. The head of state said, 'Outside is the place for those who choose to be miserable.'" (God's party is for everybody, but not everybody displays the party spirit!)

(15) The strict set met together to work out how to trip Jesus up. Then they sent some of their number to Jesus and invited some of Herod's cronies along with them. They said to Jesus, "Sir, we know how honest you are. You stick to the truth about God whether folk like it or not. It doesn't matter to you what position or qualifications people hold. So tell us, is it right for us to pay taxes to the Roman Emperor or not?" Jesus knew what they were up to and said, "Why are you trying to catch me out, you oily creeps? Will one of you lend me a coin?" When they had handed a coin to him, Jesus looked at it and said, "Whose head is this and whose name is above it?" "It's the Emperor," they said. Jesus said, "Let the Emperor have what belongs to him, and let God have what belongs to God." This took them by surprise and they hurried off.

There was an easy-going wealthy set who did not believe in any life other than this one. They came to Jesus with their question. "Sir, the laws going back to Moses say that if a man dies without children, his brother must marry his wife and give her children who will be thought of as his dead brother's. Have you heard the case of the seven brothers? The first one married and died childless, leaving his wife to his brother, and so on down the line to the seventh brother. Then the woman died. Whose wife will she be in the next life, since they all married her, one after the other?" Jesus said, "Don't be so stupid. You've obviously never read the old books and know nothing about the way God works. There'll be no separate family units in the next life. We shall all belong to God's family. You don't seem to know the words God meant specially for you. 'I am the God of Abraham, the God of Isaac, and the God of Jacob.' God is not God to people who are dead. Abraham, Isaac, and Jacob must still be alive." The people who overheard this conversation were very impressed by the way Jesus put things.

When the strict set heard how Jesus won the argument with the easy-going set, they came to see Jesus as a body. One of them, a legal expert, tried Jesus with the question, "Sir, which of all the rules in the old books is the most important?" Jesus said, "You must love God with your whole being – your mind, your feelings, and your will.' That's the first rule. The second rule is closely connected. 'Love the person next to you as you love yourself.' Everything else the rule books and God's speakers have to say is simply a working out of those two rules."

Jesus was glad of this opportunity to speak to so many of the strict set at the same time. He put this teaser to them. "How do you expect to spot God's Chosen One? What family will he come from?" They said, "He will be a descendant of David." Jesus said, "In that case why did David refer to God's Chosen as his 'Leader'? These were his words,

'God said to my Leader: Sit by me;
Then you'll have no enemy.'

In our culture, children owe complete loyalty to their parents. Since David expresses his loyalty to God's Chosen, how can God's Chosen be one of David's descendants?"

This confused them. It was the last time any of them tried to catch Jesus out with questions.

23 This is what Jesus had to say about the strict set to the people and to his friends: "The experts in the old books and guardians of public morals who make up the strict set think themselves, each one, a little Moses! If you want to please them, you have to do whatever they tell you, to the letter![14] But I don't recommend you imitate them. They don't practice what they preach. They tie up heavy parcels which they persuade other people to stagger along with, but they wouldn't dream of carrying such weights themselves, even less offer to lighten anyone else's load. They do everything for show! They like to parade in their special clothes. They love to have a place among the distinguished guests on social occasions, and they always sit up front in the places of worship where everybody can see them. It makes them feel good when people in the high street nod to them politely and say, 'Good morning, Reverend.' There's no need, my friends, to follow them by giving yourselves titles. None of you has special authority over anyone else. You're all learning together. There's only one source of life and that's God. God alone is your spiritual superior. You mustn't even allow yourselves to be thought of as experts. There is only one expert – God's Chosen. Look among the nobodies if you want to spot the most important person. Those who put themselves on pedestals will fall off them. Those who don't go after names and titles will be the truly distinguished.

"Get out of the way, Holy Joes, humbugs! You're blocking the road to the Bright New World. You've got no interest in being there yourselves, and you try to put off those who are going in the right direction.

"You're a pain in the neck, Holy Joes, humbugs! You go from one end of the world to the other to make a new recruit, then you give them a special place among you on your rubbish dump!

"Get knotted, you blinkered know-alls! You claim one item of your religion is more sacred than another. From this you argue that some of your promises are more binding than others. You're too dull to realize that everything is sacred because everything can be traced back to God.

"We'd miss you like a sore thumb, Holy Joes, humbugs! You pay your religious dues on time, but you've forgotten the really important things your religion asks of you – kindness and fair play and being true to your word. A fly falls into your drink and you delicately pick it out. Then you shut your eyes and gulp down a camel!

"Take a running jump, Holy Joes, humbugs! You wash your plates and cups in case they've been used by bad people, and the luxury food and wine you eat and drink from those same plates and cups come from the profits

---

[14] These words must be sarcastic in view of verse 8 onwards.

of your shady business interests. You're blind to real dirt, you humbugs. Clean up your lives and your cups will be clean.

"You're as false as hell, Holy Joes, humbugs! You're like whitewashed gravestones, sparkling in the sunlight, but full of rotting corpses. You impress others with your prim and proper ways, but underneath you're vicious, and crafty too.

"You stink, the lot of you! You design fine memorials for God's speakers of times past, and put flowers on the graves of those who've lived good lives. You kid yourselves that if you'd been around at the time you wouldn't have had any part in killing God's speakers as your ancestors did. At least you admit you're descendants of the people responsible for killing God's friends! You want to finish the job they started? Come on, then, get on with it! You're the same species of poisonous snake as your ancestors. The local rubbish dump is the only place for you!"

(These words of Jesus remind us of what it says in one of the old books. God says, "I'm sending you gifted speakers, wise counselors, and people with learning. Some of these you'll murder or execute, others you'll torture in your places of worship, and others you'll outlaw from your communities." Yes, it's pious people who are to blame for that dreadful history of persecution which stretches from the time of that good man, Abel, to Gary who was murdered recently by religious fanatics in the worship area of the temple.)[15]

Here are words of Jesus showing how he foresaw in his lifetime that persecution was on its way.

"Jerusalem, Jerusalem, you're famous for killing God's friends and throwing stones at God's agents! Over and over again I've tried to put my arms round you and draw you to me, like a mother hen gathering her chicks under her wings. But you wouldn't have it! Your people are now without the protection I would have given them. Believe me, you won't see me again until you're ready to join in the song, 'Welcome, God's Chosen!'"

---

[15] This translation opts for the view that verses 34-35 are not intended to be understood as words of Jesus but a comment from the Gospel-writer, in line with that writer's practice of quoting a scriptural text to underpin the narrative. Matthew may here be quoting from a writing his readers would have been familiar with, but now lost. This would make more intelligible the reference to Zacharias, who was killed by two Zealots in the temple in about 68 C.E., thirty years or more after the crucifixion of Jesus, but before the completion of Matthew's Gospel in its present form.

24

As Jesus was on his way out of the temple, his friends pointed out the new building work in progress. Jesus said, "Impressive, isn't it? Believe me, it won't last very long. It's all due to be demolished!"

Later, when Jesus was sitting down on Olive Hill, and out of hearing of the crowds, his friends raised the subject again. "When is this going to come about? Will it mean the end of the world?" Jesus said, "Don't let anyone make fools of you. Many will claim to be my successors and say, 'I'm God's representative on earth,' and they will mislead lots of people. There's no need to get excited when you hear about wars and rebellions. This is the normal course of events; it doesn't mean the end of the world. Countries will go to war with one another and rulers will engage in power struggles. There'll be natural disasters here and there and severe food shortages. These happenings are just like a woman's labor pains. They lead to better things.

"The authorities will arrest you and torture you before putting you to death. You'll be victims of prejudice in every country in the world for being loyal to me. Many will give up; others will go over to the enemy and act as spies. There'll be a lot of hate. Some will claim to speak for God and put wrong ideas into people's minds. People will use force to get their way. Love will be in short supply. But those who stay the course will achieve God's purpose for them. The Good News about the New World will be carried to every land and every race. After that the world as we know it will come to an end.

"When you see the 'Eyesore,' described in the Book of Daniel (work it out for yourself), then the people who live near Jerusalem will have to take refuge in the mountains. They'll have no time to go through the different parts of the house to collect their belongings. Anyone out in the fields had better not go home to get a coat. It will be hard on those who are pregnant or nursing young children when the time comes. Pray that it doesn't happen in winter or on a Rest Day when travel is restricted. It will be a time of great suffering, greater than ever before or ever again. Only because God plans to shorten the period will there be any chance of survivors. For the sake of God's people there'll be a limit to those days.

"Don't believe anyone who claims to be able to point out God's Chosen

One at that time. There'll be frauds and impostors who use tricks to convince people. They'll come close to deceiving God's best friends. So be on the look out, I've warned you! If anyone says, 'Cut yourself off from people – that's how you'll find him!' be very suspicious. If anyone says, 'Try meditation – you'll find him inside you,' make sure your mind doesn't play tricks. Pious exercises are like rotting corpses. They are best left for the crows to pick over. The Complete Person will come as a surprise, like a lightning flash.

"You can learn a lesson from the fig tree. When the branches grow, they become tender and the leaves come out. Then you know summer is on the way. When you see the events I've described taking place, you'll know what's going to happen next. Believe me, the world as you know it won't disappear until all these things have happened. One world will give way to another, but my words will last forever.

"No one knows when all this will happen, apart from the Loving God. Those closest to God don't know. Even I don't know. The time when the Complete Person appears will be like the time of Noah. Before the great flood came, everyone was living life in the usual way, eating and drinking and getting married. Then Noah got into his big boat and in no time a flood swept everybody away. That's what it will be like when the Complete Person comes. Sometimes two people are working together in the open air, and without warning, one of them has a heart attack. Or two people are preparing food together and one suddenly has a stroke. So you must be ready for anything. You don't know when the Leader is coming. If a householder knew the exact time a thief planned to break in, the police would be there, ready to make an arrest. But since you don't know when the Complete Person is coming, you must keep your wits about you every moment.

"Imagine two very different types of manager, each put in charge of a branch of the business, with instructions to look after the employees. One manager is pleased when the boss arrives to find everything being done properly. Promotion to a higher branch will follow. The other manager uses the boss's absence as a chance to bully those he is responsible for and to run up a huge drinks bill. One day the boss will arrive unexpectedly and give that manager the sack. No doubt such a person will complain bitterly about unfair treatment. The scrap heap is the place for all who abuse their trust."

25 Jesus said, "This is how it's going to turn out in the Bright New World. Imagine ten bridesmaids following our custom of going out to meet the bridegroom with lanterns. Five of them are silly and five of them are sensible. The silly ones forgot to take any spare oil with them for their lanterns, whereas the sensible ones took extra oil in separate containers. There was a delay, and the bridegroom took a long time getting to the agreed meeting point. So they all sat down and nodded off to sleep. In the middle of the night, someone shouted, 'The bridegroom's coming. Get ready to meet him!' Then the bridesmaids got their lanterns ready. The silly ones said to the sensible ones, 'Our lanterns are going out. Let us have some of your oil.' But the sensible ones said, 'Sorry, we've only got enough for ourselves. You'd better try and get some from the shop.' While they went off to buy some oil, the bridegroom came and the five with their lanterns burning lit the way for him to the bride's house for the party. Then the door was shut. Later, the silly bridesmaids arrived. They shouted at the door, 'Sir, let us in!' But the doorkeeper said, 'Sorry, no gatecrashers!' So keep your wits about you. You don't know how long the waiting is going to be.

"Or think about it this way. A company director goes off on an extended world tour, leaving the business in the hands of three deputies. Each was assigned a capital sum to be used for the expansion of the company. The first was given five million pounds, the second two million, and the third one million. The first used the capital to set up five new branches and the second added two new lines to the company's products. The third put the money in a fund where the interest just kept up with the rate of inflation. At last the director's holiday came to an end and the deputies were summoned to give their reports. The first presented pictures of the new branches, which had been set up with the five million. The director said, 'Well done. You've proved your worth. I'm going to make you joint director with me in the firm.' The second deputy showed the catalogues advertising the new lines. The director said, 'Well done. You've proved your worth. I'm putting you in charge of sales.' The third deputy said, 'I'm afraid I'm not up to performing the miracles you expect. Here's the audit to show your money's been kept safe.' Then the director gave the deputy a dressing-down. 'I don't pay you to sit on your backside! I expect miracles, do I? Well,

I expected at the very least you would try your hand at the stock exchange and increase the capital! You're fired! My new joint director will take over your department. In this firm those who show enthusiasm get ahead; those who don't care about anything end up without anything. There's the door. You belong with the moaners on the streets!'

"Now imagine that exciting time when the whole company of the Complete Person is met together, including those from beyond time and space.[16] The Leader will take his place. People from all nationalities will stand in front of him and he will divide them into two groups, one either side of him. Then the Leader will say to one group, 'My Parent is pleased with you. You're the people God has been planning a New World for since the beginning of time. You can join me there. I remember when I was starving, and you gave me a good meal; I remember when I was thirsty, and you bought me a drink; once I was a social outcast, and you invited me home; then I had nothing decent to wear, and you kitted me out; when I was unwell, you looked after me and when I was in prison, you visited me.' These good people will say, 'Leader, when did we ever give you a good meal or stand you a drink? When did we have you in our house or give you clothes? We don't remember you being ill or visiting you in prison.' Then the Leader will say, 'Believe me, when you did these things for people most think not worth the trouble, you did them for me. They are my family.' Then the Leader will speak to the other group. 'As for you lot, God can't stand the sight of you. You belong with thugs and bullies. When I was starving and thirsty, you shrugged your shoulders; when I was an outcast, you shunned me; you didn't care about my worn-out clothes or about my health, and when I went to prison, you said it served me right.' These people will protest, 'Leader, when was all this?' The Leader will say, 'When you ignored those you thought didn't matter, you were ignoring me.' Such heartless people can never make good the wrong they've done. But those who care for the needy will have life to the full."

---

[16] The term "Son of Man," here translated "Complete Person," is capable of carrying a collective sense, as in the Book of Daniel.

26 When Jesus had told his friends what he wanted to tell them about the Bright New World, he said, "It's only two days before the festival which celebrates the greatest event in our people's history. Then the Complete Person will be arrested and put to death on a cross." At about the time Jesus said this, the temple clergy and city councilors were meeting together in the official residence of Guy, their chief. They discussed a plan to kidnap Jesus and kill him. They said, "It had better not be during the holiday. If people got to know, we would have a riot on our hands!"

Jesus was being entertained at Dategrove, in Simon's house. This Simon was shunned by everybody because he had a skin disease. A woman came in with a glass jar filled with very expensive aromatic oil. Jesus was lying on the couch, having something to eat. The woman poured the oil on his head. Jesus' companions were disgusted when they saw what she was doing. They said, "What a waste! A lot of charities would be pleased to have the money from the sale of that oil!" Jesus sensed their disapproval and said, "Don't be so hard on the woman! She has done something wonderful for me. Your selfishness ensures a steady supply of people for you to practice your charity on. But I won't always be here to receive your gifts. This woman has embalmed my body, ready for my burial. Take special note of what I say. Whenever and wherever the Good News is spoken about, you must make sure this woman's action plays a big part in the story."

Then one of the twelve close friends of Jesus, Judas from Kerioth, went to the leading members of the clergy. He said, "How much, if I tell you how to get hold of him?" They made a deal with Judas and advanced him three hundred pounds. From then on Judas waited his chance.

(17) On the first day of the festival, when only bread without yeast is eaten, Jesus was visited by his friends. They asked him, "Where do you want us to get the food ready for the celebration?" Jesus gave them directions to the house of someone who lived in the city. They were to give this message: "The Leader says, 'The time is ripe. I'm going to celebrate the special occasion at your place. My friends will be coming too.'" The friends carried out these instructions and got the food ready.

In the evening, Jesus and his friends took their places on the couches. While they were having the meal Jesus said, "Believe me, one of you here will give me away." They were very upset by this and each of them protested, "You can't mean me, Leader, surely?" Jesus said, "One who has eaten from the same dish as me will be a traitor. The Complete Person must be true to the picture painted in times past, but heaven help the one who hands the Complete Person over to the enemy. He'll wish he'd never been born!" Then Judas, the traitor said, "Surely, you don't mean me, Leader?" Jesus said, "You should know!"

They were still eating when Jesus took a loaf of bread and said "thank you" to God. Then he broke it and gave it to his friends. He said, "Have this: it's my body." Then Jesus took a cup, said "thank you" to God, and passed it on to them. He said, "I want you all to drink from this cup; it's my blood which brings friendship with God; it will flow for many and they will know their wrongdoing has been forgiven. As for me, the next time I drink this wine with you will be at the dawn of my Parent's New World."

They sang a song, then walked toward Olive Hill. On the way Jesus told them, "You'll all run off and desert my cause tonight. As it says in the old books,

> 'When the shepherd falls dead,
> The sheep flee in dread.'

But when I come back to life, I'll go on ahead of you to Galilee." Rocky said, "The rest may desert your cause, but you can count on me!" Jesus said, "Believe me, before the cock crows at dawn tomorrow, you'll disown me three times." Rocky said, "I'd die side by side with you rather than do such a thing!" The other friends said the same.

(36) Jesus took his friends to a secluded spot near an old olive press. He said, "Sit here. I'm going over there to talk with God." He took Rocky and Zebedee's boys with him. Jesus became distressed and agitated. He told them, "My heart's breaking. I feel as if I'm being crushed to death. Please stay close to me and keep awake." Jesus went a bit further on, threw himself on the ground and began to talk with God. Jesus said, "My own Loving God, if there's another way out of this, please show me ... No, what I want doesn't matter, only what you want." When Jesus came back to the three friends he found them asleep. He said to Rocky, "Was it too much to ask you to keep awake for an hour? Keep your eyes open and ask God to let you

off the hook. You want to stand by me, but have you got the guts?" Jesus went away again and talked with God. He said, "My own Loving God, if there really is no other way, I'm ready to take it all." When Jesus came back to his friends, he found them asleep again. They could not keep their eyes open. This time Jesus just left them and went back to talk with God on the same lines as before. The he came back to his friends and said, "Still asleep? Still taking it easy? The time's come. The Complete Person is about to be handed over to evil people. Up you get! Time to go! Look, here comes the traitor!"

Then one of the closest friends of Jesus, Judas, appeared with a mob waving swords and clubs. They came from the clergy and the leaders of the community. The traitor had arranged a signal, "The one I kiss is the man you want; grab hold of him." Judas came straight to Jesus and said, "Hello, Leader," and kissed him. Jesus said, "Friend, do your job!" Then they grabbed hold of Jesus and held him tight. Then one of Jesus' companions pulled out his knife, attacked a leading officer and cut his ear off. Jesus said to his friends, "Let's have no more violence. Those who use violence come to a violent end. Don't you realize, I could ask my Parent to provide me with an army of crack fighters? But that's not the way the old books say it should be." Then Jesus spoke to the mob. "What are you doing with those clubs and knives? What do you think I am, a terrorist? You've seen me teaching in the temple every day. Why didn't you arrest me then? It's exactly the way God's speakers imagined in the old books." Then all Jesus' friends ran for their lives.

(57) Jesus was taken to Guy, the High Priest, who was joined by the experts in the old books and other leading members of the community. Rocky followed Jesus at a distance, all the way to the courtyard outside Guy's official residence. He went inside and sat down with the guards to see how things would turn out. The religious leaders and all the councilors present were busy inventing evidence against Jesus to make a case for the death penalty. But none of it would hold together. The witnesses who came forward were poor liars. Then two took the stand and said, "This man said, 'I can destroy God's temple and build it again in three days.'" Guy stood up and said, "What do you say to that? Can you give us an explanation?" But Jesus kept quiet. Then Guy said, "You are now under oath, with God as your

judge. Are you or are you not the Chosen One, God's Own?" Jesus said, "That's for you to say. But I will say this, 'Start looking now and you'll see God introducing a new humanity to the world.'" Then Guy lost his temper and said, "This is an insult to God. We don't need any more witnesses. You heard what he said. What's your verdict?" They shouted out, "Death!" Some of them spat at him and others hit him and said, "Come on, God's Chosen, guess who I am!"

(69) Meanwhile Rocky was still sitting in the courtyard. A woman came up to him and said, "Haven't I seen you with Jesus, the hero from Galilee?" Rocky shook his head and said, "I don't know what the hell you're talking about!" As Rocky was making his way through the gateway, another woman recognized him and said to the people standing around, "He's one of the gang belonging to Jesus of Nazareth!" Rocky said, "As God is my witness, I've never met the man!" A little while later, some people Rocky had been chatting with said, "You don't fool us. You must be one of them. Your accent gives you away." Rocky lost control of himself and began to use foul language. "I'm telling you, I've never bloody set eyes on him!" Then the cock crowed. Rocky remembered what Jesus had said, "Before the cock crows at dawn, you'll disown me three times." Rocky went out through the gate and cried like a baby.

27 In the early morning, the full council met together to plan the death of Jesus. They put him in chains and took him off to Pilate, the Roman Governor.

When Judas heard that Jesus had been condemned to death, he was deeply sorry for what he had done and brought back the money to the clergy in the temple. He said, "I've done a very wicked thing! I've caused the death of someone really good!" They said, "What do you expect us to do about it? It's your problem!" Judas threw the money in the direction of the altar and walked out. He then went straight and hanged himself. The clergy picked up the money and said, "We can't very well put this into the collection box. Blood money is dirty!" They discussed it for a little while, then decided to use the money to buy some land belonging to a pottery, to serve as a burial ground for immigrants. That's how it got the name it has today, "The Bloody Field." The incident reminds us of things spoken about in the old books.[17]

(11) Jesus was brought to stand trial before the governor. The governor said, "So you fancy yourself as the leader of the Jewish people?" Jesus said, "What makes you say that?" But when the clergy brought their charges, Jesus would not reply to them. Then Pilate said to Jesus, "Don't you want to defend yourself against all these things they're saying about you?" But Jesus refused to answer any of the charges. The governor was impressed.

Usually during the holiday period the governor would make a friendly gesture to the Jewish people by releasing a popular prisoner. At that time the Romans had in custody a well-known prisoner called Barry. So when the public came to watch the trial, Pilate said, "Which of your two national saviors would you like me to release for you? Savior Barry or the Savior some call God's Chosen?"[18] Pilate realized that envy was the reason the council had brought Jesus to trial.

While Pilate was conducting the trial, his wife Claudia sent him a message. "Don't get involved in the case of that good man. I had a nightmare about him last night."

Meanwhile the clergy got the mob to shout for Barry to be released and for Jesus to be killed. So when the Governor spoke to them again and said, "Which one do you want me to set free?" They shouted, "Barry." Pilate said, "What do you want me to do with Jesus, God's Chosen, so called?" They all shouted, "Put him on a cross!" Pilate said, "Why? What's he done wrong?" They screamed back, "Hang him high!"

Pilate saw that he was losing control. The mob was getting out of hand. So he poured out some water and washed his hands in front of everybody. He said, "I take no responsibility for this person's death; it's your business!" They shouted together, "Leave it to us; if there's any comeback, we'll take the blame, or our children after us."

So Pilate released Barry. Then he had Jesus beaten and gave the order for him to be hung on a cross. First the Governor's soldiers took Jesus back inside and called together the rest of their mates. They took all his clothes

---

[17] The "quotation" is a mixture of several passages from the Hebrew scriptures which are difficult to translate in a way that makes sense. We think it best just to allude to them in this way.

[18] Pilate discomforts the Jewish leaders by mocking their choice of heroes. Both are called Jesus = savior, or national liberator.

off and draped one of their red cloaks round him. Then they made a prizewinner's wreath out of brambles and put it on his head. They put a stick in his right hand and knelt down in front of him. They played the fool with him, shouting, "Three cheers for the greatest Jew of all time!" They spat at him, snatched the stick from him, and hit him on the head with it. When they had finished having their fun, they took off the cloak and put his own clothes back on. Then they marched him off to the place of execution.

(32) On the way the soldiers forced someone to help Jesus carry his cross. He was an African called Simon. When they got to Skull Hill, they tried to get Jesus to take a painkiller, but he refused it. When they had fastened Jesus to the cross, they shared out his clothes, throwing the dice for each item. Then they sat down and kept guard. The notice over his head said, "This is Jesus, the greatest of the Jews."

Then two thugs were hung either side of Jesus. The people who passed by shouted insults at him, falling about with laughter. They shouted things like, "Hey, you! Weren't you going to knock down the temple and build it in three days? How about jumping off the cross and saving yourself?" Religious people also made fun at his expense. They said, "He was good at helping other people. He's not much good at helping himself! He's supposed to be our Leader. Why doesn't he jump off the cross now? If he does, we'll support him! He's convinced he's God's favorite. If that's the case, God will come to his rescue!" Even the thugs hanging with Jesus shouted abuse.

At twelve o'clock it became very dark everywhere until three in the afternoon. At about three o'clock Jesus shouted out in Hebrew, "My God, my God, why have you left me?" The Hebrew for "My God" sounds something like Elijah, so some of the onlookers said, "He's calling for Elijah!" Someone ran and filled a sponge with some cheap wine, put it on a stick and held it up for Jesus to drink. Some said, "If we hang around long enough, we may get to see Elijah, if he comes to save him!" Then Jesus gave a loud cry and died.

(51) At that very moment the curtain in the temple was ripped from top to bottom. An earthquake split open the rocks. Many good people rejected by the community came out from their hiding places among the tombs.

They began life again with Jesus and appeared in public among the crowds on the streets of Jerusalem.

When the Roman officer on duty, and the other soldiers with him, saw the earthquake and the way Jesus died, they said, "He was just like a god!"

There were some women present, watching a little way off. Some of these were friends of Jesus from Galilee who had been of great help to him. They included Maggie, Maria the mother of James and Joseph, and Marion (Zebedee's wife).

In the evening, a wealthy friend of Jesus, Joseph from Ram, went to Pilate and asked for Jesus' body. Pilate ordered the body to be given to him. Joseph took the body, wrapped it in a clean linen cloth, and placed it in the resting place intended for himself, a chamber he had recently had cut from the bare rock. Then he put a big stone over the entrance and left. Maggie and Maria stayed there for a while and sat down near the grave.

(62) The next day, Saturday, the temple clergy and members of the strict set went to see Pilate. They said, "Sir, we remember what that fraudster said when he was alive, 'After three days I'll return to life.' So order the grave to be guarded until tomorrow, or his followers may go and steal his body and tell people he's come back from the dead. That would be the most dangerous fraud of all!" Pilate said, "I'll let you have some soldiers. Do your best to protect the grave." They took the soldiers to guard the grave, and put a seal on the stone.

28 Very early on Sunday morning, Maggie and Maria went to see the grave. Without warning there was a big earth tremor. One of God's agents came and pushed the stone out of the way and sat on it. He was dressed in white clothes that shone in the morning light. The guards were dead scared and shook from head to toe. He said to the women, "Don't be frightened. I know you're looking for Jesus who was hung on a cross. Jesus is not in there; you're welcome to take a look. He's come to life again and he's on his way to Galilee. You'll meet up with him there!"

Nervous but happy, they ran as fast as they could to get the news to the other friends of Jesus. Before they had got very far they met Jesus. Jesus said, "Hello; good to see you!" They rushed toward him, held him tight, and showed how much they loved him. Jesus said, "There's no need to be nervous. Please take a message to my folks. I'll see them when we all get back home to Galilee."

Meanwhile, some of the soldiers who had been on guard went into Jerusalem and told the clergy what had happened. The clergy had a quick meeting with the leading citizens and decided the best thing to do was to give the soldiers a large bribe. The soldiers were told to say, "His followers came in the night and stole his body while we were asleep." Then they said, "If the Governor gets to hear about it, we'll put him right so you don't get into trouble." The soldiers took the money and did as they were told. Many people still believe their version of the story.

The remaining eleven of the group who had assisted Jesus, went to a mountain in Galilee where Jesus had asked them to meet him. When they saw him, they greeted him warmly, but some still had doubts. Jesus came close to them and said, "Everyone, everywhere, must now look to me for leadership. So go and make friends for me all over the world. When you dip people, tell them about the Loving God, made known in God's True Likeness and by means of God's Spirit. Pass on to them, in full, my way of life. Look out for me, because I'll always be with you, to the end of time."

Luke's Good News

(Part One)

1 Dear Theo, in writing to you I know I'm writing to someone who loves God. Lots of people have tried to put in writing the exciting things that have been happening in our world recently. They've been setting down information they got from people who were there on the spot and wanting to talk about it. I thought, since you hold a government post, you'd like to know the facts. I've been collecting them and putting them in order. I want you to be fully in the picture, so you can check the truth of the various accounts which have come to you.

(5) Kerry lived at the time of Herod the Great. He belonged to an old family of God's helpers. His wife Lisa came from the same family. God saw that Kerry and Lisa were good people. They did their best to please God by keeping the rules of their religion. They hadn't been able to have any children and were getting on in years.

One day Kerry was at work in the central place of worship in Jerusalem. He was due to take part in the service. He was allotted the task of burning the scented crystals. To do this he had to go into the restricted area set apart to mark the presence of God. The people waited outside, holding thoughts of God in their minds. Inside Kerry got a fright. He hadn't expected to see one of God's agents standing by the table. The agent said, "Keep calm, Kerry! God has been listening to you. Lisa is going to have a baby boy. John would be a good name for him, since it means 'gift from God.' Congratulations! He'll bring you a lot of happiness, and everyone else will be pleased too. He'll be a famous man of God. He must keep away from the drink. God's Spirit will be his guide from the moment he's born. He'll bring many of your people back to God. He'll tell them God is coming. He'll be a strong character and remind them of Elijah. He'll put an end to family quarrels and help those who've made a mess of their lives back into society. He'll arrange a warm reception for God." Kerry said, "I find that hard to believe. I'm not as young as I used to be, nor is Lisa." God's agent said, "My name's Gabriel. I'm in close touch with God who sent me to you with this good news. Although you don't believe me now, you won't have long to wait. Meanwhile, you're to keep your mouth shut. You can tell people about our meeting after the baby is born."

The people waiting outside began to wonder what had happened to Kerry. He was taking so long. When at last he came out, he seemed like somebody struck dumb, as if he'd seen a ghost. He made a few weak gestures to the people, then hurried home as soon as the service was over.

Soon after, Lisa got pregnant and stayed at home. In those days, people who couldn't have children had to put up with a lot of painful gossip. So Lisa said, "God's been good to me. I don't have to be ashamed any more!"

(26) When Lisa was six months pregnant, God sent Gabriel to Nazareth in the province of Galilee. Gabriel had a message for Mary, a young woman engaged to Joseph, a descendant of King David. Gabriel came into the house and said, "Pleased to meet you, Mary. You're a special person. God thinks highly of you." But Mary was nervous, trying to think what it was all about. So Gabriel said, "Nothing to worry about, Mary. God is your friend. You're going to have a baby boy, and you're to call him Jesus. He will be famous and known as 'God's Likeness.' God will make him the true successor of David, his ancestor. He'll have the permanent care of God's people, and they will go on increasing more and more." Mary said, "I don't see how that can be. I'm not married yet." Gabriel said, "God's Spirit has it all arranged. She will be responsible. 'God's Likeness' has to be very special. You'll also be pleased to know your cousin Lisa is pregnant. It's going to be a boy! Everyone had given up hope, but she's now six months gone. There's no limit to what God can do!" Mary said, "Here I am then, ready to help God all I can. May your words come true!" Then God's agent left.

(39) Mary packed her bag and went down south to visit her cousin. Lisa and Kerry lived up in the hills, not far from Jerusalem. As soon as Mary got there she greeted Lisa with a hug and a kiss. This made Lisa's baby jump inside her. It was God's Spirit, bringing the baby to life. Lisa spoke out loud,

"What a lucky woman you are, Mary. Your baby's going to be a wonderful person. I'm very honored to have a visit from the mother of the one who's going to be my Leader. Your greeting got my baby moving. He must be pleased! It's always a good thing to believe what God tells us is going to happen."

(46) Then Mary sang this song for Lisa:

> "I sense the greatness of God
> Who makes my joy complete;
> God smiled at me and asked my help,
> And everyone will dance with glee
> At the wonderful thing happening to me.
> What a God!
>
> In every age God aids the good,
> Upsetting the plans of the arrogant:
> See how the powerful fall off their perches!
> Honor for the modest, a banquet for the hungry;
> The rich get nothing and slink away!
> God keeps promises to friends and companions –
> Abraham, Sarah, and their like today."[1]

Mary stayed with Lisa for about three months, then went back home.

(57) The time came for Lisa to have her baby. It was a boy. All her family and neighbors were happy for her when they heard the news. They put it down to God's kindness. Just over a week later it was time to give him a name. The ceremony was combined with the removal of the little boy's foreskin. Kerry was the popular choice of name, after his father. But his mother said, "No; he's going to be called John." Her friends said, "That's unusual. No one else in your family has that name." Then they asked his father, using sign language, since he was very deaf. Kerry asked for something to write on. He put down, "His name is John." They were all

---

[1] The name "Israel" signifies not only Jacob, but is inclusive of his family and their descendants. Similarly, it is not just David, but his family (house) that is referred to. The Hebrew mind understood this inclusiveness. We need to make it more obvious.

puzzled by this. Then at last, Kerry felt free to speak. He gave all the credit to God. The people in the village were excited when they heard Kerry's story. It became the talking point throughout the hill country around Jerusalem. People asked, "What sort of person will he turn out to be?" It was obvious God had a plan for him.

(67) Then Kerry was inspired by God's Spirit to sing this song:

> "What a wonderful God,
> The God of Jacob, Leah, and Rachel!
> This God has come to help us and set us free.
>
> The world will be healed by the power of love,
> By a descendant of David and Bathsheba.
> Those who spoke God's promises were right:
> The days of hate and having enemies are passing.
>
> God was generous to our ancestors,
> A loyal and reliable friend.
> God promised Abraham and Sarah
> An end to hostility and fear,
> Freedom to worship and serve.
>
> You, little baby, will speak for God;
> You will go in front of God's Chosen Leader
> And roll out the carpet.
> You'll tell people their problems are over,
> Free from guilt at last.
>
> God is kind and gentle;
> God will turn darkness into daylight,
> So we can make our way in peace."

John developed a striking character from his earliest days. He joined those who lived the harsh life of the desert, until the time came for him to make his public stand.

2 Augustus, the Roman emperor, sent out an order for a census to be made of the population within the empire. The Governor of Syria was responsible for managing the count in Palestine. Everybody went to their hometown to have their names recorded. This meant that Joseph had to travel from Nazareth in the north to Bethlehem in the south. Bethlehem was the recognized home of all those descended from David. He took Mary, his partner, with him. She was pregnant. Whilst they were in Bethlehem Mary went into labor and gave birth to her first child, a boy. She dressed him in his baby clothes and put him in the feeding trough. They were living rough in the yard with the animals, because the hotel was full.

That night, down in the fields nearby, some sheep farmers were guarding their sheep. One of God's agents approached them. There was a strange light, which frightened the farmers. The agent said, "Don't panic. I've some good news for everybody. A baby has just been born in Bethlehem. He's going to be our new Leader, God's Chosen, the one we've been waiting for. If you want to see him, he's in a feeding trough with his baby clothes on." Then a band of singers appeared. They were singing songs for God. This is what they sang:

> "Look at God's beauty around and above,
> We bring you God's peace and a bundle of love."

When the singers had faded into the distance, the sheep farmers said, "Why don't we go up to Bethlehem and find out what it's all about? God's been speaking to us." So they ran as fast as they could, and found the baby in the feeding trough being cared for by Mary and Joseph. Then the farmers told everybody what they had learnt about the baby. Their story was hard to believe. But Mary remembered their words and thought deeply about them. The sheep farmers went back to the fields, singing songs to God as they went. They had seen and heard such wonderful things.

(21) A week later the time came to give the baby boy his name and to remove his foreskin. He was called Jesus, as God's agent had suggested before he was conceived.

There were special ceremonies going back to the time of Moses, which Mary and Joseph went to Jerusalem for. Jesus had to be given as a present to God. (The old books say, "The first boy born in every family shall belong to God.") They also made the customary gift to God of two pigeons.

Simeon lived in Jerusalem. He was a good man and carried out the duties of his religion. He was looking forward to better days for his country. God's Spirit was with him, and she told him he wouldn't die before seeing God's Chosen. She led him to the worship center at the same time as Mary and Joseph were bringing in the baby Jesus. Simeon took Jesus in his arms and sang this song of thanks to God.

> *"Your helper, God, moves on content,*
> *Your plans my eyes have seen;*
> *A new day dawns for every land,*
> *Beyond your people's dream."*

Joseph and Mary couldn't believe what Simeon had to say about Jesus. He gave the three of them his good wishes, and said to Mary, "Your son will bring out the best and the worst in our people. He'll get into trouble for showing up so many in their true light. And you will share his pain."

Anne was one of God's speakers. She came from a good family. She was eighty-four years of age, a widow whose husband had died just seven years after their marriage. She lived in the worship center and did all she could to help, eating very little and talking with God on behalf of others, day and night. She came up to Mary and Joseph and said words of thanks to God for the baby. Then she pointed him out to those who had their country's best interests at heart, as their hope for the future.

When Mary and Joseph had completed their business in Jerusalem, they went back home to Nazareth in Galilee. Jesus was a healthy baby, and grew up to be a strong and bright lad. People sensed there was something special about him.

(41) Every year, Mary and Joseph went to Jerusalem, for the festival that celebrates the escape of the slaves from Egypt. When Jesus was twelve, they went up as usual. When the festival was over, and the holidaymakers on their way home, Jesus stayed behind in Jerusalem, without his parents knowing it. They thought he was with another group traveling the same way. When at last they started to look for him among their friends and

relations, they couldn't find him. So they went back to Jerusalem to look for him there. It took them three days to find him. He was in the worship center, sitting among the teachers, listening and asking questions. Everybody who heard him was impressed by his grasp of the arguments and his intelligent comments. When Mary and Joseph saw him, they couldn't believe their eyes. Mary said, "This is not the way to treat your parents! We've been worried stiff!" Jesus said, "Why the problem finding me? This is my home; there are things I have to do here." They didn't have a clue what he meant.

From then on, back in Nazareth, Jesus was careful to fall in line with his parents' wishes. Mary had much to think about for a long time to come. Jesus continued to develop a remarkable mind and grew quite tall. He was liked by everybody.

3 Tiberius had been Roman emperor for fifteen years. Pilate ruled on his behalf in south-west Palestine, Herod Antipas in the north-west, and Herod's brother Philip in the north-east, and Linus in the south-east. Hank and Guy were the official religious leaders, but it was John, Kerry's son, God spoke to. He was living in the desert at the time. He went round the villages near to the River Jordan, inviting people to be dipped as a mark of their change of heart and that their wrongdoings had been forgiven. As God's speaker says in the old books,

> "The desert hears a lonely voice:
> 'Quickly flies the time of choice,
> Repair the roads, straighten the bends;
> Now's your chance to be God's friends;
> Down with the mighty, up with the low,
> All living things their God will know.' "

This is what John said to the crowds who came to him to be dipped. "You poisonous snakes! I see you're wriggling out of the cornfield now harvesting is about to start! Let's see some change in your behavior! Don't rely on having Abraham as your ancestor to save you from trouble. God can make new children for Abraham out of people you've no more time for than these stones! The chopper's ready; it will strike at the very roots of your religion and society."

The people asked John, "What can we do about it?" John said, "Those of you with too many clothes should share them with those without any. The same applies to the food in your cupboard."

Even outcasts who collected taxes for the Romans, asked John to dip them. They said, "What advice would you give us in our position?" John said, "Collect only the right amount. Don't fiddle the books." Some soldiers asked him, "What about us?" John said, "No bullying or mugging or twisting the law to suit yourselves. You're on good wages. Be satisfied!"

There was a feeling of expectation. People were beginning to wonder about John. Was he God's chosen deliverer? John put an end to the speculation by saying, "I'm only dipping you in water. Someone is coming more able than me. I'm not fit even to untie his sandals. He will drench you with God's Spirit, and that will be like fire. When corn has been harvested, the grain has to be separated from the useless husks. That's what's going to happen to you. The one who's coming will do the job thoroughly. He'll store the grain in his barn and the rubbish left over he'll put on the fire until it's burnt to nothing." John made rousing speeches on different aspects of his message. But Herod put him in prison. This was because John publicly denounced Herod for marrying Rose, his brother's wife, and for lots of other bad things he'd done.

(21) Jesus was one of the many people who were dipped at that time. Afterwards, while he was talking with God, the clouds parted, and God's Spirit came down on him. She looked like a pigeon. A voice from overhead was heard to say, "That's my boy! You're doing fine!"

Jesus was about thirty when he set out on his new career. He was of Jewish descent, tracing his ancestry through Joseph, his father, to King David and further back to the oldest ancestors of the race, Jacob, Isaac, and Abraham. He was also a member of the human race, of common stock with the rest of humanity. God is parent of all humankind and parent of Jesus.[2]

---

[2] See footnote overleaf.

After getting God's Spirit at the River Jordan, Jesus felt ready for the task ahead. But first he was moved to spend some time in the desert. This gave him the chance to get clear in his mind which direction his life should take. He was there for about six weeks and went without food the whole time. He was near to starvation. The thought came to him, "If I'm God's Chosen, all I need to do is order these stones to become bread." Then Jesus remembered some words from the old books, "People can't live just on bread."

Then Jesus imagined himself looking down from a very high mountain where, at a glance, he could see all the countries of the world. He thought, "All this could easily be mine. I just have to be cunning, and gain the support of the right people." Then he thought again, "The old books tell us the only one we should try to please is God."

Then another idea came to him. He saw in his mind's eye the worship center in Jerusalem. "Perhaps if I jumped off the highest point I could prove I come from God? It should work like the song,

> 'God has friends who only wait
> To catch you as you fall;
> Your feet will gently touch the ground
> Without a scratch at all.' "

But then Jesus thought of some other words from the old books, "You must not push God too far." Then Jesus felt at peace. It was some while before such troubling thoughts came to him again.

(14) Full of enthusiasm, Jesus went back to Galilee, where he quickly became a local celebrity. He taught in the places of worship, and everyone

---

[2] Verses 23-38. This translates the essence of Luke's long genealogy, tracing Jesus' ancestry first to Abraham to assert his Jewish origins, to Adam (adam = man or mankind) to assert his full humanity, and to God, father of all, thus father of Jesus. The expression "as was supposed" attached to the parenthood of Joseph was almost certainly an addition to Luke's text, seeking to harmonize the genealogy with an interpretation of the birth narrative which saw a virgin birth. It is unlikely that Luke thought he was writing about a virgin birth. His genealogy is the clue. Everyone comes into the world as an act of God's Spirit, Jesus (and John the Dipper) included, just as everyone has God for parent, Jesus included. There is even less evidence for a virgin birth in Matthew. The Greek *parthenos* means "young woman," and Matthew, like Luke, also traces the descent of Jesus through Joseph. The scriptural evidence for a virgin birth thus ranges between the minimal and nil, and relies mainly on a literalist interpretation of a doubtful translation.

spoke well of him.

Then he visited Nazareth, his hometown. He went to worship on Saturday as usual. He offered to read and was given a book of one of God's speakers. The part he chose went like this,

> "God's Spirit has inspired me
> To bring the poor good news;
> She tells me, 'Get the blind to see,
> Bust the jails and set folk free;
> God's arms are open lovingly.' "

Jesus shut the book and gave it back to the person in charge. Then he sat down to teach. Everyone was watching him carefully. Jesus began by saying, "Today these words are coming true, and you're here to see it." Everyone found his style of speaking impressive, and made favorable comments. They said, "Is this really Joseph's boy? Isn't he doing well!" Jesus said, "I know what you're going to say, 'He's on to a good thing up there in Nahum town. How about doing something for the folks at home?' I tell you, God's speakers never get the backing they deserve from their nearest and dearest. There were many single mothers in our land in Elijah's day, when there was a drought for three and half years, and nobody had much to eat. Yet God didn't send Elijah to help any of them. Elijah went instead to the help of a single mother in Lebanon. Lots of our people had skin complaints in Elisha's day. The only one attended to by Elisha was Norman from Syria." These remarks drove them wild. They set on Jesus, rough-handled him, and took him to the top of the steep hill the village was built on. They were going to throw him over the edge, but he managed to get away.

(31) Jesus went back to Nahum town, a prosperous town in Galilee, and held a teaching session every Saturday. Everyone was impressed by what Jesus had to say. He spoke with confidence. In the place of worship was a man in a confused mental state, thought to be caused by an evil spirit. He shouted out, "Why are you pestering me, Jesus of Nazareth? Are you going to kill me? I know who you are – God's Chosen!" Jesus quickly dealt with him by saying, "Calm down and be yourself again!" The man fell over, but wasn't hurt. Then his mind cleared. All those looking on were stunned and

kept asking one another, "What special words did he use? He's got complete control over the powers of evil." Everyone over a wide area got to hear about Jesus.

After the meeting Jesus went home to Simon's house. Simon's mother-in-law had the 'flu. The family asked Jesus if he could do anything to help. Jesus stood by the bed and talked to her. She felt better at once, got up, and looked after her guests.

That evening, when the sun was going down, the townsfolk brought to Jesus people with many kinds of illness. Jesus touched each one and made them better. Lots of them were disturbed in their minds. Jesus cured them too. Some were noisy and shouted, "You're God's Likeness!" But Jesus told them to be quiet. They knew by instinct he was God's Chosen.

Early next morning, Jesus got up and found a quiet spot where he could be alone. But the crowds tracked him down. They tried to persuade him to stay in Nahum town. But Jesus said, "I must take the Good News of God's New World to the other towns. That's my job!" So Jesus took his message to the places of worship in other parts of the country.

5 One day Jesus was standing on the shore of Lake Galilee. The crowds around him were begging him to talk to them about God. He noticed two fishing boats moored on the beach. Their owners were nearby, washing their nets. One of the boats belonged to Simon. Jesus got into the boat, and asked Simon to push it a little way out from the shore. Then Jesus sat down and taught the crowds from the boat. When Jesus had finished speaking, he said to Simon, "Take the boat into deep water and let the nets down. See if you can catch anything." Simon said, "Teacher, we've been fishing all night and caught nothing. But just to please you, I'll give it a try." Simon and his crew landed such a big catch of fish that the nets started to break. So they called out to their partners in the other boat to come and help them. Together they piled both boats so high with fish, they began to sink. Simon (or Rocky as Jesus was to call him) couldn't believe his eyes. He fell down in front of Jesus, and said, "Sir, please go away. I'm no good!" The onlookers, like Rocky, couldn't believe their eyes. They had never seen so many fish caught at one time. Neither had James and John Zebedee, Simon's partners. Jesus said, "Stop worrying about your

faults, Simon. I've got a new job for you – fishing for people!" As soon as they brought the boats back to shore, the friends gave up their fishing business to stay in the company of Jesus.

(12) In one of the towns Jesus visited there was a man covered in sores. When he saw Jesus, he begged him, on his hands and knees, to help him. He said, "Sir, I'm sure you can cure me of my complaint if you want to." Jesus put his arm round him and said, "Of course I want to help you. You're going to be better now!" The man's sores began to heal straight away. Jesus asked the man not to tell anybody, but to report to the health officer, and to show his gratitude to God in the customary way. This made Jesus even more famous. Huge crowds came to hear him and get cured from their illnesses. Jesus escaped to quiet places whenever he could, to talk with God.

(17) One day there were members of the strict set present when Jesus was teaching. They came from every part of the country, including Jerusalem. At that time Jesus was highly successful as a healer. While Jesus was speaking, some people brought along a paralyzed man on a stretcher. They tried to get through the door to put him in front of Jesus, but there were too many people in the way. So they went up on the roof, took off some of the tiles, and let the man down right in the middle where Jesus was sitting. Jesus was impressed by their trust, and said, "Friend your wrongdoings are forgiven." The members of the strict set objected to these words. They said, "Who does he think he is? Surely only God can forgive sins?" Jesus knew what their problem was. He said, "What's upsetting you? You think, don't you, it's easier to say to someone who's paralyzed, 'Your wrongdoings are forgiven,' than to say, 'Get on your feet and walk!'? I'm going to show you the Complete Person can forgive wrongs here on earth!" Jesus, turning to the paralyzed man, said, "Get on your feet! Go home, and take your stretcher with you!" The man got up at once, picked up his stretcher, and walked home, shouting his thanks to God as he went. Everyone was amazed and gave thanks to God. They found it all hard to grasp, and said, "We've seen some strange things today!"

(27) The next thing Jesus did was to visit the tax office, where Levi was working for the Romans. Jesus said to him, "I want you to be my friend!" Levi got up, left his work, and went with Jesus. Then Levi held a big party in his house in Jesus' honor. A large number of collaborators like Levi, and

other outcasts, were lying on the couches, having a meal together. Some members of the strict set complained to Jesus' friends. "Why do you eat with such bad characters – traitors and their cronies?" Jesus had a word with them. He said, "It's those who are ill need a doctor, not those who are well. I don't ask people who think they've nothing wrong with them to be my friends. I call the people you label 'bad' to a new life."

Then the strict set raised another matter with Jesus. "John the Dipper's followers, and members of our set, often go without food, and spend the time talking to God. But your friends spend all their time bingeing." Jesus said, "Do you expect wedding guests to turn up their noses at the food? That would be rude to the host! One day the party will be over. No one will feel like eating then!"

Then Jesus gave them a riddle to think about. "You don't tear a piece from a new shirt to patch an old one. The new shirt will be ruined, and the patch on the old shirt will look odd. You don't put new wine into dirty old bottles. You'd ruin the wine that way! You need fresh clean bottles for new wine!"

6 One Rest Day, Jesus and his friends were going for a walk through the cornfields. They plucked some of the corn, rubbed it in their hands to remove the husks, and ate it. Some members of the strict set saw what they were doing, and said, "Do you realize you're breaking the rules of the Rest Day?" Jesus said, "Haven't you ever read what David did when he and his friends were hungry? He went into the house of God, took and ate the special bread which only the clergy were allowed to eat, and he gave some to his friends." Then he told them, "The Complete Person has freedom to decide what can be done on the Rest Day."

Another Rest Day, Jesus went to a place of worship to give some teaching. A man was there who had lost the use of his right hand. The strict set were watching to see if Jesus would heal the man on the Rest Day, as they wanted to catch him breaking the rules. Although Jesus knew what they were thinking, he said to the man, "Come and stand by me." He jumped from his place, and stood by Jesus. Then Jesus said to the others, "Tell me, should we help people on the Rest Day, or should we do them harm? Should we give life or destroy it?" His eyes swept the room, appealing to everybody. Then Jesus said to the man, "Hold out your hand!" As he did, the man found he could move his fingers again. The strict set were livid, and got together to work out how to put a stop to Jesus.

(12) About that time, Jesus sought out a quiet spot up in the mountains. He spent a night there talking with God. Next day he called his friends together, and chose twelve of them to help him in his work. They were Simon, who Jesus nicknamed "Rocky" and his brother Andrew, James, John, Philip, Bart, Matthew, Twin, James (Alf's son), Simon (nicknamed "Hothead"), Jude (James's son), and Judas from Kerioth who was to turn traitor.

(17) Jesus brought his band of helpers down from the mountains to a flat piece of ground, where he got together a big crowd of followers, and many interested people from all over the country and from abroad. They wanted to hear Jesus and be made fully healthy. Those suffering from anxiety or depression, found peace of mind. Everyone tried to touch him. They all felt better just by being close to him. He spoke these words to his followers in particular:

> *"You're the important ones now, those of you who haven't*
> *got much.*
> *You're citizens of God's New World.*
>
> *You're the important ones now, those of you who are hungry.*
> *You're going to have plenty to eat.*
>
> *You're the important ones now, those of you who are grieving.*
> *You'll soon be laughing.*
>
> *Think yourselves privileged when people despise and reject*
> *you, and when they insult you and call you names for being*
> *true to the ideals of the Complete Person. Hold your heads*
> *high and keep your spirits up when that happens. Better things*
> *are on the way to you in the world to come. The ancestors of*
> *those who ill-treat you, treated God's speakers in the past in*
> *the same way.*

To the back of the queue, those who are loaded with money!
You've had your prizes!

To the back of the back of the queue, those who are over-fed!
There won't be any food to spare for you!

To the back of the queue, those who laugh at others!
It's your turn to feel hurt!

To the back of the queue, those who seek to be popular
*   and famous!*
The ancestors of the type who applaud you were taken in
*   by the frauds of days gone by.*

(27) "Listen to what I say: Love your enemies, and do good to those who want to harm you. Ask God to help those who speak badly of you or treat you roughly. Instead of putting up your fists when someone picks a fight with you, lower your guard. If someone steals something from you, don't be possessive about what you've got left. Respond readily to everyone who asks a favor, and if anyone gets hold of something belonging to you, don't insist on having it back. Treat others as you would like them to treat you.

"What's so very special about loving those who love you? Even people you label 'bad' manage to do that. It doesn't count if you do a good turn to someone who's done a good turn to you. Almost anyone will do that! If you only lend money in order to make a profit, you're no better than a gambler placing a bet on the favorite. Love your enemies, do good to those unlikely to do anything for you, and lend money to people unlikely to pay it back. This will be your great reward – you'll know you're sharing God's character. God is kind to those who show no gratitude and to those who behave badly. The Loving God makes allowances. So should you!

(37) "Don't think the worst of other people, unless you want other people to think the worst of you! Don't send anyone to the scrap heap, or that's where you'll end up! Forgive and you'll be forgiven. Be generous, and generosity will come your way. Life will be so rich and full for you; you'll constantly be amazed. You get out of life what you put into it."

Then Jesus told them a story about someone who didn't know the district trying to show someone else the way. They both got lost! He said, "Students shouldn't try to give the teacher lessons before qualifying as teachers themselves. How is it you see a speck of sawdust in someone else's eye, when you're walking around with a great plank in your own? You've got a cheek to say, 'Would you like me to take that bit of dirt out of your eye?' with that plank blocking your view! You humbug! You're not qualified to help someone else with their problem until you've owned up to your own!

"You're no more likely to have a good time with prickly people than you are to find your favorite food in a bed of thistles. Only a good-hearted person can do genuine good. The 'holier-than-thou' type only cause grief. They say unpleasant things because they're unpleasant people.

"I'd rather you didn't try to flatter me with respectful titles like 'Reverend' and 'Sir' if you've no intention of doing what I ask you. I tell you, anyone who comes to me for advice, and acts on it, is like a builder who digs down deeply and sets the foundations for a house on solid rock. When the floods come and the water lashes the side of the house, it will hold firm because it's been built with care. Anyone who hears what I have to say, but ignores my advice, is like a sloppy builder who builds a house on loose soil. Just one flood, and the whole lot comes tumbling down. There's nothing left but a heap of rubble."

7 After a long teaching session in the open air, Jesus went back into Nahum town. A Roman army officer there had a houseboy he was deeply attached to. The boy was very ill and looked likely to die. The officer heard about Jesus, and sent some of the religious leaders to him, to ask him to come and heal his friend. When they came to Jesus, they spoke warmly on his behalf. They said, "He really deserves your help. He loves our people and built our worship center." Jesus went along with them, but when he was close to the house, the officer sent some friends out to Jesus with a message, "Please Sir, don't put yourself to any trouble on my account. I'm not fit to invite you into my home. That's why I didn't come to you in person. But I'm sure if you say the right words, my companion will get better. Your profession is like mine in a way. We've both been given charge over others by a higher authority. The soldiers in my unit obey my

orders. The people who look after my house do as I ask. One word from me is enough." Jesus was very impressed by the officer's way of putting things. He turned round to the people who were with him and said, "I'll tell you something. I haven't come across any of my own race with as much confidence in me!" The messengers went back to the house and found the officer's houseboy in good health.[3]

(11) Soon after, Jesus visited a pretty village called Nain. His friends and many other people walked there with him. As he came to the entrance to the village, he met a funeral coming the opposite way. The man being carried out for burial was his mother's only son. She had already lost her husband. Many friends from the village were by her side. When Jesus learnt the circumstances, he felt very deeply for her. He said to her, "Dry your eyes." Then he went over and gently tapped the stretcher. The bearers stopped in their tracks. Then Jesus said, "Come on, young man, time to get up!" The boy everyone had given up for dead, sat up and began to talk. Jesus called his mother to come and look after him. At first, a lot of people were frightened. Then they shouted their thanks to God. They said, "It's great to have one of God's great speakers among us. He's the sign of God's love for us!" This high regard for Jesus spread far and wide.[4]

(18) John the Dipper got a report from his followers of what Jesus was doing. So John asked two of them to visit Jesus to ask, "Are you the one we've been expecting, or do we have to wait for someone else?" At the very time John's friends brought the message, Jesus had just been curing a lot of people from many kinds of illness, including blindness. So Jesus answered John's friends like this: "Go back to John and tell him what you've seen and heard. Blind people are getting their sight back, disabled people are able to get about, people with skin complaints no longer feel like outcasts, deaf people can hear again, some have been brought back from the point of death, and the poor are getting some good news at last! That should cheer

---

[3] Greek *doulos* = slave. The word slave is avoided throughout this translation, in line with the principle of "cultural translation." Here a variety of words is used to throw light on the probable situation – "house boy," "friend," "companion" – the man was obviously all of these. Whether the relationship was a gay one cannot be decided for certain. The centurion's feeling of unworthiness may have stemmed from his knowledge that whereas such a relationship was acceptable in his culture, it was not amongst the orthodox Jews he admired.

[4] Nain = modern Nein. Possible Hebrew meaning "beauty spot."

you up. Don't be put off by my way of doing things!"

When the messengers had gone, Jesus spoke about John the Dipper to the crowd around him. "When you went out into the desert, what were you expecting to see? Royalty? A popular politician?[5] What then? Were you hoping to see a fashion parade? The palace is the place, if that's what you're looking for! Why did you choose such an uncomfortable destination for your day out? Did you go to hear one of God's speakers, the kind not seen since the old days? Yes, that's why you made that hard trek. But John was more than an old time preacher, wasn't he? You'll find him mentioned in the old books.

> *'Watch out! My envoy's on the way*
> *To set the stage for that great day!'*

I believe John is the most significant figure of our time. But you'll all be significant in God's New World, even more than John. Ordinary people took to John, even the social outcasts who collect taxes for the Romans. They realized John was doing God's work. That's why they went to be dipped by him in the river. But the strict set refused to be dipped by John, and so put themselves outside God's plan for them.

"Do you remember the games we used to play in the street when we were children – weddings and funerals? When our team played music, the others had to dance; but if we sang funeral songs, they had to cry. Some children got the sulks and wouldn't play. Then we would sing:

> *'To dance the tune you didn't try,*
> *And when we wailed you wouldn't cry!'*

There are people like that today. John the Dipper only ate what he could pick up in the desert, and has never touched strong drink. So you call him mad. Because, like most people, I enjoy my food with a jug of wine, you say,

---

[5] "A popular politician" – literally "a bent reed," sarcasm by which the Jewish people would have understood Herod Antipas, since it was the symbol on his coins. The pattern here suggests a humorous repartee between Jesus and the crowd. To the first two questions the crowd would have laughingly shouted out "No!" and to the third "Yes."

'Look at him, spending all his time at parties, mixing with the lowest of the low!' Intelligent folk make the right response on the right occasion."

(36) One of the strict set, called Simon, invited Jesus home for a meal. Jesus went into his house and lay out on one of the couches where the food was being served. One of the town prostitutes with a bad reputation found out that Jesus was there.[6] She came in with a jar of highly scented oil and stood by Jesus. She started to cry, and used her tears to wash Jesus' feet. Then she dried them with her hair. She kissed his feet over and over again and massaged them with the oil. Simon was very shocked by this and thought, "If this fellow were one of God's speakers, he'd know who this woman is, making advances to him like that, and what she does for a living." Jesus turned to him and said, "I've something to say to you, Simon." He said, "Alright, Teacher, let's hear it!"

"There were once two people who'd borrowed money from a moneylender. One owed five hundred pounds, the other just fifty. Neither of them could pay the money back, so the moneylender cancelled their debts. Which one of them will appreciate the moneylender most?" Simon said, "The one, I imagine, who had the biggest debt."

Then Jesus looked back to the woman again. "Take a good look at this woman, Simon. When I came in from the street you didn't trouble to provide a bowl of water for me to wash my feet, but she's washed my feet with her tears, and dried them with her hair. I've not had one kiss from you, but she's not stopped kissing my feet ever since she came in. You didn't put a spot of oil on my head as is customary with an honored guest, but she's massaged my feet with expensive perfume. So you see, she must have been forgiven for the many things she's done wrong. That's why she loves me so much. Those who think they've very little to be forgiven for, don't show much love." Then Jesus said to the woman, "You're okay by me!"

The other guests discussed the incident among themselves. Some said, "Who does he think he is, letting people off as lightly as that?" Finally, Jesus said to the woman, "Your trust in me has given you new life. From now on, I want you to feel good about yourself!"

---

[6] Greek. "Woman of the town," as today, euphemism for prostitute.

8 Jesus now went on a tour of the towns and villages, telling people the Good News about God's New World. As well as his twelve male helpers, Jesus had several women on his team. Some of these Jesus had helped with personality problems and weaknesses. They included, among others, Maggie, who had been an extremely difficult person before meeting Jesus, Joan, the wife of one of Herod's chief ministers, and Susan. These women were well off, and helped with expenses. One day a big crowd came together from towns near and far away. Jesus told them a riddle. It went like this: "A farmer was sowing his crop. As he scattered the seed, some of it fell on the path and the birds swooped down and ate it up. Some fell on rocky ground, but when the shoots came up they withered, because the soil was too dry. Some seed fell among thistles. The thistles grew and the plants were choked. Other seed fell into good soil and yielded a fine crop of grain, a hundred times what the farmer sowed. If you've got ears, use them!"

Later Jesus' friends asked him the meaning of the riddle. Jesus said, "You're the lucky ones. You get to know the solutions to my riddles about God's New World. To others they are still just riddles. The old books talk about people who look without seeing and listen without hearing."

(Here's the solution to the riddle: The seed is a message from God. The seed on the path means people who hear the words, but evil thoughts wipe them clean from their minds. They don't give themselves a chance to trust and live. The seed on rocky ground refers to people who get excited by the message and trust it for a short time, but when they meet the first difficulty, they give up. The seed among the thistles stands for those who listen, but when they get home, the cares of daily life, greed, or obsession with trivial things, prevent the message from having any relevance. As for the seeds sown on good ground, they are like people who get the message and really take it to heart. They survive all life's ups and downs, and have something to show for it at the end.)[7]

Jesus said, "You don't light a lamp, then put it under a bed or a flower pot. You put it on a lamp stand, so that when your guests arrive, they can see. There's nothing hidden that won't be exposed, and no secret that won't come to light. You must listen carefully. The more attention you pay to

---

[7] It may be noticed we do not use inverted commas for this section. The explanation of the parable is probably from the Gospel-writer, Mark, used here by Luke.

what's being said, the more you'll get out of it. Those who don't listen, end up losing their ability to listen."

One day, Jesus' mother and brothers came to see him, but the crowd was blocking the doorway. Someone got a message to Jesus, "Your family's outside. They want a word with you." Jesus said, "My true family are those who listen to God's message and do something about it."

(22) One day Jesus and his friends went out in the boat. Jesus said, "Let's go right across to the other side of the lake." They set sail, and soon Jesus fell asleep. A freak storm swept across the lake, and the boat began to take in water. They were in real danger. The friends shook Jesus and shouted, "Boss, wake up, we're sinking!" Jesus woke up and stood firm against the wind and the rough water. There was a sudden change in the weather, and everything went calm. Jesus said, "Where's your trust?" The friends were frightened and didn't know what to think. They said, "Who is this? He even has the weather under control!"

Jesus and his friends landed near the town of Kursa, which is on the other side of the lake from Galilee. As Jesus was getting out of the boat, a man who was mentally ill came to meet him. For a long time he had not worn any clothes, or had anywhere decent to live. He sheltered in the caves where the dead were buried. When he saw Jesus, he fell down in front of him and screamed, "Leave me alone, Jesus. You're God's Chosen. For God's sake stop torturing me!" Jesus quickly got to grips with the man's case. He learnt that he had frequent attacks, when he had to be guarded and tied down. Sometimes he would break loose and run off into the desert. Jesus asked him, "What's your name?" "My name's Legion," he said, "I'm so many people all in one. Please don't have me put away!" On the hillside nearby, a large herd of pigs was feeding. Confused voices from the man's mind begged Jesus, "Why can't we plague the life out of those pigs instead?!" Jesus said, "Okay, off you go!" The pigs rushed down the bank into the lake and drowned.

The farm workers looking after the pigs saw what happened and ran off to tell their neighbors in the town and the surrounding district. People came out to see what was going on. They found the man having a serious talk with Jesus. He was fully dressed, and his mind was clear. They were still afraid of him. When the farm workers told how the man had been healed,

LUKE'S GOOD NEWS (PART ONE)

the locals asked Jesus to leave the district. They were anxious about the rest of their livestock. As Jesus was getting back into the boat, the man who had been cured begged to go with him. But Jesus pointed him toward his home. He said, "That's where you should be now. Your family need you. Tell them what God has done for you." Off he went and told everyone in the town how Jesus had helped him.

(40) When Jesus got back, there was a big crowd waiting for him. He had a warm welcome. A leader of the community called Jay came up to Jesus, grabbed him by the arm and asked him to come to his house. His only daughter, twelve years old, was dying.

As he made his way, Jesus was hampered by all the people crowding round him. One of these was a woman who had been suffering from bleeding for twelve years. She had spent all her money on doctors, without success. She came up behind Jesus and touched the edge of his coat. Her bleeding stopped immediately. Then Jesus said, "Who touched me?" No one owned up. Rocky said, "Come on now, Boss, with all these people so tight around you, it would make more sense to ask who isn't touching you!" Jesus said, "I know someone touched me. I felt my energy being used." The woman realized she had been found out. Trembling with fear, she fell down in front of Jesus and told her story for everyone to hear. Jesus said to her, "Friend, your trust in me has made you well again. Don't worry. Everything's going to be alright."

While Jesus was still talking to the woman, someone came from Jay's house with a message, "No need to trouble the doctor any further. Your little girl has died." Jesus overheard and said to Jay, "Don't be afraid; trust me. She's going to be alright." When Jesus arrived at the house, he only allowed Rocky, James, and John to go with him with the child's father and mother into the bedroom. The members of the house staff were making a racket with all their crying, but Jesus said, "Stop crying. She's not dead, only asleep." They sniggered, truly believing she was dead. Then Jesus took hold of the girl's hand, and said in a clear voice, "Time to get up, little one!" She woke up and got out of bed. Jesus told the staff to bring her a snack. Jay and his wife were amazed. But Jesus asked them to keep the matter quiet.

9 Jesus held a training course to teach his twelve special helpers how to heal the sick in body and mind. Then he sent them round the country, to tell people about God's New World, and to offer healing. He gave them this advice: "Travel light. You don't need a pack or walking stick, no food or money, nor a change of clothes for that matter. If you're offered hospitality, stay in the same home until you leave the district. As for any place not giving you a welcome, leave as quickly as you can, and put the experience behind you." So they left Jesus and went on a tour of the villages, passing on the Good News and healing the sick.

When Herod, the ruler of Galilee, heard what was going on, he was puzzled. The rumor was that John the Dipper had come back from the dead, or that Elijah had arrived, or that another of God's speakers from the old days had reappeared. Herod said, "I had John's head cut off, so who's this everybody's talking about?" He tried many times to get to see Jesus.

When they got back, the friends gave Jesus a full report. Then he took them on a private retreat to Fishtown. But the crowds found out where he was, and caught up with him. He made everybody welcome, talked about God's New World, and attended to anyone who needed healing.

It was near the end of the day, and Jesus' friends came to him and said, "It's time for all these people to go on their way. They need to get to the villages to buy food while the shops are still open, or to find accommodation for the night. Jesus said, "Why don't you give them something to eat?" The friends said, "All we've got is five loaves and two fish, unless you mean us to go and buy food for this lot?" (The crowd numbered about five thousand.) Jesus said, "Get the people to sit down in groups of about fifty." When they were all in their groups and sitting down, Jesus took the five loaves and the two fish, and asked God to use them. Then he broke the bread and fish, and gave the pieces to his helpers to take round to the people. Everybody had something, and felt afterwards they'd had all they needed. The leftovers filled twelve baskets!

(18) One day Jesus was talking with God as one person to another. Only his close friends were there to hear him. Afterwards he asked them, "Who do ordinary people think I am?" They said, "You remind them of John the Dipper; others think you're like Elijah, or one of God's speakers from the old days." Then Jesus said, "And what do you think of me?" Rocky

answered, "You're God's Chosen." Then Jesus urged them, in the strongest possible terms, not to reveal this to anyone. "First of all," Jesus said, "the Complete Person is going to be cruelly treated. The leaders of all the religious groups will turn against him. He'll be killed, but three days later he'll come back to life again."

These are words Jesus spoke to all his friends: "If you want to be my followers, you must stop trying to please yourselves. Each day's task will be like carrying a cross. You must learn to do things my way. Those who try to save their lives will lose them, but those who lose their lives for me will make their lives complete. What's the point of having everything, if you aren't true to yourself? As for those who are embarrassed by me and by my ideas now, it will be even more embarrassing for them one day, when they see the Complete Person and all his helpers, brightly dressed for the great celebration, in the presence of the Loving God. But, believe me, some of you here won't die before you see the dawn of God's New World."

About a week after telling his friends all this, Jesus took Rocky, James, and John up a mountain. While Jesus was talking with God, his face looked different, and his white clothes sparkled in the strong light. Suddenly they noticed two people talking to Jesus. These must be the former leaders, Moses and Elijah! They looked radiant. They were talking about Jesus' coming death in Jerusalem, and how it would bring a new era, like the one Moses brought about. Rocky and his friends were drowsy, but awake enough to see the splendid sight of Jesus and his companions. As the two were leaving, Rocky said to Jesus, "It's great up here, Boss! Let's make three shrines, one for you, one for Moses, and one for Elijah!" Rocky blurted this out without thinking. At that moment, the clouds came down thick on the mountain and gave them the shivers. Then they heard a voice coming out of the mists, saying, "*This* is my Own, my Chosen; listen to *him*." After the voice, they saw Jesus again, but he was on his own. The friends kept quiet about this experience until some time afterwards.

Next day, after they had come down from the mountain, a big crowd was waiting for Jesus. A man in the crowd shouted, "Please have a look at my son. He's my only child. He has fits, and screams without warning. His whole body shakes, and he foams at the mouth. He's in great distress, and hardly has a moment free from anxiety. I asked your assistants to help him, but they didn't know what to do." Jesus said to his friends, "What a useless bunch you are! How long do I have to put up with you?" Then he said to the man, "Bring your boy here." The boy was seized by a fit as he was being brought to Jesus. He rolled on the ground, shaking from head to toe. Jesus spoke to him, and he recovered at once. Then Jesus told his father to take him home. Everyone was thrilled, seeing what God could do. But Jesus chose this moment to say to his friends. "Please listen carefully. The Complete Person is going to be betrayed. He'll be powerless in the hands of ruthless people." But they could not understand what Jesus said, and were afraid to ask.

(46) Once the friends of Jesus were arguing about which of them would be the most famous. Jesus understood their way of thinking, so he took a little child, and stood her by his side. Jesus said, "Whoever gives this child a place of honor as I do, gives a place of honor to me and the one I represent. It's the little people who are the most important." John said, "Boss, we saw someone who doesn't belong to us healing people by using your name, and we tried to put a stop to it." But Jesus said, "That was wrong of you. You should have recognized someone like that as your ally."

The life of Jesus was drawing to its climax. Jesus was determined to go to Jerusalem. He sent some of his friends on ahead of him to book accommodation in the places they were to pass through. They tried a village in Samaria, but the people there showed their racial prejudice by having nothing to do with him. They realized that Jesus was a Jew, because he was on the way to a festival in Jerusalem. James and John were angry, and said to Jesus, "Leader, would you like us to ask God to send lightning from the sky, to set the village on fire?" But Jesus gave them a stern talking to. He said, "You must put a stop to those angry feelings of yours. The Complete Person doesn't set out to kill people, but to bring them to life." So they went on to the next village.

As Jesus and his friends were walking along the road, someone came up to him and said, "Can I join your team? I'll stick by you whatever happens." Jesus said, "Foxes have holes they can bolt to, and birds can fly up to their nests, but there's no place of rest for the Complete Person." To another Jesus said, "Come and join me." But the reply Jesus got was, "Leader, can you give me a few days to make arrangements for my father's funeral?" Jesus said,

"Leave that to someone with nothing better to do. Your job is to tell people about God's New World." Someone else said to Jesus, "I'd like to come with you, but first I must go and say goodbye to my family." Jesus said, "In God's New World you must fix your eyes on the future. You won't make headway, if you keep harking back to the past!"

10

In addition to the men and women Jesus assigned to special duties at the start of his work, he later added about seventy others and sent them to towns and districts he planned to visit.[8] He told them, "There's a bumper harvest out there, but we're short of workers. We must ask the farmer to take on some more. It's time for you to get going. Remember you're going to find yourselves without protection in places where the inhabitants may be dangerous. You'll be safer without money or bag or sandals. Don't get talking to anyone you meet on the road. As you go into a house for the first time say, 'We're here on a friendly visit.' If they're friendly in return, seek to form a closer friendship with them. If they're unfriendly, leave them alone. Stay in the same home for the whole of your visit, and eat and drink whatever is put in front of you. If you do your work well, you'll deserve to be well looked after. But don't go moving from house to house to see if you can get anything better. And if the people of a town put on a special welcome meal for you, don't be fussy about the food. Heal the sick while you're in that town, and say to them, 'The good things of God's New World are for you.' If you get a bad reception, hold a peaceful demonstration in the street, and say, 'We're going on our way, because you have not made us feel at home. Even so, we leave you with this message, "God's New World has come near to you today." ' Believe me, that day even Sodom will rank higher than that place."[9]

---

[8] The number seventy together with the term "others" may symbolize the Gentiles. (Genesis 10 lists the number of the nations of the earth as 70, and "others" was a common euphemism for Gentiles.) Luke seems to be describing a mission to Gentile or semi-Gentile territory, just over the border from Galilee, which Jesus himself visited on occasions. The mission may be the equivalent in Luke to the feeding of the four thousand in Mark and Matthew which was probably also a Gentile or semi-Gentile occasion in the same territory. In line with this impression are the favorable comments of Jesus on his reception in Gentile towns (v. 14 Tyre and Sidon in modern Lebanon) in contrast to those in Galilee (v. 13). See also vs. 7-8 where the missionaries are not to insist on kosher food.

[9] Sodom is significant for Jesus, not for its sexual ambiguity, but for its notorious breach of the customs of hospitality.

Jesus said, "Shame on you, Dancetown! Shame on you, Fishtown! If the towns of Lebanon had seen me at work as you have, they would have speedily changed their ways. God will excuse Tyre and Sidon, but there's no excuse for you! And don't look so smug, Nahum town. You expect to be top of the class, don't you? Bottom more likely!"

Then Jesus turned again to his new helpers, and said, "Anyone who listens to you will be listening to me, and anyone who rejects you rejects me and the one I represent."

The seventy-strong team came back in high spirits. They said, "Leader, we even cured people who were mentally ill!" Jesus said, "I saw it all in my mind's eye. I saw evil quickly losing ground. My training has enabled you to cope in some very tricky situations, and to come through without a scratch! But that's nothing to boast about. You should be more pleased that you're on God's list of friends."

Jesus was in a merry mood and expressed his feelings to God like this: "I thank you, Loving God, ruler of time and space, that your truth cannot be grasped by the clever, but only by the simple and straightforward. Yes, Loving God, that was a good idea of yours! You've put me in charge, just as a parent would give a trusted child an important task. You know me better than anybody, and I'm the only one who knows you, apart from those I share my secrets with."

When Jesus was alone except for his closest friends, he said, "You're a lucky bunch! You get to see it all! Many famous people, thinkers and rulers, would have given anything to have your insights, but they never got the chance."

(25) It was about that time a member of the strict set thought of a question to test Jesus. He asked, "Teacher, how can I achieve life to the full?" Jesus said, "I'm sure you know the rule books well. What do they say?" He said, "You must love God with your feelings and your will, your strength and your intelligence. You must also love the person next to you as you love yourself." Jesus said, "That's right. Stick to those principles and you'll really live." The man felt the need to probe further, so he went on to ask Jesus, "What is meant by 'the person next to me'?" In reply Jesus told this story: "Someone was traveling the rough road from Jerusalem to Jericho and was set on by a gang of thugs. They took his clothes, beat him up, and ran off,

leaving him unconscious. The first person to come along happened to be a high-ranking religious leader. When he saw the man, he hurried by on the other side of the road. Next someone who helped to keep the worship center clean and tidy came along. He went over, had a good look at the man, then walked on. A while later one of the Samaritans you despise so much came by. When he saw the battered man, he was moved to tears. He went over to him, put wine and olive oil on his cuts and bruises, bandaged him up, and put him on his donkey. When he came to a hotel he booked a room and took care of him. Next day he gave some money to the manager and said, 'Look after him well. On my way back, if you have any extra costs, I'll pay the rest of the bill.' Which of the three travelers saw the man who was mugged as the person next to them?" The member of the strict set said, "The one who put him back on his feet." Jesus said, "Be like him!"

(38) One day Jesus visited a village and was invited by a woman called Martha into her home. She had a sister called Mary who gave Jesus the attention an eager student gives a teacher, hanging on his every word. But Martha had a pile of work to do in the kitchen. So she interrupted them and said, "Leader, do you realize that while my sister is sitting here with you, I've been left to do the cooking on my own? Ask her to give me a hand." But Jesus said, "Martha, Martha, you're trying to do too many things at once. You'll get stressed out. Come and sit here with Mary. She knows how to relax and get the best out of my visit."

11 One day, after Jesus had been talking with God, one of his friends said to him, "Leader, teach us how to talk with God. John the Dipper taught his friends!" Jesus said, "When you talk with God, say something like this:

> *'Loving God,*
> *help us proclaim your values*
> *and bring in your New World.*
> *Supply us our day-to-day needs.*
> *Forgive us for wounding you,*
> *while we forgive those who wound us.*
> *Give us courage to meet life's trials.'* "

Jesus went on to say, "Imagine one of you has a friend, and you knock on her door in the middle of the night and shout, 'Have you got any food to spare? A visitor has just turned up, and I've got nothing in the house.' She shouts back, 'Stop making all that noise. You'll wake the children. We're all in bed. I'm not getting up at this time of night.' But if you keep banging the door, putting your friendship at risk, she'll get up and give you whatever you want, just to get rid of you! So if you're determined and persistent, you'll get what you're after.

"Those who ask questions learn; those who explore discover; those who knock get invited in. Some of you have children. When they're hungry, do you give them food that's gone off? When they're thirsty, do you give them poison? You're a rotten lot, but you look after your children and give them the right things. God is the very best of parents. So when you ask for God's Spirit, you'll receive her."

(14) On one occasion Jesus was helping someone with a speech defect. Afterwards the person was able to speak normally. Those who watched were amazed. But some of them said, "He knows how to deal with evil because he's evil himself!" Others kept on asking him to do magic. Jesus knew their minds. He said, "Countries which have civil wars end up as deserts with every house in ruins. If evil is turning on itself, its end is near. I know you say I heal by using evil powers. If that's the case, what about the healers you approve of? Ask them what they think. They'll put you right! Once you accept I'm healing on God's behalf, you'll see God's New World, right in front of your eyes. We're ready for those intent on mischief, and equipped to deal with them. Make up your mind whose side you're on. Anyone who doesn't support me in the good work I'm doing is a troublemaker."

(24) Here's another story Jesus told: "Once a dirty old tramp was thrown out of an empty house where he'd been squatting. He looked all round the town for somewhere suitable to sleep, but couldn't find anywhere. Then he thought he would try his old place again. It was still empty, so he broke in. He saw that someone had cleaned up his mess while he'd been away. Then he had an idea. He invited seven other tramps even more grubby than himself to share the squat. The mess they all made together was much worse than when he had lived there on his own." When Jesus had finished

telling the story, a woman in the audience shouted out, "I bet your mother's proud of you. I'd be, if I were your mother!" Jesus said, "Save your kind remarks for those who do what God asks of them."

The crowds going to hear Jesus were getting bigger and bigger. Jesus said, "People today are very wrong-minded. They want to see something spectacular. All they'll get will be a reminder of the story of Jonah. Just as Jonah was the only chance for the people of Nineveh, the Complete Person is the only chance for the people of our time. The African Queen, who made a long journey to seek advice from Solomon, will condemn you. There's better advice to be had here today! The people of Nineveh will condemn you, because when Jonah gave them God's message, they changed their ways. The message is even clearer today! We see with our eyes. If you've got good eyesight, your whole body can move around freely. If you've got bad eyesight, you'll bump into things. So get your eyes checked! In other words, be honest with yourself. Then you'll have a light inside you shining outwards, like a lamp. Everything happening around you will be clear to you."

(37) After Jesus had finished speaking, a member of the strict set invited Jesus home for a meal. Jesus went straight into the dining room to the couches arranged for the guests. His host was put out that Jesus did not first make use of his posh bath suite. So Jesus said to him, "You strict people wash your cups in a special way, in case they've been used by bad people, but the wine you drink from those same cups is bought from the profits of greed. How stupid you are! God knows you inside and out. Deal with your greed; unload your surplus wealth; then everything about you will be clean."[10]

Jesus said, "The world would be a happier place without you Holy Joes! You pay your religious dues on time, but you've forgotten the most important thing your religion asks of you – social justice, the true love of God.

"Take a running jump, you Holy Joes! You sit up front in the places of worship, so that everybody can see how important you are, and you like

---

[10] A precise procedure of ritual washing was expected of the good Jew. The use of the word "baptizo" = dip, suggests the host possessed a bathing suite on the Roman pattern, a mark of considerable affluence.

people in the high street to greet you respectfully. You're as false as hell! You're like new-cut turf laid to hide a row of graves. You look good on the surface, but what's underneath?"

A lawyer interrupted Jesus and said, "Teacher, I find what you're saying about my companions very insulting." Jesus said, "We can do without you guardians of public morals, too. You tie up heavy parcels for other people to stagger along with, and you never offer to lighten anyone's load. You stink, the lot of you! You design fine memorials for the good people your ancestors murdered. It's a family business; some of you do the killing, some of you build the tombs."

(These words of Jesus remind us of what it says in one of the old books. "God says, 'I'm sending you gifted speakers and able leaders, some of whom you'll persecute or murder.' " Yes, it's pious people who are to blame for that dreadful persecution of God's people, which stretches from the time of that good man Abel, to Gary who was murdered in the worship area of the temple. Those guilty of these wrongs are still around today.)

Jesus continued, "You're in the way, you sticklers for the rules. When people were eager to learn, you locked the door marked 'knowledge' and threw away the key."

When Jesus got outside, the strict set made obvious their dislike of him. They bombarded him with hostile questions, and gave him no peace, hoping to catch him off his guard.

12 Sometimes the crowds became too big, and there was a danger of people getting hurt. So Jesus aimed his teaching at those who genuinely wanted to learn. He told them, "Don't be influenced by the strict set. They're play-acting. They'll be found out one day. Don't do or say anything in private that will cause you embarrassment when it's public knowledge.

"Friends, don't be afraid of those who are out to kill you. If they succeed, they won't be able to harm you any more. God is the one you need to pay attention to. It's in God's hands whether you live or die forever. Keep your minds on God! Have you heard? They've got sparrows on offer in the market, five for a pound! They may be cheap in the market, but each one is precious to God. You're precious too. God notices when you're putting weight on or losing it, before you notice it yourself. You've nothing to fear with such a God looking after you. Don't undervalue yourselves!

"I promise those who stand up for me, I will claim them as friends and introduce them to God's friends. I can't say the same for those who are ashamed to own me.

"You can have your reservations about my community if you wish. But you're in real trouble if you label 'evil' the good things that come from God's Spirit. That displays a moral blindness not open to being put right.

"When you find yourselves having to make a defense, whether in a place of worship or in the public courts, don't worry about what to say. Rely on God's Spirit; she will prompt you!"

(13) Someone in the crowd shouted out to Jesus, "Teacher, my brother's done me out of my share of the family property. Tell him to put it right." Jesus said, "I'm not a judge. I'm not qualified to decide your case. But I will say this, to you and to everybody else: Watch that monster 'Greed.' Quality of life doesn't depend on how much money or property you have."

Then Jesus told a story. "There was once a rich farmer whose farm over-produced. He was short of the storage space he needed while waiting for the prices to be right. It caused him great anxiety. 'What am I going to do?' he thought to himself. Then he made a big decision. 'I know,' he said, 'I'll pull down these old barns and build bigger and better ones. Then with room for my surplus, I'll be able to retire on the profits. I'll be able to do all the things I've always wanted to do, take holidays abroad, go to parties and have a good time.' But God said, 'You chump! This is the last day of your life. Your wealth is useless to you now. You're so thoughtless, you haven't even made a will!' That's what people are like who spend their time making money and don't give God a chance to give them things of real value."

Jesus turned to his friends and said, "So stop worrying about things of no importance. What does it matter what you eat or drink or whether your clothes are in fashion? A good life doesn't depend on going to posh restaurants or having the right wardrobe. Take a tip from the crows. They don't go to work every day, or put their money in a bank when they get paid, but God makes sure they have something to eat. You rate yourselves more highly than the birds, don't you? You won't make your life last any longer by worrying about it. What's the point of worry when there's so little you can do to change things? Be like the wild flowers. They don't earn their living, yet they're better dressed than Solomon with all his beads and bangles! Since God cares so much about the looks of the grass which ends up as stubble in a matter of days, God is bound to see to your clothes. It's more trust you need! It's time to stop vexing yourselves with questions like, 'Where shall we eat tonight?' or 'Have we ordered the right wine to go with the meal?' You'll make yourselves ill, having to make so many decisions! People who are bothered by such questions don't yet know God. God loves you, and knows what's best for you. Help to bring about God's New World. Then there'll be enough for everybody.

"Don't be frightened if the tasks ahead seem too big for so few of you. The New World is *God's* project. The Loving God will make a present of it to you. So sell all those luxuries and give the money to charity. Treasure those things that last the test of time. That way you won't need to worry about burglars or breaking things. You can tell what a person is like by what they value.

(35) "Be ready to come to the help of others at a moment's notice. You should be like a business expecting the boss to arrive at any time, or a team likely to have an inspection any day. When the boss arrives, he'll be so pleased by what he finds, he'll invite all his employees to a slap-up lunch at his expense. He'll pretend to be the waiter! Even if the boss arrives at an inconvenient moment, his team will still have smiles on their faces because they're ready for every emergency.

"Think about this: If a householder knew the exact time a thief planned to break in, the police would be there, ready to make an arrest. But since you don't know when the Complete Person is coming, you must keep your wits about you every moment."

Rocky said, "Leader are you just talking to us, your friends, or to everybody?" This is how the Leader replied: "I think of you as managers in a business. Imagine two very different types of manager, each put in charge of a branch of the business, with instructions to look after the employees. One manager is pleased when the boss arrives to find everything being done properly. Promotion to a higher branch will follow. The other manager uses the boss's absence as a chance to bully colleagues, subject the women on the staff to sexual harassment, and run up a big drinks bill. One day the boss will arrive unexpectedly and give that manager the sack. Perhaps some employees of the firm are more aware of the standards expected by the boss than others. Those who should have known better will get a severe reprimand; those with less experience will get off more lightly. So I expect those of you I've appointed to positions of responsibility to observe high standards of conduct, and I expect those who are highly gifted to do great things.

"My mission in life is to bring about a revolution, and I'm longing to see the sparks fly! I have a painful time ahead of me, and I can't wait to get it over and done with! Some of you imagine I'm going to bring peace to the world as if by magic. It's not as simple as that! What I have to say is more likely to lead to conflict. Families will be split down the middle, parents and children will fail to see eye to eye, and newlyweds will fall out with their in-laws."

Then Jesus spoke to the crowds who were listening in to all this. "You're very good at forecasting the weather. If you see clouds coming up from the sea, you say, 'There's rain on the way,' and you're right. If the wind changes to come from the desert, you say, 'We're in for a hot spell.' Right again! You have double standards! You like to show how bright you are in understanding the weather, but you turn a blind eye to what's happening in the world at large, and pretend to be dull! Isn't it time you learned to have an opinion of your own? Think things out and come to a realistic view of your situation, before matters are taken out of your hands and you find you have no choices left. Once you've lost your freedom, it's hard to get it back again."

13 Somebody told Jesus about the people from Galilee Pilate had killed while they were at worship. Jesus said, "Do you think they were singled out for that fate because they were bad people, worse than other Galileans? No, it doesn't work like that. But if you don't mend your ways, a similar fate will be yours. Remember those eighteen people who were killed when the Siloam tower fell on them? Were they more wicked than all the other people living in Jerusalem at the time? Of course not! But if you don't come to your senses, you'll all die under a heap of rubble."

Then Jesus told them this story: "A woman had a fig tree in her garden, but couldn't get any fruit from it. So she said to her gardener, 'We've had this fig tree for three years now and there's still no fruit on it. Chop it down; it's only taking up space!' The gardener said, 'May I suggest we keep it one more year. I'll loosen the roots and put some compost round them. We may get some fruit next year. If not, we'll chop it down.' "

(10) One Saturday Jesus was teaching in a place of worship. A woman came in with a bent back. She had been unable to stand up straight for eighteen years. Jesus saw her and called out to her, "Friend, you're going to have that back put right today!" Then he went over to her and put his arm around her. She straightened up and sang a song of thanks to God. But the person in charge of the worship center was angry and gave a long lecture to the people. "There are six days for you to work in. Go to the doctor on one of those days, not on the Rest Day." Then Jesus said, "Who are you trying to impress with your self-righteous play-acting? I've seen you Holy Joes taking a donkey or a cow from the stables to the water trough on the Rest Day. This woman is a descendant of Abraham. Her disability has made her a prisoner to all intents and purposes for eighteen years. What better time to release her than on God's special day?" When Jesus said this, his critics were so ashamed, they didn't know where to look. People started jumping up and down, singing and shouting their thanks to God in appreciation of all that Jesus was doing for them.

Then Jesus went on to say: "How can we describe God's New World? What picture can we use? God is like a gardener sowing a mustard seed in his garden. One day it grows to become a tree, big enough for the birds to nest in. Or God is like a woman making some bread. She mixes a tiny amount of yeast in a much larger amount of flour until it all rises."

(22) On his way to Jerusalem Jesus visited many towns and villages and spent some time teaching in each. On one occasion someone asked him, "Sir, am I right in thinking the full life you talk about is only for the privileged few?" Jesus said, "If you think the door is small, you must work all the harder to get through it. I tell you the entrance is getting blocked by all the pushing and shoving. Shall I tell you what it's going to be like for narrow-minded people like you? One day the owner of the house will shut the door, and you'll be the wrong side of it, knocking and shouting, 'Sir,

please let us in!' The owner will shout back, 'Who are you? How did you get here?' Then you'll say, 'You remember us. We invited you to lunch, and listened to you when you taught in our town.' But the owner will say, 'What are you doing here? Get off my property, you're trespassing!' You'll be so angry and upset when you see Abraham, Isaac, and Jacob and all God's other speakers arriving for the New World, because you'll be outside. People will come down the big wide roads from every part of the world to be at the big party to celebrate God's New World. Those now thought of as no-hopers will have the best seats, whereas those who think they deserve special status will be lucky to get a seat at all."[11]

Just then some members of the strict set spoke to Jesus. They said, "We advise you to get away from this place as quickly as you can. Herod has assassins out to get you." Jesus said, "Take that crafty old fox a message from me. 'Nothing is going to upset my plans. I'm getting on with my work of healing today and tomorrow, and by the day after that I'll have finished what I have to do in this town.' I'm keeping to a tight schedule. I want to get to Jerusalem in time. That's the place God's speakers get killed, not here."

Jesus said, "Jerusalem, Jerusalem, you're famous for killing God's friends and throwing stones at God's agents! Over and over again I've tried to put my arms round you and draw you to me, like a mother hen gathering her chicks under her wings. But you wouldn't have it! Your people are now without the protection I could have given them. Believe me, you won't see me again until you're ready to join in the song, 'Welcome God's Chosen!'"

14

One Rest Day, Jesus was invited to a meal by one of the leading members of the strict set. This gave the strict set an opportunity to watch his behavior closely. As Jesus was going in, he noticed a man with swollen legs, standing by the door. Jesus said to those watching, "Is it against the rules to cure people on the Rest

---

[11] Verses 23-30 require a contextual translation along these lines to be properly understood. Luke sets two contrasting agendas side by side, that of the typical Pharisee with his narrow-minded question and narrowness of vision, and that of Jesus who throws the New World open to all with a generous heart. The Victorian pictures of the "broad and narrow" ways thus got it disastrously wrong in directing the enquirer to adopt the Pharisee as role model instead of Jesus. (Enoch Powell agrees with this interpretation in his commentary on Matthew.)

Day? Let's have a clear ruling from you, yes or no?" They wouldn't give Jesus an answer. So Jesus took the man with the bad legs to one side, cured him, and sent him home. Then Jesus said, "If one of your children or one of your animals even, has a serious accident on the Rest Day, do you wait till next day to do anything about it?" They had no answer.

Jesus noticed how the guests were all trying to get the best places. He told them, "When you're invited to a posh meal, don't make straight for the best position where everyone can see you. The one who's given the invitations may have somebody else in mind for that place. She may come to you and say, 'I'm sorry, that place is reserved for a special friend of mine. I wonder if you'd mind moving?' By that time all that's left will be a crowded spot near the door, and you'll look a fool as you make your way there. I recommend you choose that spot near the door when you come in. Then the one who's invited you may come and say, 'Friend, I've reserved somewhere better for you. Come this way.' Then the other guests will be impressed as she shows you to your place. Those who try to make themselves look important only make themselves look silly; those who act with modesty earn respect."

Then Jesus said to the one who had invited him, "Next time you have a party or invite people to a meal, don't invite your family and friends or your rich neighbors. They'll probably invite you back, so you won't really be giving anything away. Instead send out invitations to those who would value a good meal – the poor, the disabled, the lonely, people with special needs. You'll get a good feeling if you're generous when there's nothing in it for you. You should wait till the end of time for your pat on the back." One of the guests said, "That will be a happy day! There'll be plenty to eat for the citizens of God's New World!" In reply, Jesus told this story: "There was once a man who had plans for a big party. He sent out lots of invitations. When he'd got in all the food and prepared it, he contacted everybody he'd invited, with the message, 'Come and get it – it's all ready!' But they all gave their apologies. One said, 'I've just bought a new property and I must go and inspect it. I'd love to come to your party. Perhaps another time?' Another one said, 'I've bought some new business equipment and I can't wait to try it out! So sorry!' Another said, 'I'm afraid you've chosen a very inconvenient date. I'll be away on my honeymoon!' These replies upset the man who'd gone to so much trouble. He used an agency to get in touch with all the poor people of the town and invited them to the party. Even so, when all these people had arrived and it was time for the party to begin, there was still plenty of room. So he sent some of his helpers out into the streets and into the country to look for those living rough in shop doorways and under hedges. He said, 'Do your best to get them to come. I'm determined to have a houseful! Those on my original list who turned down my invitation will miss the most exciting event of all time!' "

At a time when Jesus had a very large following he said, "Anyone who joins my band of followers and doesn't put me before the needs of family or personal needs, isn't up to the job. Following me involves carrying a heavy weight of responsibility. Just suppose you want to build an extension to your property. First of all you have to sit down and work out whether you can afford it. Otherwise, when you run out of materials and money soon after you've started, people will think you're someone with ambitions above your means. Imagine a country thinking of going to war with another. Its leaders find out that the country they intend to fight has twice their number of troops and armaments. If they've got any sense, they'll instruct their ambassadors to draw up a peace treaty, before it's too late and hostilities begin. So, if you want to be my friend, you'd better count the cost first. You must be prepared to give up everything for me.

"Let's think about salt. It has lots of uses, but once it loses its tang, there's no way of putting it back. It's no good for the garden or the compost heap. It's useless! If you've got ears, use them!"

15 Jesus had a special attraction for all those excluded from respectable society. They listened to what he had to say. This annoyed the strict set. Their complaint was: "He spends his time with disreputable types of people and even has meals with them!" Jesus explained what he was doing like this: "Can any of you imagine having a flock of a hundred sheep and caring so much about each one of them, that if even one gets lost you leave the other ninety-nine out in the open to go looking for it? And would you then carry it back on your shoulders, singing for joy? When you get home, would you invite all your friends and neighbors to a party and ask them to get excited over just one

sheep? But I'm telling you, God is happier with one bad person who changes for the better, than with ninety-nine people who think they have no faults!

"Imagine someone very careful with their money. One day they happen to mislay some money somewhere in the house. They will, of course, search frantically for it, in every corner and underneath every bit of furniture. But when they've found it, will they tell everybody in the street and invite them in for a celebration? Not very likely. But God's friends always party when an outcast comes back into the community."[12] Then Jesus told them this story: "Once there was a man with two sons. The younger one said to his father, 'Dad, let me have the money you intend leaving me in your will.' So the father made over to both sons the share of his estate he had decided to leave them. A few days later, the younger son packed his bags and went abroad. Away from home he soon went through his money, living without a thought for the next day. At the very moment his money ran out, there was a slump in the country where he was living and there were no jobs worth having. All he could get was a job on a farm looking after some pigs. Sometimes he was so hungry, he felt like eating the pig food. No one took pity on him. Finally he came to his senses and said, 'Back home the workers on Dad's farm get as much food as they need and more, but I'm dying of hunger. I've had enough of this job; I'm going home to Dad! This is what I'll say to him, "Dad, I've led a selfish life and I've treated you shamefully. I'm not fit to be thought of as your son. Please give me a job on the farm. I'll do anything!"'

"So he made his way back home to his father. His father saw him coming in the distance and his heart melted at the sight of him. He ran toward him and hugged and kissed him. Then the son began the speech he'd prepared, 'Dad, I've led a selfish life and I've treated you shamefully; I'm not fit to be thought of as your son ... ' But his father said, 'We must get you into some decent clothes right away. My new jacket – I haven't worn it yet – I'm sure it will fit you. And I've got a bright shirt and some new shoes to go with it. Let's have a big party and get some good food in. I thought

---

[12] These parables are meant to contrast rather than compare God's ways with human ways. They contrast the acceptance by Jesus of those classed as "sinners" with their rejection by the Pharisees. We have tried to capture the note of irony in Jesus' voice, essential for an understanding of the parables.

my son was dead, but here he is! ALIVE! I thought I'd lost him forever, but he's back where he belongs!'

"At the time the party was getting into full swing, the older son was out working in the fields. On his way back to the house he heard the sound of music and dancing. He stopped to ask those standing in the doorway what was going on. They said, 'Your brother's come home and your father's throwing a party to celebrate his safe return.' The older son was furious and refused to go in. So his father came out and tried to persuade him. But he said to his father, 'I've been working my fingers to the bone for you all these years, and I've always done whatever you asked me to do. When have you had a party for me, so I could have a good time with my friends? But this worthless son of yours comes home after wasting all your money on wild adventures, and no expense is spared to make him welcome!' The father said, 'My boy, I've got you with me all the time. Everything I have is yours as well. It's right for us to have a party and to be happy. He's not just my son; he's your brother! We'd given him up for dead, but he's alive; we thought we'd lost him, but he's come back home.' "

16 Jesus told his friends this story: "There was once a wealthy businessman who entrusted his affairs to an accountant. Someone told him that the accountant was defrauding him. So he called the accountant into his office and said, 'I've had reports that you're fiddling the books. I want a complete financial statement from you before I fire you.' The accountant said to himself, 'I don't know how I'll cope if I lose this job. I'm not strong enough for manual work and I don't fancy queuing for the dole. I think I know a way out. I must make sure that when I lose my accountant's job, there will be people willing to have me in their homes.' Then he arranged interviews with each one of those who owed his boss money. He said to the first one, 'How much was that invoice you haven't paid yet? How about cutting the sum by half? Here's a new agreement for you to sign. You can tear up the old one.' The next one had his bill reduced by ten per cent in the same way. When the boss found out what his accountant had done, he had a sneaking admiration for him. People in the world of finance are shrewder in their operations than religious people in theirs. So use all your money to befriend the friendless.

One day it will be they who'll be welcoming you into their eternal homes."[13]

Jesus went on to say, "Those who are unreliable in small matters can't be trusted with something important. If you don't use your money responsibly, you're not up to handling things of true value. If you've not looked after what's been given you in trust for others, what right have you to expect something of your own? You must make up your mind where your loyalty lies. You can't be attached to God and money."

Some members of the strict set overheard what Jesus was saying. They were very fond of money and laughed at him. Jesus said to them, "You lot know how to make a good impression, but God knows what you're like inside. The money and wealth you value is worthless to God."

Jesus said, "The rules and teachings in our old books were relevant until the coming of John the Dipper. Since then the Good News about God's New World has been made known. You should be using all your energy to be part of it. But it's easier for a new universe to replace the old than for you to ditch all those little rules you're so fond of![14]

"Those who break up committed relationships in order to play around, cause heartache and misery.[15]

"There was once a very wealthy man, called Desmond, who dined out every day, dressed in the most expensive clothes. Near the entrance to his luxury apartment, a homeless man, called Larry, slept rough. He was unwell and badly nourished and sometimes had to make do with what Desmond threw into the bin. His only friends were stray dogs. One day Larry died and was the guest of honor at a party given by Abraham. Soon after, Desmond died and was buried. He found himself in a miserable and hopeless place.

---

[13] Like all the parables, this story offers itself for numerous interpretations. If the story is taken in context with the stories which precede it in Chapter 15, and the story which follows it at 16:19, then the point seems to be that not only are the Pharisees cold-hearted in their rejection of "outcasts," but their policy also lacks good sense. (Or the story may be simply about "gumption" and the lack of it among religious people.)

[14] Verse 17 should be interpreted contextually with verse 16. That way there is no contradiction. The verses express Jesus' frustration at the inability of the Pharisees in particular to embrace the new order introduced by John and himself.

[15] Verse 18 appears to be out of context, but may not be so. It may follow on from the contrast in verses 16 and 17 between the call of God in the mission of Jesus and obsession with the minutiae of the Law. In Hebrew thought Israel was married to God. Jesus is saying that those choosing to bind themselves to the Law, instead of God, were being unfaithful.

In great distress he looked up and saw Abraham and Larry far away, enjoying their food together. Desmond cried out, 'Dear Abraham, please help me; send Larry this way with something cool for me to drink. I'm parched.' But Abraham said, 'Remember, my boy, when you were alive, you had it good, whereas Larry had a rough time of it. He's having a good time now and you're suffering. In any case there's no transport to get us to you, or you to us.' Desmond said, 'Then, Sir, please send him to my hometown where I have five brothers still alive. Tell him to warn them, so they don't end up in this horrible place!' Abraham said, 'They've got the old books. All they have to do is to take notice of what they say!' 'No, Abraham, Sir, that doesn't work. But I'm sure if someone visited them from the dead, they would take notice.' Abraham said, 'If they don't pay any attention to the old books, they won't listen to someone who comes back to them from the dead!' "

17 Jesus said to his friends, "Life is full of pitfalls and it's very easy to trip up. But we can do without people who deliberately put obstacles in the way. Anyone who makes it hard for those taking their first steps toward God should go for a swim with a brick tied round their neck to experience what they're doing to others! Make sure your behavior is helpful at all times. If one of my followers does something wrong, have a word with them. If they're sorry you must not hold it against them. If they have persistent habits which they deeply regret, you must forgive them over and over again."

They said to Jesus, "We need more confidence!" Jesus said, "A bit of trust is all you need, the sort of trust a gardener has. If you have a small seed, you can make it grow into a large plant. Or you can transplant a bush from a garden to a new position by the sea and it will thrive."

Jesus said, "Imagine you're a farmer. If one of your farm workers came in one day after plowing a field or looking after the sheep, would you say, 'I've just laid the table, sit down and have some supper with me'? Or would you be more likely to say, 'Now you've come in, you can get your apron on and cook my supper. Then stand by to serve the food and pour out the drink. You can have your supper when I've finished'? You don't think it's necessary, do you, to thank those who are only doing their job?" (So, when you've done a good job of work you must say, "We're just workers hired to do a job. We've only done what was expected of us.")[16]

(11) Jesus continued on his way toward Jerusalem and crossed the border between Galilee and Samaria. He was going into a village when a group of down and outs shouted to him from a distance. (They were excluded from society because they had skin diseases.) They said, "Doctor Jesus, please help us!" Jesus saw them and said, "Go and show yourselves to the health officers." As they went on their way, their skin infections disappeared. One of them, as soon as he realized what had happened, came back to Jesus, singing a song of thanks to God. He shook Jesus warmly by the hand and thanked him. He was a Samaritan, a despised foreigner. Then Jesus said, "I thought there were ten of you? Where are the rest? Has no one got the decency to come back and say 'thank you' to God, except someone of another race and religion?" Then Jesus said to him, "You're free to go where you want now. Your trust in me has cured you."

(20) Some members of the strict set said to Jesus, "This New World you talk about, when is it going to come?" Jesus said, "God's New World is not something you can see. It will never be possible to say, 'Look, there it is!' The New World is here already. It's in people's minds and in their relationships."

Then Jesus said to his friends, "Soon you'll be longing for that day when humanity will be complete and perfected. You'll be frustrated by the lack of progress. There'll be various groups of people who tell you, 'The way to get there is to come along with us. We are the only ones who know the way!' Don't fall for that kind of talk. Don't let anyone put you on a false trail.

"The whole world will be aware of the community of the Complete Person in a split second, in the way lightning brightens up the sky from one end to another. But first there has to be a period of great suffering and rejection. It will all come about as suddenly as the flood in the time of Noah. The people of those days just carried on with life as usual while Noah was building his big boat. When he was safe inside, the floods came, and

---

[16] It is possible the explanatory comment of verse 10 is not part of the original story. It may have been supplied by Luke, or his source. If this is the case, alternative interpretations of the original may be considered. As with other parables (e.g. The Prodigal Son, The Lost Sheep), the hearer is invited to contrast God's generous behavior with human hardness.

everybody was drowned. It was the same again in the days of Lot. People went about their business, making plans for the next day. But on the day Lot left Sodom, a cloud of volcanic ash rained down on the town, killing all the inhabitants. That's how quickly the community of the Complete Person will appear."[17]

Jesus said, "The day will come when people won't have time to go through the different parts of their house to collect their belongings, and anyone out at work won't have a chance to go home to say goodbye. Remember what happened to Lot's wife when she stopped to look back at Sodom. (She was fossilized by falling ash!) Those who put their own safety first will be lost, whereas those who risk their lives for others will live."

Jesus said, "I'm telling you, two people can be in bed together at night, then without warning, one of them suffers a heart attack. Two people can be in the kitchen preparing a meal, then one of them suddenly has a stroke." The friends of Jesus asked him, "Where do tragedies like that happen?" Jesus said, "Just as a bird of prey is drawn to a rotting carcass, so death comes to those who don't know how to live."

18

Jesus told his friends a story to encourage them to develop an up beat relationship with God.

"There was once a lawyer appointed to settle disputes between people in his community. He was an unscrupulous man and had no love for God or people. There was a woman in the town who kept bothering him, saying, 'When are you going to deal with my claim for compensation?' To begin with the lawyer kept putting her off, but at last he said to himself, 'I couldn't care less whether anyone gets justice or not, but this woman's becoming a nuisance. I'd better attend to her case, otherwise she'll drive me mad!' " Jesus said, "If a lawyer with no interest in justice can be made to do his job, then surely God will listen to those who ask for help? Does God need to be pestered like the lawyer in the story? Of course not! God will respond quickly to cries for help. It's all a matter of trust in God. It surprises me how difficult it is to find trust here on earth!"

---

[17] The term "Son of Man," usually translated by us as "the Complete Person," frequently carries with it a sense of community, referring at one and the same time to Jesus and his followers. This wider sense is evident in Luke's version of these sayings.

Here is a story Jesus told to those who thought they were good people and looked down on others: "Two people went to their place of worship to talk to God. One was very religious, and the other was an outcast from society. The first stood confidently out at the front. (He thought he was talking to God, but really he was talking to himself!) This is what he said: 'God, I thank you I'm not like other people. I don't steal or tell lies, and I don't have sex with anybody except my wife. I'm not a traitor to my country like that tax collector back there! I keep to a strict diet, and I give generously to charity.' The second stood at the back, his head in his hands, groaning pitifully. All he said was, 'God help me. I'm no good!' I'm telling you, it was the second person that went home on good terms with God rather than the first. Those who put themselves on pedestals fall off them sooner or later, but those who grieve over their faults are honored by God."

(15) Some people were bringing their children to Jesus for him to hold. His friends told them to leave Jesus alone. But Jesus asked for them to be brought to him. He said, "Let the children come to me; never try to stop them. They already belong to God's World. I tell you, anyone who doesn't naturally accept God's New World in the way a child does, has no chance of being part of it."

(18) A leader of the community asked Jesus, "Good Teacher, what must I do to have life to the full?" Jesus said, "You shouldn't be so careless with your compliments. Only God is good! You know the rules. Don't take away someone else's partner; don't kill; don't steal; don't lie or cheat; respect your parents." The man said, "Teacher, I've kept all the rules from the time I was a child." Jesus replied, "There's only one thing missing. Go and sell everything you've got, give the money to those in need, and you'll find things of real value in God's New World. Then come and be my friend!" This advice was not what the man wanted. His face dropped, since he was rather well off. Jesus looked straight at him and said, "It's exceedingly difficult for the wealthy to become citizens of God's New World. I would say it's easier for a camel to get through the eye of a needle than for anyone well off to get into God's New World!" Someone who heard what Jesus said shouted out, "There's not much chance for any of us then!" Jesus replied, "It's impossible for anyone to make it without God's help. But God makes everything possible!"

Rocky said, "We've left our homes and families to be with you!" Jesus said, "You've struck a good bargain. True, you've left your houses and families behind, but now you have a larger family and many homes to go to. And you'll have life to the full one day."

(31) Jesus spoke to his closest friends in private and said, "As you know, we're on the way to Jerusalem. Everything God's speakers in olden times said about the Complete Person will come about. He'll fall into the hands of the Romans; and he'll be made fun of and degraded and spat on. After they've beaten him, they'll kill him. But three days afterwards he'll be restored to life." At the time Jesus said these things to his friends, it didn't make sense to them.

When they were getting near to Jericho, a blind man was sitting beside the road, asking for money. He heard a crowd gathering and asked what was happening. They told him, "Jesus from Nazareth is coming this way." Then he shouted out, "Jesus, New David, help me!" The people standing where they could get a good view told him to shut up. But he shouted at the top of his voice, "New David, help me!" Jesus stopped and asked for the man to be brought to him. Jesus said to him, "How can I help you?" The man said, "Leader, I'd like to be able to see again!" Jesus said, "Have your sight back, then. Your trust in me has cured you." The man could see again from that moment on. He became a follower of Jesus, singing a song of thanks to God. Everybody joined in the chorus.

19 Jesus came to Jericho, but had no plans to stay there. Keith, the chief superintendent of taxes, lived in Jericho. He was very wealthy. He wanted to get a good look at Jesus, but there were so many people with the same idea, he had no chance, especially since he was short. So he ran ahead of everybody else and climbed a tree where he would have a good view of Jesus coming along the road. When Jesus got to the tree he looked up and said, "Keith, come down quickly. I've decided to spend the day in your home." Keith leapt down and greeted Jesus warmly. But there was a lot of murmuring from the crowd. They said things like, "He's chosen to go home with a traitor." But Keith said to Jesus, so that everyone could hear him, "I want you to know, Leader, I'm going to give half of everything I own to charity, and if anyone thinks I've cheated them,

I'll give them back four times the amount." Then Jesus said, "Today Keith and his family begin a new life. Keith is a descendant of Abraham like the rest of you. My job is to get alongside those who've lost their way in life and restore them to the community."

Jericho was the last stage of the journey on the way to Jerusalem. A lot of the people traveling with Jesus thought God's New World would come at any moment. So Jesus told them this story: "Once a local leader went a long way from home to the center of government, to have his position confirmed. Before leaving he called ten of his deputies into his office and made over to each of them a large sum of money. He said, 'This is for your use while I'm away. See if you can make a profit!' The leader was very unpopular with the people and they sent representatives to the government to say, 'We don't want this person as our leader.' However, his position was confirmed, and when he came back he called his deputies into his office to find out how they'd used the funds he'd granted them. The first said, 'Sir, I've made a thousand per cent profit on the money you gave me!' The leader said, 'Well done. You've proved your worth as my deputy. I'm putting you in charge of a district which includes ten large towns.' The second said, 'Sir, with your money I've managed to make a five hundred per cent profit.' The leader said, 'I'm putting you in charge of a district covering five big towns.' The next one said, 'Sir, I've kept your money safe. You can check the accounts. I didn't like to take any risks, since you're very hard on those who fail.' 'Hard on those who fail, am I?' the leader said. 'In that case why didn't you make a sound investment with the money? At least when I came back I would have got some interest.' Then he said, 'Transfer the money from this waster's account to the account of the deputy who made the thousand per cent profit.' (There was a cry of protest, 'Leader, he's got plenty in his account already!') The leader said, 'The way I run things, those with initiative get ahead, and those who slack get fired. But now we must deal with those who opposed my appointment. I'm going to put an end to their games.' " After telling that story, Jesus joined the pilgrims on their way to Jerusalem. He walked out in front.

(29) Jesus came near to the villages of Figland and Dategrove, which were close to Olive Hill. He sent two of his friends on an errand. He said, "Go into the village over there and outside one of the first houses you come

to, you'll find a donkey that's never been ridden. Untie it and bring it here. If anyone says, 'What do you think you're doing?' just say, 'The Leader needs it.' The words worked, just as Jesus said they would. When they had brought the donkey to Jesus, they put their jackets on its back and helped Jesus on to it. As Jesus rode along, people put their coats on the ground for the donkey to walk over. When Jesus came to the path that goes down from Olive Hill, all his followers began to sing songs of thanks to God for all the wonderful things they had seen Jesus do. They sang:

> "Welcome the king who comes with God's love,
> Peace matched with beauty, below and above."

Some members of the strict set said to Jesus, "Teacher, tell your followers to stop making such a noise." Jesus said, "I'm telling you, shut these people up and you'll have a riot on your hands!"

When Jesus saw the city, his eyes filled with tears. He said, "If only you would adopt the policies which lead to peace, now while you have the chance. But you can't see what's in front of your eyes. The days are coming when your enemies will attack you from all sides. They will massacre your inhabitants, including the children, and turn your fine buildings into a heap of rubble, and all because you didn't recognize the mission from God to save you."

Then Jesus went into the temple and drove out those who were selling religious objects and souvenirs. Jesus said, "It says in the old books,

> 'This house is the place to meet with me;
> You've made it a den of iniquity.' "

Every day Jesus taught in the temple. The religious and civic leaders were all trying to think of a way to kill him, but they couldn't touch him because he was such a big hit with the ordinary people.

20 One day, Jesus was teaching the people in the worship center, telling them the good news. Some of those in charge of the center, together with some experts in the old books and some of the city councilors, said to him, "What right have you to take over like this? Who gave you permission?" Jesus said, "Let me ask you a question. Was John inspired by God to dip people, or did he get the idea from someone else?" They talked among themselves and realized that if they said, 'John was inspired by God,' Jesus would say, 'Why then didn't you accept his teaching?' But if they said, 'He got his ideas from someone else,' they were afraid the people standing by would attack them, because they believed John was a true messenger from God. So the officials said they did not know where John got his ideas. Jesus replied, "In that case, I'm not going to tell you who gave me the right to do what I'm doing."

Then Jesus told the people this story: "Someone planted a vineyard, let it out to tenants, then went abroad for a long time. At harvest time the owner sent an agent to collect the produce due as rent. But the tenants beat him up and sent him away without any of the rent. Then the owner sent another agent and they beat him and called him names. He got nothing out of them either. They seriously wounded the third agent the owner sent, and threw him out. Then the owner said, 'What can I do? I know – I'll send my son. I love him so dearly; they're sure to respect him!' But when the tenants saw him, they said to one another, 'This is the owner's boy; come on, let's kill him and the property will be ours.' So they threw him out of the vineyard and killed him. What do you think the owner will do to them? I think he'll get rid of those tenants and find new ones." The people who were listening said, "Oh no! Please, not that!" But Jesus looked at them straight and said, "Then what do the old books mean when they say,

> 'The stone the builders thought was useless
> Is the stone which takes the stress'?

Watch out for the stone you've neglected and left lying around. You may fall over it and hurt yourselves! Watch out for that stone you're trying to pull down from its place. It may fall on top of you!"

The clergy realized from these remarks that Jesus had told the story with them in mind. They longed to get their hands on him, but they were afraid of what the people would do to them. However, they kept a close eye on Jesus and briefed people in the crowd to ask leading questions. They hoped to trap Jesus into saying something seditious they could use to bring him on a charge before the governor. One of them questioned Jesus like this, "Teacher, we know you always make things clear and don't mind who you offend. You teach the truth of God exactly as you see it. Is it right for us to pay taxes to the Roman emperor or not?" Jesus saw this was a trick question, so he said to them, "Show me a coin. Whose head is this and whose name is above it?" They said, "The emperor's!" Jesus said, "Give the emperor what belongs to the emperor, and give God what belongs to God." The people who were listening appreciated how skillfully Jesus avoided the trap, so that his questioners could not fault him.

Another trick question was put by members of a group who did not believe in life after death. They said, "Teacher, the laws from the time of Moses say that if a man's brother dies, leaving a wife but no children, the man shall marry the widow and produce children who shall be thought of as his brother's. Just suppose there were seven brothers. The first one married and died childless, leaving his wife to his brother, and so on down the line to the seventh brother. Then the woman died. Whose wife will she be in the next life, since they all married her one after the other?" Jesus said, "Marriage has to do with the way society is organized at the present time. It will not be an issue for those who prove themselves worthy of being citizens in the New World, and there is no such thing as marriage in the life after death. There will be a different form of existence where all are regarded as members of God's family. Moses made it quite clear that this life is not the only life. In the story of the burning bush he calls God 'the God of Abraham, the God of Isaac, and the God of Jacob.' God isn't God of the dead, but of the living. In the presence of God they are all still alive!" This answer impressed some of the experts in the old books. They said, "Well done, Teacher, you put that very well!"

Jesus then put a tricky question to his critics. He said, "Why do the experts say God's Chosen will be a descendant of King David? David says in a song he wrote,

> 'God said to my Leader: "Sit by me;
> Then you'll have no enemy." '

In our culture children owe complete loyalty to their parents. Since David expresses his loyalty to God's Chosen by calling him 'Leader', how can God's Chosen be one of David's descendants?"[18]

Then, with everybody listening, Jesus said to his followers, "Don't trust your clergy. They like to parade around in their distinctive clothes and have everyone make a fuss of them when they appear in public. They like to have the best seats in the places of worship and sit at the top table when there's a banquet! They take advantage of defenseless women and coax money out of them. They say long prayers in order to impress everybody. Instead of the good reputation they seek, they're getting to be known for the humbugs they are!"

21

At one point during his teaching in the worship center, Jesus drew the attention of his audience to the collection box. Many of the people putting their money in were well off. A poor woman, as she passed, put in two small coins. Jesus said, "I'm telling you, that woman has given more than all the others. They've still got plenty to live a comfortable life, but she gave everything she had left from her small income."

The guides showing visitors round the worship center were pointing out the beauty of the stonework and the tasteful fittings patrons had donated. Jesus said, "Take a good look at it all. It will soon be nothing but a heap of rubble."

Someone asked Jesus, "Teacher, when will this temple be destroyed, and what events will bring it about?" Jesus said, "Don't let anyone fool you into thinking they can predict the future. There will be many claiming to speak for me, and some who even try to impersonate me. They will say things like, 'The end of the world is near!' Don't fall for that kind of talk. When you see wars and revolutions, keep your heads. It's the normal pattern of history. It doesn't mean the end has come.

"There'll be great political changes, there'll be natural disasters, severe food shortages, and outbreaks of infectious diseases over wide areas, and there'll be freak weather conditions. But first, as my followers, you'll be

---

[18] Jesus is not here indulging in biblical literalism, but rather making fun of biblical literalists, tying them up in knots!

arrested and badly treated. You'll be condemned by those who claim to act in the name of God; you'll be put in prison and stand trial in the highest courts. It will be your opportunity to get your message across. Don't fret beforehand about what you're going to say. I'll give you the words and a skill that will be more than a match for your opponents. Sometimes members of your own family will betray you, and some of you will be executed. Everyone will think badly of you because you are my friends. But you won't suffer any permanent loss. All you have to do is stand by your principles and you'll come through, full of life.

(20) "When you see armies approaching Jerusalem from all sides, then you'll know the city is going to be destroyed. Those who live in the surrounding area would be wise to seek refuge in the mountains, and those in the city will have to get out before it's too late. People in the farmlands must not take their goods into market. The consequences of folly will be clear for all to see. The old books are full of warnings. It will be a dreadful experience for expectant mothers and those with the care of children. The people of this land will face indescribable sufferings. Many will be killed; others will be captured and taken far from their homes. Jerusalem will be occupied by people of other races for a long time to come. It will seem as if the whole universe is falling apart. Many will suffer from breakdowns and fears they cannot control. In all this confusion the Complete Person will emerge, like someone appearing out of the mists. The sight will be powerful and dazzling. You'll get your confidence back and see the new life you've been longing for becoming a reality."

Then Jesus said: "Think about the trees, a fig tree for example. When their leaves start to sprout, you can see that summer is on the way. So, when you see the things I've described happening, you know God's New World is on the way. Believe me, the world as you know it won't disappear until all these things have happened. One world will give way to another, but my words will last forever.

"You must keep your wits about you. Watch out for those things that sap your energy and drag you down – late nights, heavy drinking, anxiety. Don't miss the wonder of the great things happening all over the world. Keep your eyes open. Ask God to give you strength to get through the difficult times, so that you'll be ready for the Complete Person."

Jesus taught in the worship center every day. Each evening he returned to Olive Hill. People got up very early in the morning to get a good place in the center to hear him.

22 It was the time of the Jewish festival when only bread without yeast is eaten. The clergy were trying to think of a way to assassinate Jesus, because they feared a popular revolution. Judas from Kerioth was one of Jesus' closest companions. Evil thoughts entered his head, and he sneaked off to talk to the clergy and their security guards. He offered to make it easy for them to capture Jesus. They were delighted, and agreed to pay him for the job. Judas clinched the deal, and from then on looked for a chance to hand Jesus over to them when there would be no crowd to prevent it.

On the special day when the lambs for the festival meal were being killed, Jesus gave Rocky and John the task of preparing and setting out the food. They asked Jesus, "Where are we going to meet?" Jesus said, "When you go into Jerusalem, a man carrying a jar of water will be on the lookout for you. He'll lead you to a hotel. Follow him in and ask to speak to the owner. Say, 'The Teacher has sent us. Please show us to the function room he's booked to celebrate the festival with his friends.' The owner will show you a big room upstairs. The couches and tables will be set out ready. All you have to do is prepare the food." John and Rocky went into Jerusalem, and everything went according to plan. They got the food ready.

(14) When everybody had arrived, and it was time to begin, Jesus moved to his place on the couch near the table, and his friends grouped round him. Jesus said, "I've really looked forward to having this meal with you, before facing my ordeal. But I'm not going to eat anything now. I'll eat with you next in God's New World. Then you'll appreciate the full significance of what we are celebrating here tonight!"[19]

Then Jesus took a cup, thanked God for it, and said, "Share this among yourselves. No wine for me until God's New World has come!"

---

[19] This is just one of many conflicting possible interpretations of what is happening at this point, according to Luke's distinctive account. This interpretation suggests that Jesus is deliberately going on a fast, possibly as a wise precaution of keeping his gut clear for the ordeal ahead, something Luke, as a doctor, would be likely to appreciate.

Then he took a loaf of bread and said "thank you" to God. He broke it, gave it to them, and said, "This is my body."

Then Jesus said, "Have a good look round. Someone sitting right here at the table with me is going to help my enemies. What's going to happen to the Complete Person has already been decided. There's no going back. It's the one who's going to betray me I feel sorry for!" Then Jesus' companions started to discuss among themselves who would do such a thing. They soon got on to the question of which of them ranked as number one. But Jesus said, "You know how many countries have leaders who bully their subjects, despite calling themselves 'friends of the people.' You must not imitate them. Anyone who wants an important role must humbly seek the advice and experience of others, and anyone who thinks they have leadership qualities must show they are not above doing the dirty jobs. The needs of the customers in a restaurant come before the needs of the waiter. I'm showing you how to act like the perfect waiter.

"I want to thank you for standing by me in so many difficult situations. Here and now I'm inviting you to share with me the responsibilities of the New World, and I'm inviting you to the party to celebrate its coming. You're going to be in charge of looking after God's People."

Then Jesus turned to Rocky and said, "Simon, please listen to what I'm saying. It's crunch time for this circle of friends. But I've asked God to help you keep your cool so that, when things come right again, you can be a source of strength to others." Rocky said, "Leader, I'm ready to go to prison with you, and to die by your side!" Jesus said, "Believe me, Rocky, the next time the cock crows at sunrise, you will already have said three times that you don't know me."

Then Jesus said to them all, "Do you remember when I sent you on tour without a bag or money or shoes on your feet? How did you cope like that?" They said, "We had no problems at all!" Jesus said, "It's going to be different tonight. You'd better make sure you've got your money with you and a travel bag. A knife is more use than a heavy coat to those on the run! What's going to happen reminds me of what the old books say, 'He kept company with criminals.' " They said, "We've got our weapons ready, Leader." Jesus said, "That's enough talk of weapons!"[20]

(39) Jesus left the hotel and took his usual route to Olive Hill, with his

friends close behind him. When he came to his favorite spot, he said to his friends, "Ask God to keep you out of trouble tonight." Then he went a little way from them and talked with God. Jesus said, "Loving God, please don't let me have to go through with this. But if it's what you want me to do, I'm ready." As Jesus said this, he experienced a great upsurge of strength, and he knew God had not left him on his own. But the pain of grief and anxiety was so intense as he opened his heart, the sweat fell from him in great big drops. Then Jesus got up off his knees and went back to his friends. They had found escape in sleep; the sight was too distressing for them. Jesus said, "This is no time to be asleep. I told you to ask God to keep you out of trouble."

As Jesus said this, a group appeared led by Judas, one of the twelve closest companions of Jesus. He tried to kiss Jesus, but Jesus said, "Judas, do you mean to trap me with a kiss?" This alerted the others to the danger and they said, "Leader, shall we fight them off?" One of them attacked a boy who worked for the High Priest, and cut his right ear. But Jesus said, "No more violence!" He touched the boy's ear and it healed up. Then Jesus said to the mixed band of councilors, clergy, and police who had come to arrest him, "Why are you fully armed, as if I were a terrorist? You've had plenty of opportunity to get me in the temple. I've been there every day. Why didn't you arrest me then? But this is your moment, and the world's darkest hour!"

(54) Then they arrested Jesus and took him to the place where Guy, the religious chief, lived. Rocky followed, keeping out of sight. There was a big fire in the middle of the yard, with lots of people sitting round it. Rocky joined them. One of the women who worked for Guy caught a glimpse of Rocky in the light of the fire. She pointed to him and said, "Here's one of Jesus' gang!" But Rocky said, "Woman, I've never met him!" Later on, someone else recognized him and said, "I'm sure you're one of them!" But Rocky said, "No mate, you've got it wrong!" About an hour later, someone else kept teasing him, saying, "Come on, stop pretending. We can tell you're

---

[20] The words of Jesus to the disciples to have their swords ready is not a call to arms, but realism on his part. Since his followers are not going to adopt his peaceful ways as they did on the mission tour, they might as well, as befits their desertion, provide adequate physical protection for themselves. The word of Jesus, "enough," is a cry of frustration and sadness.

one of Jesus' friends. You've got a northern accent!" But Rocky said, "You're talking a load of crap!" Just then a cock crowed. Jesus turned round and looked at Rocky. Rocky remembered what Jesus had said, "Before the cock crows at sunrise, you will have said you don't know me three times." Rocky went outside and burst into tears.

While they held Jesus, the policemen made fun of him and knocked him about. They blindfolded him and said, "Let's see how psychic you are! Tell us who's hitting you!" And they abused and insulted him over and over again.

In the morning there was a meeting of the councilors and clergy. They had Jesus brought before them. They said to him, "If you're God's Chosen, then tell us." Jesus said, "You've already formed your opinion, so what's the point in telling you anything? You're not open to a meeting of minds. But from now on God's giving the Complete Person control of everything, not you." Then they asked, "So you're God's True Likeness, are you?" Jesus said, "Stop trying to put words into my mouth!" Then they said, "Dodging the question is proof of guilt. Now we've got all the evidence we need!!"[21]

23

The meeting broke up, and Jesus was taken to stand trial before Pilate, the Roman Governor. Those speaking for the Council said, "We have evidence that this man has been trying to provoke a rebellion by encouraging people not to pay their taxes to the emperor. He calls himself 'God's Chosen,' which amounts to a claim to be head of state." Pilate said to Jesus, "Are you this people's head of state?" Jesus said, "That's your way of looking at things, not mine." Then Pilate said to the clergy, and to those who had come to watch the trial, "There is no case against this man." But his accusers would not be put off. They said, "He's been spreading anti-government propaganda from one end of the country to the other. He started up in Galilee."

This gave Pilate an idea. He asked if Jesus was a Galilean. When he found out that Jesus was from the area Herod was responsible for, he sent him to Herod who was in the city on a visit. Herod was pleased to see Jesus,

---

[21] Some interpretation has to be put on these words. The Greek translated literally "you have said" is meaningless. "You said it, not me" is also possible, or "You've hit the nail on the head!"

because he had been trying to get hold of him for some time. He had heard a lot about him and wanted to see how good he was at performing miracles. He spent a long time asking Jesus questions, but Jesus refused to answer him. At the same time, the clergy kept up a barrage of accusations against Jesus. Then Herod and his soldiers made fun of Jesus. They dressed him up in robes of state and sent him back to Pilate. Pilate and Herod had been enemies, but their involvement in the trial of Jesus led to more friendly relations between them.

Then Pilate called everybody back. He said, "You've brought this man before me as a political agitator. I have questioned him here in front of you and come to the conclusion that he is not guilty of the charges you have made against him. Herod is of the same opinion. That's why he sent him back to me. There are no grounds whatsoever for the death penalty. I propose to have him beaten; then I will let him go."

Then everybody started shouting at once, "We don't want this man! We want Barry!" (Barry was in prison for causing a riot in the city, and for murder.) Pilate wanted to let Jesus go, so he spoke to them again. But they started to chant: "Hang him high! Hang him high!" Pilate tried a third time to get them to change their minds. He said, "What have you got against this man? What's he done wrong? I really don't think he deserves the death penalty. I'm going to have him beaten; then I'm going to let him go." But they kept up their chants, calling for his death. At last Pilate gave in to them. He let out of prison the dangerous criminal they had shouted for, and let them have their way with Jesus.

(26) As they led Jesus off to the place of execution, they grabbed hold of an African called Simon, a visitor to Jerusalem. They forced him to walk behind Jesus, carrying the crossbeam for the gallows. Many of Jesus' supporters followed on behind him, including some women. They were all in tears. Jesus turned to them and said, "People of Jerusalem, don't cry for me. Cry for yourselves and for your children. The time's coming when it will be better to be without children. People will be scrambling to find hideouts in the mountains. If a government which takes pride in good order treats us so unjustly, what will happen when there's a bad government?"

Two criminals were taken to be executed at the same time as Jesus. When they came to Skull Hill, they fastened Jesus and the criminals to their crosses. Jesus was hung between the other two. Then Jesus spoke to God. He said, "Loving God, forgive them. They don't know what they're doing." The soldiers threw dice for his clothes. The ordinary people standing by watched in silence. But the leaders tried to make fun of Jesus, shouting things like, "He was good at helping other people. If he's God's chosen leader, let's see him help himself!" The soldiers made fun of him too. They paraded in front of him and offered him some of the free wine they got for doing the job. They said, "If you're the leader of the Jews, where's your rescue party?" They said this because there was a poster on top of the cross with the words, "The Leader of the Jews."

One of the criminals who was hanging beside Jesus mouthed abuse at him, saying things like, "You're supposed to be God's chosen leader. Let's see you get yourself out of this! You can give us a helping hand while you're at it!" But the other one told him to shut up. He said, "You should have more respect for God. We're all in the same boat. We deserve it because of what we've done. The man you're abusing is innocent!" Then he said, "Jesus, put in a good word for me when your New World comes." Jesus said, "I promise, you and I will keep one another company today, in God's Garden."

At about twelve o'clock midday, the sun went in and black clouds settled over the whole country until three in the afternoon. At the worship center, the big curtain designed to keep people from God's presence, was ripped in two. Then Jesus let out a big cry and said, "Loving God, I'm in your hands now." Then he stopped breathing.

The Roman soldier in charge was very impressed by the way Jesus died. He thanked God and said, "He was a good man – one of the best!" All those who had gone to watch the execution went home feeling very depressed. Jesus' friends, especially the women who belonged to Jesus' closest band of helpers from Galilee, continued to watch what was happening from a convenient distance. Among the friends was Joseph from the town of Ram, near Jerusalem. He was known as a good and honorable man. He was a member of the Council, but had spoken against the decision to arrest Jesus and have him executed. He was looking forward to God's New World. Joseph went to Pilate and asked for Jesus' body. He took it from the cross, wrapped it in a linen sheet and put it in a new grave that had been cut out of solid rock. It was Friday evening, the time for getting ready for the Rest

Day on Saturday. The women from Galilee went with Joseph and saw Jesus being put in the grave. Then they went to their lodgings and got the ointments and spices ready to embalm Jesus. They could not do the embalming the following day because it was the Rest Day.

24 On Sunday morning, as soon as it was light, the women made their way to the grave, carrying the ointments they had prepared for the embalming. They saw that the stone, which sealed the entrance to the grave, had been moved to one side, but when they went in, there was no body. While they were wondering what to do, two strangers in bright clothes emerged out of the darkness. The women were startled and went weak at the knees. But the strangers said, "Why are you looking in a grave for someone who's alive? Jesus isn't here; he's come back to life! Don't you remember what he said when he was with you in Galilee? He told you the Complete Person would be mistreated by evil people and be executed, then come to life again three days later." This stirred the women's memories, and it all began to make sense. They left the grave and told the other friends of Jesus about their experience. The women who had been to the grave included Maggie, Joan, and Marion, and several friends of theirs. The men belonging to Jesus' inner circle would not believe the women's story. They thought it wishful thinking. (Some say that Rocky ran to the grave to check out the women's story. He looked into the grave and saw the sheets the body had been wrapped in, then went back to his lodgings not knowing what to think.)

(13) The same day, two friends of Jesus were on their way to Emmatown, a few miles from Jerusalem.[22] They were discussing the events of the weekend. As they were talking, Jesus met up with them, going the same way. They didn't recognize him in the failing light. Jesus said, "You were deep in conversation as you were walking along. What were you talking about?" They hesitated for a moment and their faces were sad. Then one of them called Clover said, "You must be the only visitor to Jerusalem who doesn't know what's been happening the past few days!" Jesus said, "What do you

---

[22] Emmaus is usually identified with modern Kulonieh, which is under four miles from Jerusalem and a more plausible walk. The seven of the Greek text is probably a symbolic number like most of the numbers in the Gospels.

mean?" They said, "Haven't you heard of Jesus from Nazareth, a great speaker from God, who did wonderful things which were seen by everybody? Our clergy and politicians handed him over to the Romans to be tried and executed. We hoped he was going to be our national liberator. All this happened three days ago now. But some women we know have come up with a very surprising story. They visited the grave early this morning and found that the body was gone. They came back and told us they had seen messengers from God who said that Jesus was alive. Then some friends of ours went to the grave and found it was indeed empty, but they saw no sign of Jesus."

Then Jesus said, "How could you be so dim? How long is it going to be before you piece together the clues in the old books? Don't you know the passages which speak about the way God's Chosen would suffer before becoming famous?" Then Jesus began to explain how the words of Moses, and all the other speakers from God in days gone by, pointed to himself.

As they came near to the village, Jesus walked on, as if he intended to continue his journey. But the two would not hear of it. They insisted, "You must stay at our place. It's nearly night; there's no light left for traveling." Jesus accepted the invitation. When they were having supper, Jesus took a piece of bread, said "thank you" to God, broke it and handed it to them. At that moment they realized who he was. Then he left them. They talked to one another about it and said, "What a wonderful experience that was! How he cheered us up on that walk together! We understood the old books for the first time!" They went out again straightaway and walked back to Jerusalem. They found a gathering of all the close friends of Jesus. The two were told, "It's true, the Leader's come back to life. Rocky's seen him!" Then they told the others how they had met Jesus on the road, and how they had recognized him when he broke the bread.

(36) While they were talking, they suddenly realized that Jesus was there with them. They were frightened and thought they were seeing a ghost. Jesus said, "Why are you so nervous? What's the problem? It really is me. Look at my hands and feet. You can touch me if you like. Ghosts don't have flesh and bones like me." Then he let them have a good look at his hands and his feet. They were very happy to see him, but still found it difficult to believe. Jesus said, "I could do with something to eat." They brought him

some grilled fish and part of a honeycomb. He took the food and ate it while they watched.

Then Jesus said, "Do you remember what I taught you when we were together? All the important events of my life find an echo in the rules of Moses and in the things God's speakers and the songwriters said." Then Jesus explained the old books to them and said, "The old books say that God's Chosen will suffer and that he will come back to life after three days. They also say that his message of new life and forgiveness must be taken all over the world, to every race, starting with the people of Jerusalem. You have a vital role, because you've seen it all. I'm going to send you the special gift promised to you by my Parent. So stay here in Jerusalem until you get the confidence you need for the job."

Then they walked out together to Dategrove. Jesus waved goodbye to them and assured them of his love. Then he left them and returned to God. The friends were filled with love and admiration for Jesus, and went back to Jerusalem feeling very happy. They attended the worship center regularly, to give thanks to God.

Verses Omitted

The scriptures are based on several manuscripts and the manuscripts differ from each other in the inclusion or exclusion of some texts. Scholars differ as to which texts should be included or excluded. Here is a list of the texts we have decided not to include. They do not appear in all the manuscripts. Our decisions may not have been the right decisions. We hope that at least some of them are. We have included (in brackets) the doubtful 24:12, on the advice of Bishop John Shelby Spong.

5:39. Does not make a lot of sense in the context. Sounds like a Pharisee getting the last word, or possibly Jesus making fun of the Pharisee's conservative position. Its inclusion does not add anything and confuses the issue.

11:33. Verse 33 already occurs at 8:16. It is unlikely that Luke, always sparing of space, repeated his material in this way. Its presence is not essential and interrupts the flow of the argument.

17:36. This verse seems to be added from Matthew's Gospel. It adds nothing to the thought.

22:19b, 20. This translation follows the "shorter text," the more likely original, reflecting an alternative pattern for the celebration of the communal meal, in which cup precedes bread, as in 1 Corinthians 10:16, 21.

23:17. An addition copied from the accounts of Mark, John, and Matthew.

Luke's Good News

(Part Two)

1 (From Luke) When I wrote you my first book, Theo, I was writing to someone who loves God. So I told you the things Jesus did and what he taught, right from the start to the day he passed beyond time and space. Before he left, he handed on some guidelines from God's Spirit to the friends he had chosen as his special helpers. There was no answer to the proofs Jesus gave to show them he was alive after he had been dead. They saw him many times for well over a month, and he talked to them about "God's New World." Once when Jesus was having a meal with his friends, he told them, "Don't go away from Jerusalem. Wait till you get what my Parent means to give you. I've talked about it before. John dipped people in water, but in a matter of days you'll be drenched with God's Spirit."

At a time when they were all together, the helpers asked Jesus, "Leader, are you now going to give political power back to the Jewish people?" Jesus said, "The future course of the world's history is none of your business! It's a matter for the Loving God. Your job, when God's Spirit gives you confidence, will be to stand up for me in Jerusalem and the surrounding district, in Samaria and all over the world." Soon after Jesus said this, the friends watched him go up the mountain and disappear among the clouds. As they were straining to get a last look at Jesus going on his way, a couple of people wearing bright clothes came up to them and said, "What are you folk from Galilee looking up there for? You've only lost sight of Jesus for a while. He'll come back the way he went, and he'll still be the same Jesus!"

(12) Then they went back to Jerusalem from Olive Hill, just a short walk. As soon as they got there, they went straight to their headquarters in the room upstairs. They included Rocky, James and John, Andrew, Philip,

Twin, Bart, Matthew, James (Alf's son), Simon the Hothead, and Judas (James' son). Some women were there too, including Jesus' mother Mary. They all spent a lot of time together, talking with God.

On one occasion, there were about a hundred and twenty people in the room. Rocky stood up to make a speech. He said, "Friends, you can't stop the old books coming true. God's Spirit spoke through David and foresaw that Judas would help to get Jesus arrested. Judas was one of us and helped us in the work." (You may like to know what happened to Judas. He bought a field with the money he was given for betraying Jesus. He had a bad fall there and was fatally injured. When the people of Jerusalem got to hear about it, they called his field "The Bloody Field.") Rocky went on, "One of our songs goes like this,

> 'His house will be empty,
> Its owner gone:
> And his job will be going too ... '

We need a replacement to join us in the job of convincing people Jesus is alive. It must be someone who belonged to our group all the time Jesus our Leader shared his life with us, from the time John was dipping in the river, to the day Jesus went out of our sight up the mountain." There were two candidates, Joseph (sometimes known as "Honest Joe") and Matt. Then they spoke to God like this, "God, you know what each of us is really like inside. Show us who you'd like to have in this special job, which Judas gave up to go his own way." Then they put the names in a bag and Matt's name was picked out. He joined the other eleven friends of Jesus with special duties.

2 It was the spring holiday, and they were all there. It was just like a hurricane sweeping out of the sky. You could hear the noise all over the house. Sudden streaks of light darted about and lit up one friend after the other. They were all filled by God's Spirit, and she gave them the ability to communicate in new ways.

There were many Jews staying in Jerusalem at that time, from every country in the known world. The noise attracted a big crowd. It was strange that, though they spoke different languages, they could all understand what the friends were saying. They found it incredible and said, "They're ordinary working people from Galilee! How can they communicate with us? They're talking about the exciting things God has been doing, and we can understand every word, just as if we were hearing it in our own language!" (There were people there from the countries round the Persian Gulf and further east, from the Celtic lands, from north Africa, Arabia, Crete, and Rome, as well as from districts nearby. Some had been born Jews, others were Jewish converts.) They were impressed and confused at the same time, anxious to know what it was all about. Some thought the whole thing funny and said, "It looks as if they've had a few drinks!"

(14) This was the cue for Rocky to stand up where he could be seen, with the other eleven special friends around him. He shouted to the crowd, "My own people, and everyone here in Jerusalem, if you listen carefully, I'll explain what's going on. We haven't been drinking; it's only nine in the morning! What Joel said in his book is coming true:

> 'One day,' says God, 'I will fill every living thing in a special way. My Spirit will move your children to speak for me; she will excite teenagers with new ideas and give old people dreams about the future. Even those who have no rights, my favorites, will be full of me and speak my words. There will be earth-shattering events. The sun will be eclipsed and the moon appear red, as signs of God's coming among us. Then anyone who acknowledges God will be healed.'

"My people, listen to me: I'm going to tell you about Jesus from Nazareth, someone you remember being impressed by, because God did great things through him, proving he was God's agent. He fell into your hands. God knew that was going to happen and made plans. You used foreigners to kill Jesus, by hanging him on a cross. But God brought him back to life forever. Death couldn't hold him down. One of the songs David sang has words which could be Jesus talking:

> 'God, I follow you,
> You're with me all the time;

Nothing breaks my back,
Always feeling fine.
Sing a song of joy;
Future holds no fears;
You will not let me rot,
Nor give my loved-ones tears.
You've told me what life's all about:
With you I'll always sing and shout.'

"Brothers and sisters, it's not very likely our hero David was talking about himself. He's dead and buried; you can go and see his grave any time you like. He was looking into the future and remembering the promise God had given him, that one of his descendants would carry on where he had left off. David foresaw God's Chosen would come back to life after being dead. That's what he meant by the words,

'*You will not leave me dead,*
or let your Chosen rot.'

"Jesus is the one he was talking about. God brought Jesus back to life, and every one of us here can swear to the truth of it. He has been granted the highest honor by God his Parent, and God has given him the promised Spirit to pass on to us. That's the explanation of what you're seeing and hearing today! David didn't become one with God in this way, but he said,

'*God said to my Leader, "Sit by me,*
Then you'll have no enemy." '

"So now you all know the truth. Jesus, the one you hung on a cross, God has marked out as the Chosen Leader."

When the people heard this they were deeply shocked and said to Rocky and the others "Friends, what can we do about it?" Rocky said, "You can all turn over a new leaf and be dipped in the name of Jesus the Chosen. All the wrong things you've done will be forgiven, and you'll have the gift of God's Spirit. She is promised to you and your families, including those who live a long way away. God's invitation is for everybody." Rocky went on speaking to them and appealing to them, saying things like, "The society we live in is rotten to the core. It's time to take a stand and be different!" All those who took notice of what Rocky was saying were dipped, and the number of Jesus' followers was increased by about three thousand. They spent their time learning and getting to know one another. They shared their meals and talked with God together.

(43) Everybody was very excited because the friends of Jesus were doing lots of remarkable things. All those who accepted the Good News lived closely together and shared everything they had. They sold their valuables and used the money to help those who were hard up. Every day they spent a lot of time together in the temple and took turns to have one another into their homes for a meal. These occasions were great times. Everybody enjoyed the food and gave their thanks to God. The friends were popular with ordinary people, and because of Jesus there were more people finding a better life every day.

3 One day, at about three in the afternoon, Rocky and John were going into the central place of worship for a service. A disabled man, who had never been able to walk, was carried to the spot where he begged every day from the people going in to worship. It was right by the well-known "Beautiful Gate." As John and Rocky passed he asked them for money. Rocky and John both stared at him, catching his attention. He thought this meant he was going to get some money. But Rocky said, "I haven't any money on me, but I've got something better to give you. I represent Jesus from Nazareth, God's Chosen; so stand up and walk!" Rocky took hold of his right hand and pulled him up, and he found that his feet and ankles had a new strength in them. He bent his knees and tried a few practice steps. Then he followed John and Rocky into the temple, walking and jumping up and down, shouting his thanks to God as he went. Everybody turned to look, and when they recognized the beggar from the Beautiful Gate, they were puzzled and couldn't make out what had happened. The man hung on tight to Rocky and John as they went through Solomon's Arches, because everybody was running toward them to be in on the excitement. So Rocky faced them and spoke to them.

"What's up, my dear people? Why are you looking at us? There's nothing special about us. We haven't got this man to walk! God, who Abraham, Isaac, and Jacob and the rest of our ancestors worshiped, has given pride of place to Jesus. Jesus is God's Likeness. He's the one you handed over to the Romans and gave the thumbs down to in front of Pilate, even though Pilate had decided to set him free. You rejected this good man of God, and asked to have a murderer set free instead. You killed the bringer of life. But God has brought him back from the dead and we have seen him since. You all know this man here; you've seen him many times before. He got his new strength by relying on the reputation of Jesus. Because he trusted Jesus, he's now in perfect health. You can all see the difference!

"I realize, friends, neither you nor your leaders knew what they were doing. God's speakers in days gone by said the Chosen One would be badly treated. So it all went according to expectations. It's time for you to show you're sorry and to seek God's friendship again, so the wrong things you've done can be put behind you. If you do this, God will give you a period of recovery and then send you Jesus, the Chosen One. He must belong to the world beyond time and space until that time when everything is made new again. God's speakers told us about this long ago. It was Moses who said, 'God will give you a speaker just like me. He will be someone you can relate to, and you should take notice of what he says. Anyone who doesn't listen will find themselves out on a limb.' All God's speakers have seen these things coming, from Samuel onwards. You're the lucky ones on the receiving end of the promises made by God's speakers, and you've inherited the special relationship God had with your ancestors. God said to Abraham, 'Your descendants will be a good influence for everyone all over the world.' It's all happening! God's representative has come to influence *you* first of all, by getting you to give up your bad ways."

4 While Rocky and John were still speaking, some members of the clergy, and some leading public figures, came with the security officer and objected to their teaching the people. In particular they were annoyed the case of Jesus was being used to prove there is life after death. They arrested them both and, because it was late in the day, they locked them up till next morning. But a lot of people accepted what John

and Rocky had been saying. The numbers by this time had grown to about five thousand.

The next day a special court was held in Jerusalem. Most of the high-ranking clergy were there, all related to one another. John and Rocky were brought before them. They asked, "What's the trick? Who's put you up to it?"

Rocky felt inspired by God's Spirit and said, "I want all you important people to know, since we're being had up for an act of kindness shown to a disabled person, and since there's some doubt about how he was healed, it's Jesus from Nazareth, God's Chosen who has put us up to it, the one you strung up, but God brought back to life. It's Jesus you must thank that this man stands in front of you in full health! As the old books say about Jesus:

> 'The stone the builders tossed away
> Stands in the central spot today.'

Jesus is the only one who can give complete healing. There is no one else like him anywhere else in the world."

Those conducting the hearing were impressed by the courage shown by John and Rocky, and very surprised to hear they had no formal education. The only explanation was that they had got it from Jesus. It was difficult for them to say anything, because the man who had been healed was standing right there. So they cleared the court and discussed the case in private. They asked, "What on earth are we going to do with them? Everybody in Jerusalem knows they've done something quite extraordinary. We can't deny it. But we've got to stop this movement from spreading. So let's caution them and forbid them to talk about Jesus."

The court called back John and Rocky and gave them an order not to teach or speak about Jesus. But Rocky and John answered, "What do you think God would prefer? For us to do what you want or to do what God wants? We can't stop talking about the things we've seen and heard." So after warning them in even stronger language, the court let them go. It was obviously impossible to punish them, in view of what had happened. Everyone was thanking God. The man who had been healed was over forty years old.

(23) As soon as they had been allowed to go, John and Rocky went to

their friends and told them what the religious leaders had said. Then together they spoke to God: "Wonderful God, you brought about the earth, the sea and the skies, and everything in them; your Spirit inspired our ancestor, David, your helper, to sing

'Leaders of all peoples known
In anger risen agree their plan;
Tyrants strutting side by side
Challenged God and mocked God's Own.'

In this city Herod and Pilate united Jews and non-Jews against Jesus, your special agent. But they couldn't defeat your plans. We are your agents now. Look how they're threatening us! Give us the guts to speak your words. Let's have more big surprises and more people healed when we use the name Jesus."

When the friends had finished talking to God, a tremor of excitement went round the room, and they were inspired by God's Spirit to speak God's words with confidence.

Those who accepted the Christian message were a very united group of people. They shared all their belongings and kept nothing for private use. The leaders spoke with great conviction from their first-hand knowledge that Jesus had returned to life, and everybody felt good. No one went short of anything, because those who owned property put it up for sale and gave the money to the leaders who used it to help anyone in need. That's how Joseph from Cyprus, one of the temple assistants, got his new name. The leaders called him "Cheery," because he sold his field and gave them the money.

5 A married couple, Nye and Sapphire, sold some of their property. Nye made out he was bringing all the money from the sale to the leaders, but actually kept some of it back. His wife knew what he was up to. Rocky challenged him, "Nye, why are you behaving in such an evil way? You've pocketed part of the money you got from the sale of your property! Do you think you can play a trick on God's Spirit? It was your property before you sold it, and afterwards you were free to do what you

liked with the money. Why all this deceit? It's not us you're trying to cheat, but God!" Rocky's words caused Nye to have a heart attack, and he collapsed dead on the floor. Everybody who got to hear about it was very shocked. Some of the younger people took charge, wrapped him in a sheet, and took him away to be buried.

About three hours later, Sapphire arrived, not knowing what had happened. Rocky challenged her. "Did you and your husband sell your land for the amount you told me?" "Yes" she said, "that's what we got from the sale." Rocky said, "Why did you two plan together to find out if God's Spirit could catch you cheating? The people who've just buried your husband will be back any minute for you!" She then collapsed in front of him and died. The young people came in, made sure she was dead, then carried her out to bury her beside her husband. The members of the church and others who got to hear about it were very frightened.

The followers of Jesus continued to impress the people by their actions. They met under Solomon's Arches. People who were not members of the group were too frightened to join them, though they talked of them with respect. Despite this, the numbers of those who put their trust in Jesus, the Leader, continued to grow, women and men. Sick people were carried out into the streets and put on mats and camp beds so Rocky's shadow could fall on them as he went by. Lots of people came in from the towns round Jerusalem, bringing those who were unwell or mentally disturbed, and they were all made better.

(17) The Chief of the clergy decided it was time to act. He and those who held the same religious views as he did felt they were being upstaged. They arrested the leading followers of Jesus and put them in the public jail. But in the night someone sent by God organized their escape, and told them, "Go and stand in the worship place and tell people how your life has changed." So they went there as soon as it was light and carried on teaching. The Chief and his colleagues called a special meeting with all the important people in the Jewish community. They sent to prison for the followers of Jesus to be brought before them. But when the police got there, they couldn't find them in the prison. So they came back and told the meeting, "We found the prison was locked and well guarded at every door, but when we opened the doors there was no one inside." This puzzled the chief of

police and the religious leaders. They could not work out how it was possible to escape. Then someone came in and told them, "Your prisoners are standing in the worship place and teaching the people." Then the police officer went with some of his squad and brought them to the meeting. The police did not use violence. They were too afraid of having stones thrown at them!

When the followers of Jesus had been brought in, they were made to stand in front of the meeting. The Chief started to question them. "We made it quite clear you were not on any account to teach in the name of this leader of yours, but you've done the very opposite. You've been all over Jerusalem spreading his teachings and making it look as if we are responsible for his death." But Rocky, backed up by the others, answered him by saying, "We intend to do what God wants, rather than listen to people like you. The God our ancestors worshiped brought Jesus back to life, the one you strung up on a piece of wood. He's now God's number one, the Leader and Healer who will bring God's people to a change of heart, and make their bad behavior a thing of the past. It's our job to make this known, with the help of God's Spirit. She has been given to those who do what God asks them to do."

These words caused the members of the meeting to lose control of their feelings, and they wanted to kill the followers of Jesus. But one of the strict set who was at the meeting, Liam, an expert in the Rule Books and highly thought of by the ordinary people, stood up and asked for the followers of Jesus to be taken outside for a while. Then he spoke to the meeting. "I'm speaking to you as members of my own race. I think you ought to be careful how you deal with these people. You remember Ted and his gang? He claimed to be somebody special and attracted about four hundred followers. But he was killed, and his gang went into hiding. And that was that. It was the same with Judas from Galilee. He led a protest against the Poll Tax and came to a sticky end. So your best course with these people is to leave them alone. If their movement is just a political thing, it won't last. But if God is behind it, then there's no stopping it. Try and you will find yourselves up against God!"

Liam won his point. They called the followers of Jesus back and had them flogged. They ordered them not to mention Jesus in their public speaking, and let them go. As they left the meeting, the followers had smiles on their faces. They felt privileged to have been badly treated because of their loyalty to Jesus. Every day they carried on teaching in the place of worship and in their homes. They called Jesus "God's Chosen."

6 At the same time as the followers of Jesus were growing in number, those whose first language was Greek complained they were being discriminated against by those who spoke the Jewish language. They thought their people who had no means of support from a family were not getting their fair share of the food handed out each day. The twelve leaders called everybody together and said, "We've got enough to do telling people the truth about God, without having to act like waiters. So friends, we suggest you choose seven responsible people to be in charge of this work. They must have the right motives and carry the respect of everybody. We will spend our time keeping in touch with God and passing on what God has to say." Everybody thought this made sense, so they chose Stephen, known for his strong convictions and closeness to God, and with him Philip, Russ, Norman, Tim, Craig, and Colin (a convert to the Jewish religion from Antioch). These were introduced to the leaders, who asked God to help them and gave them a hug. God's message reached more and more people, and there were new followers joining all the time, including many of the temple clergy.

(8) Stephen was a strong and attractive person, and people soon became aware of his abilities. But some didn't like him, especially those who went to a place of worship which was more like a private club. They argued with Stephen, but couldn't match his quick mind and convincing way of speaking. So they spread rumors that he had spoken disrespectfully of Moses and God. They got a gang together to grab Stephen when he was off guard. They had the backing of the clergy and the experts in the old books. He was taken to court, where the witnesses they brought forward told lies about him. They said, "This man spends all his time running down the temple and the rules of our religion. We've heard him say that Jesus from Nazareth will pull down the temple and change the way Moses told us to do things." Everybody there eyed Stephen closely. You could tell from the way he looked what a good person he was.

7 The Chief of the clergy asked Stephen, "Is it true what they're saying about you?" Stephen conducted his own defense in this way:
"I ask you, as my own people, to give me a fair hearing. Our wonderful God appeared to Abraham when he lived near the shores of the Persian Gulf, before he moved north to Haran. God said, 'Leave the country where you were born, leave your friends and relations behind, and go in search of a new land. I will show you the way.' Abraham traveled from the Persian Gulf, north up the river Euphrates, to Haran. After his father died, God directed him into this part of the world, where you now live. God never allowed Abraham to own even the smallest piece of land here, but promised his descendants would own it, even though he had no children. This is the way God put it, 'Your descendants will be asylum-seekers in a foreign land. They will suffer discrimination and have no rights for four hundred years. But I will settle the score with the nation which turns them into slaves, and they will escape and worship me here.' Then God introduced Abraham to the practice of removing the foreskin, and he did this to his son Isaac a week after he was born. Isaac did the same for his son Jacob and then Jacob for his twelve sons, who we think of as the founders of our race.

"Jacob's sons were envious of their brother Joseph, and sold him as a slave to the Egyptians. But God looked after him, and helped him through all his difficulties. He was able to impress the Pharaoh of Egypt with his attractive personality and good sense, so that he became Prime Minister and Head of the Royal Household. Then there was a severe famine, which struck Egypt and Palestine and caused great hardship. Jacob heard that Egypt had stocks of grain, so he sent his sons there for the first time. On their second visit, Joseph told his brothers who he was, and introduced them to the Pharaoh. Then Joseph sent an invitation to his father Jacob and the rest of the family, to come and live with him. There were about seventy-five of them altogether. Jacob moved to Egypt and died there. So did the rest of his family at that time. Their bodies were brought back to Samaria and put in a grave Abraham had bought from the Hamor family with money. The day was coming when God would keep the promise made to Abraham.

"Our people in Egypt had grown in number. Another Pharaoh came to rule over Egypt. Joseph meant nothing to him. He exploited our people, and made them leave their children out in the open to die. That was when Moses was born. He was a beautiful baby. For three months he was brought up at home, and then, when he was put out in the open, Pharaoh's daughter adopted him and brought him up as her own son. Moses was educated as an Egyptian and was very talented. When he become a man, he had an urge to visit his true relations. When he saw one of them being beaten up by an Egyptian, he jumped in to protect him, and this ended in the death of the Egyptian. His own people were more embarrassed than pleased by this incident. They didn't realize Moses was the one God would use to help them. The next day he tried to put an end to a fight between two of them. He told them, 'You ought not to be fighting one another. You're comrades!' But the one who had started it gave Moses a shove, and said, 'Who do you think you are? Are you going to kill me, like you killed the Egyptian yesterday?' Moses in panic left Egyptian territory and went to live as an alien in Midian. It was there his two sons were born.

"After many years Moses had a strange experience in the Sinai Desert when a bush caught fire. The sight intrigued Moses, and as he went closer to get a better look, he heard God's voice. 'I am the God of your ancestors, the God of Abraham, Isaac, and Jacob.' Moses was frightened and started to shake. He didn't dare look. Then God said to him, 'Take your sandals off, as a mark of respect for my presence here. I've seen the cruel treatment my people have had in Egypt, and I've heard their cries of pain, and I've got a plan to rescue them. I want you go to Egypt for me.'

"Do you see what I'm trying to say? Moses was rejected by his own people. Their words were, 'Who do you think you are?' But he was the very one God sent to lead and free our people after the experience of the burning bush. Moses led our people out of Egypt, performing remarkable feats in Egypt, at the Red Sea, and for many years in the desert. It was also Moses who said to our people, 'God will send you another speaker, one of your own number, like me.' Moses continued to pass on to our people his experiences of God when they met together, and he told them the instructions he had received on Mount Sinai. But our ancestors wouldn't follow his lead. Instead they pushed him out of the way, and told him they wished they were back in Egypt. They said to Aaron, 'Make us some gods to lead us. We don't know what's happened to Moses, the one who led us out of Egypt!' That was when they made a statue in the shape of a bull. They offered food to the statue and held a party for it. God turned away in disgust while they went on to worship the sun, moon, and stars. As it says in the old books, 'Did you honor me with your gifts all that time in the desert, people of Israel? No, you made statues of shameful gods, just like the foreigners, and carried them in special tents. You deserve to be exiled to Babylon.'

(44) "The tent our ancestors were supposed to care about was the tent for God's worship, which was set up in the desert according to the directions God had given Moses. Our ancestors brought it to this country under the leadership of Joshua, when God moved the other nations to make room for them. The tent was kept till the time of David, who pleased God. David asked God's permission to build a more permanent place of worship for the Jewish people. But it was Solomon who built God a house. But our God is too big to live in a house made by human builders. According to one of God's speakers, God says, 'Space is my throne, and I use the earth to rest my feet on. How can you possibly build a suitable house for me? What size do you intend to make the living room? Have you forgotten I made everything there is?' "

Then Stephen said, "Oh, what a stubborn lot you are. It's much easier to get foreigners to listen and change their hearts. You oppose everything God's Spirit seeks to do, just like your ancestors. Can you name a single one of God's speakers your ancestors didn't treat badly? They killed those who said God's Special Representative was coming, and now you've murdered him by handing him over to the enemy! You've been told what God wants of you by God's messengers. But you've done the opposite!"

Stephen's words made the members of the court lose their temper. They were so angry, you could hear their teeth grinding. But Stephen was only conscious of God's Spirit inside him, and as he looked into the distance, his mind was filled with thoughts of God's beauty, and Jesus in the place of honor at God's side. "Do you see what I see?" Stephen said, "Look, the clouds are parting! It's the True Human in the place of honor, right next to God!" But they put their hands over their ears, screamed, and rushed straight at him all at once. They dragged him out of the city and started to throw stones at him. They left their jackets in charge of a young man named Saul. As the stones came at Stephen, he spoke to Jesus. "Jesus, my Leader, let me come to you." Then he knelt down and shouted loudly, "Leader, forgive them for this wrong!" The next moment he died. Saul thought that killing Stephen was the right thing to do.

8 That day marks the beginning of a rough time for the followers of Jesus in Jerusalem. All except the leaders left their homes and moved out into the country. A group of people, well known for their devotion to God, took charge of the funeral arrangements for Stephen, and led the mourning. Saul, on the other hand, led the harassing of the Christians, breaking into their homes one after the other and dragging men and women off to prison.

Those who had been forced to leave their homes, spread their ideas wherever they went. Philip went to a town in Samaria and spoke to the people there about God's Chosen. Large crowds gathered and listened attentively to what Philip had to say. They were impressed by the remarkable things he was doing. People who had been mentally disturbed found peace, and some of the disabled, the lame, and the paralyzed, were healed. The whole community shared in the happiness.

In the same town there was a famous magician, a popular entertainer, called Simon. Everybody took notice of him, including the leaders of the community. They believed his powers were supernatural. Simon's abilities as a magician were amazing. He had the power to hold people's attention for a long time. But their attention was now drawn to Philip and his good news about Jesus and God's New World. When women and men accepted what Philip had to say, they were dipped. Simon was one of these, and when he had been dipped he went everywhere with Philip. He was amazed by all the wonderful things he saw happening.

When the leaders back in Jerusalem heard the people of Samaria had accepted God's message, they sent Rocky and John to find out the facts. The first thing they did when they arrived was to ask God to give the new converts the Spirit. Up to now God's Spirit had not entered any of them. Only the name of Jesus the Leader had been used when they were dipped. Rocky and John hugged each of them and they received God's Spirit.

When Simon saw people could get the Spirit just by being touched by the leaders, he said to them, "I'd like to be able to pass on God's Spirit by touching and hugging people. How much do you want?" But Rocky said, "Get out of my sight! And you can take your money with you! God's gifts aren't for sale! You're not one of us. You haven't got the right attitude. You'd better change from your bad ways and beg God to forgive your unworthy thoughts, if you can. I can see you're a thoroughly bad lot." Simon said, "Please speak to Jesus for me, so I escape the dangers you talk about."

When Rocky and John had told their stories and handed on the Leader's teachings, they went back to Jerusalem. They gave the good news to many of the Samaritan villages they passed through on the way.

(26) Philip had a strong feeling he should now go south on the desert road that leads from Jerusalem to Gaza. He got going and had not been long on the road before he met an African. He was a castrated man, the court treasurer of the queen of the Ethiopians. He had been to Jerusalem to worship and was now on his way home. He was sitting in his carriage and reading aloud from the old book called Isaiah. Philip felt an urge to run up to the carriage and ask for a lift. When he heard what the man was reading, he asked, "Are you making any sense of it?" "Not much," the African said. "I could do with someone to explain it to me." So he invited Philip to sit by him in the carriage. The castrated man was reading this passage:

> "He was driven like a lamb to the slaughterhouse –
> A sheep cannot argue with the shears.
> With nothing to say, put to shame in every way,
> There was no one to calm his fears.
> His life was cut off; hope of children gone –
> Never was such injustice done."

The castrated man asked Philip, "I'd like to know who God's speaker is talking about. Is he talking about himself or somebody else?" Then Philip used this extract from the old book to explain to the castrated man how the Good News of Jesus applied to *him*.

Soon after they came to an oasis beside the road. The castrated man said. "Look there's a pool of water! There's no rule which says I can't be dipped, is there?" He stopped the carriage. Philip and the castrated man went down into the water together. Then Philip dipped him. As soon as they had come out of the water, Philip realized it was time for him to leave. They never met again, but the African went on his way a very happy man. Philip next turned up at Azotus and traveled from there to Caesartown, passing on the good news in all the villages on the way.

9 All this time, Saul kept up a hate campaign, promising to put an end to all the followers of Jesus. He went to the Chief of the clergy and asked for warrants to take to the Jewish places of worship in Damascus, so he could arrest any men or women he found there with the new ideas and bring them back as prisoners to Jerusalem.

Saul was on the outskirts of Damascus when, without warning, he was overcome by the strong sunlight. He collapsed on the ground and heard a voice saying, "Saul, Saul why are you giving me all this hate?" Saul said, "Who are you, Sir?" The voice said, "I'm Jesus, the one you're out to destroy. Get up now and go into the town, where you'll be told what to do." The guards with Saul did not know what to say. They heard a sound but did not see anything. Saul got to his feet, but when he opened his eyes he could not see. He had to be led by the hand into Damascus. He was blind for three days and had nothing to eat or drink all that time.

In Damascus there was a friend of Jesus called Ian. He had a dream in which Jesus spoke to him by name. "What is it, Leader?" he asked. Jesus said, "Go to Jude's house in Straight Street, and ask for a man from Tarsus called Saul. He's spending his time talking with God. He's dreamt that someone called Ian will come and touch him, so he can see again." Ian said, "Leader, I've heard a lot about this man. He's been big trouble to your people in Jerusalem. He's come here with warrants from the clergy to arrest anyone who uses your name in worship." But Jesus said to him, "It's safe for you to go. I've picked this person to be my representative to those who are not Jews. He will act as my ambassador to heads of state. He'll speak for me to his own Jewish people too. I'll have to warn him about all the suffering he'll get when he stands up for me."

Ian made his way to the house and went inside. He hugged Saul and said, "Saul, my friend, Jesus our Leader, the one you met on the way here, has asked me to visit you. You're going to be able to see again, and you'll be filled with God's Spirit." At once the film over Saul's eyes began to clear, and he could see again He got up and was dipped. After having something to eat, he began to feel stronger. Saul spent a few days with the followers of Jesus in Damascus. He started straightaway to speak in the places of worship, saying, "Jesus is God's Likeness." All those who heard him were astounded and said, "Isn't this the man who's been giving a bad time in Jerusalem to those who worship using the name of Jesus? Wasn't he supposed to come here to take such people back to the religious leaders as prisoners?" As Saul became more confident he argued skillfully that Jesus is God's Chosen. The Jews in Damascus did not know what to think about it. In the end they made a plan to murder him, but he got to hear of it. They kept up a round-the-clock lookout on the town gate, so they could get him as he went through. But one night Saul's friends came for him and let him down through a hole in the wall in a basket.

(26) Saul made for Jerusalem and tried to join the followers of Jesus there. But they were all afraid of him and thought it was a trick. It was Cheery who befriended him and introduced him to those in charge. Cheery told them how Saul had met the Leader on the road, and how the Leader had spoken to him. He also told them about Saul's courage in speaking for Jesus in Damascus. Saul got to know the friends of Jesus well, and went all over Jerusalem speaking on behalf of the Leader. He had discussions with the Greek-speaking Jews, but they tried to murder him. When the friends realized the danger Saul was in, they arranged transport for him to Caesartown, and from there to Tarsus. For a while the Christians in the whole of Palestine had a breathing space. With the help of God's Spirit they grew in numbers and confidence. They showed their allegiance to the Leader in the way they lived.

(32) At this time Rocky toured the whole country. On a visit to God's people in Ludd, he came across a man called Aidan, who had been in bed for eight years, unable to move. Rocky said to him, "Aidan, Jesus, God's Chosen, has made you well again. You can get up and make your bed!" Aidan got out of bed straightaway. When they saw Aidan well again, the whole community in Ludd, and the plain of Sharon round about, became followers of Jesus.

In Jaffa there was a friend of Jesus whose name was Gazelle. She was always helping other people, especially poor people. At this time she had a serious illness and died. Her body was laid in a room upstairs. Ludd was not far away, so when the Christians in Jaffa heard Rocky was there, they sent two messengers to him, asking him to come as soon as possible. Rocky packed his belongings and went straight back with them to Jaffa. When he got there he was taken upstairs straightaway. Some poor women were in the bedroom. They crowded round Rocky and showed him the coats and dresses Gazelle had made while she was alive. Rocky sent everybody out of the room. Then he knelt beside the bed and talked with God. He looked at the body and said, "Come on, Gazelle, it's time to get up!" Gazelle opened her eyes, and when she saw Rocky, she sat up. Rocky held her hand as she got out of bed. Then he called for the other friends to come up, including the women who had been there. He showed them that Gazelle was alive. Soon everyone in Jaffa was talking about what had happened, and many put their trust in Jesus. Rocky stayed on in Jaffa, lodging with a leather-maker called Simon.

10

Neil was a soldier, stationed at Caesartown. He was a captain in the Italian Regiment. He and his family were very religious, and had respect for God. Neil used his wealth to help those in need, and set aside time to talk with God. One day, at about three o'clock, he was visited by a messenger from God who came into his house and said, "Neil, isn't it?" Neil jumped quickly to attention and said, "Yes, what can I do for you, Sir?" The messenger said, "God has taken notice of your words, and has seen your help to those in need. You are to send some of your people to Jaffa to fetch someone called Simon, better known as Rocky. He's in the home of a leather-maker, also called Simon. His house is on the sea front. When the messenger had gone, Neil sent for two people who worked in his house, and one of his soldiers who shared his religious enthusiasm. He told them about the message and sent them to Jaffa. They came within sight of the town the following day at twelve o'clock.

About the same time Rocky went up to the patio on the roof to talk with God. He was feeling hungry and fancied something to eat. While lunch was being prepared, he began to daydream. He looked into the distance and saw what seemed like a great sheet being spread out on the land, held by its four corners. It had all sorts of animals in it, including snakes and birds. Then he heard a voice, "How about something there for lunch, Rocky?" Rocky said, "With respect, I couldn't possibly. I only eat kosher food. Everything else is dirty." The voice spoke again, "You mustn't call the food God has prepared 'dirty.'" This happened three times; then the picture disappeared.

At that very moment, when Rocky was trying to make sense of what he had seen with his mind's eye, the messengers from Neil arrived. They were standing at the outside gate, asking if it was Simon's house, and if Rocky was at home. Rocky was still deep in thought, when God's Spirit drew his attention to the three people down below who were asking for him. He rushed down to meet them, feeling they'd been specially sent to him. When Rocky got to the bottom of the steps he said, "I'm the one you're looking for. How can I help you?" They said, "You've probably heard of Neil, because he's got a good reputation among your people. He's an officer in the regiment, a good man, who respects God. He's been advised to ask you to visit him, so he can hear your ideas." Rocky invited them in and put them up for the night.

Next day, as soon as they were ready, Rocky, the messengers, and some other friends from Jaffa, set out for Caesartown. They arrived the following day. Neil was waiting for them. He had invited all his friends and relatives along. When Neil met Rocky, he bowed down respectfully. But Rocky said, "There's no need for that. I'm only human." They chatted together as they went into the room where everyone was waiting.

Rocky said, "You realize as a Jew I'm not supposed to mix with non-Jews or visit their houses. But God has shown me I shouldn't look upon anyone as inferior or treat them like an outcast. So I've come here willingly today in answer to your request. What can I do for you?" Neil said, "Three days ago, at three o'clock, the same time as now, while I was talking to God, a man in bright clothes came into my room. He said, 'God has heard what you've said, and seen what you've done for other people. I suggest you send to Jaffa for Simon, better known as Rocky, who's staying with Simon the leather-maker in his house on the sea front.' So I sent for you straightaway, and you've kindly accepted my invitation. All of us sense that God is here, and we're all eager to hear what God has asked you to tell us."

(34) This is what Rocky said to them. "I now know God hasn't any favorites. All who honor God and do what's right, no matter what their race or religion, are accepted by God. You've heard of the special message sent to the Jews? The Good News is that Jesus, God's Chosen, brings peace. He's the one we all look to now. I'm sure you know the story of what happened after John told people to be dipped in the river. It started in Galilee and spread all over the country. God gave the power of the Spirit to Jesus from Nazareth. He went everywhere doing good, and healing people from very severe illnesses. It was obvious God was with him. We saw everything he did, in and around Jerusalem. They killed him by hanging him on a wooden post. But God brought him back to life three days later, and made it possible for him to be seen, not in public, but by a group of us specially chosen to tell other people afterwards. We actually ate and drank with Jesus, after he returned to life. We had instructions from him in person to tell people about him, and to make it clear he's the one chosen by God to decide the fate of those who are alive and those who've died. All God's speakers point to him. From them we learn that those who trust Jesus are forgiven by him for the wrong things they've done."

Before Rocky had finished his speech, all those taking notice of what he was saying received God's Spirit. The Jewish followers of Jesus who had come with Rocky were very surprised that non-Jews were included. They heard them thanking God in several different languages. Then Rocky said, "Does anybody object if I dip these people? They have received God's gift, just like us!" So Rocky gave instructions for them to be dipped as followers of Jesus, the Chosen. The new Christians asked Rocky to stay with them for a few days.

11 The followers of Jesus in the south heard that people who were not Jews had responded when God spoke to them. When Rocky next visited Jerusalem, those who thought people needed to become Jews before they could be followers of Jesus, spoke angrily to him. "You've been visiting the homes of people who don't keep our rules!" So Rocky took pains to explain to them in detail what had happened. "It was in Jaffa, while I was talking with God, that everything became clear to me. I saw what looked like a big sheet coming out of the

sky, held by its four corners. It came quite close. All sorts of animals were in it, snakes and birds among them. Then I heard a voice saying, 'Time for lunch, Rocky!' I said, 'God, I can't eat that. I don't eat dirty food.' Then the voice came again. It seemed to come from the sky. 'You mustn't call the food God's prepared "dirty."' This happened three times and then the sheet disappeared up into the sky. Just then, three people from Caesartown arrived at my lodgings. They were looking for me. I was quite sure God's Spirit wanted me to go along with them. She was urging me to get rid of my prejudices. I've six friends here who'll back me up, because they came with me. We went together into Neil's house. Neil told us how a messenger from God had come into his house and said, 'Send to Jaffa for Simon, better known as Rocky. He will tell you things which will bring life and health to you and all the people who live with you.' When I spoke to them, God's Spirit came into them, just as she did to us when it all started. I remembered the Leader's words, 'John dipped people in the water, but you will be drenched with God's Spirit.' Since God was giving them the same gift he gave us when we put our trust in Jesus, I wasn't going to be the one to stand in God's way." This put a stop to their criticism. They thanked God and said, "It seems God has given people who are not Jews the ability to change, and to experience true life."

(19) Those who had to leave their homes because of the troubles following the death of Stephen, moved north into Syria as far as Antioch, and to Cyprus. They only gave God's message to the Jewish people. But some who came from Cyprus and northern Africa went to Antioch and spoke about Jesus the Leader to people who were not Jews. They felt the presence of Jesus, and a large number put their trust in him. When the followers of Jesus in Jerusalem heard about this, they sent Cheery to Antioch. When he got there and saw God at work, he was delighted and told them all to be true to the Leader and do their very best for him. Cheery was a fine character. He had high ideals, and God's Spirit could be seen in everything he did. He introduced a lot of people to Jesus.

Then Cheery went to Tarsus to find Saul. He took Saul back to Antioch with him, and for a whole year the two of them were guests of the group there. Lots of people came to the classes they held. It was at Antioch the followers of Jesus were first called "Christians."

About the same time, some people who often spoke for God came to Antioch from Jerusalem. One of them, called Hopper, stood up to speak. God's Spirit moved him to tell the group there would be a serious shortage of food throughout the Mediterranean world. This came about in the reign of the Roman Emperor Claudius. The meeting decided to send gifts to their friends in and around Jerusalem. Everyone was encouraged to join in, according to their means. Cheery and Saul were given the task of taking the gifts to the leaders of the Christians in the south.

12

The same time as all this was happening, Herod used his position to launch a vicious attack on some of the friends of Jesus. He had James knifed to death. James was John's brother. When this turned out to be popular, Herod arrested Rocky and put him in prison. This was during the Jewish holiday. Four groups of soldiers were set to guard Rocky. Herod's plan was to stage a trial in public after the holiday was over. While Rocky was in prison his friends begged God to help him.

It was the night before Herod was going to stage the trial. Rocky was held by a chain at each wrist. He was asleep with two soldiers standing either side of him, and there were guards in front of his cell door. One of God's special agents came quickly into the cell, holding a bright light. He tapped Rocky on the shoulder, woke him up, and said, "Quick! Get up!" Rocky's handcuffs were unlocked. The agent said, "Put your jacket and shoes on, and come with me." Rocky went out after him in a daze. The rescue by the agent did not seem real – more like a dream. They crept past one guard, then another, until they came to the iron gate which led to the city outside. This opened for them and they went through and started to walk down the street. At the junction with the next street the agent quickly disappeared. By this time Rocky had woken up and said. "It's for real! God has sent his agent to help me escape from Herod and the nasty death the mob were looking forward to."

As soon as Rocky got his bearings, he made for the house of John Mark's mother, Marie, where a lot of people had come together to talk with God. When Rocky knocked at the front door, a girl called Rhoda who worked in the house, went to see who was there. When she recognized

Rocky's voice, she was so excited, she forgot to open the door and ran back to tell everyone he was there. They told her she was letting her imagination play tricks. But she stood her ground. "He's jumped out of his body, then!" they said. All this time Rocky kept on knocking, and when at last someone opened the door, the friends could hardly believe their eyes. Rocky asked them to be quiet, and then told them how God had got him out of prison. He said, "You had better tell James and the others." Then he left and went somewhere safer.

In the morning there was panic among the soldiers over what had become of Rocky. Herod called for a search, but it led nowhere. So Herod interrogated the guards and had them put to death. Then he went north to Caesartown for a while.

Herod at this time was making life difficult for the people of Tyre and Sidon. They sent a delegation to him and used the influence of Bud, one of Herod's officials, to bring about an agreement. (Their territory was dependent on Herod's territory for its economic survival.) Herod made a great occasion of the new accord, dressing in style, sitting high up on a platform, and making a grand speech. The people responded by shouting, "He can't be human. He sounds more like a god!" Because Herod was allowing himself honors that should have been given to God, he immediately began to feel very ill, and died soon after of a painful stomach complaint.

God's message got across to more and more people. When Cheery and Saul had done what they had set out to do, they went back to Jerusalem and took John Mark with them.

13 Among the Christian community at Antioch there were teachers and speakers. They included Cheery, Simeon – nicknamed "Blackie" because of his dark skin, another African called Lucius, Sturdy who had been a childhood companion to prince Herod, and Saul. At a time when they were going without food to keep their minds on God, God's Spirit spoke to them. She said, "It's time for Cheery and Saul to get on with the special job I want them to do." The group went a little longer without food and talked with God again. Then they all gave Cheery and Saul a hug and said goodbye.

God's Spirit directed Cheery and Saul to the nearest port, where they caught the boat to Cyprus. They landed at Salamis and talked about God in the Jewish places of worship. John Mark went along to help. They went right across the island as far as Paphos. There they met a magician, a Jewish confidence-trickster known as "Slippery Al." He hung around the governor of the island, George Paul. George Paul was an intelligent man, and he invited Cheery and Saul to talk to him about God. But Slippery kept interrupting and trying to put the governor off. Saul, who from now on called himself Paul, was inspired to look Slippery straight in the eye and say, "You little devil, you stand in the way of everything that's good. You're up to all sorts of tricks. When are you going to stop twisting God's truth into something crooked? I'm telling you, God's not going to let you get away with it! Let's see how you like being blind! No sunshine for you for a while!" Straightaway Slippery Al found himself in a thick fog, and everything went black. He had to grope about, trying to find somebody to hold his hand. The governor was impressed and put his trust in Jesus. Then Paul and his friends caught the boat back to the mainland and landed at Perga. But John Mark left them and went home to Jerusalem.

(14) They moved on to a town with the same name as the town they started from, Antioch. On Saturday they went to the Jewish place of worship and found somewhere to sit. After reading from the old books, the leaders passed them a message. "Friends, if you have anything to say to cheer these people up, we'd like to hear it." So Paul stood up and spoke to them: "What I have to say is for my own people and for people of other races who respect God. The God of the Jews took special care of our ancestors. They were a people to be reckoned with when they lived in Egypt. God gave them the means to escape from Egypt, but had a lot to put up with from them as they traveled through the desert. Only by displacing seven different nations in Palestine were our people able to settle in the land God intended them to live in. It took about four hundred and fifty years. Then for a period God inspired a series of able leaders. At the time of one of those leaders, Samuel, the people decided they wanted a monarchy. God's choice for king was Saul (Kish's son, a descendant of Benjamin). He was king for forty years. Then God replaced him by David. This is what God said about David. 'David, Jesse's son is the sort of person I like. He will

do what I want him to do.' God has given us a descendant of David to be our Healer, as promised. His name is Jesus. Before Jesus came, John the Dipper called all the Jewish people to be dipped, to show they were sorry for their bad ways. When he had done his job, John said, 'I hope you've not made the mistake of thinking I'm the Chosen One! Someone is coming after me. I'm not fit to untie his shoelaces!' Those of us here who are descended from Abraham, and any others here who honor God, have all been sent this life-giving news. The people of Jerusalem didn't recognize Jesus. Nor did their leaders. They didn't understand the words of God's speakers, read out loud every Rest Day. In fact they carried out what the speakers said would happen and condemned Jesus to death. They gave him a sham trial, then asked Pilate to execute him. When they'd made sure they'd done everything the old books say would happen to him, they took him down from the gallows and buried him. But God brought Jesus back to life. For several weeks he appeared to the friends from Galilee who had come to Jerusalem with him, and they're making sure people know the facts. We're here to bring you the Good News that God has kept the promise given to our ancestors, by bringing Jesus to life. You may remember some words from the old song which refer to Jesus:

> 'You're my Child today:
> By my side to stay.'

"There is more I could quote from the old songs – these words, for example, about his returning to life and his body not rotting:

> 'The promise I made to David
> I'll make come true for YOU.'

And

> 'Your Chosen One will not be found
> A rotting corpse beneath the ground.'

These words can't refer to David, because after David had played his part in

God's plans in his own day and age, he died and was buried alongside his ancestors. David did become 'a rotting corpse beneath the ground'! But the one God brought back to life didn't rot. So I'm telling you, friends, it's through Jesus you're going to be forgiven for the wrong things you've done. If you trust Jesus, you can be free from all the guilt you couldn't get rid of by trying to keep the rules Moses laid down. You'd better watch out, otherwise the words of God's speakers may apply in your case!

> *'Those of you who laugh,*
> *The laugh'll be on you.*
> *The work God's doing today,*
> *The things God's going to do,*
> *When someone tries to tell you,*
> *You won't believe it's true!'* "

On their way out, people asked Cheery and Paul to come back next Saturday, to explain things in greater detail. After the meeting was over, many Jews and others who had been converted to the Jewish religion, went after them. They chatted together, and Paul and Cheery encouraged them to stay close to God.

Next Saturday, nearly everyone in the town came to hear God's message. This made the local Jewish leaders jealous of Paul and Cheery. They greeted them with insults and tried to shout them down. Then the two of them put it very plainly. "We thought it right to give God's message to you first. But you don't want to hear it. That shows you're not ready for 'Life to the Full.' So we'll offer it to those who are not Jews instead. God has told us to do this. God says:

> *'To every race you'll be a light;*
> *Earth's farthest shore will greet the sight.'* "

When those who were not Jews heard this, they cheered. They gave Jesus their trust, and took the road to full life. So God's message spread rapidly in that part of the world. But the Jewish leaders used their influence with the town councilors and with some of the religious women from the upper classes. These made trouble for Cheery and Paul, forcing them to leave. So they turned their backs on Antioch, and went on to Konya. They were happy in their work, and kept their spirits up.

14

Much the same thing happened in Konya as in Antioch. Paul and Cheery went to the Jewish place of worship. They spoke so well, a lot of people there, Jews and non-Jews, put their trust in Jesus. But those Jews who were not willing to do this, worked on those who were not Jews and turned their minds against the two friends. So they had to stay at Konya a long time. They spoke bravely on behalf of Jesus. He gave them the words, and backed them up by helping them do remarkable things. But the townspeople were split into two camps. Some agreed with Cheery and Paul, and others with their Jewish opponents. There was a plot, which involved leaders from both communities, to set upon Paul and Cheery and kill them by throwing stones at them. But the two found out about it and got going quickly. They made for the towns of Lester and Derby. They carried on talking about the Good News there.

In Lester there was a man who had no feeling in his feet and had never been able to walk. He sat there listening to what Paul had to say. Paul caught his eye and realized the man was in a right frame of mind to be cured. Paul shouted across to him, "Get on your feet!" The man jumped up and started walking. When the crowd saw what Paul had done, they started shouting in the local language, "The gods have turned into humans and come to see us." They thought Cheery was Jupiter, their chief god, and because Paul did the talking, they thought he was Mercury, their messenger god. The temple where Jupiter was honored was just outside Lester, and the one in charge there brought cows and bunches of flowers to the entrance of the town. They wanted to worship the two friends. When Cheery and Paul realized what was happening they were upset and ran about in the crowd shouting, "Friends, please stop! We're just ordinary people like you. This is our good news. You should leave behind the sort of things you're doing now and get to know the God who's truly alive, the one who made everything – earth, sea, and sky. In the past, God let different races invent their own religions. But there have always been clues to God's good character – the weather, the harvest, plenty of food, and much else for you to be happy about." They had great difficulty in preventing themselves from being worshiped, even by saying things like this. By this time some of the Jewish leaders from Antioch and Konya had arrived. They worked on the crowds and got them to throw stones at Paul. They were dragging him out of the town, thinking he was dead, when his supporters made a human shield round him and he got up and walked straight back into the town. Next day Paul and Cheery moved on to Derby.

When they had handed on the Good News to the people of Derby, Cheery and Paul went back the way they came to Lester, Konya, and Antioch. As they went, they firmed up the new Christians, and encouraged them to build on what they had been taught. They told them, "You can't become part of God's New World without having trouble on the way!" They chose leaders for each group of Christians and asked God to help them. They trusted Jesus to look after them. He was to be their Leader from now on. Then Cheery and Paul made their way back down toward the coast. They stopped to speak to the people of Perga, then caught a boat back to Antioch from a port nearby. This was the Antioch they had started from, and now they were going back with their work done. God had helped them from beginning to end. As soon as they got there, they called all the Christians together and gave a full account of what they and God had done together, and how God had made it easy for people who were not Jews to put their trust in Jesus. Paul and Cheery stayed on in Antioch as part of the community there for some time.

15 Some people from the south, near Jerusalem, came to Antioch and started to argue that only men whose foreskin had been cut off, as Moses taught, could expect any help from God. Paul and Cheery strongly disagreed with them, and the matter was hotly debated. So Cheery and Paul, and some others, were sent on a delegation to Jerusalem, to discuss the question with the friends of Jesus there. The Christians in Antioch met to say goodbye to them. They traveled via Syria and Samaria, and when they told the Christians in those parts about those who were not Jews who had put their trust in Jesus, everybody was delighted. When they arrived in Jerusalem, they got a warm welcome from the Christian leaders. They gave a full account of what they and God had done together. But some Christians who belonged to the strict set butted in and said, "They must have their foreskins cut and keep all the other rules of Moses." The Christian leaders held a meeting to discuss the matter. After much argument, Rocky stood up to speak.

"Friends, you know the story of how God chose me to be the first to pass the Good News to people who weren't Jews, so they could put their trust in Jesus? It's quite an old story now. God, who knows our thoughts and feelings, accepted them and gave them the Spirit, just like us. Because of their trust, God has made their minds clean and counts them in with us. So why are we annoying God by trying to make our Christian comrades do something which was a nuisance to our ancestors and a nuisance to us too? The truth is that all of us, including our ancestors, can only experience life to the full as a free gift from Jesus, our Leader."

The whole meeting was very quiet while Cheery and Paul talked about the remarkable things they and God had done together, with people who were not Jews. When they had finished, James, Jesus' brother, gave a summing up.

"Listen carefully, friends. Rocky has reminded us of the first occasion when God convinced us that non-Jews are alright to mix with, and that some of them belong to God already. This is in line with what God's speakers say in the old books.

> *'I'll come back again,' says God,*
> *'The faith of David to restore.*
> *This time it will be set to last,*
> *And be an empty shell no more.*
> *I want a larger family –*
> *It's been my plan for many a year.*
> *All races will belong to me.'*
> *God has no pets, that's very clear!*

"This is how I think we should approach this issue. We shouldn't make things difficult for non-Jews who are turning to God. We should write to them, asking them not to eat food which has come from the temples; to behave responsibly in sexual matters; and not to eat meat which still has blood in it. That will do. Moses doesn't need any more supporters. His words are read every Saturday in all our places of worship."

Then the whole meeting agreed to choose representatives to send to Antioch with Paul and Cheery. The two they chose were respected leaders of the Christian community, Jude and Silas. The letter they took with them read like this:

> *This letter is to those from a non-Jewish background who trust in Jesus, in Antioch and the surrounding districts. It comes to you from the leaders of the Christian community and friends of Jesus in Jerusalem. We are sorry to hear that some people from our number visited you and, without our backing, said things to upset you and cause trouble. The representatives we are sending you have the support of all of us. They will travel alongside our much loved Cheery and Paul, who have risked their lives in the cause of Jesus, our Leader. Our representatives are Jude and Silas. They will explain the contents of this letter to you. God's Spirit and we ourselves are now agreed as to what should be done. Like her, we think you should not be weighed down with a long list of do's and don'ts. All we ask is that you avoid food from the temples and any meat that contains blood because the animal has been strangled, and that you behave responsibly in sexual matters. If you follow these guidelines, everything will be alright.*
> *Best Wishes.*

So the four friends were sent north to Antioch. When they arrived, they invited the Christian community to a special meeting, and handed on the letter. When the Antioch Christians read it they were delighted by its contents. Jude and Silas were both used to speaking for God, and they had some very encouraging and helpful things to say. When they had stayed a good while there, they set off again for Jerusalem. They had won the hearts of the Christians in Antioch. Paul and Cheery stayed on in Antioch and were part of a large group who taught and spoke God's words.

After a while, Paul said to Cheery, "How about going back to all the towns where we spoke God's message, to see how the new Christians are getting on?" Cheery wanted to take John Mark with them, but Paul was against this, because Mark opted out of the previous venture part way. There were such bitter words between Paul and Cheery that they ended their partnership. Cheery teamed up with Mark and they took the boat to Cyprus. Paul asked Silas to be his companion. They set out together, and the Christians asked God to look after them. They started by visiting the churches in Syria and the districts beyond.

16 Paul went on to Derby and then Lester. Lester was where Timothy lived. He was a new Christian. His mother was Jewish and his father Greek. His mother was a Christian too. Timothy was popular with the Christians in those parts. Paul asked Timothy to join his team. Paul cut off Timothy's foreskin to please the Jews who lived in the area. They suspected Timothy had not had this done to him earlier because his father was Greek. In every town they visited, they told the Christians about the guidelines agreed by the leading Christians in Jerusalem. The churches continued to grow in numbers and in confidence.

The team went further inland, then westwards and north. But wherever they tried to go, they felt God's Spirit was trying to stop them. They ended up in Troy, on the farthest western coast of Asia. During the night, Paul dreamt he saw someone across the water in Europe, saying to him with great feeling, "Come over here and help us." (This was when I, Luke, joined the team.) When Paul woke up, we decided straightaway to cross the sea to Europe. We were quite sure God wanted us to take the Good News to the people over there.

(11) The boat from Troy took us straight across the Aegean Sea and next day up the coast to Newtown. After we had landed, we made for Philiptown, the largest town in those parts. The population is largely Italian. We spent a few days getting to know the place. Then on Saturday we went down by the river outside the town, where we heard people were in the habit of meeting to talk with God. It turned out to be a women's group, so we sat and chatted to those who had come along. One of them, Lydia, was a businesswoman, who owned a company that made high quality purple cloth. God was already important in her life, so she listened very

carefully to everything Paul said, and took it all in. Lydia, and the people who lived with her, were dipped in the river. Then she invited us back to her house. She said. "Now I've put my trust in Jesus, you're welcome to come and stay with me." So we went home with her.

One day when we were on our way to the same meeting place, we met a fortune-teller who used a large snake to pass on her messages. She was exploited by her employers, who made a lot of money out of her. She started following Paul and our team, shouting, "These people belong to the greatest God of all! They have a life-giving message for us!" She made a nuisance of herself like this for several days, until Paul became quite annoyed. At last he turned round and said, "You're sick! Jesus, God's Chosen, is going to make you better!" She was a new person from that moment on.

But when the girl's employers found they had lost their means of making money, they grabbed hold of Paul and Silas, and dragged them to the town hall. They made a complaint to the magistrates and said, "These Jews are causing trouble in our town. The things they're telling us to do are against our Roman laws." The crowd started to get nasty, so the magistrates ordered Paul and Silas to be stripped and flogged. They got a bad beating and then they were put in prison. The warder was given special instructions to keep an eye on them. So he put them in a maximum-security unit and chained them to the floor.

In the middle of the night Paul and Silas talked with God and sang songs. The other prisoners could hear it all. Suddenly there was a violent earthquake, which shook the foundations of the prison. Doors came off their hinges and the prisoners' chains were loosened. The warder woke up with a start, and when he saw the prison doors wide open, he grabbed his sword to kill himself. He thought the prisoners had escaped. But Paul yelled out to him, "Don't hurt yourself! We're all here!" The warder had the lights put on, and in a state of shock, ran into the cell and fell down shaking in front of Silas and Paul. Then he brought them out and asked them, "How can I learn to cope with life, like you?" They told him, "Put your trust in Jesus, and you will know true health and happiness, and so will the others in your house." Paul and Silas then gave God's message to the warder and the people who lived with him. It was still night when the warder washed their wounds. Without waiting for the morning, he and all his family were dipped. He took Paul and Silas into his house and gave them a meal. Everyone in the house was very excited and happy because the warder had put his trust in God.

In the morning the magistrates sent the police to the prison. They said, "You had better let those two prisoners go." The warder went to tell Paul. "The magistrates have sent to say you're free to go. They're dropping the charges." But Paul said, "They're not going to get away with this! They've beaten us in public and sent us to prison, all without a trial. You can't treat Roman citizens like that! If they think they're going to hush it all up, they can think again! Let them come and fetch us!" The police took this message back to the magistrates, who had a fright when they learned that Paul and Silas were Roman citizens. So they came to the prison and apologized. They gave them an escort out of the prison, and then requested them to leave the town. After their release from prison, Paul and Silas went back to Lydia's. They met their Christian sisters and brothers again, and put them in good heart. Then they left Philiptown.

17 Paul and Silas traveled a hundred miles west along the high road from Philiptown to Tessatown. At Tessatown there was a Jewish place of worship, so Paul went along as he usually did. For the next three Saturdays he had discussions with the people he met there. He pointed them to parts of the old books, which showed that God's Chosen had to suffer death and return to life again. He said, "I know who God's Chosen is. His name is Jesus!" Some of them were convinced and became friends of Silas and Paul. Also they won over a lot of the Greeks there who were keen to know about God, and a number of the leading women. But the Jewish leaders resented Paul and Silas, and with the help of some shady characters from the back streets, they got a riot going. They attacked the house of a new Christian called Jason, expecting Paul and Silas to be there. When they could not find them, they dragged Jason and some of his friends before the town magistrates, shouting, "Paul and Silas are revolutionaries, and they're trying to start a revolution here! We've brought you Jason, because they've been using his house as their base. They're all breaking the laws of the emperor by saying someone called Jesus should be the ruler!" This got everybody even more worked up, magistrates and people. Jason and the others had to find money for bail. Paul and Silas left Tessatown under cover of night and traveled further west again toward Berea. Once again, when they arrived, they made straight for the Jewish place of worship. The Jews of Berea were more tolerant than those in Tessatown. They listened eagerly to what Paul and Silas had to say, and spent days looking carefully through the old books, to check what the friends were saying was true. Many of them put their trust in Jesus, including several Greek women who were highly respected members of the community, and some Greek men as well. But when the Jews back in Tessatown got to hear that Paul and Silas were passing on God's message in Berea, they came to cause trouble, using their usual mob tactics. The Christians of Berea got Paul away to the coast, while Timothy and Silas stayed behind. Paul was accompanied by friends from Berea all the way to Athens. Then they went back to Berea with a message from Paul for Silas and Timothy to join him as soon as possible.

(16) While Paul waited for his friends to arrive, he went sightseeing in Athens. He was saddened to see so many competing religions. So he had discussions with the Jews in their place of worship, and with others who wanted to find out more about God. He also talked with people he met in the main street each day. Some of these were students who spent their time searching for the meaning of life. They did not know what to make of Paul. Some said, "He's just talking hot air." Others, "He's come from overseas to sell his religion." That was all they managed to make of the Good News Paul was giving them about Jesus and life after death. Then they invited Paul to give a talk in the large courthouse on Mars Hill. They said, "We'd like to know a bit more about these new ideas you're spreading around. Some of what you have to say seems rather odd to us. Perhaps you can explain it?" The people who were born in Athens, as well as others who came to live there, liked nothing better than to spend their time hearing and discussing the latest ideas.

So Paul stood up in the big arena and said, "It strikes me you people who live in Athens take religion to extremes. As I was walking round your city, looking carefully at the shrines where you worship, I came across an altar which had on it the words, 'This is for an unknown god.' You may not know what you are worshiping. But I'm here to tell you. The God who made the world and everything in it, and is responsible for what you see whichever way you look, cannot be made to fit into any of the places of worship we make with our human skills. There is nothing God needs from us. God gives us life and breath and all the abilities we have. God made us all from the same pattern, no matter what we call ourselves, or where we live. God decided how long our human lives should last and the limits we can travel. God has set a test for us. We are to go exploring, and if we look hard enough, we will find God. It's not really difficult because God isn't far from any of us. Doesn't one of your poets say,

> *'In God we thrive,*
> *In God we strive.*
> *Apart from God*
> *We're not alive'?*

And another one said,

> *'We're all God's children.'*

"If we really are God's children, why do we think God can be portrayed by a sculptor, working in gold or silver or stone? God has been very patient with our ignorance. But now God calls people everywhere to step out boldly in a new direction. There is a time set aside, when God will bring everything to light, and sort things out in a just and fair way. God has chosen someone special to set this in motion, and has let us know who it is, by bringing him back to life after he has died!"

When Paul spoke about someone dying and coming alive, some of them started to laugh. Others said, "Very interesting. We must have you to speak again." Paul realized it was time to go. But some joined him afterwards, and put their trust in Jesus. These included Dennis, who was a member of the court, a woman called Pet, and a few others.

18 Paul went on from Athens to Corinth. There he met a Jewish couple, Cilla and William, who came originally from the Black Sea coast. They had recently moved to Corinth from Rome because the Emperor Claudius had turned all the Jews out of Rome. Paul went to see them and they took him in as a lodger. They got on well because they were all skilled tentmakers. They set up business together. Every Saturday Paul went along to the Jewish place of worship. He would start a discussion, and try to win over the Jews and Greeks who were there. When at last Timothy and Silas arrived in Corinth, that was where they found Paul, in the middle of making a speech.

He was explaining to the Jews that their promised Chosen One was Jesus. They responded by shouting insults at him and saying he was talking rubbish. Paul turned his back on them and said, "I've had enough of you. You're on your own from now on. It's other peoples' turn!" Then he walked out, and to make his point went straight to the house next door where Titus lived. Titus loved God although he was not Jewish. Paul was joined by Cris, the Jewish leader. He put his trust in Jesus and so did all the people who lived with him. Paul persuaded a large number of the people of Corinth to become Christians and be dipped.

One night Paul saw Jesus in his dreams. Jesus said to Paul, "Don't be afraid. Don't let anyone shut you up. I'm with you and everything will be alright. I've got a lot of friends in this town." So Paul stayed in Corinth for a year and a half, teaching people the truth about God.

When Leo became the governor of the province, the Jews got together and took Paul to court. They accused Paul of trying to introduce an illegal religion. Paul was just about to defend himself when Leo told the Jews, "If this were a criminal matter or some serious wrong had been done, I should be bound to listen to what you have to say. But it strikes me, you're just playing with words over your religious rules. I think you should sort it out yourselves. I don't want to get involved in these matters. Go away, all of you." But before the court could be cleared, Sonny, the Jewish leader, was jumped on and knocked about. Leo did nothing to stop it. After a long stay in Corinth, Paul said goodbye to his Christian friends in the town and went by sea to Syria. Cill and Will went with him. Paul had been letting his hair grow long to show he was on special duties for God. But at the seaport he had his hair cut short again before boarding the boat. When they arrived at Ephesus, Paul decided to put Cill and Will in charge of operations there and leave them to it. But first he visited the Jewish place of worship and talked to the people there. They wanted Paul to stay longer, but he said, "No, I must say 'Goodbye' for now. I'll come back and see you again, if it's alright with God."

(22) Paul took the boat to Caesartown. After a brief visit to Jerusalem to keep in touch with the Christians there, he went back to Antioch. He stayed in Antioch for a while, then went on a tour of a district where the Celtic people lived, to boost the confidence of the Christians among them.

Meanwhile, in Ephesus, a Jew from northern Africa called Ray arrived. He was a good speaker and knew the old books well. He had been instructed in the basic truths of Christianity, and was very keen to pass on what he had learnt. His knowledge of the facts about Jesus was very accurate. He seemed, however, not to know about any dipping of people since the time of John the Dipper. He courageously spoke his mind in the worship place. Cill and Will were among those who heard Ray. They invited him home, and explained to him aspects of Christianity he had not come across. Ray wanted to visit Greece. So the Christians of Ephesus made things easier for him by writing letters of introduction to the Greek Christians. When Ray arrived in Greece, he was a great help to those Greeks who had accepted God's gift. He entered into public debate with the Jewish leaders, and was able to show, by using the old books, that Jesus is God's Chosen.

19 While Ray was in Corinth, Paul traveled on from the Celtic lands to Ephesus. At Ephesus Paul came across some Christians he had not met before. He asked them, "Did you receive God's Spirit when you became Christians?" They said, 'No, we've never heard of that!" He asked, "What happened when you were dipped then?" They replied, "We were just put under the water the way John the Dipper always did it." Paul said, "John's dipping was just about saying sorry. He told people to put their trust in the one coming after him. That's Jesus."

When they heard what Paul had said, they were dipped again. This time the name of Jesus, the Leader, was used. Afterwards Paul hugged them and

God's Spirit came inside them. They lost all their shyness and spoke God's messages freely. There were about twelve of them.

Paul went back to the Jewish place of worship, and for about three months spoke there forcefully. His main topic at this time was God's New World. Some of the people there refused to listen and said unpleasant things about the Christians to the others who were there. So Paul left the worship place and took his friends with him. From then on, for two years, Paul shared the lecture room of a Greek teacher called Tyrone. Paul held discussions there every day. This gave the chance for everybody in those parts, of whatever nationality, to hear God's message.

God helped Paul to do many remarkable things. When towels or cloths Paul had used were taken to people who were ill, they got better, and those who were confused were able to think clearly again.

(13) A group of Jewish healers, who advertised themselves as the sons of someone on the temple staff in Jerusalem called Sheba, went around from place to place offering to cure people. Once they tried to help some mentally disturbed people by using the name of Jesus. They said, "We're going to put you right in the name of Jesus, the one Paul talks about." One of them shouted back, "I've heard of Jesus and Paul, but who are you?" Then the healers were attacked violently. They ran out of the house badly beaten and without their clothes.

When the people of Ephesus in both the Jewish and Greek communities got to hear about this, they were impressed, and the reputation of Jesus, the Leader, increased. Many who became Christians admitted to doing things they were ashamed of. Some of them had dabbled in black magic. They burned their books in front of everybody. These books were very valuable – enough to employ a thousand workers for a year. This shows the value that was now being put on the truth from God.

After all this, Paul made plans to visit Greece and Macedonia again and from there to go back to Jerusalem. He said, "Then I want to see Rome." Paul sent two of his assistants, Timothy and Rastus in front of him to Greece, while he stayed a little longer in Turkey.

(23) This was the time the presence of the Christians led to a riot in Ephesus. A silversmith called Des had a contract to make images for the worshipers of Diana, the mother-goddess. He employed a large number of

workers at good wages. He called his employees and associates together, and said, "Comrades, we've got a good business going here. But now our jobs are under threat, because in Ephesus and all the districts around, Paul has been saying the gods we make are not real gods at all. A lot of people are listening to him. This doesn't only affect our trade. It threatens the temple of the great goddess. People will stop believing in her. Ephesus will lose all the visitors who come from near and far. When they heard what Des had to say they all started chanting. "Diana for ever!" "Save Ephesus!" They went on the rampage in the streets and ran toward the theater. On the way they grabbed Harry and Guy, two Greeks who had made friends with Paul on their travels together. Paul wanted to talk to the crowd, but the other Christians would not let him. Some of Paul's friends among the local officials also sent him a message warning him not to go into the open-air theater. People were shouting different things, and most of the crowd did not know what it was all about. It was all very confusing. Some of the Jews pushed their leader Alexander to the front and told him to make a speech. He called for the crowd to be quiet and did his best to explain his point of view. But when they realized he was a Jew, they kept up their chant for about two hours, "Diana for ever! Save Ephesus!" Then the town clerk got everybody to be quiet and said, "People of Ephesus, our town will always be world-famous because we look after the temple of Diana, where the meteorite which landed here is on show. Nobody is going to rob us of our fame. So calm down and make sure you don't do anything you'll be sorry for afterwards. These people you've brought here haven't robbed the temple, or said anything disrespectful about our religion. If Des and his workers have a complaint, they should bring it before the authorities on one of the days when the court is sitting. That's the right way to go about things. Anything else we can settle by holding a proper public inquiry. Our behavior today has put us outside the law, and we could be accused of making a riot. There's no excuse for this kind of behavior." Then he told everybody to go home.

20 After the rioting had calmed down, Paul called a meeting of the Ephesus Christians. He praised them for their conduct, said goodbye and left for Europe. He traveled first through

Macedonia, encouraging the Christians there. Then he went south to Greece and stayed for three months. He was going to catch the boat to Syria, when he heard that some Jews were out to get him. He dodged them by changing his plans and going back north. Paul now had a full team of helpers from the places he had visited, including Timothy and me, Luke. I stayed with Paul while the others went on ahead. We caught the boat from Philiptown just after Easter. The boat took five days to get to Troy where the others were waiting. We stayed in Troy for a week.

On Sunday, when we met to share food together, Paul gave us a talk. This was because he was thinking of leaving the next day. Paul was still talking at midnight. The room upstairs where we were meeting was lit by a large number of oil lamps. A young man was sitting on the window ledge. He began to feel drowsy as Paul went on and on. Then he went right off to sleep and fell out of the window, down three floors. When his friends got to him they thought he was dead. But Paul came down, put his arms round him and hugged him tight. "Nothing to be worried about," Paul said, "He's still alive!" Paul led everybody back upstairs. Then he broke the bread and ate with those who were there. Afterwards he chatted with them till morning. Then Paul left the house. The young man, whose name in Greek means "a lucky fall," was taken home none the worse for his experience, and everybody was very relieved.

(13) We took the boat from Troy to Assos just round the coast. Paul went by land part way and joined us on the boat at Assos as planned. We then made our way around the coast. It took a few days because we called in at several ports. Then we docked at Miletus. Paul had decided to sail past Ephesus, being pushed for time. He hoped to be in Jerusalem by Whitsun.

However, from Miletus Paul sent a message to the Christian leaders in Ephesus, asking them to come and meet him. When they came, this is what he said to them: "Friends, I want you to remember how I lived alongside you the whole time I was in these parts, working hard for our Leader, and trying not to make myself appear important. They were difficult times, and I was often in tears because of the trouble my own people made for me. I did my very best to help you, passing on the message, teaching in public and in your homes. I told Jews and Greeks how important it was to make a new start and put their trust in Jesus, our Leader. Now I have to do what the

Spirit is telling me to do. She wants me to go to Jerusalem. I've no idea what will happen to me there, except that she warns me everywhere I go to expect to be put in prison or punished in some way. I don't put any great value on my life. It's just that I want to finish the job Jesus my Leader has given me. I want to spread the Good News of God's wonderful generosity. I've spent so much time with you talking about God's New World. I seem to know that none of you will see me again. Nobody can blame *me* if things go wrong from now on. I've told you everything there is to know about God's plans. Look after one another and all the people God's Spirit has made you responsible for. Jesus, God's Likeness, died for them all. I expect when I'm out of the way, the people in your care will be attacked by those who want to do them harm. Even some of *you* will twist the truth and try to get other Christians to go along with you. So watch out. Remember I spent three years saying these things to you, night and day, often with tears in my eyes. Now I'm asking God to look after you. Remember what I've told you about God's goodness. That will help you have confidence and know you're members of God's big family. I was never after your money or your personal property. You know how I had my own business, which was enough to keep me, and my friends. I tried to set you a good example in helping those who are less well off. Our Leader Jesus said, 'More happiness comes by giving than by getting.'"

When Paul had finished speaking, they all joined together to talk with God. There was a lot of crying and each of them hugged and kissed Paul. They were especially upset because he said they would not see him again. Then they saw him on to the boat.

21 After we had said our final goodbyes to the Ephesus Christians, we sailed south round the coast, past the island of Rhodes. At the next port, we changed onto a boat making for Syria. This took us just in sight of Cyprus. We landed at Tyre because the boat had to unload its cargo there. We found out where the Christians were living, and stayed with them for a week. They gave Paul a message from the Spirit. She said Paul should not go to Jerusalem. After our stay in Tyre, we got ready to continue our journey. All the Christians, men, women, and children, came with us as far as the beach outside the town. We spent some time together, talking with God, then we said goodbye. We got onto the boat, and the friends from Tyre went home. We had one more stop, at Acre, and spent a day with the Christians there. The following day we got off the boat at Caesartown and stayed with Philip, the one who is so skilled in spreading the Good News. (You remember, he was one of the seven helpers chosen by the Jerusalem Christians.) Philip had four daughters who were not married. They were very gifted, and handed on messages from God. During the few days we stayed with them, Hopper, one of God's speakers from the Jerusalem region, came to see us. As soon as he met us, he undid Paul's belt and used it to tie up Paul's hands and feet. Then he said, "I've got this message from God's Spirit. She says, 'This is how the people of Jerusalem will tie up the one this belt belongs to and take him as a prisoner to the Romans.'" When we heard this we all tried to argue Paul out of going to Jerusalem. But Paul said, "All this crying is breaking my heart. I'm quite willing to become a prisoner and even to die in Jerusalem if it helps the cause of Jesus, my Leader." There was nothing we could say to make Paul change his mind. So we stopped trying and just said, "We hope you really *are* doing what God wants!"

(15) So we hired some horses and started out toward Jerusalem. Some of the Caesartown Christians came with us, and when we got to Jerusalem they showed us the way to the house of Mason from Cyprus, one of the very first Christians. He was able to put us up. The Jerusalem Christians gave us a warm welcome. The next day Paul visited James, Jesus' brother. The other leaders were there. After asking how they all were, Paul gave a complete account of the way peoples of all races had responded to God through his efforts. When they heard this they thanked God. Then they said to Paul, "Friend, there are thousands of Jews here who've put their trust in Jesus. But they all believe in keeping the old rules and regulations. They've heard that you tell the Jews in other countries to forget all about Moses and not to cut the foreskins of their boys and other such customs. We don't really know what to do to prevent you having trouble from them. They're bound to find out you're here. What about this for an idea? Four of our men have grown their hair long because they're on special duties. If you sponsor these in the customary ceremony for bringing the special duties to an end, and if you pay for them to have their hair cut, people will see that the rumors

about you are false. They'll notice you joining in and keeping the rules. People of other races who have become Christians are another matter. We sent them that letter we all agreed on, directing them not to buy food from the temples or to eat meat which has blood in it, and to behave responsibly in sexual matters." So next day, Paul acted as sponsor for the men. He went through all the special washings and went with them to the temple. He made the announcement that the special period had come to an end and that a gift would be made to God on behalf of each of the men.

These ceremonies lasted for a week. When they were almost through, some Jews from abroad who had recognized Paul in the temple, called on the crowd of worshipers to get hold of him. They shouted, "Anyone who calls themselves a good Jew, come quickly and help. This is the man who goes everywhere slandering our people, telling them to throw away our rules and get rid of our temple. Now to crown it all he's brought his stinking foreigners into the temple." (Someone had seen Paul in the city with Tommy, a friend from Ephesus, and made the mistake of thinking Paul had brought him into the temple.) The commotion spread out into the city. People ran to see what was happening. Paul was taken hold of roughly and dragged out of the temple. The temple doors were shut behind him. The crowd were out to beat Paul to death. But the commander in charge of the Roman soldiers was told there was rioting in Jerusalem. Quickly he brought a unit of soldiers with their officers to the trouble spot. When the rioters saw the commander with his soldiers, they took their hands off Paul. Then the commander arrested Paul, put handcuffs on him, and asked who he was and what he was up to. The people in the crowd were shouting several different things at once, making it impossible for the commander to make any sense of it. So he ordered Paul to be taken to the soldiers' barracks. When they came down the temple steps, the pressure of the crowd was so strong, the soldiers had to carry Paul. The crowd followed all the way shouting, "Kill him."

Just as they were going into the barracks, Paul whispered to the commander, "Can I have a word with you?" The commander said, "So you speak Greek? You can't be the Egyptian who caused trouble some while ago and took his army of a thousand cut-throats out into the desert!" Paul said, "I'm a Jew from Tarsus in Turkey. I'm also a citizen of a very important city.

Please let me speak to the people." The commander gave his permission. Paul stood on the steps of the barracks and put up his hand for silence. When everyone was quiet, he spoke to the crowd in Hebrew.

22 Paul began, "Friends, old and young, please listen to what I have to say." When they heard Paul talking to them in Hebrew, you could have heard a pin drop. He said, "I'm Jewish. Although I was born abroad in Tarsus, I was brought up here. I went to Liam's School, where I was given a thorough training in all the rules of our ancestors. I was a keen God-supporter, just like you are now. I gave the Christians a rough time of it. I wanted to kill them. I arrested them, men and women, and put them in prison. If you don't believe me, you can ask your leaders. They were the ones who gave me warrants to show to the Jewish leaders in Damascus. I went to arrest the Christians there to bring them back to Jerusalem to be punished. It was about twelve o'clock midday and I was within sight of Damascus, when suddenly the light became too strong to bear. I collapsed on the ground and heard a voice saying, 'Saul, Saul, why are you giving me all this hate?' I said, 'Who are you, Sir?' The voice said, 'I'm Jesus from Nazareth, the one you're out to destroy.' The others with me saw how bright the light was, but didn't hear the voice. I said, 'What am I supposed to do, Sir?' Jesus said to me, 'Get up and go on to Damascus where you'll be told what to do.' Because I couldn't see in the strong sunlight, the others had to lead me by the hand to Damascus. In Damascus there was a man called Ian who kept all your rules and had a good reputation among the Jewish community. He came to see me. I could feel him close beside me as he said, 'My dear friend Saul, you're now going to see again!' At that precise moment I got my sight back and could see him clearly. Then Ian said, 'The God of our ancestors wants you to be part of the plan. You're going to see the best person who ever lived and hear what he has to say from his own mouth. You're going to travel all over the world telling people what you've seen and heard. So what are you waiting for? Come on, let me dip you, so you can wash away all the bad things of the past. Ask Jesus for help.'

"Then I went back to Jerusalem and went to the temple to talk with God. As I was fixing my mind on God, I saw Jesus. He said to me, 'Get away from Jerusalem as quickly as you can, because they won't listen to what you say about me.' I said, 'Leader, they know very well I went round the places of worship arresting those who trust you. I put them in prison and had them beaten up. While your champion Stephen was being killed, I stood by watching, liking what I saw. I kept an eye on the jackets of those doing the killing.' Then Jesus said to me, 'You must get out of here. I want you to go abroad to meet people of other races.'"

(22) The crowd had listened to Paul respectfully up to this point. But now they started shouting, "Let's get rid of him. The world would be better off without him!" They started taking their jackets off and throwing clods of earth, so the commander ordered Paul to be taken into the barracks. He directed that Paul be questioned while he was being beaten to find out why he had so many people's backs up. But as they were tying Paul up, Paul said to the officer standing there, "Is it legal to beat a Roman citizen who has not been tried and found guilty?" Then the officer went to the commander and said, "Are you sure you know what you're doing? This man's a Roman citizen." So the commander came and asked Paul, "Is it true you're a Roman citizen?" Paul said, "Yes." The commander said, "It cost me a fortune to get my citizenship." Paul said, "But I was born a citizen." Straightaway those who were just going to torture Paul jumped back from him. The commander was frightened when he realized he had tied up a Roman citizen. But he had to find out what Paul was being accused of by his own people, so next day he released him, and called for a full meeting of all the leaders. Then he got Paul to address the meeting.

23 Paul looked straight at his audience and said. "Friends, I've always tried to do what is right in the sight of God." Then Ninus, the Chief of the clergy, told his guards to punch Paul in the face. Paul said, "God will do that to you, you two-faced toad! You aren't fit to be my judge! You've just broken the law yourself by ordering me to be hit!" The guards said. "How dare you insult God's mouthpiece!" Paul said, "Oh, my dear friends, I didn't realize I was speaking to God's mouthpiece. I didn't expect God's mouthpiece to have anything to say against a leader of God's people. It's against the written code of practice."

Paul noticed there were two rival groups present. Some belonged to the strict set, and others belonged to the well-off, easy-going set. So Paul shouted out for everybody to hear, "Friends, I'm one of the strict set. That's the way my parents brought me up. I'm actually on trial here because I believe there is life after death." This set the two groups arguing with one another. The strict set believes in an after-life and in supernatural beings, whereas the easy-going set thinks nothing exists beyond what they see. There was a lot of noise, and some of the strict set took Paul's side and said, "This man's okay! It's possible someone from God in the world of the spirit has spoken to him!" A fight broke out, and the commander was afraid Paul would be severely injured. So he ordered the soldiers to pull Paul away, and take him back to the barracks.

In the night Jesus stood by Paul's bed and said, "Don't lose your nerve! You've stood up for me here in Jerusalem. Now you're going to stand up for me in Rome!"

(12) Next morning some Jews got together and vowed they wouldn't have anything to eat or drink until they'd killed Paul. There were more than forty people in this plot. They went to the Jewish leaders and told them, "We're absolutely determined not to eat anything until we've killed Paul. You can help us by getting the council to ask the commander to bring Paul to you. You can say you need to ask him some more questions. We'll make sure he doesn't reach you alive." But Paul's sister's son found out about the plot. He was allowed to visit Paul in the barracks and told Paul what he knew. Paul called one of the officers and said, "Take this young man to the commander. He has some important information." The officer took Paul's nephew to the commander and passed on Paul's message. The commander took the boy by the hand and led him to a place where they could talk quietly on their own. Then the commander asked, "What special news have you got for me?" Paul's nephew said, "The Jewish leaders have decided to ask you to bring Paul before the council tomorrow. They'll pretend they want to know more about the facts. Don't let them take you in. They'll have over forty waiting to ambush Paul. They've said they're not going to eat or drink until they've killed him. The leaders will be here any minute to get you to fall in with their plans." The commander told the young man to be on his way, and said, "Don't tell anyone you've spoken to me."

Then the commander called two of his officers and told them, "Get ready to leave for Caesartown by nine o'clock tonight. You'll need two hundred regulars, seventy horse riders, and two hundred with spears. Get some horses for Paul. Your job is to take him to the governor, Felix." Then the commander wrote a letter. This is what it said:

> *Claude Lewis to his Excellency, the governor Felix, good wishes. This man was attacked by the Jewish mob and would have been killed had I not rescued him with my guards. I intervened because I learned he was a Roman citizen. I had him brought before their council hoping to find out what they were accusing him of. I found it was all to do with their religious rules. There was nothing in the case that warranted death or imprisonment. When I was given secret information that there was a plot to kill him, I sent him to you straightaway. I have told those who are bringing the case they must present their accusations to you.*

The soldiers obeyed their orders, and took Paul that night to a fortress ten miles to the north. Next day they returned to barracks, except the horse riders who took Paul on the rest of the journey. When they got to Caesartown, they gave the letter to the governor and handed Paul over to him. When he had read the letter he asked Paul where he was from. When Paul told him he came from Tarsus, he said, "I'll hear your case as soon as those who are bringing the charges get here." Then he ordered Paul to be kept safe in quarters reserved for heads of state.

24

Five days after Paul had been moved to Caesartown, Ninus arrived with some of his colleagues and a lawyer, to present the case against Paul to Felix. When Paul was brought in, the lawyer began his speech for the prosecution like this: "Sir, we owe it to you that we have enjoyed peace for such a long time. Your able rule has brought many benefits to our people. These things mean a lot to us, and we want you to know how grateful we are. I shall not keep you long, but I hope you will listen to what I have to say with your usual patience. This man is a threat to public order. He causes fighting in the streets wherever there are Jewish communities. He is the leader of a secret terrorist movement, which has its headquarters in Nazareth. He even behaved in a scandalous manner in our most sacred place of worship. So we arrested him. If you cross-examine him carefully, you will find that what we are saying is the truth."

The Jewish leaders shouted their agreement to what the prosecuting counsel said. Then the governor called on Paul to make his defense. This is what Paul said: "I happily make my defense, since I know you have experience of trying cases amongst the Jews over many years. You will have no difficulty in checking the facts. Less than a fortnight ago I went to Jerusalem to worship. I was not found quarrelling with anyone in the temple, nor did I cause trouble in any of the places of worship or on the streets. These people can give no proof for the charges they are bringing against me. I freely admit belonging to a group my opponents here think is way out. But I worship the same God as they do, our ancestors' God. I accept everything in our Rule Book, and the writings of God's speakers from times past. I have the same hope they have, that one day, everybody who has died, good and bad, will be brought back to life. So I try to make sure I have nothing to be ashamed of, either in God's sight, or in the sight of other people. After being away from Jerusalem for a long time, I came back with some money for people in need. I also wanted to join in the temple services. It was while I was doing these things they spotted me in the temple. I was taking part in an act of worship, which was just coming to an end. I was on my own and causing no trouble at all. There were just a few Jews from abroad, worshiping alongside me, and you notice that none of them is here to make any complaint. So it's up to my opponents before you to say what crime I committed when I explained my beliefs to their council. I think what upset them was that I said, 'I'm on trial here because I believe there is life after death.' "

Then Felix, who had taken the trouble to find out about the Christian movement, brought the hearing to a close and said, "I'll give my verdict when commander Lewis arrives." He ordered the officer in charge to guard Paul. He was to be given as much freedom as possible and his friends allowed to look after him. A few days later, Felix and his Jewish wife Drew sent for Paul and asked him to explain what it meant to put your trust in Jesus the Chosen. Paul touched on the subjects of good conduct and self-control, and spoke of the time when all wrongs would be put right. This made Felix nervous and he said, "I think we'd better leave these matters for a while. We'll talk again when we have another chance." He was hoping Paul would try to bribe him. That's the real reason he sent for Paul so often for a chat. Two years passed, and Festus replaced Felix as governor. Festus was anxious to get on the right side of the Jews, so he kept Paul in prison.

25 Three days after Festus had arrived in the province, he traveled from Caesartown to Jerusalem. The Jewish leaders took the opportunity to repeat their charges against Paul. They asked Festus, as a very special favor, to transfer Paul to Jerusalem. They had a plan to kill him on his the way there. Festus said, "I intend to keep Paul at Caesartown. I shall be going back there soon. Some of you can come with me, if you like. Then you can say what you find wrong in the man to his face."

After a stay of just over a week, Festus went back to Caesartown. The next day he sat in court and called for Paul to be brought before him. When Paul came in, the leaders from Jerusalem shouted their charges at him from all sides. But they could not prove anything. Then Paul made his defense. "I have not broken any law, either against the Jews, the temple, or the emperor." Festus was still trying to please the Jews, so he said to Paul, "How would you like to go to Jerusalem and face these charges there? I will try the case." Paul said, "This is the right place for me to be tried, since it is one of the emperor's courts. You know quite well I have done no wrong to the Jewish people. I would be the last to try to escape from death if I had done anything wrong and deserved it. But these are all empty charges and I don't intend to end up in the hands of that lot! I appeal to be tried by the emperor!" Festus had a few words with his advisors, then said. "You have appealed to the emperor; to the emperor you will go."

Several days later, Griff (a member of the Herod family) came with his sister Bernice to Caesartown to welcome Festus. They stayed for several days, and this gave Festus the chance to talk to Griff about Paul's situation. This is how he put it: "There's a prisoner here from the time of Felix. When I was in Jerusalem the leaders there told me about him and pressed me for a sentence. I told them it was not the practice of the Romans to hand anyone over before they had the chance to confront their accusers and make their defense. So when they got here I held a court and had Paul brought in front of me. When the accusers had their turn, I was surprised they did not charge him with any recognized crimes. It turned out to be some dispute over their religion – something to do with someone called Jesus who had died, but who Paul insisted was alive. I found I was out of my depth in these matters, so I asked him if he would prefer to be tried in Jerusalem. But Paul appealed to the emperor, and asked to be kept in custody here meanwhile. So I gave the order for him to be held here until we can arrange for him to be sent to the emperor." Griff said to Festus, "I'd rather like to hear the man myself." Festus said, "I'll arrange for you to hear him tomorrow."

The next day, Griff and Bernice, in their robes of state, came in procession to the courtroom with the high-ranking military officers and the leading citizens of Caesartown. Then Festus called for Paul to be brought in. Festus said, "Noble Griff, ladies and gentlemen, here is the man the Jews everywhere have been complaining to me about. Their slogan is 'Death to Paul.' In my opinion he's not done anything to deserve the death sentence. He's appealed to the emperor for trial, so that's where I'm going to send him! I don't know what to say to the emperor about him. I've brought him for you all to hear, especially you, Griff, to get some idea what to write. I can't very well send a prisoner on, without saying what the charges are."

26 Griff said to Paul, "This is your chance to speak up for yourself." Paul waved politely to Griff and began his defense: "I am very grateful, noble Griff, for this chance to clear myself of the charges made against me by the Jewish leaders, especially since you are an expert on Jewish customs and controversies. I must ask you to listen patiently to what I have to say.

"All the Jewish people know about my upbringing among my own people, and my time in Jerusalem. They know perfectly well, though they are reluctant to give you the facts, that I was a keen member of the strict set. I'm here on trial because of my trust in the promise made by God to our ancestors, a promise every strand of Jewish tradition hopes to see fulfilled. It is the basis of our worship, which never stops, day or night. It is because I have this hope, your Highness, that the Jewish people are out to get me.

Why do any of you here think it ridiculous to say that God brings the dead back to life? At first my convictions led me to do my best to destroy the reputation of Jesus of Nazareth. I went at it with a will in Jerusalem. I had permission from the clergy to put many of God's people in prison. When they were being condemned to death, I cast my vote against them. I tried to force them to change their beliefs while having them beaten in the places of warship. They made me so angry, I even went to foreign towns to smoke them out.

"I was on one of these expeditions, riding toward Damascus with arrest warrants from the Jewish leaders. It was the middle of the day, your Highness, when the sun became unbearably intense. We were all affected by it and got down on the ground. I heard someone saying to me in our own language, 'Saul, Saul, why are you giving me all this hate? You'll make your head ache if you keep banging it against the wall!' I said, 'Who are you, Sir?' He answered, 'I'm Jesus, the one you're out to destroy. Get off the ground and stand up straight! I've met you here for a special purpose. I want your help to tell other people about me, what you know already, and what you will come to know. I'm going to set you free from all your enemies, and I'm going to send you to people of other races. You'll get them to see the world in a new light. Evil will lose its grip on them and they'll discover God's power. They will put the past behind them and join my circle of friends.'

"From that day on, noble Griff, I've tried to be true to that experience which came from beyond time and space. I started in Damascus and Jerusalem; then I went through the whole country and overseas, telling everyone to turn their backs on wrongdoing, to acknowledge God, and to show it by leading a better life. That's why the Jewish leaders caught hold of me in the temple and tried to kill me. God has been with me helping me up to this very moment. I'm here to tell you, whether you are thought of as important or unimportant, that what Moses and God's other speakers said would happen, has happened. They said God's Chosen would suffer death and then come back to life. They said he would bring a new dawn for Jews and non-Jews alike."

While Paul was putting his case across, Festus shouted out, "Paul, you've lost your grip on reality. You've been reading too many books!" Paul said, "No, your honor, I'm telling you the plain facts. His Highness knows what

I'm talking about. I'm sure I make sense to him. He will be familiar with the story. It was all public knowledge at the time. Griff, do you accept what God's speakers said in times past? Of course you do!"

Griff said to Paul, "You don't think you can turn me into a Christian in such a short space of time, do you?" Paul said, "I don't know how long it would take. I'm just asking God that you, and everybody else listening to me, will come to the point where I am now, except I wouldn't want you to be a prisoner like me."

Then the distinguished guests rose to take their leave. As they went out they said to one another, "This man doesn't deserve the death penalty, nor should he be in prison." Griff said to Festus, "A pity you can't let him go. He's lost his chance by appealing to the emperor!"

27 At last the order came for us to sail to Italy. Julius, an officer in the emperor's own troop, was put in charge of Paul and some other prisoners. We caught a boat making for the Asian ports on the Aegean sea, and set out straightaway. Paul had me and Harry from Tessatown for company. Next day, we landed at Sidon, and Julius kindly allowed Paul to go ashore to visit his Christian friends. They gave him some things he needed for the journey. We left Sidon and went east and north of Cyprus to avoid the full strength of the wind. Then we went along the mainland coast to the port of Myra. The officer found a boat on its way from Egypt to Italy and put us on board. The going was slow for the next few days, because we now had the full strength of the wind coming at us. We managed to get to Crete and struggled along the coast as far as a place called Fairhaven.

We were now very behind time and it was the middle of October, long past the season when it was safe to put to sea. Paul made his feelings known to those in charge. "Boys, it's too dangerous to go any further. We'll be putting the cargo and our lives at risk." But the officer was more inclined to listen to the boat-owner and the captain than to Paul. Most on board thought since Fairhaven was not a very good harbor to spend the winter in, it would be better to try to get to the port of Phoenix, further round the coast, which had a harbor protected from all winds. With a light wind behind them, they thought they would be able to make it. So they pulled up the anchor and started to work along the coast of Crete, keeping close to the shore. But suddenly a very strong wind, known locally as a "north-easter," came at us from the island. The boat could not turn into the wind, so we had to give way and be driven along. We used the small island of Gavdos to shield us from the full blast. Even so we got blisters on our hands, hauling in the dinghy. The next job was to send ropes underneath the boat to hold it together. The sailors were afraid of being blown toward the sandbanks of north Africa, so they lowered all the rigging and allowed the boat to drift. Next day we made such heavy weather, the sailors started to throw the cargo overboard. On day three it was the turn of the boat's fittings to go over. It was too dark to see the sun or the stars for many days, and the storm showed no sign of slacking off. We thought we were done for!

It was a long time since anyone had had anything to eat. So Paul called for everyone's attention. "There you are, boys – what did I tell you? If we'd stayed in Crete we wouldn't have got into this mess! My advice now is for you to keep your spirits up. We're going to lose the boat, but we're all going to stay alive. I had a message last night from the God who employs me and who I work hard for. 'Don't lose your nerve, Paul, You're going to face the emperor. Those traveling with you will survive as well.' So cheer up, boys. I know God can be trusted to make it all come right. I expect we'll be castaways on an island somewhere."

We had been drifting for a fortnight and were somewhere in the Adriatic Sea. In the middle of the night the sailors had a hunch we were near to land. So they started to measure the depth of the water with a weight and line. They found it was quite shallow, and a further testing showed even shallower. They were afraid the boat might end up on the rocks, so they let down four anchors from the back of the boat, and hoped they would live to see another day. Then the sailors tried to play a dirty trick. They lowered the dinghy saying they were going to put down the anchors from the front of the ship. But really they meant to escape. Paul shouted to the soldiers with their officer, "If the sailors don't stay on board, there'll be no chance of surviving!" So the soldiers cut the ropes of the dinghy and it drifted away. It was nearly day, and Paul tried to get everybody to have something to eat. He said, "You've been in a state of tension for a fortnight without eating anything. You need to eat something to build up your strength. You're all going to escape without a scratch." Then Paul took a piece of bread and held it up for all to see. He said "thank you" to God, broke the bread and started eating. This boosted morale, and everybody on board joined in, two hundred and seventy-six in all. When they had eaten all they wanted, they threw the cargo of wheat into the sea to make the boat lighter.

When it was light, nobody recognized the coast, but they saw a sandy cove and thought it might be possible to get the boat to run aground there. They cut off the anchors and left them in the sea, and got the oars ready. Then they put up the sail in front of the boat and we started to move toward the beach. But we got stuck on some rocks under the water. The front of the boat would not move, but the back was being broken by the waves. The soldiers wanted to kill the prisoners to stop them swimming away. But the officer would not let them, because he wanted to save Paul. He ordered all those who could swim to jump overboard and swim to land. The rest followed using planks and rafts made from pieces of the boat. That's how we all managed to get ashore safely.

28 When we were all safely on dry land, we found we were on the island of Malta. The people there were very kind to us. It had started to rain and it was very cold, and they lit a fire and welcomed us all round it. Paul had twisted together a bundle of sticks to put on the fire. The heat frightened an adder out of the wood and it clung to Paul's wrist. When the local people saw the snake hanging from Paul's hand, they whispered together, "This man must be a murderer. He's escaped from the sea, but he's not going to escape justice." But Paul shook the snake into the fire. The snake had done him no harm. The people were expecting Paul to swell up any minute or fall down dead, but when, after a while, it was obvious nothing of the kind was going to happen, they altered their opinion of Paul and started calling him a god.

Near the place we came ashore were the estates of the ruler of Malta, who was called Lee. He invited us to his home and looked after us with great kindness for three days. At that time his father was suffering from gastric fever and had to stay in bed. Paul went to his room, put his arms round him, and asked God to make him better. As soon as he recovered, everyone else on the island who had an illness came to see Paul, and they were all made better. The islanders treated us like royalty, and when the time came to set out to sea again, they brought onto the boat everything we needed for the voyage.

Three months later, we boarded another boat from Egypt, which had spent the winter in Malta. The boat had carvings of the star twins, Castor and Pollux, on its bow. We called at Syracuse in Sicily and stayed there three days. Our next port was Reggio, on the southern tip of Italy. We spent one day there and then a wind from the south took us on to Naples. We found some Christians in Naples who invited us to stay with them for a week. At last we arrived at Rome. The Christians of Rome heard we were coming, and some of them traveled thirty and forty miles down the Appian Way to meet us. Seeing them put Paul in a very good mood and he thanked God. When we arrived in Rome, Paul was allowed his own accommodation. The only condition was that a soldier was appointed to stay with him.

Three days later, Paul asked the leaders of the Jewish community in Rome to meet him. Paul said, "Friends, I did nothing in the way of harm to our own people, nor did I challenge the way of doing things we got from our ancestors. Yet they arrested me in Jerusalem, and handed me over to the Romans. When they had questioned me, the Romans were anxious to let me go, because they realized I had done nothing to deserve the death penalty. But my own people kept up the pressure. The only way out was for me to appeal to the emperor, even though I didn't want to put my own people on trial in this way. I've asked you to meet me, to explain the position to you. In fact, the reason I'm a prisoner has to do with the special hope you and I share as Jewish people." They said, "We've not had any letters about you, and none of our people who've come here from the homeland has linked your name with any scandal. But we'd like to hear what you have to say, because our information is that the group you belong to has a bad reputation everywhere."

Paul made a date for them to visit him at his lodgings. They came in large numbers. He spoke with them all day, going into great detail. He told them about God's New World, and explained how the story of Jesus tied up with what was said in the old books. Some accepted what Paul said, others did not. They ended by disagreeing amongst themselves. Paul's parting shot was this, "God's Spirit was right when she spoke to your ancestors through Isaiah:

> 'The sight of God closed their eyes.
> Their minds then inward turned:
> When clear and plain the issues stood,
> The key to life they spurned.'

I'm telling you now. God's gift of healing is being announced to people who are not Jews. They will listen."

Paul lived for two years in Rome. He earned enough to pay his own rent and entertain everyone who came to see him. He told people about God's New World, and about the Leader, Jesus, God's Chosen. He spoke with great confidence, and no one tried to stop him.

PART TWO

PAUL AND HIS FRIENDS

Paul's Letter to Rome

1 This letter comes to you from Paul, a helper of Jesus, God's Chosen. God has asked me to pass on the Good News of Jesus to other people. This "Good News" was promised by God's speakers a long time ago. Their words can be found in the old books. It's all about God's Likeness, someone who is truly human by being descended from David, but seen by those with special insight to be God's Likeness, because he has power over death. God's Chosen is Jesus, our Leader. Jesus has given my team the special task of getting people of all races to trust in God. And it's Jesus who has given us what we need to carry out the task in the way he wants. You are some of the people who've received the invitation to be his friends. I'm writing to you who live in Rome. God loves you all; you're all invited to be God's people!

Greetings from the Loving God, and our Leader, Jesus, God's Chosen.

First of all, Jesus moves me to thank God for you all, because your trust in God is talked about everywhere. I'm keen to spread the Good News about God's Likeness, as God knows. When I talk with God I never fail to mention you. I'm asking God to let me visit you. I can't wait to see you, so I can be a good influence on you, and help you to be strong – or rather, I ought to say, so we can help and encourage one another to trust in God. I want you to know, my friends, I've made plans to visit you often, but something has happened to upset them each time. I was hoping to have a good crop of converts in your part of the world, as I have elsewhere. I owe a great deal to people of all types – some highly cultured, others with little education; some very clever, others not so bright. It's the mixture of people in Rome that makes it so attractive to me as a place to spread the Good News.

As I take round the Good News, I hold my head up high. It's God's way of bringing complete well-being to everyone who accepts it. The Jews got the Good News first; now other races are getting it. The Good News tells how God is putting right what has gone wrong. It's all a matter of trust, from beginning to end. As the old books say, "The way to real life is through trust in God."

(18) God's fierce opposition has been declared against all the evil and wickedness done by people who shamefully suppress the truth. Everything it's possible to know about God has been made known to humankind – God has made sure of that. Though God's character is too wonderful for us to understand, from the beginning of time it's been easy to grasp something of it through the world of nature. There's no excuse for complete ignorance! Though people can tell what God is like, they take no notice. They aren't grateful for God's gifts. Instead they've filled their minds with nonsense and gone wandering down every dark alley. They thought they were being clever while making fools of themselves. In the place of God who lives forever, they put statues of people, who live for no time at all, or even animals, birds, or snakes. God has watched them go on from this to despise one another and to practice all kinds of abuse. Because they've twisted the truth about God, their attitude to the material world is twisted too. They've forgotten that the source of lasting good is God, not things! God let them go on to pursue their selfish desires. Women use their charms to further their own ends. Men, instead of being friends, ruthlessly exploit one another. Their stressful lifestyle makes them ill.[1]

When people have no interest in getting to know what God is really like, God has no option but to leave them to their own evil thoughts, which lead to every kind of inhuman conduct. There is no end to their wickedness. Such people are greedy and envious, they commit murder, they quarrel and deceive; they play dirty tricks, they gossip and slander one another; they hate the very idea of God; they're arrogant, with no respect for their

---

[1] These verses have been shamefully used as a basis for the discomforting of those with a same-sex orientation. Undoubtedly Paul had uppermost in his mind the callous exploitation associated with the sex-trade, centered in his day in the pagan temples. He was not addressing the issue of loving same-sex relationships. Our translation strives to refocus on Paul's concern with the ill treatment of one human being by another, of which sexual abuse is one example, the persecution of minorities another.

parents; they're silly, unreliable, lacking any tender feelings or scruples. They know they're offending God and that they don't deserve to live. Yet not only do they persist in their evil ways, they encourage others to do the same.

2   But you've no excuse either, if you think you're in a position to criticize other people, because your critical attitude shows you're as bad as they are. We know God is a fair judge when people behave badly. Do you think when you criticize other people for behaving in the same way as you do, it will somehow put God off the scent? Shouldn't you be more appreciative of God's kindness, patience, and tolerance in your own case? Don't you realize that God's kindness is intended to get you to change your frame of mind? But your hard, unbending attitude means you're going to be in for a nasty shock on the day God's fair judgment is announced. God will take into account the whole pattern of your life. To those who have patiently tried to be a permanent influence for good, God will give life to the full; while for those who've been selfish and ignore the truth about their own wickedness, the consequences will be unpleasant in the extreme. There will be a time of grief and suffering for all who behave badly of whatever race. But it will be an exciting time, with a sense of achievement and contentment, for all who've done what is right, whatever their religion or culture. God has no racial bias.

For those who've done wrong because they don't know the rules, ignorance is no excuse. The future is empty for them. Those who know the rules, and still do wrong, will have the rules quoted against them. It's not enough to know the rules. Only if you keep them will God be impressed!

When people who don't know the rules do what is right, as if by instinct, they are accepted on their own merits. The fact that they've never read the rules does not matter. They have a natural sense of right and wrong, and their conscience tells them whether or not they've made the grade. This is close to the way God looks at things. Through Jesus, God looks deep into our most secret thoughts.

(17) Do you think you're one of God's people because you're never without the rulebook and always talking about God? You think you know God's mind inside out and know what's right and wrong because you've

studied the rules. You're so sure you're a guide for the blind, a light for those in darkness, correcting those who've got it wrong and putting beginners through their paces! You've got it all neatly tied up, haven't you? Isn't it about time you gave yourself a few lessons? You tell others it's wrong to steal. Can you put your hand on your heart and say you've never stolen anything yourself? You hold strict rules on the matter of personal relationships. Have you never stepped over the line? You believe God should be the only object of worship. Have you never made any financial gain from your religion? In fact, you make a mockery of those rules you're so proud of, and you give God a bad reputation. To use the words of the old books, "You make God's name a laughing-stock all over the world."

Being without a foreskin is your badge of office. You'd deserve a badge if you kept all the rules! But since you break the rules, your badge doesn't count for anything. Those who don't have the badge, but keep the rules, display the true badge. They're in a position to take you to task, because all you have is a meaningless badge. Belonging to God isn't a matter of outward show. It's got nothing to do with badges! God's people are those who have their hearts in the right place. God's Spirit is what makes them stand out, not rules. Such people aren't out to impress others. What God thinks of them is all that matters.

3 Is there any advantage, then, in being born into the community of God's people? Is there any value in having a distinct identity? Quite a lot, I would say. You must remember, in the first place, that God's messages were entrusted to a special community of people. Just because some of them let God down, it doesn't mean that God has opted out of the relationship. God can always be relied upon, even if everyone else turns out to be unreliable. As the old books say, "Your words stand up to the stiffest cross-examination, and you always win your case." Our bad conduct shows how good God's conduct is. Does that mean God is at fault to be displeased with us? (I hesitate to use such human talk in relation to God. God's view on the world cannot be questioned.) There is an argument which goes like this: "If our dishonesty serves to highlight God's honesty, can that be so bad on our part? Doesn't the end justify the means?" Some accuse *me* of saying this. They couldn't be more wrong!

What if we put it another way? Are those of us who are members of God's community in a position to feel superior? Far from it! I've already made it clear that insiders and outsiders are equally enthusiastic when it comes to doing wrong. The old books say, "There's no such thing as a good person, or a wise one for that matter; no one who is true to God. Everyone has gone off the track, everyone is corrupt; no one knows what it is to be kind. They're foul-mouthed, fork-tongued, poisonous like snakes. They only use words to sting and wound. They only hurry anywhere in order to kill. They leave a trail of misery wherever they go. They have no wish to live in harmony with others. God means absolutely nothing to them!"

Everything in the book of rules refers to those who take the rules as their standard. So no one is in a position to talk about their achievements. The whole world stands accused by God. Nobody succeeds in looking good in God's eyes by keeping the rules. The rules only point out where you've gone wrong.

(21) But recently, God has announced another way of putting right what is wrong, an idea foreseen in the Rule Book and by God's speakers in the past. This is God's way of putting things right by means of a relationship with Jesus, God's Chosen. It's for all who put their trust in him. There are to be no special categories, because we've all made a mess of things and failed to live up to God's intention for us. Everybody is now to be put right by means of God's loving action. It's like receiving a gift, or being released from prison. Jesus, by his death, has made us one with God. All we have to do is to trust him! By doing this, God shows supreme goodness. All the wrongs of the past are overlooked, and a new way shown of dealing with the wrongs of the present. Anyone who puts their trust in Jesus is acceptable to God. God cannot do better than that!

The "holier than thou" attitude is out! Why? Because we don't get any credit for what we do. It's all a matter of trust. The right relationship with God comes only through trust, not by keeping the rules. God is not a special mascot for the insiders. God belongs to everybody. There's only one God, who will put things right for insiders when they trust and for outsiders when they trust. Does this mean that if we trust we can throw away the rules? No, that's not the right way of looking at it. Trust will help us appreciate the rules.

4 Abraham, the ancestor of the Jewish people, is a good example of what I'm talking about. If Abraham had made a good impression by the things he did, he could have been pleased with himself. But it was not what Abraham *did* that impressed God. The old books say, "Abraham put his trust in God and that's what God liked about him." Workers receive their wages as a right. They're not a gift, but have to be earned. But when God accepts people who have nothing to their credit, trust becomes the deciding factor. This is what David meant when he described the happiness of those God accepts, despite what they've done:

> *"It's great to know you've been forgiven*
> *And your mistakes forgotten;*
> *It's great to be sure*
> *God's not keeping a score;*
> *That would be truly rotten!"*

Is this feeling of well-being only meant for those who keep the rules in the old books or do the rest of humanity get a chance? Since it was Abraham's trust that counted with God, it's important to note that this was before and not after he kept the rule about removing the foreskin. The acceptance of the rule was a mark of the relationship with God that already existed on the basis of Abraham's trust. This means that Abraham is the ancestor of all those who have a relationship with God not based on keeping the rules. He's also the ancestor of those who keep the rules, but, like him, think trust is more important than rule keeping.

God promised Abraham and his descendants that one day the world would be theirs. This promise was not based on what it says in the Rule Book, but on a relationship of trust with God. If only those who keep the rules are to enjoy God's New World, then trust counts for nothing and the promise was false. The Rule Book only leads to frustration. When there are no rules, there's no upset when they are broken! So the promise depends on trust and on God's delight in giving. It's for all the descendants of Abraham, not only for those who keep the rules, but also for those who trust God like he did. Abraham may be regarded as the ancestor of all of us. The old books put it clearly, "I've made you the ancestor of many nations."

Abraham stands in the presence of the one he trusted, the one who brings the dead back to life, the same God who makes worlds out of nothing. Abraham clung on to the hope that he would be the ancestor of many nations, even when it seemed impossible. When he heard the words, "Your descendants will be too many to count," he was very old with not much longer to live. What's more, Sarah was incapable of having children. But none of this put him off. He went on trusting in God's promise, and this trust renewed his physical strength and his delight in God. He never doubted for a moment that God would be able to keep the promise. It was this trust that kept him on good terms with God. The words "on good terms with God" don't only apply to Abraham. They apply to us too, since we trust the same God who brought Jesus, our Leader, back to life. He was arrested and executed as a result of our wrongdoing, and was brought back to life to restore our relationship with God.

5 We're now on good terms with God by means of trust, and Jesus helps us maintain our relationship with God, so that we no longer have to fret. Jesus made us aware of God's way of loving those who don't deserve it. And we're sure we'll share the thrill of God's success. We keep our spirits up, even when we're having a bad time. Trouble forces us to put up with things. Putting up with things helps our personalities develop and we become more confident. We know we won't be let down, because we've experienced God's love flooding into our hearts through the gift of God's Spirit.

In the nick of time, when we were getting into more and more of a hopeless mess, God's Chosen died for the sake of those who couldn't care less about God. Not many would offer to die for a righteous bore. Now and again someone has the courage to die for a person whose qualities they admire. Jesus died for us when we were rotten to the core, and that puts God's love in a class of its own! By his death we've been put back on good terms with God. Thanks to Jesus, we'll escape the dreadful fate we had coming to us! By the death of God's True Likeness, we've changed from being God's enemies into being God's friends. Now we're God's friends, new life from Jesus helps us become complete people! We ought to go over the top in celebration because of what God has done for us through Jesus.

He's arranged for us to be God's friends!

(12) Being human seems to mean doing wrong. Doing wrong leads to death. That's why death affects everybody. There was plenty of wrongdoing in the world before there were any rules, but since nobody knew the rules, no one could be held responsible. Nevertheless, death held everybody in its grip from the dawn of humanity to the time when Moses introduced the rules, including those who did wrong without realizing it. The development of conscience was a pointer toward the day when a new humanity would appear.

The extent of humanity's wrongdoing doesn't affect God's loving action on our behalf. Death is a feature of our flawed humanity, and touches everybody. In the same way, everybody is touched by Jesus, God's gift of love. God's gift upsets the principle that wrongdoing must be followed by a verdict of "guilty." Despite a great amount of wrongdoing, God's gift amounts to a verdict of "not guilty." Up to now, our link with one another as humans meant we shared the consequence of our common failure. That consequence was death. But now we also have a link with Jesus who is human too. This means God's love is being given to us in a new relationship and in a new life.

So, since the flawed humanity we all share meant a verdict of "guilty" for everybody, the goodness of one member of the human race reversed the verdict, bringing life for all. Just as the failure of one meant the failure of all, so now the fine performance of one means we can all make something of our lives! Rules were introduced to produce a sense of failure. But no matter how many rules were broken, God's love was always one step ahead. Death made it look as if failure had the upper hand, but God's goodness has won through to put things right, bringing life to the full through Jesus.

6 Some of you seem to think it's okay to carry on behaving badly so as to give God a chance of being even more generous. What an outrageous idea! Wrongdoing has been given a fatal blow deep inside us, so how can we let it gain control over our lives again? Don't you realize that when we were dipped as friends of Jesus, we were acting out his death? We went down under the water just as Jesus went down into the grave. We are showing that just as Jesus was brought back to life, good as

new, by the Loving God, so we too are beginning a new life.

Only if we share in Jesus' death can we share his coming to life. Each of us has to imagine that the person we were has been put with Jesus on the cross. All the bad in us has been destroyed and lost its control over us. If you're dead, you're immune to all bad influences. But if we take the death of Jesus as our starting point, then we trust his new life will be ours too. We know Jesus came back to life and will never die again. Death has no more power over him. His death put paid to wrongdoing forever. He lives God's life. It should be the same with you. Your bad old lives are a thing of the past. Now you live the life God wants you to live, with the help of Jesus.

Wrongdoing should have no more attraction for you. You should no longer be selfish. Your physical and mental powers should not he used for any wicked purpose. You should be completely at God's disposal for doing good, now that death is behind you and life in front of you. The overriding influence in your life is God's kindness to you, not bad impulses or slavish obedience to rules and regulations.

Because we no longer need rules and are in God's good books, does that mean it's alright if we behave badly? Of course not! If you enter someone's employment, you're expected to work for them. Wrongdoing is like a firm specializing in death. "Doing Good" is the firm that produces the right relationship with God. Thank God, though you were once employed in the business of wrongdoing, now you've learnt from your mistakes and you're making up for lost time. You've changed your occupation, from wrongdoing to doing good. (I'm using language I hope you'll understand.)

When you were engaged in wrongdoing, the firm of "Doing Good" had no claims on you. You're ashamed now at the thought of what you were expected to do for such a poor wage. Your only prospect was death! But now God is your employer, the old firm has no claim on you. Your conditions of work are excellent, and your prospects for promotion unlimited. Death is the payment in the firm of wrongdoing. Everybody in God's firm gets a free bonus – life to the full with Jesus.

7 Friends, you've had experience of the law, so you'll know that laws only apply to people during their lifetime. For example, a woman is only married to her husband according to the law as long as he is alive. If he dies, then legally she is no longer married. She will be breaking the rules of society if she leaves him for someone else while he's alive. But if he dies, society will not blame her for finding another partner. I would like to apply this, my friends, to your relationship with Jesus. He brings about an alteration in your legal status. Instead of being tied to rules and regulations, you're now free to have a relationship with the one who's come back to life. That's a better arrangement in God's eyes! In the days when selfishness prompted our actions, rules and regulations drove us to despair of making anything of our lives. The rules were like a bully standing in our way. Now the bully's dead, we're free to make a new relationship, and God's Spirit shows us how to go about it.

Does this mean rules are always a bad thing? I'm not saying that. But it's true that without rules there's no such thing as doing wrong. For example, I would not have been aware of craving for something that belongs to someone else if the rules had not told me I shouldn't have that feeling. The rule encouraged me to want the things I'm not supposed to have even more. No rule: no problem! Without rules I lived a carefree life, but as soon as I was made aware of the rules, doing wrong became an obsession. It ruined my enjoyment of life. The rule that was supposed to show me how to live, drove me to despair. It's as if the rule and wrongdoing got together to make a fool of me and make me wish I were dead! The rules and regulations come from God and are godly, fair, and good. So did something good bring me to the point of despair? That can't be right! The wrong use was being made of something good, showing just how crafty wrong can be, manipulating a rule to make matters worse instead of better. The rules come from God, but I am selfish, addicted to bad ways. I don't understand what I'm doing. I don't do what I really want to do, but what I hate doing. Doing what I don't want to do means I agree with the rules, but wrong has got such a grip on me, I'm no longer in control. It seems there is no good in me – in my human nature, at any rate. Although I want to do what is right, I can't make it. I can't live up to my ideals. Wrongdoing has taken over.

There seems to be a rule that whenever I want to do good, I can only do what's wrong. I can't help myself. I appreciate God's rules with my mind, but something else is going on inside me that tips the balance toward wrong. It's like being a prisoner. I'm all mixed up. How do I get out of the mess I've got into? My aim is to please God; my conduct does the opposite. Jesus is the answer. Thank God! Jesus is now in charge of my life.

8 Those who have a relationship with Jesus are off the hook. There's a new spirit of freedom and an escape from all those deadly old rules. We weren't up to keeping the rules, so God has done things a different way. God's Likeness has been put in the form of a human being with the same weaknesses as everybody else. A human body was used to tackle human wrongdoing, so we could achieve what the rules were aiming at, not by trying harder, but by having a different attitude. You can try and live the human way and get bogged down in human failings, or you can live God's way with God's new approach. It's deadly trying to do things your way, but doing things God's way brings life and peace. If you try to do things your way, you're really working against God. You're not letting God influence your life. Self is acting like a barrier. Those who please themselves cannot please God.

But you are overcoming your selfish instincts and allowing yourselves to be guided by the Spirit of God who lives in you. Anyone who does not have the same way of thinking and feeling as Jesus is not a friend of his. Even if your bodies have been ruined by selfishness, the Spirit brings a new lease of life based on a good relationship with God. If God's Spirit has taken possession of you, then just as God brought back Jesus from the dead, so the same Spirit will give your humanity a new lease of life.

So, friends, we don't have to carry on being selfish. That road leads nowhere! But if you allow the Spirit to kill off the selfish side of your nature, you'll know what it means to live! Those guided by the Spirit of God are members of God's family. The Spirit is not a bully. She doesn't rule by fear. She brings about a sense of belonging, so that we can call God Mum or Dad. It's the Spirit makes us sure we're members of God's family, so that we share in God's ownership of everything, just like Jesus. We share the suffering of God's Chosen, so that we can enjoy a better quality of life with him.

(18) As I see it, what we have to put up with now is nothing compared with the experience of happiness coming to us soon. The physical universe

has been evolving toward a point where God's family will be established. There's been a lot of frustration on the way, but God has been at work through it all. The mess and muddle was the breeding ground of a vision for the future. The whole universe will break out from the prison of its self-destruction and share the joyful freedom of God's children.

It's as if, up to now, the physical universe has been groaning like a woman having a baby. The Spirit makes us aware of being part of that universe, so we share in the birth-pains. We can't wait to emerge into freedom and become part of God's family. It's hope that keeps us on the road to complete well-being. If we've already got what we were hoping for, there's no point in hoping any more, is there? But since we're hoping for something we can't see yet, we're able to relax and wait for it.

The Spirit is a big help when we're finding it hard to cope. Sometimes it's difficult to put our feelings into words to God. That's where the Spirit comes in. She interprets the deep desires we can only express as groans. The Spirit is the link between us and God. By means of the Spirit, God sees right inside us. The Spirit enables God's people to make their wishes known to God and brings their wishes into line with what God wants.

(28) Those who love God are in partnership with God, working for good in every part of life. There's a special job for each one of us. God knows our potential and chooses us carefully. First we go through a period of training to take on the same character as God's True Likeness. So God's True Likeness turns out to be the first of a big family. After God has selected us for our tasks, we're invited to join the team. We find ourselves on good terms with God and have a new sense of dignity as people.

What does it all add up to? God is our friend. That means we've got no real enemies. God came to us completely in the gift of the True Likeness. God's not a stingy giver. The sky's the limit! Do we have to worry what people say about us? Since God is on our side, it doesn't matter what others think. Jesus isn't in the business of condemning. The one who died and came back to life is shoulder to shoulder with God and shoulder to shoulder with us!

Can anything get in the way of the love of Jesus for us? Bad times? Depression? Persecution? Hunger? Poverty? Danger? Murder? As the old song goes:

"We look death in the face for you each day:
Like sheep to the slaughterhouse taken away."

No, we come out smiling from every kind of difficulty, with the help of the one who loves us. I'm absolutely certain that neither death nor life, the rulers of this world or other worlds, the world as we know it or the world as it may become, no power, no authority, no hidden force, nothing in any form of existence can ever come between us and the love of God shown to us in Jesus.

9 What I'm going to say now is the absolute truth. Christians do not tell lies. My conscience is controlled by God's Spirit. I'm heartbroken and suffer continual mental anguish. So strong are my feelings for my own people, the Jews, that I would forfeit my own lifeline with Jesus, if by so doing they could experience his new life. They're the descendants of Jacob; God looks on them as adopted children. They've experienced God's presence and have a special relationship. God gave them a set of rules, taught them how to worship, and made promises to stand by them. They're the descendants of the first people to worship the true God, and God's Chosen is of the same race. The God who is God of everybody and everything should be praised for all this.

God's ideas have not failed just because not all Jacob's descendants are the real thing. Not all Abraham's descendants are descendants in the special sense God intended. The old books say, "It's through Isaac your true descendants will come." This is a way of saying that physical descent doesn't produce God's children. It's a matter of living up to God's intentions. God promised, "At the right time I'll make sure that Sarah has a son." The same process of selection was at work in the case of our ancestors Rebecca and Isaac. Even before their two children had been born, or done anything good or bad, God told Rebecca, with the long term in view, "The older will have a lower status than the younger." The old books say, "I preferred Jacob to Esau." This doesn't mean God is unfair. God told Moses, "I shall be kind and forgiving to whoever I want." It's God's nature to be generous. You can't twist God's arm. In the old books the Egyptian Pharaoh was told, "I made you king to show what I can do, to let the whole world know about me."

Some people experience God's kindness, while others cannot because of their stubborn attitude.

Someone may argue like this: "If God has control over everything, how can we be blamed if we don't do what is right?" We can't call God into question, because as humans we're not on a level with God. It would be like a work of art criticizing the artist and questioning the use of materials for particular objects. The fact is that God, instead of expressing anger and a display of power, has shown a lot of patience to people who deserve to be thrown out. This is part of the overall strategy. By treating bad people so well, God gives us a hint of what's in store for those due to receive the full package of kindness. It's all been worked out. People of all races are included. God said, "I will call those outside my family 'My people,' and I will call those no one loves 'My loved ones.' In the very place where they were regarded as outsiders, they will be recognized as children of the True God."

God's speaker used strong language to make the point about the Jews. "Though the descendants of Jacob are as many as the pebbles on the beach, only a small number will survive. God will soon put matters right in the world." "If God had not left us a few survivors, we would have vanished altogether, just like Sodom and Gomorrah."

What does this all add up to? Those who've never tried to be on good terms with God, now have a special relationship with God by means of trust. But those who've tried so hard to get on the right side of God by keeping rules, missed the whole point of the rules. How could they go so far wrong? Because, instead of trusting God, they relied on their own efforts. They've fallen flat on their faces, just as it says in the old books,

> "*Some slip on my rock in Jerusalem,*
> *But those who trust need feel no shame.*"

10 Friends, I long to see my own people being healed, and I'm asking God to help them. I know, from my own experience, they are enthusiastic about God, but their enthusiasm is based on ignorance. They don't want to know about God's special offer of a new relationship, and they persist in doing things their own way. It's as if they knew better than God! Jesus has got rid of the old rules and made it possible for everyone who trusts to be on good terms with God. Although Moses suggested that rules can put things right when he wrote, "Those who keep the rules will really live," the old books also talk about the way of putting things right by trust.

> *"You cannot climb a rocky steep*
> *And drag God's Chosen down;*
> *No use to wallow in guilt's deep,*
> *Unless you want to drown."*

Do you remember the rest of the song?

> *"The answer's at your finger tips,*
> *Close to your heart*
> *And on your lips."*

If you recognize Jesus as Leader and believe that God brought him back to life, you will be healed, without any doubt. What we say with our lips and what we sincerely trust in our hearts go together to bring complete well-being and good relations with God. The old books say, "No one who trusts God will be let down." It doesn't matter what our racial background is. We all have the same God, and we only have to ask to find complete satisfaction! Here's another extract from the old books. "Anyone who asks God for help will get it."

(14) But how can people ask God for help if they have no trust? And how can they trust someone they've never heard about? And how will they get to know unless someone tells them? And how can the news be passed on unless someone is given the task? The old books say, "Those with Good News find it easy to run." But not everyone has listened to the Good News. As God's speaker complained, "Has anyone got the message, God?" Trust comes by listening to the story of Jesus. Have my people not had a chance to hear the story? Of course they have! Just as we sing,

"Round the world the words have gone:
The news has been heard by everyone."

Or perhaps they haven't understood? Moses answers that question. "I will use foreigners to make my people jealous, and those they looked down on will show them up." And God's speaker puts it even more bluntly when he imagines God saying, "I was found by those who weren't looking for me; I introduced myself to those who'd never even asked if I existed." The same speaker imagines God saying about our race, "I've had my arms wide open all day, ready to embrace a people who despise and ignore me."

11

Does this mean God has no time for the Jews? Not at all! God cares about me, and I'm a Jew! I'm descended from Abraham and belong to Ben's tribe. God doesn't play fast and loose with people. Do you remember the story of Elijah? He tried to persuade God to stop caring for the Jews.

"God, they've killed your messengers and vandalized your
places of worship. I'm the only one who's stayed true to you,
and they want to kill me."

And what was God's reply?

"I've made sure there are still seven thousand who haven't
worshiped the false god."

In the same way God has today made sure a sufficient number have remained true. God's loving actions have made this possible. It's got nothing to do with what we've done. If we place importance on our achievements we rob God of all the credit.

This is how things stand. The Jewish people as a whole haven't found what they were looking for, only some of them. The rest are stuck. As it says in the old books, "They responded to God by shutting their minds. It's as if they were blind and deaf." They're no different today! I'm reminded too of the song David composed:

> "Let their table be a trap,
> Poison all their meat;
> Let them blind and senseless rise,
> Shaky on their feet."

The question is, have they fallen so badly that they'll never be able to get up again? No, it's not like that. Their mistake has given people of other races the chance of healing, and this will give my own race fresh motivation. They will be envious! As it happens, their slip-up has done the world a good turn. If one false move on their part has done other people so much good, what a great day it will be when they get things right!

(13) Most of you reading this letter are not Jews. As you know, my special assignment is to people like you, and you get most of my attention. But I'm always hoping this will make my own people envious and so bring healing to some of them. If leaving my own race to one side means the whole world can be on good terms with God, when their turn comes again, the revolution will be complete! According to our Jewish way of thinking, if the first loaf from a piece of dough is offered to God, then the whole batch from the same dough belongs to God too; and if a tree is offered to God, any cuttings from that tree belong to God.

Let's take that idea a bit further. A cutting can be taken from an olive tree and a shoot of wild olive grafted in its place. The new graft will take life from the root of the olive tree, but only if it accepts the root as its source of life. People who aren't Jews ought not to say in an arrogant way, "You're out and we're in!" Although it's true the Jews were cut off because they failed to trust, it should not be a matter of pride but of wonder and amazement. God had to be ruthless in pruning the branches of the tree. God may have to deal with you in the same way! Sometimes it's necessary to be ruthless in order to be kind. God had to be ruthless toward those who were in the wrong, in order to show kindness to you. You had better be kind yourselves, or it might be your turn for the chop! There will be an opportunity for Jewish people who give up their prejudices to be grafted back on to the tree. God is capable of doing that. It stands to reason that cuttings from the original tree will take more easily, if they are grafted back on, than cuttings from a wild tree. So friends, don't try to be superior and think you know it all. I'm letting you into the secret. The stubbornness of my people is only temporary, to give an opportunity for others to come to God. Then *all* God's people will be healed! The old books say, "The Deliverer will come from Jerusalem and rid this people of their ungodly ways. I'll form a new relationship with them when I take away their wrongdoing."

(28) Because my people are biased against the Good News, God has used that bias to your advantage. But God still loves the Jews and regards them as special because of their ancestors. God isn't fickle and doesn't give with one hand and take back with another. You people ignored God's invitation in the past, but you've done well because the Jews have taken to behaving as you used to. This means that, although they're failing to respond to God at the moment, they, like you, will get there in the end! It's as if God had arranged for everyone to be locked up, so as to have the opportunity to set everyone free! The skill of God's operations leaves us speechless! What brilliance! What an expert God is!

> "Who can match God's line of thought?
> Or by whom can God be taught?
> Who has given God gifts enough
> To match the love God gives to us?"

Since God is responsible for everything, God must be given all the credit, now and forever!

12 Because God has been so good to you, you should respond by making your whole life a gift to God. That would be a worthy present. Don't just go with the crowd. Use your imagination to find out exactly what God wants. There must be no second-best! I recognize I owe everything to God, so you must not get big ideas about yourselves. Be sensible, and remember, it's your trust in God that counts. A human body has many parts with different functions. In the same way we, together with Jesus, form one body. We all depend on one another. God gives us different abilities. Some of you are good at speaking; so be confident about it. Some of you are good at getting things done; so get on with the job. Those who are good at explaining things should be teachers, and those who know how to cheer people up should get alongside those who are feeling down. Those who have money to spare should give generously; and those who are natural leaders should lead in a responsible way. If helping others is your thing, do it with a smile.

Let's have real love! Hate the nasty things and hold on to the good things. Let love breed love. Go out of your way to put other people first. Don't let your spirits sag. Keep up your enthusiasm by remembering that you are assisting the Leader. Hope and be happy: endure and be patient. Keep your lines open to God. Share what you have with those in need, and open your homes to strangers. Have good words for those who wish you harm and don't say bad things about them. Share the joy of the happy and the sorrow of the sad. Get on with one another. Don't be snobbish, but mix with those others look down on. Don't try to be clever! Never pay back wrong with wrong. The way you behave should look good to everybody. As far as possible, be on good terms with all the world. Friends, never try to get your own back. Let God be in charge of discipline. In the old books God says, "Righting wrongs is my concern. Leave it to me." The old books also say, "If your enemies are hungry, give them something to eat; if they're thirsty give them a drink. That will give them something to think about!" Don't let evil beat you. Get the better of it by doing good.

13 You should all respect those in government. Stable governments are part of the good order God has planned for the world. Anyone who is out to cause trouble is going against God's good order and will suffer the consequences. Those in authority are not there to frighten good people. Only those who behave badly have any reason to fear. If you want to be free from anxiety, behave yourself. You will find the government on your side. Governments assist God to promote your well-being. But if you engage in criminal acts, then you should be afraid, because the government can inflict penalties, and these reflect God's disapproval of wrongdoing.

But being a good citizen is not just a matter of being afraid – it's a matter of conscience. You pay taxes because governments, as God's assistants, need money to look after you. Make sure you pay your taxes on time, and give respect and approval to those who deserve it. Don't get into debt. The only thing you should be aware of owing is love for one another. If you truly love somebody else, you can forget the rules. The rules about not taking away another's partner, and about not killing or stealing or hankering after what doesn't belong to you, are all summed up in the one rule, "Love others as you love yourself." Love doesn't hurt anybody. Love is a better way of bringing about what the rules are for.

You know what an important time it is. It's time to be alert. We're nearer now to the day when the world will get healing than when we first put our trust in God. A new day is dawning. So let's get off our nightclothes and put on our day clothes. Let's have our wits about us. This is not the time for behaving irresponsibly, for getting drunk or flirting or fooling around, nor a time for picking quarrels or being jealous. You should reflect the character of Jesus. Stop trying to please yourselves!

14

You should welcome into your community those who only have a hesitating trust in God. The fact that they don't see things the way you do shouldn't be a matter for falling out. Some people believe it's okay to eat anything, whereas others with a tender conscience are vegetarian. Those who eat meat shouldn't sneer at vegetarians, and vegetarians shouldn't adopt a superior attitude. God accepts everybody. It's not your place to voice an opinion about people who are not your employees but someone else's. They only have to answer to their employer. God, their employer, will stand up for them and give them a good name.

Some people like to keep a special day for worship, whereas others think one day is as good as the next. People must think it out carefully for themselves. Those who keep a special day do it out of regard for Jesus the Leader. Those who have a good meal have regard for Jesus too, for they say "thank you" to God before eating. Those who make a special point of going without food also do it out of regard for Jesus. They're simply expressing their thanks in a different way.

We're not on this earth to please ourselves, and for that matter our death isn't our own business either. We're responsible to the Leader both for our living and our dying. It's to Jesus we belong. That's why God's Chosen died and came back to life again, to be the Leader of those who are alive and those who have died.

Why do you criticize your Christian brother? Why do you look down on your Christian sister? We'll all have to answer to God. As the old books say,

> " 'As truly as I live,' says God,
> 'All life will worship me,
> And every tongue then sing aloud,
> "To God the praise shall be." ' "

I repeat, it's to God every one of us will have to answer!

(13) So let's put a stop to the criticism and make sure we don't make difficulties for one another. I believe I'm being true to the ideas of Jesus when I say that all taboos are unreasonable. But they're very important to some people. If, for example, you cause distress to those close to you by what you eat, then you are not being loving. Don't let your personal preferences cause the downfall of someone Jesus gave his life for. You must take care your private conviction about what is right doesn't appear scandalous in the eyes of others. God's New World isn't about eating or drinking, but about fairness and good relationships and the happiness we can share because we have God's Spirit. Anyone who follows Jesus in being sensitive to the feelings of others will be alright in God's eyes and stand high in the opinion of other people. So let's do those things that help us get on together and give one another confidence. Don't upset God's work because of some fad. There are no taboos, but you mustn't hurt others by the choices you make. It's not good to eat meat or drink alcohol or do anything likely to hurt another member of your community. Cherish the convictions God has helped you arrive at. Those who sincerely do what they believe to be right will experience contentment and freedom from guilt. But if there's any doubt about a particular course of action, there is cause for guilty feelings because practice isn't stemming from conviction. It's wrong to do anything without conviction.

15 Those of us who have strong convictions should help those who have difficulties. We shouldn't just please ourselves. We should all try hard to please other people, to do them good and build up their confidence. Jesus didn't please himself. As the old books say, "The insults meant for you have landed on me." The writings of previous times are there to teach us. They give us patience, encouragement, and hope. God, who is the source of patience and encouragement, will help you get on with one another in the same way that Jesus got on with people. Then, as one happy family, you'll be united in promoting the reputation of God, Parent of our Leader, Jesus, the Chosen One.

It will help God's reputation if you accept one another just as Jesus has accepted you. Jesus made it his life's work to pass on God's truth to the Jewish people, in line with the promises God made to their ancestors. Jesus also had those who were not Jews in mind. He wanted all races to be grateful for God's loving-kindness. Here are some quotations that make the point:

"I'll sing your praise for all to hear:
I'll shout your name out, far and near!

"Come on, you outsiders.
Share the joy of God's people!"

"Let's have an all-round cheer for God
– a song of praise from every race!"

"One of David's family
will have world-wide authority.
He'll bring good relations
To all the tribes and nations."

If you trust in the God who brings hope, you'll experience true peace and happiness, and your hope will get stronger and stronger with the help of God's Spirit.

(14) I'm quite sure, my friends, that you're good-hearted, well-educated and capable of teaching one another. So I hope you'll understand my underlining one or two points, just to jog your memory. God has given me the special task of being the mouthpiece of Jesus to those who aren't Jews.

I'm part of the whole operation of making sure everybody gets God's Good News. I'm helping other races to come to God and feel at home. God's Spirit is preparing them for this. I'm proud to work for God in the same way Jesus did. I need only mention the way Jesus has used my words and deeds to win over different races. So many wonderful things have happened by means of God's Spirit. From Jerusalem to Greece and beyond, I've spoken in public the Good News about God's Chosen. It's always been my aim to pass on the Good News where Jesus has not yet been heard of, so that I don't interfere with somebody else's work. As the old books say, "Those who have never been told about God's helper will see him, and those who have never heard his voice will understand his message."

(22) I hope that explains why I've not managed to come to you yet. But since there's nothing more for me to do in these parts, I'd like to achieve my ambition of paying you a visit. I could call to see you on my way to Spain and be helped on my way by you after I've had the pleasure of your company. First of all, though, I'm off to Jerusalem to help God's people there. The Christians of Macedonia and Greece have been so good as to provide money to help the Christians in Jerusalem who badly need it. They decided to do this themselves, feeling they owe it to the people of Jerusalem. The Jews have shared the good things they've had from God with other races. It's only fair for those other races to pay something back when they can. So when I've carried out the job of handing this nice present to them, I'll be on my way to Spain, calling to see you on the way, and bringing with me all the good things of Jesus.

Now, I've got something special to ask of you, friends. If you are true to Jesus, and have the love God's Spirit brings, join me in asking God to protect me from the bad sort in the Jewish homeland, so that my efforts to help the people in Jerusalem may be well received. Then I'll come to you in a good mood, and relax in your company. God is close to you and will give you peace.

16 I want to introduce you to our friend Phebe, leader of our community in the dock-land district of Corinth. Welcome her in the name of Jesus in a way that will bring credit to you as God's people. Give her whatever help she may need from you, for she has been a good friend to many people, including me.

Give my kind regards to Cill and Will, my Christian workmates. They risked their lives for me. I'm grateful to them, and so are all our groups. My regards to the Christians who meet in their house. Also to Wayne, the very first Christian from the western tip of Asia; to Mary, who has been working very hard among you; and to Andy and June, my relations, who were in prison with me. They're in the first rank of Christian leaders, and were Christians before me. Special love to my dear friend Lee.

Regards to Urban, another Christian workmate, and Stan, another special friend. Regards to Les who has proved his worth. Regards to Bill's family. Regards to Rod, another relative of mine, and to Cecil's family. Greetings to those two ladies whose names mean "delicate and dainty" but who work so hard; and to another hard worker, Percy, who I'm very fond of. Regards to Rufus who has special qualities, and I must not forget his mother who has been like a mother to me. Regards to Chris, Sparky, Mervyn, Paddy, Massy, and the rest of their group. Regards to Phil, Julie, Neville, and his sister, Olympia, and all their friends. Hugs and kisses all round! Regards from all the other groups.

(17) Friends, please keep a look out for those who want to cause divisions and bad feeling. That's not how you've been taught to behave. Don't get involved with them! People like that are not working for our Leader. They're on their own ego trip! They use flattery and smooth talk to trap simple-minded folk. Everybody knows about your loyalty, and it makes me so happy! But I want you to be wise as well as good, so that it's impossible for evil to outwit you. The God who brings peace will help you get the better of evil's power. Jesus is with you and will help you.

Regards to you from Timothy, my assistant; also from Lucien, Jason, and Pat, my relations.

(I, Terry, who wrote this letter down, send my Christian kind regards.)

I'm staying with Gus. He holds the meetings of our community in his house. He sends his regards. So does Rastus, who has a high position in local government, and our friend Kurt.

The Good News about Jesus will give you strength. Thank God, the secret is out. What God's representatives in times past knew, is now common knowledge right round the world. God wants everyone to know, so that all can trust and respond. How wise is the one and only God made known through Jesus! Be thankful, now and always!

Paul's Letters to Corinth

First Letter (1 Corinthians)

Introduction

Many scholars believe that the letters to the Corinthians as they stand in traditional translations of the Bible are a collection of many fragments from the long correspondence Paul had with the Christians of Corinth. It is a pity we do not also have their letters that prompted Paul's, and their replies! But sometimes what traditionally appear as statements of Paul summarizing his beliefs, may have been his quoting of the Corinthians' questions, which he then goes on to discuss. Sometimes he refutes the beliefs implied by their questionings, e.g. "It is good for a man to have nothing to do with a woman" (7:1). It is not always possible to identify these examples with accuracy, but we have tried to pay attention to them where the context renders them obvious.

More difficult is the question of how many letters Paul wrote to Corinth. The evidence of the letters themselves is that he wrote at least three, possibly four or more, and we may have parts of all these letters. It is not our purpose to provide a critical commentary, but we incline to the view held by many scholars and popularized by William Barclay that 2 Corinthians 10–13 represents a letter sent in between the first letter as we now have it and 2 Corinthians 1–9. Whatever the scholarly arguments to and fro, the fact of the matter is that the letters in their current sequence do not make sense, whereas the amended form, which produces three distinct letters, makes very good sense on the whole. Since the purpose of this translation is to make sense, the three letters format is the one we adopt.

1 This letter comes to you from Paul. Sonny, my friend and yours, is helping me to write it. God has asked me to spread the Good News about Jesus. Those of you who are God's friends in the city of Corinth are very special people because you have come under the influence of Jesus. Everyone is special who uses the name of Jesus in worship and, like us, accepts him as their Leader, wherever they happen to live. We want to pass on to you the goodness and peace we've got from the Loving God and Jesus.

I'm always saying "thank you" to God for the goodness you've got from Jesus. You are much better people because of him. Your knowledge is wider and you express yourselves more freely. You have made the truth you've heard about God's Chosen your inner strength. That's why you've had all the gifts on offer from God, and you can't wait to see Jesus himself. He will keep you going so that on that day you won't have anything to be ashamed of. God can always be trusted. It was God who invited you into the community of God's True Likeness.

(10) Please dear friends, stop falling out among yourselves, and learn to get on with one another. I know this is what Jesus would want me to say. You all have the same aims, so you should be able to come to a common mind. The group who meet in Chloe's house have told me that you are squabbling. It seems you have adopted labels. Some of you say, "I'm for Paul" or "I'm for Rocky" or "I'm for Ray" or "I'm a real Christian – I belong to Jesus." Do you think you're behaving like Jesus if you cut off yourselves from others?

Was Paul hung on a cross for you? Was the name of Paul used when you were dipped? Thank God, I didn't dip any of you, except Cris and Guss. So no one can say you were dipped as my followers. O yes, I've just remembered, I did dip the people who live in Steve's house. I can't think of anybody else. Jesus didn't ask me to dip people. He asked me to pass on the Good News.

I know I'm not the best of speakers or good at arguing the case. That means it's not me but the message about Jesus on his cross that gets the results!

(18) The message about Jesus on his cross is meaningless to those who are going nowhere. But to those of us who are on the path to completeness,

it shows how resourceful God is. It says in one of the old books,

> *"I'll make the clever look a fool,*
> *And the scholar dim."*

The reputation of society's brilliant thinkers has vanished overnight. God has made them all look silly. God has outwitted those who set store by their intelligence, by ruling out intelligence as the means of discovering God. Instead God has chosen to give life to those who accept what seems to be a foolish tale. Those of the Jewish religion always want clear proof before they believe in anything, whereas the Greek thinkers try to work out a system of belief by using their minds. But we talk about God's Chosen on a cross. That's the opposite of the proof the Jews are looking for, and an insult to the intelligence of the Greeks. But to God's friends, whether Jews or Greeks, it's God's stroke of genius. God playing the fool outwits the highest human mind, and God becoming weak defeats the greatest human strength.

Just think, sisters and brothers, what sort of people you were before you became the friends of God. Not many of you were intelligent as society rates intelligence; not many of you were people of influence; not many of you were from the ruling classes. God chose the simple in the community to make fools of the clever; God chose the weak of the world to bring the strong to their knees; God chose the failures and outcasts of society, people regarded as nobodies, to bring the accepted order crashing to the ground. No one can show off in front of God. God has given you Jesus as your friend. He's God's bright idea. He restores our relationship with God and gives us status and freedom. So, as the old book says, "If you must show off, let people know what God has done for you."

2 When I came to see you, friends, I didn't make a mystery of God's truth by using big words or clever talk. I kept to the simple story of Jesus hung on a cross. I was not well at the time and so nervous, I couldn't stop shaking. My words were so poor, their success was sure proof of the work of the Spirit. This means your trust in the message wasn't based on skillful argument, but on God's power. The Christian message does have

an appeal to those who think deeply about things. But it doesn't fit the thinking of today's leading authorities. They'll soon count for nothing. We speak God's mind, which until now has been hidden. Long before history began, God was planning great things for us. Those in government haven't been in tune with God's mind, otherwise they wouldn't have put the one who rules over everything on a cross. One of the old books says something like this,

> "For God's lovers are prepared
> Experiences rare;
> Eye not seen, ear not heard,
> Way beyond compare."

(10) We have an insight into these things by means of the Spirit. The Spirit gets to the bottom of everything, even the mind of God. Just as you're the only one who knows what you're thinking, so only God's Spirit knows what God is thinking. We don't have knowledge of things in the conventional way. Our knowledge comes from God's Spirit inside us. This means we have a special appreciation of all the other things that come from God. We use words different from the world's great thinkers. We use words we're given by the Spirit that can be understood by people who have the Spirit.

If you don't have the Spirit, you can't receive the special gifts she brings. You can't appreciate their value because they don't make sense. Those who have the Spirit appreciate the true value of everything. They don't need someone else to put them right. Who knows what God is thinking? Who has ever been in a position to give God advice? Jesus gives us a window into God's mind.

3 Friends, I had difficulty in knowing how to talk to you. You seemed not to have been affected by the Spirit. Your way of talking was crude. Compared with Jesus, you were children at the nursery stage. You still needed breastfeeding; you weren't ready for solids. You're not ready yet! You're still squabbling over your toys and competing for attention. When are you going to grow up? Those rival fan clubs of yours,

"I'm in Paul's gang!" or "I'm in Ray's gang!", just show how immature you are! What's so big about Ray or Paul? We're only helpers, doing the job God has given us. I put the plants in their pots, and Ray came along with the watering can. It was God who got the plants to grow. The one who pots, and the one who waters, are nothing compared with the gardener who produces the plants. Planting and watering are all part of the process, and those of us who do these elementary tasks get paid for it. We're expected to work as a team in the potting shed. You're God's potting shed!

(10) Or you can think of yourselves as a building. God gave me the task of setting the foundation. Now someone else is laying the bricks. The bricklayer must be careful to build up from the foundation already in place. No one should try to replace it with another. The foundation is Jesus, God's Chosen. A variety of materials can be used on top of a foundation, gold, silver, rare stone, wood, or thatch. Some materials will stand the test of time better than others. A big fire will reveal the quality of the work. If the building survives, the builder will get a good name. If it's destroyed by fire, the builder's work will be in ruins. Even though there's no penalty for shoddy work, the builder's reputation will suffer. You're like a building that stands to remind people of God. God's Spirit lives in you. God will deal severely with anyone who does you harm. You're special because you are where God lives.

(18) Don't kid yourselves. The worst fools are those who think they know it all. If you really want to become wise, start by looking upon yourselves as fools. All the wisdom of our civilization put together is foolish to God's way of thinking. Two quotations will make my point,

> "God confounds the boffins
> Despite their clever wafflings"

and,

> "For all your craft,
> God thinks you daft."

So please don't put any of us on a pedestal. We don't own you; you own us,

Paul, Ray, and Rocky. Everything belongs to you now, the world, life and death, the present and the future. Only, don't forget, you belong to Jesus, which means that, like him, you belong to God.

4 Here is another way of thinking about us. We're in the employment of Jesus, as God's private secretaries. The chief requirement is that we can be trusted with confidences. I don't have to answer to you or anyone else apart from God. I think I'm doing alright, but it's not for me to say. It's the Leader who makes the assessment. You mustn't jump to conclusions. Stand by for the Leader's report. It will be fully comprehensive and very revealing. We all have to wait till then for God's pat on the back.

I've been using pictures to describe the work Ray and I've been doing. I'm sure I speak for both of us when I say we hope you will come to order and do away with the fan clubs. You must not use your enthusiasm for either of us as the means of giving you a sense of importance. None of you is anything special over against anyone else. Anything you possess has been passed on to you. It's not right to be so cocky about something you've got from others. You acknowledge no help from us. The way you behave, anyone would think you'd come into some money, or joined the aristocracy. If that were the case, you could share your good fortune with us! It seems to me that, as God's workers, we are right at the bottom of the social scale, on a level with criminals sentenced to death. We're on show for high and low to laugh at. A good name for us would be "The Jesus Fools." You, on the other hand, are such clever Christians! We are weak, but you are strong! You are the important ones, and we are a joke! At this very moment we're hungry and thirsty; our clothes are shabby; we have bruises from being knocked about; we don't know where we're going to sleep tonight; and we're aching all over from our hard work. Yet when people throw insults at us, we wish them well; when they do everything they can to make life difficult for us, we put up with it; when they call us names, we respond politely. We're treated like rubbish waiting to be disposed of.

I'm not writing this to make you ashamed of yourselves. I'm talking to you as members of my family. I'm telling you how it is. Although there are many other Christian teachers to give you good advice, not many of them have the same close relationship with you as I do. Because I was the first to give you the Good News, I'm like a parent to you, and recognized by Jesus as such. So please, try and do things my way. That's why I've sent Timothy to you. I love him dearly; he's been like a son to me. He will take you back to the type of Christianity I teach in all the churches I visit.

Some of you are getting a bit above yourselves. That's because you think I'm not coming to Corinth. Well, let me tell you, I'm on my way, if it's okay with the Leader. Then we shall see whether you self-important ones are as big as your talk! It's what you get done, not what you say that matters in God's New World! It's up to you. Do you want me to use the big stick? Or will you have calmed down enough for me to use the way of love?

5 It has been reported to me from a reliable source that some of you are behaving badly in the matter of personal relationships, worse indeed than anything people who are not Christians get up to. Someone is fooling around with his stepmother! And you just shrug your shoulders! You should be ashamed of yourselves. Why hasn't the offender been asked to leave the group?

It makes no difference that I'm not there with you to give my opinion. I can exercise my influence from a distance. On behalf of Jesus, our Leader, I have already pronounced this man guilty for behaving so badly. Next time you meet, you're to act as if I were there, with the strength I have from Jesus. You must declare this man to be a danger to the community until his urges have been controlled. Only then can he be fit to meet with Jesus.

Don't be so sure of yourselves! Just as a bit of yeast makes the bread rise, so a few people can make a difference to the quality of life. You must try to be a healthy influence in your community, not a bad influence. Jesus invites us to celebrate in the presence of God. Let's have a great party, with good food and pleasant company!

Remember I wrote to you before, telling you not to mix with bad people. Please don't misunderstand me. I did not mean the bad people you meet in the street, people who are out for themselves, people who cheat, people who put other things in the place of God. You could only avoid them by cutting yourselves off from society altogether. I want to make it clear, I was talking about being friendly to Christians who are irresponsible or pursue their own goals – greedy, gossipy, drinkers, frauds. Don't express your friendship by having a meal with them. What people who are not Christians do is not for us to judge. (God will decide what to do about those who are not Christians.) But we have a duty to assess the behavior of members of our Christian family. So, GET RID OF THAT WICKED MAN!!

6 I cannot understand how anyone of you could step so sharply out of line as to take a complaint about another Christian to a court that does not recognize our beliefs. Why didn't you have the matter dealt with by your Christian friends? As God's people you are responsible for putting the world to rights. So why can't you handle little problems amongst yourselves? We may well be called upon to make decisions at the highest level of God's management of the world. How are we going to do that if we can't even cope with routine business? How can you bear to expose your petty squabbles in front of those who are not members of the Christian community? What have I got to say to make you blush? Is there no one in your group capable of settling a dispute between one Christian and another, so that you are driven to the extremity of involving those who don't have our trust in God?

Going to court is an admission of failure. Isn't it more Christian to put up with a wrong? What's so terrible about being cheated? Unless, of course, it's you Christians who are doing the cheating!

(9) It's time you realized that people who choose not to control their conduct aren't ready for God's New World! I'm talking about people who mess around in frivolous relationships, people who worship things instead of God, those who set out to steal another's partner, those who make money out of sex or abuse the young, thieves, loan-sharks, those who eat and drink too much, those who make fun of others. Don't associate with people like that. Many of you used to be as grubby as them. Now you've had a bath, you're God's people! Jesus has put you on the right path, and God's Spirit is helping you on the way.

Some of you say, "Now I'm a Christian, I can do what I like!" Yes, but not everything is good for you. I think a better motto would be, "I can do what I like, but I won't be a slave to anything!" Another of your favorite sayings is, "Food is for my guts and my guts are for food!" Yes, and one day

God will take away your food and your guts! Your body is not for playing about with. Your body belongs to the Leader, and he should be in control. God brought Jesus back to life. That same power can give us new life.

(15) Think of your bodies as part of Jesus' body. Do you want Jesus' body to be infected by a tart? It doesn't bear thinking about! Prostitutes share their bodies with their customers, and the other way round. They become one body, as it were. Those who become friends of the Leader become one with him in a unity of thought and will. So avoid casual sex. Most of the bad things we do, we do to other people. But casual sex is harmful to yourself. Your body is the home of God's Spirit. You're not the owner, to do what you like in it. God paid a big price for you, so make sure your body is fit for God to live in.

7 I now turn to the questions you raised in your letters to me. Some of you think the best way to cope with sex is for men and women to keep right away from one another. I think that is more likely to lead to sexual offenses. My advice is for everyone to have a regular partner. Husbands and wives should strive to meet each other's sexual needs. They should submit to one another for that purpose. It's not good to refuse a partner, though it's fine if partners agree in a friendly spirit not to have sex for a while. You may think that by doing this you can get closer to God. But make sure you don't overdo the keeping apart, otherwise you may get into trouble because you can't control yourself. I'm saying all this as a sympathetic counselor; I'm not trying to lay down the law. We all like other people to be just like ourselves. But we are all different, each with our own special personality that we get from God.

You asked me about those who do not have partners, or who have lost them. There's nothing wrong with remaining single, like me. But if you know you have strong needs, get yourself a partner. Better than being frustrated!

I do have clearer advice for those who are already in relationships, based on the teachings of our Leader. Neither partner should be the cause of bringing a relationship to an end. In the case of a relationship that has broken down, the partners should try to get together again, or else stay out of committed relationships in future.

(12) You also had questions about "mixed marriages" between Christians and non-Christians. I don't know what the Leader would have to say about this. I can only give you my own opinion. If a Christian has a non-Christian partner, that's no grounds for breaking up. Providing they are happy with their relationship, they should stay together. Christians bring their partners into contact with God, and their children too. But if a non-Christian partner wants to leave the relationship, they should be allowed to do so. The Christian partner must not feel guilty about it. God wants us to have peace of mind. Sometimes one partner is able to lead the other to the full life God wants us to have.

(17) Make sure you follow the pattern God has set you as an individual. I tell everyone in all the churches, "Be yourself!" If you had your foreskin removed before you became a Christian, don't try and pretend otherwise. If you still had your foreskin when you became a Christian, there's no need to have it cut off. It should no longer be an issue. The only thing that matters is doing what God wants. Be at ease with your own pathway to God.

(21) Some of you were slaves when you became Christians. Don't feel bitter about it. By all means work for your freedom. At the same time, make the best of things as they are. Jesus alters our feelings about our status. Slaves who belong to Jesus are free, and free people who belong to Jesus think of him as their master. Jesus paid a big price to set you free, so you shouldn't feel like slaves anymore. Friends, be content with whatever God had in mind for you when you became Christians.

(25) You asked me about those who, up to now, have no sexual experience. Again, I'm not sure what the advice of the Leader would be. I can only give you my own opinion as the Leader's trusted friend. In view of the critical situation we are in, it's probably best for everyone to stay as they are. If you have a partner, keep the relationship going. If you are on your own, try not to get involved. But if you do find a partner, there's nothing wrong with that, not even if previously you didn't think yourself the type. Those in relationships have extra problems, and I feel for you.

We need to put everything on hold, since none of us may have much time left. In such times our relationships, our feelings of sorrow and joy, our financial and commercial dealings, do not carry the same weight. The world is falling about our ears.

I want to save you unnecessary anxiety. If you are single, you have more freedom in the present emergency to be of help to the Leader. You can give it all your attention. Those who are in relationships have their partners to worry about and lots of things to see to, as well as their loyalty to the Leader. I'm not trying to tell you what to do or what not to do, but simply to help you understand the options. Then everybody will appreciate the role the other has to play, and the Leader will be served to the best advantage.

Is it right, in view of all this, to break engagements off? Not if a couple are passionately looking forward to living together. Let the ceremony take place at once! But if they are not yet ready to enter a firm commitment, and not suffering any emotional strain from having to wait, they can remain just good friends for the time being. It can be good to get married or not to marry, depending on the situation. It's just that life is simpler for those who don't get married!

Finally, what should happen when a partner dies? Partners should stay together for life. If one dies, the one who is left can take another partner, if they wish, providing they seek advice from the Leader. My personal opinion is that they would do better to remain single. I suspect I'm in line with God's Spirit on that one.

8 Some of you have a problem about buying meat that has been to places where people worship other gods from ours. We each have our own opinions based on our view of the facts. What I would say is, "Opinions give you a big head: love gives you a big heart." Those who are sure of the facts have usually missed something. Those who love God are acknowledged by God.

For example, with regard to this particular problem, we know for a fact there is only one God. That means the other gods do not actually exist. Some people use the word "gods" to describe important people in the world or beings in other worlds – there are many of them, many gods, many rulers. But for us there is only one God, the Loving God who brought everything into being. We exist to serve that God's purposes. And there is only one ruler in charge of the world, our Leader, Jesus, God's Chosen. He holds everything together and we wouldn't be here were it not for him.

But not everybody looks at it like this. Some of our Christian family used to worship the other gods and cannot easily put the experience behind them. Food from the places where they used to worship remind them of their experience, and they feel guilty or threatened. Some of you think this silly. You say, "What has eating something got to do with relating to God?" Your view is that it makes no difference whether we eat the food in question or not. I would say to you, be careful the freedom you prize does not cause distress to those who are struggling with their consciences. I grant that you are right in your way of looking at things. But if people see you eating in the places where the other so-called gods are worshiped, they may be encouraged to do the same. For them it may be the means of the old gods regaining power over their lives. Make sure your perfectly correct way of looking at things isn't the means of destroying Christians who are not as strong as you are, the very people Jesus died for! If you harm members of your Christian family and cause them distress of mind, it's Jesus you're hurting. This is the rule I've made for myself. If what I eat causes problems for someone else, I'll do without it. I'm not in the business of making life difficult for others.

9 I'm a free agent, one of God's Special Branch. I've with met Jesus. You're living proof of the value of my work for the Leader, even if some Christian groups don't have any time for me.

I want to say this to my critics. Don't those of us who work for Jesus have a right to live above the poverty line? Don't we have the right to expect hospitality for our wives, as partners to encourage us, like the other friends of Jesus and his brothers and Rocky? Why is it only Cheery and I have to make ends meet by having a part-time job? Have you ever heard of soldiers paying their own way? Surely a gardener can eat some of his own vegetables, or a farmer drink some of the milk from his own cows?

This is just common sense. But I also have the old books on my side. Among the rules Moses gave us is one which says, "You must not put a gag on an animal when you're using it to work for you." God is not just concerned about animal welfare, but our welfare too. People, as well as animals, should have a right to eat as they work. We've planted a good crop on your land. Is it too much to expect some of the produce? I realize other workers have had a hand in it as well. But I think we've done more than anybody to deserve a share. We've never insisted on getting our dues. We put up with anything rather than make trouble that would stop the Good News from getting across. Think about those in the temple in charge of receiving the animals brought as gifts. They get their food from a share of the meat. The Leader wants those who spread the Good News to be looked after by those who receive it.

I've never asked you for financial help, and I'm not asking now. I'm too proud of my independence – I'd rather die! I'm not proud of the way I pass on the Good News. It's something I have to do. I would be miserable if I didn't do it. I don't get the thrill people get when they do something of their own accord. I do something because I'm told to do it. So what do I get out of it? Well, I get the satisfaction that I'm passing on the Good News for free and not insisting on my rights!

(19) Yes, I'm a free agent. I don't have to do what anybody tells me. I've chosen to be at everybody's beck and call, so as to win the hearts of as many as possible. When I'm talking to Jews, I behave like a Jew, so I can get across to them. I'm no longer obliged to keep the Jewish rules, but I keep them, so I can relate to those who think the rules important. When I'm with non-Jews, I can relax and behave like them, though I'm still bound by instructions from God handed on to me by Jesus. When I'm with people who are simple-minded I put things in a simple way, so they can grasp the message. I've learnt to adapt, using every method at my disposal. That way, in every situation, I can usually reach some. The Good News is what counts. I want everybody to share its benefits.

Some of you enjoy going to the races. You know that in each event there are lots of competitors, but only one gets the prize. Run your Christian life as if you were determined to be first! Athletes have to undergo a strict training. They do it to get a token prize. Somebody else may get the prize next time. We're going for the prize that will be ours for keeps. When I run, I have my eyes on the finishing line, and when I throw a weight, I make sure of my aim. I keep fit and exercise regularly, so that while I'm coaching others, I'm still in the running myself!

10

Let me remind you, my friends, of the history of those of us whose origins are Jewish. A cloud showed our ancestors the way to go. They found a path through the sea. Those experiences of the cloud and the water gave them a relationship with Moses. They were bound together by special food and drink, which God provided. They got their drink from God's Rock, which they found everywhere they went. However, most of them didn't live up to God's hopes, and they died at various stages on the journey through the desert. (Today we think of Jesus as God's Rock.)

Our history is a warning to us. We must not make the same mistakes as our ancestors. Don't worship material things like some of them. We're told, "The people held wild parties which got out of hand." We must not be irresponsible in our sexual behavior, like some of them. On one day a great number died as a result of over-indulgence. We must not try our Leader's patience as our ancestors did. Some of them died from snakebites. Nor must we be always looking on the gloomy side, like them. They lacked the will to live. We're meant to learn a lesson from the stories of what happened to those people, even though we live at a much later time. So don't be too sure of yourself, or you'll fall flat on your face. What you are going through every one of us has to go through, at some time or another. God is reliable and won't let you get into any trouble you can't cope with. God will also give you any extra toughening up you need and show you the way out of your difficulties.

(14) So dear friends, turn your backs on things that don't matter. I'm sure you have the intelligence to understand what I'm saying. Work it out for yourselves. When we pass round a cup at our meetings and say "thank you," we're sharing together in the life of Jesus. It's the same when we each break off a piece of bread. We're joined together with him. We use just one loaf of bread, and that helps us to think of ourselves as one family. The Jewish people have the same idea when they worship. They have a meal together with the food they bring as a gift to God. I wouldn't go so far as to suggest that similar celebrations among those of other religions have the same significance. They could well be getting themselves involved with evil forces. I don't want that to happen to you. Don't get confused. You can't eat at the Leader's table and at the table of his rivals! Don't try and do the

Leader's job for him. He's the one who can defeat evil in its stronghold. We're not up to it!

I can hear you saying, "This from the one who told us all the rules have been abolished?!" Yes, all the rules have been abolished. It doesn't mean that everything is good for us! It's not yourselves you should be thinking about, but other people. If you buy some meat from the market, there's no need to create a problem by asking where it's come from. Don't forget our old song says, "Everything in the world belongs to God!" If a friend who is not a Christian invites you home for a meal and you accept the invitation, eat what's put in front of you and don't ask awkward questions! But if at some other time someone says to you, "Don't eat that, it comes from a temple!" you should fall in line with their feelings and not eat it. It doesn't matter what you think about it. It's the other person's feelings that count. It doesn't mean you've lost your freedom, just because you've taken somebody else's feelings into consideration! And there's no need to feel guilty when you've had a good meal, providing you thank God for it!

Everything we do should bring credit to God, including the way we behave at parties. There's no need to upset people, whether they're Jewish, Christian, or of other religions. Be like me! I do my best to please everybody. I try not to think what's best for me, but for the many different sorts of people I meet. I want them all to have God's full life!

11 Try doing things my way. I aim to be like Jesus. You deserve credit for the respect you give me, and for the way you model your community on what I taught you. It's important to give respect where it's due. Everyone should respect God's Chosen. You should also respect your life partner. Jesus has shown us how, in his respect for God.

It's important for men and women to worship in a way that respects local customs. For us this means a woman should cover her head in worship. Her elaborate hairstyle may prove a distraction. It's less necessary for a man to cover his head. Men and women derive their beauty from God, and pass it on from one to the other. Our old books tell us woman was made out of the same material from which man had first been made. She was meant to be man's friend. Whether a woman wears anything on her head is her own choice, but she should remember she is being watched. Christian men and women must respect one another's feelings. They cannot just do what they want. Despite what the old books say, it's possible to argue that women come first, since they give birth to men. Whichever side you take, everything comes from God first of all. You must make up your own mind about customs to do with what people wear in public worship. Some think it's more natural for a woman to have long hair than for a man, and that men should only let their hair grow as a sign of humble devotion to God. On a woman long hair is attractive, a special decoration God has given her. These are not questions to get worked up about. It's all a matter of opinion. The various Christian communities differ from one another in their customs.

(17) Now I want to talk about something more serious. Your meetings are not helping you to improve your manners, quite the reverse! I've been told that when you come together as a community, you divide into rival groups. That doesn't surprise me! You seem to think competition is the way to find out who's in the right! When you meet, you're supposed to share a meal in memory of the Leader. Instead of which, you each eat your own food. Some go hungry and others get drunk! Anyone would think you haven't got homes where you can indulge yourselves! It looks as if your object is to bring disgrace on God's people and to make needy people feel unwanted! I'm lost for words! You expect me to give you a pat on the back? No way!

(23) This is what the Leader told me, and what I passed on to you. That very evening when his enemies were told where to find him, Jesus held some bread in his hands and thanked God for it. Then he broke it and said, "Think of this as my body. It's yours! Use it to remember me by." When they had eaten, Jesus held the cup in the same way and said, "This cup celebrates the new relationship with God, sealed by my blood. Use it to remember me by." So then, whenever you eat bread together and drink from the same cup, you're telling the story of the Leader's death, till he comes.

So anyone who eats the Leader's bread, or drinks his cup, in a way he would not approve of, is wounding him again. Think carefully about the way you've been behaving, and only then join in the meal. All those who eat and drink without consideration for other members of the Christian family harm themselves. No wonder some of you are feeling so unwell! Perhaps your selfish behavior accounts for some of the recent deaths among you! If we criticized ourselves more, we'd be less open to criticism from elsewhere. If we allow our Leader to hold us up to criticism, then we shall mend our ways and escape the fate awaiting those who have no regard for God.

Here's my advice. When you come together for your special meal, act like hosts to one another. If you have a healthy appetite, have something to eat before you arrive, then you won't make a pig of yourself! I will talk to you about the other things you mentioned in your letters when I visit you.

12

Now friends I'm going to talk about those special talents we are given by God. I want you to understand their significance. Do you remember the time before you became Christians? You were so gullible! You were hooked on fake gods who couldn't even speak to you. You can hear God's Spirit speaking every time someone calls Jesus "Leader." You can be quite sure she would not say anything bad about him.

There are many different talents, but they're all given to us by the same Spirit of God. We have separate tasks to perform, but we all have the same Leader. There are different ways of going about things, but it's the same God who starts us off. We are each aware of God's Spirit in our own way, yet her purpose is the same, to show us how to be of help to others. She may give words of wisdom to one, and useful information to another. She may give someone a strong conviction, and someone else the ability to heal. God's Spirit gives one person the strength to do things nobody thought possible, and God's Spirit shows another how to put God's truth into words. She gives to some people the sense to know which things come from her, and which do not. She helps some to speak in foreign languages, and others to translate. It is one and the same Spirit who does all this. She makes sure everybody can do something.

(12) Think of the way the human body works. There are many parts, but they fit together to make one body. Those of us who belong to Jesus, whatever our race or place in society, became parts of his body when we were dipped. The same Spirit of God has entered each of us, just like having the same drink from the same cup.

A body has many parts, not just one. A foot cannot say, "I'm not a hand, so I don't belong to the body!" An ear can't say, "I'm not an eye, so I don't belong to the body!" Parts of the body cannot detach themselves in that way. If you were nothing but eye, how could you hear? If you were all ear, how could you smell? God has skillfully put the different parts of the body in the right places. A body that was just one part would not be a body. Lots of different parts are needed to make a body.

An eye can't say to a hand, "You're no use!" or the head to the feet, "Get lost!" What's more, it's the delicate parts of the body you can least do without. We take special care with jewelry and make-up on those parts of our bodies we feel need a bit of help, and we disguise parts we are shy of with extra clothes. We show off the parts of our body we're proud of whereas God looks at the body as a whole and brings into focus the parts we hardly notice. Instead of competing, each part of the body should help the other parts to keep healthy. A pain in one part of the body extends to other parts. If one part feels good, we feel good all over.

Think of yourselves as together making up the body of Jesus. Each of you is a vital part in that body. In the Christian community, God wants everyone to count – leaders, speakers, teachers, artists, healers, administrators, enablers, and communicators. No one can do all those jobs at the same time! It's a good thing to aim high and develop your talents. But there's something even more important. (Read on.)

13 I may be an impressive speaker, but if I haven't got love, my words will be like an unpleasant banging sound that gets on your nerves. I may be able to predict the future, or share the most penetrating insights; I may know all there is to know, or have such strong convictions I can shift mountains around, but if I haven't got love, I might as well not exist. I can give everything I have to those in need, and even neglect my health working for charity, but if I haven't got love, I'll be wasting my time.

Love is patient; love is tender-hearted; love doesn't resent someone else doing well; love doesn't try to impress; love doesn't embarrass others or bully; love doesn't easily lose its cool or hold a grudge; love doesn't enjoy finding things to criticize, but is happy when everything is honest and genuine. Love puts up with all kinds of difficulty; love is open-minded and looks on the bright side; love sticks at it and never admits defeat.

Smart predictions will prove wide of the mark; those who impress with their fine words will be speechless; all our knowledge will be out of date. Everything we know is a tiny fraction of what there is to know; in our deepest understanding of events we only scratch the surface. But on the day everything comes to completion, we shan't need our little bits of knowledge any more.

Once upon a time I was a child. Then I spoke baby language and had childish thoughts and feelings. Now I'm grown up I've completely forgotten what being a child feels like. What we know now is like seeing a blurred reflection in a piece of shiny metal. One day we'll have a clear picture. I don't know very much at present, but one day my knowledge will be complete. I will know about things in the same way that God knows all about me.

Until that time comes, there are three great pillars that stand firm. They are TRUST, HOPE, and LOVE. The best of these is *LOVE*.

14

Love is the talent you should be trying to develop. The other talents God's Spirit gives are worth having too, especially the ability to explain God's truth. The language some people use is so difficult, only God can understand it. If you know how to communicate, you can stimulate, encourage, and comfort people. Those who use fancy language give themselves a treat, but those who give a clear message benefit the whole community. I would like all of you to have language skills, but getting the point across is even more important. The one who explains things, so that everyone understands, is more valuable to the community than the one who uses big words and long sentences, unless there is someone who can put what has been said in more simple terms afterwards.

So friends, what use is it if, when I come to see you, you can't understand a word I say? I can only help you if I make things clear, or give you some information or insight you can grasp immediately. Those of you who play musical instruments, like the flute or harp, will understand what I mean. If the tune is too complicated, people won't be able to sing along.

Soldiers need to be able to recognize the tunes their trumpeters play, otherwise they'll misunderstand their orders. How can people expect to know what you're talking about if you don't use language they can understand? Your words will go in one ear and out the other! There are lots of different languages in the world, and they all mean something to somebody. But if I can't understand the words someone is using, and they can't understand me, it will be difficult for us to become friends. So if you're serious about developing a talent, choose a talent helpful to others.

Someone who uses language that is difficult to follow, must ask God for the ability to be simple. Sometimes when I'm talking with God, I'm so wrapped up, I'm not aware of what I'm saying. Something that has nothing to do with my mind has taken over. What should I do about this? It's okay to get worked up and express your emotions when you talk with God. But you should keep a firm grip on your mind at the same time. Sing heartily, by all means, but think carefully about what you're singing. If you're speaking words of thanks to God, how can visitors to your meeting respond by shouting their agreement if they don't know what you're talking about? It's no good making what you consider to be a fine speech if other people can't understand you. I owe it to God that I can speak more languages than any of you. But when I'm in a meeting with other Christians, I'd sooner speak a few carefully thought-out words, so the others who are there learn something, than babble on at great length in a language nobody can understand!

Don't be childish, dear friends. It's good to have a childlike innocence. But your thinking should be grown up. As the old books say,

> "People of different tongues will speak
> Truths to my people so proud;
> But though it's done on my behalf,
> They'll be deaf to every word."

This shows the need to develop language skills for taking the Good News to people of other cultures, whereas the ability to explain God's truth in greater depth is needed for the benefit of those who are already Christians. If when you meet together, everyone is spouting off in different languages, visitors will think you very peculiar. But if everyone is out to explain some aspect of Christian truth, visitors will see where their lives have been going wrong. (If they don't take any notice, it will be their own fault.) They may come face to face with themselves for the first time in their lives. They may end up joining in the worship and say, "We know God is here with you!"

(26) This is the way you should do things when you meet together. Everyone can have their turn, providing their contribution is helpful to everybody else. Someone can sing a song, someone can explain some Christian truth, another can share an insight they have had, someone can speak in a strange tongue, and another can translate what they've said. It's not a good idea to have too many languages in the same service – three at the most I would say – and then they should take their turn and a translation be given after each. If there is no translator to hand, those who are eager to speak in a strange language must control the impulse. They must occupy themselves with their own thoughts and talk quietly with God. Then two or three who have a special message from God may speak, followed by a time of open discussion. If someone suddenly feels they have something important to say, whoever is speaking at that moment should give way to them. Everyone has a right to their say, but everyone should wait their turn. That way you will learn together what God is saying to the group, and everyone will feel better for having been there. Those who speak for God must choose their words carefully and not go on too long. God likes order, not chaos.

The general rule in Christian groups at this time is for women not to speak in meetings. A woman may, of course, have a discussion with her husband at home. For a woman to speak in an assembly goes against our social customs.

In all these matters you should realize that others heard the Good News before you. You're not the only Christians on the face of the earth! Anyone who thinks they are one of God's speakers, or have a special talent from God, will recognize that what I'm saying comes from God too. Anyone who doesn't accept that what I'm saying comes from God, should not be listened to.

To sum up, the most important talent you should develop in your meetings is how to pass on God's message. The use of different languages is not forbidden, but everything must be done in a decent and orderly way.

15 I think I need to remind you, my friends, what the Good News is all about. I gave it to you; you accepted it, and based your lives on it. This Good News will bring you to full life and health, if you keep on trusting it. But perhaps you're beginning to think it's all a waste of time?

Let me give you a summary of the essentials you learned through me. Our wrongdoing caused the death of God's Chosen. There are hints this would happen in the old books. After being in a grave for three days, he was brought back to life again. You can find that in the old books too. Rocky saw him alive, and so did the other friends in that group. On one occasion Jesus was seen by more than five hundred of his followers at the same time. Most of these are still alive to vouch for what I say, though a few have gone to their rest. He also visited his brother James, and all his close friends. Then, last of all, he came to me, though I didn't make things easy for him! That's why I should be thought of as the least important of all his special friends. I don't deserve the title "friend," because I caused God's people such dreadful trouble. I'm a Christian today because of God's goodness. I've done my best to make up for lost time. I've worked harder than the lot of them put together, but I mustn't claim any credit for it, since it was God doing all the work through me. What does it matter who does the work, providing it's done? We have the same message, the message you accepted.

(12) The fact that God's Chosen came back to life after being dead is the central theme of the Christian message. So how can some of you say that death is the end of everything? If that's true, Jesus could not have come back to life. If it never happened, we've all been wasting our breath, and your new confidence has no basis. It means we've been telling lies about God. We've given God the credit for bringing Jesus back to life. But God couldn't have done that if the dead remain forever dead. If life after death is impossible, as some of you think, then Jesus is not alive today. Without Jesus nothing makes any sense, and you are as rotten as ever you were. It means too that Christians who have died are gone forever. If the hopes we've pinned on Jesus only apply to this present life, we deserve everybody's pity.

But Jesus did come back from the dead. And he is only the first to do so. Death is part of being human. But now life after death is also part of being human. Just as we all die because we're all of the same human stock, now we all come to life because we're part of the same new stock as God's Chosen. We have to wait our turn. Jesus is just the beginning of new life from the dead. The day will come when all who belong to him will be included. That will be the end of things as we know them now. Jesus will present the New World to the Loving God when all the world's bullies and thugs have been put in their place. One by one, Jesus will get rid of all those things that prevent life. Finally, death itself will be abolished. God has put complete control of everything into his hands, everything, that is, except the central being of God. When the operation is complete, the one who is God's true likeness will return to God the overall leadership he was given. There will be no more rivals to God.

(29) I'm not sure about the practice of those who register a Christian commitment on behalf of others who have died. At least, by going to such trouble, they are declaring their belief in life from the dead. For that belief I face danger every moment of the day. I'm so proud to be the one who brought your lives into a relationship with Jesus. You don't think I fought with animals in the arena here in Ephesus just to prove myself a man, do you? If there's no life after death, there's no point in bothering. In the words of the old proverb, "Let's eat and drink all we can today, because tomorrow we won't be here!"

How could you fall for such silly ideas? You must have been in bad company! Start using your minds, and check your mistakes. I've come to the conclusion that some of you don't know God at all. With the opportunity you've been given, you should be ashamed!

(35) I can hear someone asking, "How can the dead come back to life? What sort of body do they have?" That's a silly question, but I'll try to answer it. When you sow a seed in the soil, it doesn't start to sprout until the case around it rots away. The seed you sow is just a small plain looking object. It's difficult to tell whether it's wheat or some other seed. The seed gives no clue as to what the plant will look like when it's full-grown! God has in mind the final plant that will develop from the seed and sees to it that different seeds turn into the various forms of plant they are meant to be.

The same is true of forms of life more like our own. Animals come in all shapes and sizes. We have two legs, other animals have four legs, birds have feathers, fish have fins, and so on. The stars and the planets in the sky have their own particular shapes that we recognize as beautiful. Things down on the ground have quite different shapes, but we recognize them as beautiful too. Even among the things we see in the sky we can distinguish different types of beauty, as between sun, moon, and stars. This should help us understand the mystery of life after death. When our bodies are buried they rot; but they will appear again in a form that won't rot. The bodies we bury are like rubbish we have no more use for. When they reappear, they will be good-looking and fit. The bodies we bury belong to the world we know now. When they reappear, they will belong to the world beyond time and space. There are different bodies for different forms of existence. The old books tell us how God gives life to human beings. But the new life that begins with Jesus has an added dimension. Our living bodies are composed from elements we find on this earth. Jesus brings a new humanity that comes from beyond time and space. When we only have the old humanity, we're bound to this earth. But if we belong to the new humanity, pioneered by Jesus, we lose all restrictions. Up to now we've all conformed to the same basic pattern we call human. In future we'll conform to the new pattern introduced by Jesus. We cannot be full citizens of God's New World in our present form. We need that new dimension!

(51) I'm letting you into a secret. We shall not all die but, just as if we were obeying a trumpet-call, we shall undergo a change, in a split second. At that moment, what was dead will come to life and won't die again. This change will come about for everybody. The bodies we have now which die and rot, will have a new form, so they'll never die or rot. This event will remind us of the words in the old books, "Death has lost the battle once and for all."

> "Death, you're a bee that's lost its sting!
> A weak, defeated, helpless thing!"

Blind obedience to the law has given birth to great evil, resulting in death. We can put all that behind us now, thank God, because of what Jesus has done. So then, my dear friends, stand your ground, keep your nerve. Let your work for the Leader be a full-time job. Nothing you do for him is ever a waste of time!

16 You asked me in your last letter what to do about the fund for Christians in need. I'm going to give you the same advice I gave the churches over here. Every Sunday each of you must hand in part of your weekly wage. This money must be kept in a separate account, so there will be no need for any special fund-raising efforts when I come to see you. When I come, I'll give letters of introduction to the representatives you've chosen to take the money to Jerusalem. I'm half-inclined to go there myself, in which case we can keep one another company.

I want to visit Macedonia on my way to you. I'm thinking of spending a good long time with you, perhaps the whole of the winter. Then you can see me on my way, wherever I go after that. If I were to come now, it would only be hello and goodbye. I would prefer the chance to get to know you really well, if it's okay with the Leader!

I'm going to stay in Ephesus until summer. Things are going really well for us here, despite the opposition from many quarters. If Timothy drops in to see you, please make him feel at home. He's working for Jesus as hard as I am. Make sure no one makes fun of him and that when the time comes for him to leave he's relaxed for his journey home to me. I can't wait until he and the other boys get back.

You were asking what has happened to Ray. I tried to get him to visit you with the others, but he didn't want to this time, for some reason. He'll come when he feels up to it.

Keep your eyes open; hold on to your convictions; be courageous and determined. All your actions must be loving.

(15) I'm sure you know Steve and his family. They were the very first Christians in your part of Greece and have given their lives to caring for others. You would do well, friends, to follow the example of such hard-working people and take their advice.

I was pleased at the arrival of Steve here with Lucky and Greg. It almost made up for the loss of not seeing you. They made me feel good. I'm sure they do the same for you. People like them are worth their weight in gold!

The churches in this part of the world send their best wishes. Will and Cill, and the Christian group which meets in their house, send their warmest greetings, as do all the Christian friends who are here with me. Don't forget to give one another big hugs and kisses.

You'll notice from the handwriting that I'm writing this part of the letter myself. The Christian community is for those who love Jesus. We look forward to seeing him. May you now feel his loving presence. I send my love to you all, on his behalf.

Paul's Letters to Corinth

Second Letter (2 Corinthians 10-13)

1 (2 CORINTHIANS 10) Dear Christians of Corinth, this is a very personal letter from me. I want to choose my words carefully. I hope they will be kind and gentle, as Jesus would wish. You joke, so I'm told, that I'm brave at a distance, but a coward when I come face to face with you. I hope I don't have to prove you wrong! I feel like giving a piece of my mind to those who accuse me of having unworthy motives in the work I do. Nobody's perfect; we live in an imperfect world. That doesn't mean my companions and I are out to benefit ourselves, like the rest of society. We don't use the same methods as other people. We use God's methods, which work against even the most stubborn resistance. We tear every cunning argument to shreds; we puncture every bloated ego that thinks it knows better than God; we take every bit of information the mind throws up, and use it in the cause of Jesus. We're going to make you come into line, and any who don't will be dealt with!

You can only see how things look on the outside. Some of you think you're first-class Christians. Well, let me tell you, that goes for me too, and the members of my team! I can look anyone in the face! Perhaps I have made a bit too much of the special assignment Jesus has given me. I don't mean to be heavy-handed. I aim to give you confidence, not take it away. I'm not trying to bully you with my letters, if that's what you think! I know what people say, "Paul writes great letters, full of punch. But he's not much to look at, and a hopeless speaker!" You'd better tell them they're in for a shock. I will hit them as hard in person as I've done by post!

I would rather not be put in the same class as some of those who have such a high opinion of themselves. They only look good to their mates.

To anyone else they look stupid. Unlike them, I'm trying to keep a check on advertising myself. I do, however, have clear responsibilities, which God has given me, and they include looking after you. My friends and I have done nothing out of order. We were the first to come all the way to you with the Good News about God's Chosen. We don't interfere in the good work others are doing or try to take credit for it. We'd like to extend the work we've done among you and we hope your trust will increase enough to make it possible. You could be the springboard for us to take the Good News into districts that haven't yet been reached. There's no need for competition on the same patch. If you want to make a noise about something, how about making a noise about Jesus? It's not for you to give yourself a medal! Wait to see who the Leader commends!

2 (2 CORINTHIANS 11) I know you find me a bit odd, but I beg you to make allowances. I feel very protective toward you on God's behalf. I was the one who introduced you to Jesus and vouched for your sincerity. I'm afraid you may not prove the good friends of Jesus you promised to be. Your minds are being got at in the same way the snake got at Eve. Someone only has to come along with a different view of Jesus, or a religious experience or message that doesn't match what I taught you, and you're completely carried away! What have these "experts" got that I haven't got? I admit I'm not a very good speaker, but I know my stuff! You've had plenty of opportunity to find that out.

Perhaps I made a mistake in not charging for the lectures I gave you on the Christian message? Perhaps I was too humble? Perhaps I was too anxious to make you feel important? Other groups of Christians paid my expenses to come and speak to you. I feel as if I've robbed them now! When I was staying with you and needed this or that, I didn't bother you. My friends from Macedonia helped me out. I'm going to make sure everyone for miles around knows about this, even if it sounds like bragging. Why am I carrying on like this? Because I don't love you? No, it's because I do love you, as God knows!

And I'm going to carry on! They need to be cut down to size – those experts who reckon they're on a par with me. They're frauds, confidence tricksters, not friends of Jesus at all. People with evil intentions can be real charmers! That bunch of crooks has got looking like kind-hearted do-gooders down to a fine art. They'll come to a sticky end one day.

I'm not the fool some of you think. But if you must think of me as a fool, at least recognize that I'm a fool who's got something to be proud about! I know I wouldn't get the Leader's approval for blowing my own trumpet – it's a silly thing to do. I'm lowering myself by speaking up on my own behalf.

Talking of fools, you're not so very bright yourselves, to be taken in the way you are. You seem not to mind when someone bullies you, or tricks you, or manipulates you, or treats you like dirt, or punches you in the face! I admit, neither I, nor my assistants, were up to doing the same. I suppose you think that's weakness! But if they want a competition, I'm game, though I know it's foolish.

(22) Let's compare our qualifications! Are they Jews? So am I! Are they purebred? So am I! Can they trace their ancestry back to Abraham? So can I! But are they friends of Jesus? Perhaps I'm off my head to talk like this, but let's see if they can match my record as a friend of Jesus! I've worked harder than they have, I've been in prison more often, I've been flogged more often and near to death more often; five times I was given the thirty-nine strokes with whips by my own people; three times I was beaten with sticks. Once I had stones thrown at me. I was shipwrecked three times; I was once a whole day and night in the water. I've traveled far and wide, risking my life crossing swollen rivers, looking out for thugs lying in wait. I've been hounded by my own people and by foreigners, in town and out in the desert, and even at sea. I've been let down badly by people I trusted as friends. I know what hard work means; I know all about sleepless nights. I know what it's like to be hungry and thirsty with nowhere to go, cold and short of clothes. On top of all this I've been plagued with constant anxiety for all the Christian communities. Every problem is my problem. It makes me angry when I hear that weak Christians are being brainwashed.

I don't see why I should keep quiet about these things. They show how vulnerable I am. God, the Parent of our Leader Jesus, deserves all the credit and knows I'm not making it up. Did you ever hear how I escaped from Damascus? The leader of the local Arabs had an ambush laid for me outside the town, but I was let down in a basket through a hole in the wall and got away.

3 (2 CORINTHIANS 12) I can't help blowing my own trumpet, even though it won't make much impression on you. But I'm going to tell you about the special experiences I've been privileged to have from the Leader. Fourteen years ago I was so close to Jesus that I found myself transported beyond the world of time and space. Whether it was real or my imagination, God only knows. I was in God's Garden, and I heard things it's impossible to put into human language. I'm not claiming I've got any special qualities that made this happen. It was my relationship with Jesus that brought it about. The only thing exceptional about me is my weakness. I could use this experience to impress people, since it's nothing but the truth. But I usually keep quiet about it, so people can assess my character from what they actually see and hear of me. I've been saved from getting above myself by becoming aware of a side to my personality I'm not at ease with. I've asked the Leader three times to free me from my problem. But he said, "All you need is to have me by your side. I can turn your weakness into a source of strength." So I'm not ashamed of my human failings any more, because they make me rely on the resources I have from Jesus. In the same way, I put up with everything that exposes my weakness – teasing, people making life difficult, downright bullying, and the complete wrecking of all my plans. I can take it because I represent God's Chosen. The more pathetic I appear, the more successful I turn out to be.

There you are! I've made a fool of myself! You are to blame! You are the very people who should have been standing up for me. I'm nothing special, but I compare well with those "experts" you rate so highly. You saw what extraordinary things a true friend of Jesus was capable of, though I sometimes had to wait for your appreciation. Can you really say you've had less of my attention than other groups of Christians? It's true I didn't pester you for money. Forgive me if that was a mistake!

I'm now making plans to come and see you for the third time. I shan't be making any financial demands, because it's you I want, not your money. Children shouldn't be expected to put money by for their parents. Parents should look after their children. I'll be only too pleased to be out of pocket for you. Are you going to reward my showing you more love by loving me even less? You may have a notion that, though I didn't cost you anything, I was still trying to trick you in some way. If that's what you think, please explain. Have you any cause to complain about my deputies? I had to beg Titus to visit you and sent a friend with him to keep him company. Titus didn't behave badly, did he? We all work to the same code of conduct.

Do you think I'm being paranoid? I'm talking to you in the presence of God, on behalf of God's Chosen! Everything we do, dear friends, is for your benefit. I'm afraid that when I come, I'll discover you're not my sort of people, and that I'm not your sort of person. I'm afraid of finding myself in the middle of rows, jealousy, bad temper, selfishness, rudeness, malicious talk, arrogance. I'm afraid of finding utter chaos. It would be a humbling experience for me to have my heart torn again by many who are behaving just as they did in the past, making no effort to change their outrageous and irresponsible lifestyle.

4 (2 CORINTHIANS 13) I'm on my way to you for the third time. Be ready for me to hold court. The rule in the old books is that a charge needs the evidence of two or three witnesses. I warned those badly behaved people when I was with you last time, and I'm warning them again from where I am now, and any others who've followed their example. Next time I come I shall take firm action with the lot of you. No one will escape. I'll show you that I speak on behalf of Jesus. You will be left in no doubt! You'll find out how effective Jesus is. He's no pushover. It's true that his public death as a criminal was a display of weakness of a sort. But his coming to life again showed that God is in control. In company with Jesus we too are weak, but like him we have resources outside ourselves and you're just about to get a taste!

It's time you took a good look at yourselves and asked whether you are real Christians. Are you sure you have Jesus in your hearts? Will you pass that simple test? I hope it will become obvious to you that I, and my companions, have passed the test. I've expressed my hope to God that you will not continue to do wrong. Although it would give us an opportunity to show how successful we are at dealing with bad behavior, we'd much prefer you to mend your ways. We have no quarrel with the truth and hope to find it on our side. We're quite happy to let our muscles waste away for lack of use, if it means you are using your muscles in the right way. My hope is for you to become the very best sort of people.

I'm writing all this from a distance, so that when I come to you, I won't have to take the big stick. I would rather use the special competence Jesus has given me to help you improve than use it to pull you apart.

Time to say goodbye, friends. To be real Christians is the target you should aim for! Please listen to me. Learn to get on with one another and understand one another. Then you'll experience God's love and peace in your community.

Hugs and kisses all round – that's the way! All the Christians over here send their best wishes.

May you all know first-hand the beautiful character of our Leader, Jesus, God's Chosen, and the love of God, and the special being together God's Spirit brings.

Paul's Letters to Corinth

Third Letter (2 Corinthians 1–9)

1 From Paul, a friend of Jesus, God's Chosen, (a friendship only God could have made possible!), and from Timothy, my friend and yours. To the Christian community in Corinth, and to all God's people in that part of the world. May you know, like us, the goodness and peace of the Loving God and Jesus our Leader.

It's God who must have all the credit, the Parent of Jesus, our Leader, God's Chosen. It's the Loving God who gives new meaning to life and keeps our spirits up. God brings us through every unpleasant experience into happiness. What God does for us, we can do for other people who are going through a bad patch. We have to put up with rough times, like Jesus. But this means we also get the benefits Jesus had at the end of the day. When we get hard knocks, it's all for your well-being; when God cheers us up, it's so we can bring smiles to your faces when you take the knocks. Though life is difficult for you at the moment, we're confident you'll come through your difficulties and find happiness, just like us.

(8) It's important for you to know, friends, how much trouble we had, just across the sea from you in Asia. Things were so bad, we truly believed we'd come to the end of the road. It was like hearing our death sentences. We were quite helpless. Our trouble threw us back on God, the one who brings the dead to life. The God who got us out of such a scrape can do it again, and again. It's a big help if you remember us when you're talking with God. Many will have cause to thank you, if you're a source of strength to us by that means.

Our good reputation means a lot, and helps us to be easy in our minds. We've always conducted ourselves in public openly and honestly, not trying to impress people with our knowledge, but allowing God to make use of us. We've behaved toward you in the same straightforward way. We use a simple style in our letters, so you can follow the argument through. You got the gist of it at any rate. When we meet up with Jesus we'll be able, I hope, to give each other a good report.

I was so confident of my standing with you, I was sure if I visited you twice, you'd count it a double pleasure. My plan was to visit you on the way to Macedonia and on the way back again. You could then send me on my way to Jerusalem. Perhaps I seemed to you not to know my own mind, saying "yes" one minute and "no" the next, like so many people. One thing you can be sure about, as sure as God, is that there's nothing "yes and no" about the message we have for you. There's nothing "yes and no" about Jesus. Silas, Timothy, and I all told you about him. Jesus is one great "YES." He makes all God's promises come true. He's the one who gets our applause. We appreciate God because of him. God has brought us all together in a strong relationship with Jesus and given us a job to do. God's Spirit is like an identity card which doubles as a gift voucher.

God knows that I changed my plans about coming to Corinth to save you trouble. You do not need us to tell you what to believe. Because your convictions are secure, we can all work happily together in partnership.

2 I changed my plans to avoid an awkward meeting with you. It would have upset me to upset you, and then we should all have been upset. I need you to cheer me up and that explains the tone of my last letter. I want us all to be happy together. I'm sure that's possible. I was in quite a state when I wrote that letter. It was hard to write and I shed many tears over it. I didn't want to hurt you. I just wanted to show how much I love you.

The one who behaved badly did me no personal harm, but he disturbed your community. Perhaps it's unfair to put all the blame on him. You all came down hard on him, so he's probably suffered enough. It's time to forgive. I suggest you show him a bit of love. My letter was a test for you, to see how far you're willing to follow my lead. Whenever you forgive somebody I want to be in on the act. We must not always be looking for faults to forgive, but when we do forgive we're very close to Jesus, and it does us a lot of good. If we're slow to forgive, we allow our bad side to get the better of us.

When I went to Troy with the Good News about Jesus, I had no difficulty in getting anyone to listen. But I was disappointed not to find my friend Titus there, and I couldn't relax. So I said goodbye to the people of Troy, and came over to Macedonia.

Thank God, traveling round the world for Jesus is like being awarded a triumphal procession. We throw flowers to the crowds as we pass along. Their heavenly scents are for those on the winning and the losing sides. Flowers can celebrate new life or a funeral – amazing, isn't it? We're not like some we could mention, who peddle God's message for a quick profit. We're God's appointed agents, and we have God's confidence. Everything we do is done openly, as Jesus would wish.

3 It sounds as if I'm blowing my trumpet again for myself and for my team. I shouldn't need to do this. You'll be asking us for our character references next! You can't be too careful with some people; but that doesn't apply to us, surely? *You're* our character reference! Your open hearts can be read by everyone. You're like a letter from Jesus that we've been asked to deliver safely. It's been written by God's Spirit, a living pen! The paper it's written on is alive too – your inner selves! It's Jesus who's given us the nerve to think about God in this kind of way. We can't do anything on our own. God has shown us how to help people to a new relationship, not based on hard and fast rules, but on how they are inside. Rules only get us down. When we have God's Spirit inside us, she brings us to life!

The dead old religion was written down on blocks of stone. Yet that experience of God was so exciting, God's people in those days caught something of it in the look on Moses' face. The wonder of that occasion has long since faded. The new religion is brought by the Spirit. The excitement she gives is here to stay. The old religion was exciting, even though it only told us how bad we are. Far more exciting is the new religion that tells us we can be good! Our experience has made the past look tame!

Now we can look on the bright side and take risks. We mustn't be like Moses who was so timid, he wore a mask, so people couldn't see the look on his face when he was losing his nerve. They were very hard to impress, the people of those days. Their descendants are just as bad. When the old books are read to them, it's as if Moses' old mask is still there to stop them seeing what it's all about. Jesus does away with the mask!! When we become Christians, there is no need for any kind of cover-up. The Spirit is in charge of everything. There is always complete freedom wherever she is at work. She gets us to take our masks off, so others can see how wonderful God is. It's just like watching a play on the stage. As the show goes on it gets more and more exciting and our feelings become involved. By seeing God so clearly, we become more and more like God.

4 We're doing this job of work because God asked us to. That's why we don't give in to fits of depression. We've got nothing to be ashamed of and nothing to hide. We don't play tricks or twist the words God has given us to say. God is watching to see we stick to the truth. We appeal to the highest ideals in others. Sometimes people can't see what's good about the "Good News" we offer. That's because they don't want anything better. Their minds are blocked to anything that isn't shoddy. Although the Good News is set in bright lights, and though the sight of Jesus, God's Likeness, is truly beautiful, they just can't see it. We're not offering ourselves as the object of attraction. Our slogan is "Jesus for Leader!" We're his promoters. God, who called light out of darkness, has done the same thing again, lighting us up inside. Now we can tell how wonderful and beautiful God is, by looking at Jesus.

We're like parcels with expensive presents inside them. We're nothing remarkable on the outside, as you can see, but inside we have God's resources. That's why, no matter how many troubles pile on top of us, they don't flatten us; however confused we are, we never give up trying to find the way. We never have to face the bullies on our own; when we're knocked off our feet, there's always someone to pick us up. Though, with Jesus, we walk the road to the gallows over and over again, we also share his life-force. Every day of our lives we dice with death to test the strength of the new life Jesus has given us. Like Jesus, we face death, to pass life on to you.

We know what we're talking about. Our confidence is backed by experience. We know that God, who brought Jesus back to life from the dead, will do the same thing for us. We will all be together with Jesus, in the presence of God. Yes, it's all happening for you! And we want more people to be aware of God's loving generosity, so there will be more thankful people who realize how wonderful God is.

We're feeling good! Even if our physical health gives cause for concern, we feel better in ourselves every day. What we have to put up with now will seem no more than bruises when we enter the wonderful life being got ready for us. So instead of getting bogged down in the present, let's think about the future. The things bothering us now will soon be gone. The things we scarcely imagine now will last forever.

5 The human body is like a tent. The time comes for the tent to be taken down and for campers to go home. God has a proper house for us, not something makeshift like a tent. We get fed up with roughing it in our tents and long for home comforts. We look forward to taking off our sweaty camping clothes and putting on something clean and comfortable. It's natural for us to moan when we're camping out, and to long for something more permanent. God's Spirit is like a letter from home telling us God has everything ready.

So we're in good spirits. We put up with life in our bodies, because one day we'll leave them behind and go home to God. We don't have a map or guidebook for our lives. But we know where we're going. We're on our way home to a better life than the one we have now. Although we'd much prefer to be there, our job is to please the Leader wherever we are. We will each have to report to Jesus, and give an account of the good or bad we've done while living in our bodies. He'll decide what reward we get.

(11) With this daunting prospect in mind, we get on with the task of making new recruits. God knows what sort of people we are, and so should you by now. We're not going to blow our own trumpets again. We're giving you the chance to do it for us! Give those humbugs something to think about! They believe I'm unbalanced. If they're right, it's because I've been working so hard for God. But I hope my mind is still sound, for your sake. My passion is Jesus and his love. One man gave his life for the whole of humankind. His death marks a turning point in the history of every one of us. We are all touched by his death. Everyone alive should now give up the

life of selfishness and greed and live for the one who died for them, and
came back to life for them.

(16) We have to stop putting labels on people. (We thought once upon a
time we could put a label on Jesus. We now know we'll never understand
him by doing that.) Anyone who's a friend of Jesus is a new person, living
in a new world. None of the old labels apply. God has made this possible by
seeking a relationship of friendship with us. Jesus was the matchmaker God
used to make friends with us. Now Jesus calls on us to be matchmakers,
getting people to be friends with one another. Jesus was God in person,
making friends with the world. Everyone's past conduct was overlooked.
We've been given the job of spreading friendship far and wide. Jesus has
appointed us to speak on God's behalf. We're bringing you the special
invitation from God that Jesus has entrusted to us. God's message is,
"Please let's be friends!" Jesus always acted from the highest motives. He
was thought a rogue because he mixed with rogues like you and me. He
accepted that bad label in order to share with us his quality life in God's
company.

6
We're partners in a joint venture with God. Make sure you don't
waste this wonderful opportunity God has given you. In the old
books God says:

> "I was there for you in the time of need
> Proving myself a friend indeed."

Now it's your turn to lend God a hand with the work of bringing new life
to the world. There's not a moment to lose. As for me and my friends, we're
doing our best not to make things hard for those willing to respond to the
call. We don't want any faults on our part to put you off. As God's helpers,
we always try to use God's methods of winning recruits. This means
putting up with all sorts of trouble, physical abuse, time in prison, and the
anger of the mob. We're overworked, short of food, and often miss a good
night's rest. We check our motives and make sure we've got the facts at our
fingertips. We're patient and kind. The sincere love we show proves we
share God's Spirit. She gives truth to our words and power to our actions.

We use the right tools and both hands. Despite all this, we get a mixed reception. Sometimes we get the V.I.P. treatment, sometimes we're shunned; one day we have a bad report, next day a good one. We're the fraudsters who speak the truth, the nobodies who've got a reputation. Sometimes a rumor goes round that we've died, but you see, here we are! We've been knocked around enough times, but never knocked out; there are many things to make us feel sad, but we're happy nonetheless; we're poor, yet make others rich; we've nothing to call our own, but we've got the world in our pockets.

I've been very frank with you, dear friends in Corinth. I've let you see right into my heart. I've always been open with you. It's you who've been cagey! Come on, be fair; you're like my own flesh and blood. I've dropped my defenses – now it's your turn!

You must not be in league with people who have no respect for our beliefs. There's no common ground between right and wrong. Light and darkness can't exist together. Jesus is opposed to every form of evil. Those who trust God and those who don't are on different planes. There cannot be rival attractions in the place where God is recognized! Together we stand as the sign that God is in the world. God says,

> "I'll live among my people,
> And share their lives each day;
> Since as God they worship me,
> I'll count them in my family.
>
> Don't get caught in evil's snares
> Or join with those who sell its wares.
> Then we'll know, as best of friends,
> A life where loving never ends."

7 God has promised to come and live with us, so we should make sure every part of our lives is clean and tidy. Out of respect for God, our guest, we should pay attention to our physical hygiene, and curb the ugly side of our personalities. Everything should be at its best. I'm also going to ask you to make a room ready in your hearts for me and for my friends. We've done no harm; we haven't put anybody on the wrong track; we've never taken advantage of anyone. I'm not trying to give you a guilty conscience. You have a big place in *our* hearts; indeed our future, whether we live or die, is completely tied up with yours. I sing your praises everywhere I go – I'm so sure I can depend on you. Despite all the problems we've faced together, I'm bubbling over with happiness.

When we arrived in Macedonia recently, hoping for an easier time, we had to put up with no end of trouble. There were so many people wanting to start a fight, that I quite lost my nerve. But God, who picks us up and comforts us, just like a parent with a child, arranged for Titus to come along and cheer us up. He arrived in the nick of time.

It was not just seeing Titus, which made me feel better, but his report of how you'd encouraged him, and of how you were looking forward to seeing me. He told me you were truly sorry for all the trouble I'd been put to, and that now you were backing me all the way. That sent me over the moon! That last letter I wrote probably had something to do with it.[1] I regretted what I'd written afterwards. I knew it would upset you. But I don't regret it now. I can't be happy about upsetting you. But I'm happy because your distress led you to change your ways. There are tears God can use to bring us to our senses. We don't need to worry about those tears. They help us to the new life God wants for us. Other tears are bad temper and they destroy. Just think for a moment how God has used your tears. You're so alive to the situation, so keen to make amends, so angry, and so put out by the wrong done, so passionate and determined to put matters right. No one can point the finger at you now!

When I wrote to you, I was not so much concerned as to rights and wrongs with regard to particular individuals. I was offering you a way of testing yourselves. I'm delighted to say you've passed! A particular pleasure has been to see the change in Titus. He had a good time with you, and it did wonders for his confidence. He was pleased to find you hadn't let me down. Just as you know everything I say to you can be trusted, so now Titus knows my glowing report of you was spot on. Titus has very happy memories of

---

[1] Paul is referring to the second of the three letters to Corinth as presented in this edition. (In traditional editions, 2 Corinthians chapters 10-13.)

you, which are turning into love. He was so moved by how attentive you were to what he had to say, and how you helped him to get over his nerves. It's great to know I have such dependable friends!

8 Now I'm going to tell you about the Christian communities in Macedonia. They've been a tremendous advert for God, displaying God's love in a practical way. Although they were going through very bad times, and despite having so little to live on, they enjoyed the chance to be generous in a big way. I know first hand how they gave as much as they could, and more, without any pressure being put on them. They insisted on being allowed to play their part in what was being done for Christians in need, and wouldn't take "No" for an answer. They went well beyond what we'd expected of them. Because they had declared themselves friends of Jesus, they were anxious to prove they were our friends as well, since we're all trying to do what God wants. This gave us confidence to suggest to Titus, who is in charge of the project, that he might also get a generous response from you. You're outstanding in everything else – trust in God, speaking, expertise, enthusiasm, and love for me and my companions. Now we want you to be outstanding in emptying your pockets!

Let's be clear about this. I'm not giving you orders. I'm giving you another chance to put yourselves to the test, to find out how real your love is. You should measure yourself against Jesus. His love was practical. Though he ran a profitable business, he left it for a life of poverty. He deprived himself, and you're the ones to profit. I'm doing no more than making a suggestion. You showed yourselves willing when you started collecting last year. How about getting a move on? No one expects you to do what you're not able to do. It's the spirit that counts, not the size of the gift. You can't give what you don't have. I appeal to your ideals of equality and fairness. This is not a matter of taking money from one group of needy people and giving it to another group. It's a matter of righting the balance. You've got money to spare and they're penniless. One day it may be the other way round. One of the old books tells how God's people were fed in the desert. It says,

"No one got fat, and nobody starved."

Thank God, Titus is as keen on you as I am. I haven't had to persuade him to visit you again. He can't wait! He'll be joined by another member of our team, who is very popular among all the Christians communities for the special contribution he has made to spreading the Good News. This is Luke, the Christian friend who's been chosen by our communities, to be part of the delegation, along with myself, to take the gifts to their destination.[2] What we are doing will be an act of honor to the Leader, and an expression of our humanity.

We're being very careful to avoid any hint of suspicion that these funds are not being used properly. Everything is being done openly, in God's sight and in everybody else's. The friend I've just mentioned has proved himself to be keen and reliable. He also has great confidence in you. As for Titus, don't forget he's a member of my team and wants to help you. The other friends who'll be with him are representatives of the various Christian communities, all of them good adverts for Jesus. So this is your opportunity to show to the whole Christian community the quality of your love, and to let them see for themselves why I speak so highly of you.

9 Really I don't need to go on like this about the collection for Christians in need. I know you're all for it. I told the Christians in Macedonia that you in Greece had started collecting last year, and that helped to get most of them going. I'm sending you this group of friends to make sure that the good things I've said about you don't end up being wide of the mark. I want you to be ready with your money, just as I said you would be. It would be embarrassing for me, and for you, if some of the Christians from Macedonia were to come with me when I visit you, only to find I'd been misleading them. I've thought it best for Titus and his companions to see you first, to make sure the big contribution you've volunteered to make actually exists. We don't want to have to do some last minute high-pressure fund-raising!

Those who sow a few seeds get a small crop, whereas those who sow a

---

[2] Luke is not named in the text, but the identity is almost certain.

lot of seeds get a big crop. Each of you must make up your own mind what to give, not wishing you didn't have to, or feeling you've no choice in the matter. God loves to see people giving with smiles on their faces. God will make sure you have everything you need. You'll always have enough for yourselves and enough on top to give to others, whenever you're called to do so. One of our old songs says:

> "God scatters seed to feed the poor;
> With love that lasts forever more."

God gives you seed to sow for your bread. God will also give you the seed of generosity, so that from it you'll produce a worthy sum of money. Think of all the people who'll be thanking God because God keeps you supplied with enough money to be generous, and because I'm able to direct your gifts to where they're needed! So it's not just money you're supplying, but thankful hearts as well! You're going to be the proof that the Good News works. God's reputation will stand high because of your generosity in this good cause, and in many others. People will talk with God about you with love in their hearts because of the wonderful things God is doing through you.

Let's all give thanks to God for the gift money cannot buy!

Letters from Paul's Team

First letter to Tessatown

1 This is a letter from Paul, Silas, and Timothy, to the Christian community in Tessatown. We're writing on behalf of the Loving God and the Leader, Jesus, God's Chosen. It comes with our best wishes and concern for your happiness.

We never miss you out when we talk with God. We thank God for you, and remember your way of life based on trust, your good works based on love, and your loyalty based on the hope you have in Jesus. We have no doubt, dear friends, that God loves you and has a special work for you to do. You not only listened to the Good News, but you let God's Spirit use the words to change your personalities and give you complete confidence. When we visited you, you took note of the sort of people we are, and you set yourselves to copy us. You accepted the message with a light-hearted spirit, in spite of all the trouble you knew it might get you into. You are an example to all the Christians in Macedonia and Greece. You've not only broadcast the Leader's voice all over Macedonia and Greece, but your trust in God has gained you a reputation far and wide. We don't have to tell other people about you. They already know about the good reception you gave us, and how you changed your religion to become helpers of the God who is alive and real. You're looking forward to meeting God's Likeness from beyond time and space, the one God brought back from death to life, and who will bring us through whatever may come, however dreadful.

2 Friends, as you know, our visit to Tessatown was a rattling success, unlike our experience in Philiptown, on our way to you. We had a rough time there; indeed our treatment was outrageous. But that experience didn't put us off from passing the Good News on to you, with God's help, despite the odds stacked against us. Our approach was straightforward; there were no tricks, no hidden agenda. We are licensed by God to deliver the Good News, so we stick close to God's way of doing things. We're not out to impress people, but to please God, who sees deep inside us. You saw it all, and so did God. We didn't butter you up, or try to get money out of you; we were not out to be popular with you or anybody else. We might have thrown our weight around as special representatives of God's Chosen, but we chose the soft approach, like a mother cuddling her children. We don't only want to share the Good News with you. We want to share our lives with you too. We love you so much!

Do you remember, dear friends, how we worked round the clock to meet our expenses, so we could hand you the Good News without making any financial demands? You and God can vouch for our conduct. We behaved with the highest standards toward our converts. You got individual attention, like a father spending time with his children one by one. We encouraged, and coaxed and challenged you to bring credit to God by the way you live. You belong to God's New World and share God's status.

We always thank God that, when we spoke to you, you recognized it as God's message rather than somebody's opinion. Because you made that leap of trust, you now speak God's words yourselves. Friends, you remind me very much of the Christian communities in and around Jerusalem. You've got into trouble with your own people, just like them. It was members of their own race who killed Jesus, our Leader. They killed God's speakers in times past, and now they've made things too hot for us! They frustrate God, and act in everybody's worst interests. They try to stop us talking to people of other races. They don't want others to have full life and health. They're out to make trouble all the time. They've not escaped God's notice – you'll see! When, dear friends, we had to part company with you for a while, we still felt one with you at heart, and couldn't wait to see you again. For myself – PAUL SPEAKING NOW – I made plans several times to come to you, but my health prevented me from traveling. What will we count as our greatest achievement, and what will we boast about when we meet with Jesus? Why, you, of course! You are the feather in our cap!

3 I couldn't stand the suspense of not knowing what was happening to you. Although it meant my being left on my own in Athens, I sent Timothy (my friend and companion in God's work of spreading the Good News about Jesus), to give you support and confidence. I was anxious that the pressures you've been under would prove too much for you, even though you'd been warned what to expect. When we were with you, we foresaw a hard time ahead, and you've seen our predictions come true. I was so worried, I just had to send somebody to find out how you were coping. I was half afraid the test had been too much for you, and our work undone.

But Timothy has just come back with good news of your loving trust. He says you have fond memories of me, and are as keen to see me as I am to see you. So, friends, although I too have been having a rough time, you've cheered me up by remaining true. By being loyal to the Leader, you make life worth living for me and my helpers. When we say "thank you" to God, we feel so very happy, we don't know how to put it in words. You've done so much for our state of mind. We keep talking with God about you, at all times of the day and night. We tell God we can't wait to see you, to help with any doubts or problems you may have.

Here and now, we ask the Loving God to make it possible for us to come to you. And we ask the Leader to increase your love for one another and for everybody. We are certainly brimming over with love for you! The Leader will put new heart into you, and help you carry on being the good and special people you are. You will be ready then to meet the Loving God, when Jesus and all his friends gather together.

4 Friends, you learned from us how to live in a way that pleases God, and you're doing alright so far! Keep going! The cause of Jesus, the Leader, is at stake! I'm sure you remember the rules we gave you, based on his teaching. If you want to be God's special people, you must behave responsibly in sexual matters. It's important to have control over your body. There are good ways and bad ways of having sex. If you're just out to satisfy yourself, you're acting like people who don't know God. Don't take advantage of a friend in that way. As we warned you, God will not allow such behavior to pass. The life God has in mind for us is not a life of self-indulgence, but a life in which we conduct ourselves with special care. Please don't ignore what I've just said. If you do, you'll be ignoring God, and refusing God's gift of the Spirit.

I don't need to write anything about the love you should have for one another as Christian brothers and sisters. God has been teaching you how to do it. Your love extends to the whole Christian family throughout Macedonia. But love can always be improved on. Lead a quiet life, mind your own business, and work hard to earn a living, as we've told you before. Treat those who are not to our way of thinking with respect, and don't be a nuisance to anybody.

(13) Friends, we want to make sure you know the truth about those who have died. They are just having a rest. There is no need for you to be overcome with grief, like those who have nothing to look forward to. We believe Jesus died and came back to life. In the same way, God will take care of those who die as friends of Jesus. This is the truth. It comes to us from the Leader. Those who die before us will meet with Jesus before we do. This is my picture of what it will be like at the end of time. The Leader will announce that he is ready. Then, to the sound of stirring music, he will pass through the barriers of time and space. The friends of Jesus who have died will join him first, then those of us who are alive will meet them and the Leader, midway between this world and the next. We shall be with the Leader forever. Think about that together and cheer one another up.

5 Friends, you should know me better than to ask me to supply a detailed plan of future events. The Leader's coming will be a complete surprise, as unexpected as having your house broken into in the middle of the night. A burglar waits until everything is quiet and the family safely in bed before breaking in and turning everything upside down. A pregnant woman's labor pains come suddenly and take her off guard. But from that moment on, nature takes its course, and life can never be the same again. It's good to know you're never in the dark, dear friends. It's always daytime with you, and you can see what's going on. We Christians must make sure we don't doze off like those around us. We have to keep our wits about us. Night is the time for being unconscious; it's at night that people get drunk. But since daylight is our natural habitat, let's

keep our heads clear. Let's guard our hearts with trust and love, and our minds with the hope of new life. God doesn't want us to suffer any kind of harm, but will bring us to complete life and health through Jesus, our Leader. Jesus died for us so that, whether we're awake or asleep, we're in his company and alive with his life. Carry on as you are doing, keeping one another cheerful as you make progress together.

(12) It's most important, friends, that you respect the leaders of your community. They are working so hard in your best interests. It's their task to give you advice in the name of the Leader. All of you should seek to be on good terms with one another.

And I say to the leaders, get those lazy members off their backsides. Give a pat on the back to those who are unsure of themselves and a helping hand to the weak. Be patient with everybody.

All of you must make sure you don't pay back wrong with wrong, but always try to do good to one another and to everyone you meet.

Be noted for being happy people; be in touch with God all the time; whatever happens to you, find something to be grateful for; show that God has an influence on your lives through your relationship with Jesus. Don't pour cold water on the efforts of others or sneer when they're passing on messages from God. Think carefully about everything they say, then hang on to what makes sense. Rule out bad behavior of every kind.

The God who loves peace will bring you up to the highest standards in every aspect of your personality. Then you'll have nothing to worry about on the day Jesus comes. You can rely on the God who calls you "friends" to do this. Please, sisters and brothers, speak with God on behalf of myself and my colleagues. Make sure everyone gets a hug and a kiss! I have the backing of the Leader in asking that this letter be read in your meetings for everyone to hear.

The goodness which comes from Jesus, God's Chosen, be yours!

Letters from Paul's Team

Second letter to Tessatown

1 This is another letter from Paul, Silas, and Timothy to the Christian community in Tessatown. We're writing on behalf of the Loving God and the Leader, Jesus, God's Chosen. We want to share with you the good things we've had from them.

We can't help being thankful to God for friends like you. Your trust is coming on from strength to strength, and so is the love you show to one another. That's why we use you as an example to other Christian communities of what it means to stand firm and keep trusting, in spite of opposition and unpleasantness. You've survived it all! Because God is standing by you, you know you're on the right side. You're being prepared to be citizens of God's New World. Your suffering is part of the training. Those who cause suffering, bring suffering on themselves. That's part of God's way of ordering the universe. God also gives relief to those who are suffering, and that includes you and us. We'll see the pattern clearly when we see Jesus face to face. God's special agents will deal severely with those who don't respect God, and who won't listen to the Good News of Jesus, the Leader. Their moment of humiliation will be an eternity for them, and they'll miss the thrill and enjoyment of the occasion when Jesus receives the love and admiration of his people. You'll be there, because you believed what we told you.

So every time we talk with God, we mention your names. We ask God to make you splendid examples of what it means to be a Christian. "See that they stick to their good resolutions, God!" We're sure you'll give Jesus a good name, and get a good name too. God and Jesus will be there to help you.

2 I want to say something about the time we're looking forward to, when we'll all be together in the presence of Jesus, our Leader. Don't be thrown by reports that the promised day has come. You're mistaken if you think we said anything of the kind. Don't let anyone make fools of you. Certain things have to happen before the time is ripe. There will be great political changes, and evil people will come to power, though they'll be overthrown in the end. Atheism will be state policy, and the one in charge will have complete power over everybody, just like God. All faiths will be outlawed. Don't you remember? I told you all this when I was with you! It may seem to you like a delay, but time is needed for events to unravel. It's already possible to detect the forces of chaos at work, but for the time being we have a stable government holding them in check. When the restraints of law and order break down, then chaos will reign. Only the words of Jesus will be able to put things right. The presence of Jesus with us will overcome the most extreme form of wickedness. This wickedness will combine the cruel use of force with cunning propaganda. People will be open to deception and abuse, because they've shut their eyes to the truth that brings life and health. God has control even over the use of mass hypnosis and hysteria. The peddlers of lies, and those who've fallen for them, will all be exposed, in God's good time.

(13) Friends, we thank God for you, over and over again. The Leader loves you because you were first in line for the new life. You staked your future on the truth, and the Spirit made you up to the mark. It was she who brought you on board, through the Good News we spoke to you, and she will make sure you become beautiful people, like Jesus himself. So, friends, be true to the ideals we passed on, either in what we said, or what we wrote to you.

I'm asking our Leader, Jesus the Chosen, and the God who has shown a parent's love by giving us so much to help us, and so much to hope for, to give you encouragement and strength, to do and say the right things at all times.

3 Last of all, friends, when you talk with God, ask for special help to be given us, so that what the Leader says will spread quickly, and be appreciated everywhere, just as it is by you. And ask for us to be rescued from those with bad intentions. Not everyone trusts us. The Leader can be relied on. He will give you strength, and protect you from evil forces. We trust you because our Leader is your Leader. We're sure you're carrying out our wishes, and will continue to do so. May Jesus give you the staying power he himself showed, and inspire you with love for God.

Some Christians have downed tools. Friends, don't let them influence you! We never told anybody to stop working! Remember that we weren't idle for a moment when we were with you. We had money to pay for our board, because we worked around the clock. We were determined not to put any financial strain on you. We had every right to ask you to keep us. By not asking, we were setting you an example. The principle we gave you when we were with you was, "No work: No food." Remember? We've heard that some of you have got bone-idle, and spend your time getting in other people's way. We know we have the support of the Leader in saying, "Back to work, and stop being a nuisance!" I say to all of you, brothers and sisters, there should be no getting bored doing what's right!

It's possible some won't listen to what we're saying in this letter. Sort them out; show your disapproval; make them ashamed of themselves. There's no need to treat them like enemies, but, as Christian friends, let them know the danger they're in.

Our Leader stands for peace. May he give you peace in every situation, and at every moment of the day. He will be with you.

I'm taking over from my secretary to write this final greeting in my own handwriting. I finish every letter this way. The goodness that comes from Jesus, our Leader, God's Chosen, be yours.

Letters from Paul's Team

Paul's Letter to some Celtic Christians

1 This letter comes from Paul, a key worker who gets his instructions not from any human agency but from Jesus, God's Chosen, and from the Loving God who brought Jesus back to life after he had died. All the members of my team of Christian workers join with me in what I have to say.

To the Christian communities among the Celtic peoples:

May you share in the goodness and peace that come from the Loving God and from Jesus the Leader. Jesus followed the plans of the Loving God and gave his life to free us from the oppressions of today's evil society and our own selfishness. Such a wonderful act will never be forgotten!

(6) I find it hard to believe you're turning your backs on me so soon, since it was I who passed on to you the good things that come from Jesus. You're accepting a different package of "Good News," although there's only one "Good News." Some people are trying to muddle you by offering you bad news instead of good news. But if anyone, including a member of my team, or even a being from beyond time and space, gives you a version of the Christian message that contradicts the message we gave you, you should tell them to get lost! I can't say that enough times or put it too strongly!

My job is not to please everybody, only to please God. If I were not clear about that I'd have no right to count myself a helper of Jesus. Friends, I must stress that the Good News I passed on was not an invention of the human mind. I didn't get it from other people, or from any teacher. Jesus revealed it to me.

(13) I expect you've heard about my younger days when I practiced the strictest form of the Jewish religion. I went all out to destroy the new

movement, making trouble for God's people. I was much more strict than most young people of my age, and intolerant of change. God, who had me in mind before I was born, was kind enough to ask for my help. I came face to face with God's Likeness and was given the job of sharing my experience with people of other races. I insist, I didn't discuss it with anyone else. I didn't even go to Jerusalem to get the opinion of those who were leaders of the Christian movement before me. I went into the Arabian Desert for a while and then back to Damascus. It was not until three years later that I visited Rocky in Jerusalem and stayed with him for a fortnight. The only other Christian leader I saw at that time was James, Jesus' brother. (I'm determined to set down the truth in writing. God will vouch for my honesty.) Then I went to live in the border country to the north of Syria. The Christians of Jerusalem and district never caught sight of me. They simply heard the rumor, "Our mortal enemy has become one of us. He's spreading the ideas he once tried to destroy." They thanked God for me!

2 After fourteen years I visited Jerusalem again together with Cheery. I had Titus as my personal assistant. I was convinced it was the right thing to do. I had a private meeting with the Christian leaders and gave them an account of the message I'd been giving to those of other races. I wanted to make sure I was on the right lines. My friend Titus is Greek. But none of the leaders so much as suggested that he should have his foreskin removed. But then we had some trouble from spies, supposed Christians, who infiltrated the meeting. They resented the freedom Jesus has brought us and wanted to take away our liberty. We stood up to them for your sake. You could have lost the Good News. I'm not impressed by the titles people give themselves, nor is God. Those who stood out as the true leaders were satisfied with my message and had nothing to add to it. More than that, they recognized I had a special mission to non-Jews, just as Rocky had a special mission to the Jews. It was the same Jesus who worked through both of us, each in our own sphere of operations. To settle matters, when James (Jesus' brother), Rocky, and John, the true leaders, were convinced I had been given special talents by God, they warmly embraced Cheery and myself and shook us by the hand, agreeing that we should continue our work among people of other races while they would be

responsible for the work among our own people. The only thing they asked of us was to provide funds for those in their group who were in need. I had already made plans to do that.

(11) When Rocky visited Antioch I challenged him face to face because he willfully acted in breach of our agreement. He quite happily had meals with peoples of other races until some associates of James arrived. Then he stopped eating with non-Jews because he was afraid of offending the prejudices of the strict group. Other Jews joined in this two-faced cowardly behavior, including, it pains me to say, Cheery. When I saw they were not behaving in the spirit of the Good News, I said to Rocky, "Who are you to insist that people from other races fall into line with us, when we all know you've been living like one of them? Although you and I are Jews by birth and not outcasts – as we've been brought up to think of non-Jews – we now know that someone becomes a friend of God not by keeping our rules and regulations but by putting their trust in Jesus, God's Chosen!"

(16b) My friends, we've put our trust in Jesus. That's how we became friends of God, not by keeping rules. No one can become a friend of God that way. If, instead of having rules, we keep company with Jesus, we may sometimes make mistakes; it doesn't mean we're on the wrong track. If, on the other hand, we start going back to the old way of doing things, that really is bad. It was by trying to hold fast to the rules that I came to realize how useless they were. In order to live as a friend of God I had to dump the rules. They only make you feel bad about yourself. The miserable person I was had to die with Jesus on the cross. Now I'm a new person. Jesus occupies my mind and heart. I've still got the same body, but what makes me alive is my trust in Jesus, God's Likeness. He loved me and gave his life for me. I must not turn my back on the love God has shown me. If we could have become friends of God by means of the rules there would have been no point in Jesus dying!

3 How could you Celts get things so wrong, of all people? Who's been tampering with your minds? Some of you were there when Jesus was hanged on a cross. You saw it all. I only have one question to ask you: Did you get God's Spirit by keeping rules or by accepting the Good News? You're doing things the wrong way round and making fools of

yourselves. You started with the experience of the Spirit, now you've gone back to do-it-yourself religion. In spite of all your amazing experiences, you haven't learnt a thing! I ask you again: The Spirit who made so many wonderful things happen for you, did she come in response to something you did or because you opened your hearts to the Christian message?

It was Abraham's trust that impressed God. Those who trust like Abraham are Abraham's true descendants. The old books foresaw a time when people of other races would come to trust God and so have God's approval. God gave the Good News to Abraham long ago and said, "You will spread happiness all over the world." God's words have come true. Those who trust like Abraham are now sharing Abraham's happiness.

On the other hand, those who try to live by a set of rules come to grief. The old books say, "Break just one rule and you've had it!" It's quite clear; you can't earn God's "well done" by tying yourselves up with rules. Trust is what God looks for. Trust and rules don't mix. If you choose to live by the rules, all your energy will be taken up in trying to keep them. Jesus has freed us from that hopeless struggle. He suffered the humiliation due to a criminal of the worse type. The old books say, "Anyone hanged on a tree is a public disgrace." Jesus joined the ranks of the rule-breakers so that Abraham's happiness could be shared by other races. We now have the promised Spirit simply by trusting.

(15) It's not easy for a human being to explain. Here's one way of thinking about it. A will is legally binding. It can't be set on one side or be added to once it is signed. God made a will leaving something to Abraham and his descendant. Since "descendant" is singular, not plural, I take it to refer to the Chosen One. The Rule Books did not appear until about four centuries later, so they can't set aside God's bequest to Abraham. The bequest has nothing to do with the Rule Books. It stems directly from God's provision for Abraham.

(19) So why the books of rules? They were a temporary measure to check an increase in wrongdoing. They were only meant to be in force until Abraham's descendant arrived to claim the bequest. In any case, the rules were put together by a group of people acting on God's behalf, whereas the bequest was made by God alone.

It looks as if the Rule Books and the provisions of God's will contradict each other. That's not the case. The rules were never intended as a way of life to earn God's approval by scoring points. They were a temporary measure during a very bad period. Jesus came to share the promised bequest given in trust with those who were ready to trust.

Before this invitation to trust, we were tied to the rules. It was like being in prison. The rules kept us under tight control until the coming of Jesus. He showed us how to relate to God by means of trust. Now we have trust, we no longer need such a harsh regime. Jesus has brought us into the family of God through trust. All of you who declared your trust in Jesus share his identity. Differences of race, sex, and class no longer matter. You all belong to one another because you belong to Jesus. That also means you belong to Abraham and get your share of what was promised.

4 I want to take this line of argument a bit further. Those who inherit don't get control over the property which is legally theirs until they come of age. Until that time their parents provide for them to be looked after by guardians and for the property to be held in trust. It's the same with us. When our spiritual development was at the child stage, we were directed by guardians appointed to look after us. But when the time was right, God arranged for someone to be born into a human family who would show us God's true character. He learnt the rules of his parents' religion in order to free his own people from those very rules, so making it possible for us to be adopted as sons and daughters of God. As proof that you're God's children, God has put the Spirit in you which produces the family likeness we share with Jesus. Now we can use familiar names when we talk with God, just as a child uses the words "Daddy" or "Mummy." You must stop thinking of yourselves as God's employees. You're God's children now. That means you're due for a share in God's promises.

(8) Getting to know God is a new experience for you. You used to be hooked on false religions. Now that you have a real relationship with God, I can't understand why you're still bothering with fakes. Do you want to get hooked again? You've gone back to being slaves to a strict round of religious duties. I've got the awful feeling that all I've tried to do for you has been a waste of time!

(12) Why can't you be like me? After all, I did my best to be one of *you*!

I'm not accusing you of doing me any harm, far from it. Remember how we came to know one another? Illness forced me to break my journey. It gave me the opportunity to pass the Good News on to you. My illness must have seemed a poor advertisement, yet you didn't allow it to put you off. You gave me a welcome fit for one of God's special agents. I might have been Jesus himself, you treated me so well. What has happened to the warm feelings you had for me then? You would have donated your eyes to me if such an operation could have been performed. Are you mad at me because I'm putting my finger on the truth? There are people who are acting very friendly toward you, but they have bad motives. They want to destroy your friendship with me, so as to get you to themselves. I'm quite happy that people are caring for you, providing their intentions are good. You need looking after. I can't be with you all the time. I care for you as if you were my children. I feel a mother's pain for you. I long for you to be like Jesus! I wish I could be there with you now. Perhaps then I would find there is nothing for me to be so anxious about. I don't know what to think.

(21) Perhaps those of you who are so keen on tying yourselves down with rules will listen to me if I use a story from the Rule Books as if it were a parable. In one of the books it says that Abraham had two sons, one by a slave woman and the other by a free woman. The child of the slave was only a son in a biological sense. It was the son Abraham had from his wife who inherited the promises. Let's think of these two women as symbols. Hagar, from Mount Sinai, was the slave, and her children became slaves. Mount Sinai stands for the present city of Jerusalem whose people are slaves. The other woman (Sarah) stands for the Jerusalem of the heart and mind. That Jerusalem is free and we are its citizens. Remember the song?

> *"Cheer up, unhappy childless one;*
> *Laugh and shout and sing a song.*
> *With many births your rival groans;*
> *You have a husband; stop your moans!"*

You, friends, are children of God in fulfillment of a promise, just like Isaac. Isaac had a slave brother who made life difficult for him. There's a slave inside of every one of us, challenging our freedom. What does the old book recommend? It tells us to get rid of slavish attitudes and develop those of free people. Freedom is our heritage, not slavery. The future belongs to the free!

5 God's Chosen has set us free. So stand your ground and make the most of your freedom. You're free people. Don't let anyone make you slaves again.

Please listen. It's me, Paul; I'm telling you, if you bow to tradition and let them cut off your foreskins, you'll be saying, in effect, that Jesus is no use to you. I want you to know the full implications of what you're doing. Any man having his foreskin cut to satisfy the rules of his religion, thereby vows to obey all the rules of that religion. When you choose rules as your way of life, you're turning your backs on Jesus. It means God's goodness and love have left you cold.

Our quest for completeness is Spirit-driven and depends on trust. What your sexual parts look like has nothing whatever to do with your relationship to Jesus. The only thing that matters is trust based on love.

You were running the race so well. Who put you off track? Not Jesus. He entered you for the race! You know the saying, "A little yeast makes a lot of dough rise." I'm sure you're going to see sense, for the Leader's sake. Whoever's causing you all this hassle will pay for it dearly. Friends, I'd have an easy life if I went around calling for all foreskins to be cut. It's the message of the cross that gets me into trouble. So my word to those who are bothering you is, "Why don't you go all the way and get the lot cut off?"

(13) Yes, friends, you've been set free. That doesn't mean you have to go wild. Use your freedom to love and help one another. All the rules can be put into one simple rule, "Love the person next to you as you love yourself." If you compete with one another, you'll become victims of each other's selfishness.

Instead of going for what you want all the time, let the Spirit be your guide. What you want to do and what the Spirit wants you to do are very different things. The Spirit often stops you doing what you want. If she's in charge, you don't need rules.

Selfish behavior is easy to spot: uncontrolled sex, deceitfulness, hooliganism, attachment to material things, playing with evil, gang warfare, violence, jealousy, bad-temper, cliques, envy, over-indulgence, wild parties, and so on. Let me make it clear. Those seeking to be citizens of God's New World don't get involved in such selfish behavior.

A life which shows the marks of the Spirit is also easy to spot: you will see love, peace and happiness, patience, kindness, generosity, loyalty, gentleness, and self-control. These things are not tied to rules. The friends of Jesus get rid of their selfish side, the side that does just what it feels like. We've taken the Spirit for our guide, so let's allow her to guide us! Let's not be snobbish or pushy or resentful of one another.

6 Dear friends, you may see other Christians doing something they shouldn't. If your lives are guided by the Spirit you'll deal gently with them and make it easy for them to get back on track. Make sure *you* aren't the ones who go wrong. Face the hard tasks of life together as a team. That's the Jesus way. Anyone who thinks they're more important than anyone else is making a big mistake. All should assess themselves by their own rate of progress, not by where others have got to. You should be pleased you've achieved something rather than pleased you've beaten someone else. Comparing one person with another is unfair since each of us has different problems to cope with.

If someone is sharing their knowledge of Christian truth with you, you should share what you have with them.

Be very clear about this: you can't play tricks on God. God's universe runs on the principle, "You reap what you sow." If you sow the seed of selfishness, you'll end up by yourself, alone. If you sow the Spirit's seeds, you'll reap the full life they contain. You shouldn't get bored doing what's right. Keep at it and you'll see the results. Seize every opportunity to be of help to others, especially your Christian friends.

(11) *I've taken over from my secretary now, as you can see by the large handwriting!*

Those who want to perform that little ritual on you with a knife are just using you to score points. By spending their time on such a trivial matter they avoid telling others about the death of Jesus, which would get them into trouble. They may have lost their foreskins, but they're no better at keeping the rules. They want your foreskins as a trophy to gloat over. I hope I never gloat over anything except that piece of wood on which Jesus, our Leader, hung. That's what turned my world upside down and what turned me upside down too. Foreskin or no foreskin, what does it matter? God is making a new world! Those who get excited about the big thing God is doing are God's true people. They will have peace of mind and warm hearts.

Let's have no more trouble from any of you. I've got marks on my body to show I've been beaten like Jesus.

Let the beauty of Jesus, our Leader, God's Chosen, affect you deep inside, dear friends.

Yours truly, Paul.

Letters from Paul's Team

Paul's Letter to Philiptown

1 This letter is from Paul and Timothy, workers for Jesus, God's Chosen, to all the Christians in Philiptown, leaders and helpers. May you share in the beauty and peace that come from the Loving God and from Jesus the Leader, God's Chosen.

Every time I think about you, I say "thank you" to God. When I talk with God, I say how happy I am with you all. This is because you've been by my side, sharing the Good News, from day one. And you're still doing it! I'm sure the friend who did the good job of bringing your community together, will have you ready for inspection by Jesus, when he comes. I can't help having good thoughts about you, and I know you feel the same way about me. That's because we've been through so much together. We've all tried to get the Good News accepted, and stood up for it when it was attacked, even though it meant going to prison. God knows how much I long for your company. Such deep feelings for one another come from Jesus. I tell God that I want your love to keep on growing and growing. That's the way to become understanding and sensitive, and make the very best choices. Then you'll get no bad marks when Jesus comes to inspect your work. You'll be able to show all the good things you've produced as a result of his influence. You'll be a credit to God.

(12) Since you're my friends, you may be worried about what's happened to me. It's turning out all right. I've been placed in an ideal position to spread the Good News! Everybody's got to know, even the emperor's personal bodyguard, that I'm in prison for taking my stand with Jesus. My loss of liberty has encouraged most of the other Christians here to conquer their fear and be bolder in passing on the Christian message.

Some promote the cause of Jesus for their own ends, as if they were in competition with me. Others do it out of the goodness of their hearts. These are inspired by love; they recognize I'm being punished because I argue the case for the Good News. There's not much good news in the way some people advertise God's Chosen. They seem to be more keen to advertise themselves. They take advantage of my being in prison to make things more difficult for me. So what! At least people are getting to know about Jesus, whether the means are worthy or not. That makes me happy.

I intend to go on being happy. I've got you speaking with God on my behalf, and I've got the Spirit of Jesus. That should be enough to get me out of prison! I hope, indeed I'm certain I shan't let the side down. Whether I'm given more time to live, or whether I'm condemned to death, I shall speak up for Jesus. I only live for him, so I look on death as promotion. If I'm allowed to carry on living in my present body, it means there are still worthwhile things for me to do. To be honest, I don't know which I would choose, if I had the choice. I'd like very much to leave this life, for that means going to live with Jesus. It's the option that suits my own best interests. But it's better for you I stick around. That seems to me the right choice. I can then spend more time with you all, helping you travel the road toward the true happiness that springs from trust. If I get to visit you again, you'll have an extra reason to be fans of Jesus.

Just make sure that, like the Christian message, you add up to "Good News." Whether I get the chance to visit you or have to rely on reports, it will be good to know you're getting on well together, and working side by side for the cause. Don't let the opposition get you down. They will collapse when they see the quality of new life God has given you. God has given you two special gifts – the ability to trust Jesus, and the ability to suffer for Jesus. You're facing the same challenge I had when I was with you, and, as you've heard, I face a similar challenge here.

2 It's your relationship with Jesus that gives you strength for living. It's his love which holds you when things go wrong. The Spirit binds you together in community. She gives you care and concern for one another. Now try to agree among yourselves, and make sure no one goes short of love. That will make me really happy. Don't throw your weight

about, or scheme to get your own way. Regard everyone else as someone to cherish. Spend your time seeing to others' needs, rather than your own.

Jesus, God's Chosen, is your role model. Adopt his attitude. He was God's Likeness, but he didn't try to play God (like our political leaders).[1] Of his own free will, he shared the life of people without rights. He was human just like us, and accepted his human limitations. He walked the path set out for him, even though it led to his death as a criminal. That's why God's put him in charge of the universe. He's going to be more highly praised than anyone before or after him. One day, everyone in this world, and every other world, will recognize the debt they owe him and give him their full support. They will all accept Jesus as Leader, and appreciate how wonderful the Loving God is.

(12) Dear friends, you've always taken my advice, when I was there with you, and even more now I'm away from you. So keep working to become complete. But go carefully to avoid harm to yourselves or others. You've got God to help you, giving you enthusiasm and the skills you need. I'm sure God will be delighted with the final result. Get on with the job without squabbling or looking for faults. There should be no scandals or sleaze in God's family, none of the corrupt behavior so common in the world today. You should stand out as being different. If you carry on being true adverts for the new way of living, then, when Jesus comes, I'll hold my head up high and feel that all my efforts have been worthwhile.

(17) Maybe I'm about to die for the cause that has made such a difference to your lives. I'm quite happy about that, and you must try to be happy about it too.

If Jesus the Leader sees fit, I'll send Timothy to you soon. I hope he'll bring back some news from you to cheer me up. He's my best friend, and he's the only one who cares for you like I do. The other visitors you receive are just out for themselves. They're not concerned about the cause of Jesus. You know what a good friend Timothy is. He and I have been like a team of father and son in the work of spreading the Good News. As soon as I know what's going to happen to me, I'll send him to you. I'm sure it won't be long

---

[1] "Like our political leaders." Contrast with the style of the Roman emperor is implicit throughout this passage, but it would not have been safe for Paul to make it explicit.

before the Leader lets me come to see you.

(25) I've decided to send Charming back to you. He's your friend and mine, and he's stood shoulder to shoulder with me in the work. You sent him as a special envoy to help me in my time of need. He misses you all very much. He was upset when he was told you'd heard about his illness. He has in fact been very ill, and we nearly lost him. But God was kind to him and to me too. I'm not sure I could have taken another blow like that. I want very much to send him home, as a treat for you, and to ease my own anxiety. The Leader would wish you to give him a great welcome and have a party in his honor. People like him deserve to be well thought of, especially when, like him, they risk their lives for the cause of Jesus. Charming did all he could to help me on your behalf, because you couldn't be here to look after me yourselves.

3 More than anything else, friends, I want you to be happy. That's what the Leader wants too. So I'm going to say some things I've said before. I don't mind making this extra effort, if it means saving you from trouble.

Watch out for people who do nasty things. I'm talking about those who want to change the way you look. We fans of Jesus relate to God through the Spirit. We're not obsessed with our bodies. *We're* the healthy-minded, not them. I say this, even though I've had the operation myself.

I could be superior, if I wished. My qualifications are more impressive than theirs! My foreskin was cut when I was eight days old. I'm a true Jew, a descendant of Benjamin, racially pure. I was a member of the strict set, and shared their passion for the rules and regulations. I was so keen, I even bullied Christians. If keeping the rules can make you good, I was perfect, as I kept every one.

(7) I've left all that behind for Jesus. To me, everything else is rubbish, compared with the privilege of knowing the Leader, God's Chosen. I've exchanged those worthless things for his friendship. Now that Jesus and I are friends, I've stopped trying to be good by keeping the rules. I trust *him* to keep me close to God.

I want to get to know Jesus better. I want to experience the new life he brought with him from the grave. I want to share his pain, and die with his attitude. I hope that, for me, death will be the gate to a fuller life, as it was for him.

(12) I'm far from perfect; I have a long way to go. But as Jesus looks on me as his prize, I'm running as hard as I can, to get the prize Jesus has ready for *me*. No, friends, I'm not there yet. I'm just putting the past behind me, and setting my sights on the future. I'm running God's race. The prize at the end includes a place with Jesus in the grandstand.

This is the way of looking at things all grown-up Christians should adopt. We can't expect to agree about everything. God will show us where we're going wrong. We must simply make sure we don't go backwards.

I suggest you copy me, dear friends. Or copy others who've taken me as their role model. It grieves me greatly, how many there are who oppose the teaching about the death of Jesus as a criminal. Their way is completely negative. Their bodies are their object of worship, and what they regard as important is not worth bothering about. Their minds are on material things.

Our home is beyond time and space. That's where our helper will come from – Jesus, the Leader, God's Chosen. He'll change our old worn-out bodies, and give us fit and beautiful bodies, like his. He'll be able to do that, because he has complete control over everything.

4 I can't tell you how much I miss you, dear friends. You're my prize converts, and just thinking about you makes me happy. I love you very much. Stay loyal to the Leader.

It's time for Edna and Cynthia to put an end to their disagreement. That's what the Leader wants. I'm asking Lydia, the one who worked with me to establish your community, and who has my trust, to give them some support.[2] They all worked hard with me in spreading the Good News. So did Clem, and the others in the team. God has made a note of their names.

The Leader always gives you plenty to be happy about, so cheer up! Be

---

[2] 4:3. Lydia is the best bet for the identity of the key person who worked with Paul to establish the Christian community at Philippi. The first Christians at Philippi were a group of women with Lydia as their leader. Euodia and Syntache (Edna and Cynthia) would have been among their number. Did an early copyist opposed to female leadership remove her name? Surely Paul would not have named Clement (Clem), possibly the prison warder at Philippi and the first significant male convert, and not Lydia who was converted before him?

kind to everybody. The Leader is close beside you. Avoid being anxious about anything. Talk with God about all your needs and problems, and don't forget to say "thank you" often. The inner peace God gives cannot be described. It will be yours, as friends of Jesus.

(8) There are plenty of good things in this world for you to appreciate and enjoy. There are many forms of truth, many causes that deserve support, campaigns for justice, societies with a good name, projects which benefit the community. These are the things you ought to be interested in. At the same time, continue with the program I gave you when I was with you. Then you should be able to relax in God's company.

I'm so pleased you've expressed your concern for me recently. You used your first opportunity. Not that I'm feeling sorry for myself. I've learned to take life as it comes. I've been through needy times and prosperous times. I've learnt how to survive, hungry or full-up; money in my pocket or penniless. I can handle any set of circumstances, because there's someone by my side giving me help. Even so, I appreciate your kindness in my time of trouble. As you know, in those early days, when I brought the good news to Macedonia, you were the only Christians who threw in their lot with me and sent me on my way with what I needed. You even sent provisions on to me in Tessatown several times. I'm not greedy for myself. But it's good to see you doing things that earn the thanks of others. You've paid my wages with bonuses. The gifts Charming brought from you met all my needs. They were a beautiful gesture, like a bunch of flowers. I'm sure God thought so too. The God known to me will take care of your needs, just as you took care of mine. Jesus can make all God's resources available to you. The God who loves us like a parent should have all the credit, now and always. I hear you saying "YES" to that!

Give my best wishes to everyone in the Christian community where you are. The friends who are keeping me company here send their best wishes. Some of them, you'll be especially pleased to know, work for the emperor, in his palace.

May the beauty and love of Jesus, the Leader, God's Chosen, be yours.

Letters from Paul's Team

Letter to Quaketown

1 This letter comes from Paul and from his friend Timothy, employed by God to work for Jesus, God's Chosen. It's for the loyal Christian community in Quaketown. May you have the goodness and peace that come from the Loving God.

When we talk with God, Parent of our Leader Jesus, we always say "thank you" when we mention you. That's because we've heard about the trust you have in Jesus and the love you have for one another as Christians. You have great prospects in the future life God is getting ready for you. You've heard that before, when you got the Good News, the message you can rely on. The Good News is having a big effect the world over, and it's had a big effect on your lives too since you heard it and realized how generous and loving God is. Charming, a much-loved colleague of ours, was your teacher. As a loyal helper of Jesus, he's made it his job to care for you. Charming has been telling us how God's Spirit has made you into loving people.

Ever since we got such a good report from Charming, we've mentioned you often when we talk with God. We hope you'll get a clear idea of what God wants of you, so you can do your best for the Leader and make him happy. You'll get to see the results of all your hard work and learn more about God's ways. Aim to be reliable. The one famous for being reliable will help you. Then you'll be ready for anything that comes your way. Show your appreciation to the Loving God by being bright and cheerful. You're going to get a share of the wonderful things being got ready for God's people. We've been rescued from evil's grip and become citizens of the New World. The one we all love, Jesus, God's Likeness, has brought this about.

We've been set free and waved goodbye to our feelings of guilt.

(15) Yes, Jesus is like a portrait of God come to life, showing us God's character for the first time. Jesus is the model of what we shall all become. What we see in Jesus is the life force that brought everything into being, both in our world and in worlds unknown to us. Jesus is the clue to what it's all about. There is nothing that does not relate to him, including world politics. Jesus comes first and everything else falls into place around him. He is the head of the Christian community. He was the first to turn death into life. He is number one in every sense. He expressed God completely through his human personality, and that was God's way of making friends with all living things, in this world and worlds beyond time and space. The violent death of Jesus was the key event in God's peace process. You were once enemies of God and strangers to God's ways. You did terrible things to prove it. The arms of Jesus stretched out in death are the arms of God open to you in friendship. Jesus wants you to be shining examples of God's new friends. You will be, if you keep trusting, and don't lose the hope you got when you heard the Good News. The Good News is for everybody, everywhere.

(23) PAUL SPEAKING NOW. I'm pleased to have had a hand in spreading the Good News. I'm quite happy about all the trouble I'm going to for you. I'm suffering like Jesus, though on a much smaller scale. He did the hard work; I'm filling in the gaps. It's all for the sake of the Christian community, which now carries on his work. I've been employed by God on a job that gives me responsibility for you. My job is to make sure God's message is fully understood. The truth about God was not clear to people of past generations, but now God's people are coming to understand it. For the first time we're realizing that people thought of as outsiders are capable of appreciating God's treasures. The greatest treasure we have is Jesus, our guarantee of a better life to come. God's Chosen is our prime topic. We're out to teach people and to advise them, using the most skillful methods. We aim to help them become mature, like Jesus. That's why I work so hard and give it all I've got, using every bit of energy Jesus gives me.

2 The anxiety I've had for you and for the Christians in Banktown, and for many others I've never met, has felt like a wrestling match. I'm so concerned about your morale, and for your unity as loving communities. You need to draw on the best fund of knowledge, if you're to grasp what God is doing in the world. Jesus should be your teacher. He holds the key to every form of knowledge and understanding. Watch out for people who try to tie up your minds with clever talk. Although I've never had the pleasure of your company, I feel I'm one of you. I'm so pleased to learn you're standing your ground, and being loyal to God's Chosen. You've taken Jesus as your Leader, so stick close to him. He's the foundation of your beliefs and conduct. That's what you were taught, isn't it? Jesus is the one you ought to thank!

Make sure no one traps you in a closed system of beliefs or fobs you off with slick answers. That type of religion does not come from Jesus, but from old-fashioned ways of thinking, with fixed ideas. If you want to know what God is truly like, you can find out by looking at the human Jesus. It's all there! He's given you life to the full. He has much more to offer than anyone with political power or a good education. Jesus has arranged for you to be God's people, not by keeping rules, but by becoming like him. When you were dipped in the water, it was like going down into the grave with Jesus and saying "goodbye" to your old life. When you came to the surface, it was like coming out of the grave with Jesus and saying "hello" to a new life. You put your trust in what God can do. A life of wrongdoing had scarred your character, but God gave you a new start and overlooked your past. All those rules we failed to keep, no longer count. Jesus has scrapped the rules. He gave them a public execution. His death was like a Roman victory parade. Heads of state and religious leaders were disarmed and made to look foolish in front of everyone.

(16) So don't let anyone tell you you're not a Christian because of what you eat or drink, or because you do what they think you shouldn't on Sundays, or because you don't attend every religious service. That's not what it's all about. Being a Christian means making Jesus the center of your life. And don't be made to feel inferior by those who aren't at ease with their bodies and wallow in guilt, or by those who claim special relations with extra-terrestrials, or have weird dreams or whatever. They're trying to be

one up on you. There's nothing Christian about that sort of thing. It's all too human! Stick close to Jesus. He's the boss! The Christian community gets its life-blood from him. We're a mixed bunch, but he keeps us together. Only by taking our cue from Jesus, do we make the progress God wants of us.

When you met Jesus, you left behind the fears that made you depressed. So why are you still letting them occupy your minds? It's as if you haven't made the great leap from one world to another. Why all those taboos? "Do not touch," "Don't go there," "You can't eat that!" They're just social conventions that one day will be out of date. Their origin is human. You may have rational arguments for your taboos. You can tell me they're good for holiness, humility, and self-discipline. I say they simply replace one form of self-indulgence with another.

3 You have come out of the grave with Jesus, so make sure you enjoy his new life. You can share his special relationship with God. Don't get bogged down in trivial matters. Since your experience of death and rebirth, your life is one with the ongoing life of God. When the curtain goes back to reveal the reality behind everything, Jesus will be seen as the key to life, and you'll be there, in his company.

Get rid of those things that don't fit in with your new life: irresponsible relationships, selfish motives, the desire to control and manipulate others. Don't be greedy for more and more personal possessions. That's a false religion. God will deal severely with those who make the wrong choices. You made all the wrong choices at one time. You led a really dreadful life. It's time to put the past behind you, including bad temper, angry words, prejudice, gossip, and name-calling. Don't tell lies to one another. You used to be lies all over, like a set of clothes. You've got new clothes now. You're learning to look how God meant you to be. In your new clothes, there are no differences of race, religion, culture, or class. Your relationship to Jesus is all that matters. You each have a family likeness to him!

You have a special place in God's heart. So show off those new clothes. Be sensitive and kind, quiet, gentle, and patient. Put up with each other's little quirks, and overlook your grievances. The Leader has forgiven you, so you must forgive one another. What you need most of all is love. It's the secret of getting on well together. Adopt Jesus' peaceful attitude of mind. That's what first attracted you and formed you into a community. Treasure the teachings of Jesus. Put your minds to work and help one another understand their meaning. Express your thanks to God in music, singing, and dancing. Even your simplest words and actions should display loyalty to the Leader, and mark your appreciation of what God has done for you.

(18) Those of you who are in committed relationships, should work hand in hand with your partners. That's what the Leader wants. Give each other lots of love. No bullying.

Children, pay attention to everything your parents say to you. The Leader wants you to respect their wishes. Parents, don't be too critical of your children, or you may undermine their confidence.

Workers, always carry out the instructions of your employers, not only when they're checking up on you, or when you have an eye to promotion. Do your very best at all times, as a good advert for the Leader. Put everything you've got into each job of work, as if the Leader were your boss. In fact the Leader is your true employer. He will give you your wages and arrange your pension. Those who do shoddy work will have to make good the firm's losses out of their pay packet. That's only fair.

(4:1) Those of you who are employers, treat your workers fairly and humanely. Don't forget that *you* have a boss – Jesus!

4 Spend lots of time talking with God, and think carefully about what you're saying. The most frequent word on your lips should be "thanks." Don't forget to mention us. Ask God to make the way open for us to get the message across – the truth about Jesus. It's that message which has put me in prison. Ask God to help me find the best words.

Be considerate in your approach to those who don't see things the way you do. Wait for your opportunity. Always be polite; a touch of humor helps; use words the one you're talking to will understand.

Lucky will give you all my news. He's a dear friend and works full time for the Leader. My main purpose in sending him is to get up-to-date news from me to you and from you to me. Handy is also a dear friend, and has proved his loyalty. He's well known to you, I believe. Between them, they'll be able to answer all your questions.

Harry sends his best wishes. He's in prison too. Mark (Cheery's cousin) also sends his greetings. (I've already asked you to give a warm welcome to Mark, if ever he visits you.) Justin sends his kind regards. These are the only Jewish Christians here willing to work with me to bring about God's New World. They've been a tremendous help! Charming, who belongs to your group, and works for Jesus, sends his best wishes too. When he talks with God, he shows great anxiety for you. He wants you to be well balanced and adult in your determination to do what God wants. I know very well how hard he's worked for you and for the groups in Banktown and Templetown.

My very good friend, Dr. Luke, and Demas, send their greetings. Please send on my greetings to our friends in Banktown, and to Bridget and her house group. When you've read this letter, make sure the folk in Banktown get to read it. You must also read the letter they will send on to you.[1] I have a special message for Captain Rider: Make sure you finish the job the Leader gave you.

I, Paul, am taking over the pen to write this bit of the letter myself. Please remember me while I'm in prison. May you know God's goodness and love.

---

[1] 4:16. Possibly the circular letter we know as Ephesians, called by Marcion "the letter to Laodicea."

Letters from Paul's Team

Letter to Phil, Ava, and Captain Rider

This is a letter from Paul and his friend Timothy. Paul is in prison for being a follower of Jesus, God's Chosen.

The letter is for Phil, our dear friend and colleague, Ava, his sister, Captain Rider, and all the Christians who meet in your home.

May you share in the goodness and peace, which come from the Loving God and from Jesus the Leader, God's Chosen.

Whenever I talk with God about you, I always express my gratitude. I've been told about the love you show one another as Christians, and the trust you have in Jesus, the Leader. I ask God to help you realize that this experience is meant to give rise to good projects, to further the cause of God's Chosen. Already, one result of your love can be seen, in the happiness and encouragement it's given me. Phil, my dear friend, you've been a tonic to other members of the Christian community.

I dare to give orders on behalf of Jesus, as you know.[1] But what I'm going to ask you is a special favor, in line with our loving relationship. I'm an old man now, and in prison for Jesus. I want to put in a good word for Handy. He and I have been like father and son during my imprisonment. I know you found him useless, but with me Handy's been living up to his name. You'll be surprised at the change in him. I'm sending him home to you, and in doing this, I'm sending a part of myself. I've been

---

[1] Verse 8. Paul's use of military language here seems to suggest that Archippus had been a member of the armed forces. Traditional translations have Paul describing himself and Archippus as "soldiers of Christ." Archippus = Master of Cavalry, ace-horseman, or something similar. John Henson thinks he was a converted soldier, now in charge of the slaves in Philemon's household. This would explain why he is included in the address, since he may, like Philemon, have been aggrieved by Handy's past behavior.

tempted to keep him while I serve my time in prison for the Good News, to give me the care you would give me, if you were here. But that would be taking advantage. I'd sooner ask you first. Perhaps everything is working out for the best. You lost him for a while, but now you'll have him for keeps.

There should be a new relationship between you. He's no longer just a handyman; he's your Christian friend. He's shown his love to me, and now he's ready to show it to you, both as a human being, and as a Christian.

I know, Phil, you think of me as a colleague, so I ask you to give Handy the same welcome you would give me. If he's wronged you in any way, or owes you money, put it on my account. As you can see, it's me, PAUL, writing this letter myself. I'll see you right with regard to Handy. Of course, I could argue that you owe everything to me! But I won't! Please, friend, do this one thing for me, for the sake of the loyalty we both share to the Leader. Cheer me up by being like Jesus! I'm sure you'll do what I'm asking of you. Knowing you as I do, you'll go over the top!

One more favor. Get the guest room ready for me. With you and God on my side, I'm sure we'll get the chance to enjoy one another's company again.

Charming is serving a prison sentence for Jesus, like me. He sends his best wishes. Greetings also from the rest of the team – Mark, Harry, Demas, and Luke.

May you have the goodness and love of Jesus, the Leader, God's Chosen.

Letters from Paul's Team

A Circular Letter[1]

1 This letter comes from the Mission H.Q. of Paul, appointed by God as a special representative of Jesus, God's Chosen. It is for communities loyal to Jesus. May you know God's goodness and love, and the peace that comes from accepting God as our Parent and Jesus as our Leader.[2]

What a wonderful God we have, the Parent of Jesus our Leader. God, who planned long ago that we should share the goodness and love of Jesus, now gives even more! We can join God's family as sisters and brothers of Jesus. Our hearts jump for joy at this relationship of love, which God enters so freely, and with so much pleasure.

Jesus died to set us free, overlooking our wrongdoing at the same time. What generosity! What love! In one brilliant stroke God revealed the plan. God's Chosen would become, at the right moment, the one to bring everything in the universe together. Suddenly our lives took on a new significance, as we saw ourselves part of the plan.

We are strong in our support of Jesus, because we were the first to realize that the future depends on him. And you, like us, have made a firm response. The moment you heard the truth, the Good News of a better life,

---

[1] There is wide agreement that this letter, traditionally known as "the letter to the Ephesians" was not intended for Ephesus. The address "to the Christians in Ephesus" does not appear in all the manuscripts. It may be the letter to Banktown (Laodicea) mentioned in the letter to Quaketown (Colossians), and/or a circular letter intended for the Christian communities in Asia Minor (modern Turkey).

[2] 1:1. Paul's authorship of Ephesians is doubted by many scholars, mainly on grounds of language. It should be remembered that Paul rarely put pen to paper himself, except to sign his signature, sometimes with a few personal comments. He possessed a team of scribes to do his writing for him. These were well versed in his theology, knew his mind, and after receiving instructions from Paul as to content would likely have had considerable freedom of expression. They may have continued writing letters in his name after his death, confident that Paul wished them to continue spreading his teaching.

you put your trust in Jesus and received God's Spirit. She's the guarantee of our freedom as God's people. Let's show God our appreciation!

(15) I've heard of the way you've put your trust in Jesus, the Leader, and the love you show one another, as members of the Christian community. I thank God for you over and over again, and ask for you to be open to discover for yourselves the loving and beautiful God Jesus portrayed. Let your hearts be torches to light the way ahead. The future is full of hope; there's a store of good things waiting for God's people; unlimited resources for those who trust. God has given us a demonstration by bringing Jesus back to life, giving him the key role in the universe. No power or force can touch him. He is the greatest, now and for all time! God has given him the last word in everything, and he's the one Christians must look to for guidance. With Jesus as head, the Christian community carries on his work. The universe is full of him, so Christians should be full of him too.

2 At one time you were so selfish, you were as good as dead. You went with the crowd and blindly accepted popular prejudices. Those who won't listen to God still carry on like that. There was no difference between them and us before we became Christians. We did whatever we fancied, using other people for our own ends. We made no effort to control our temper. The God who is all love took pity on us, and gave our lives meaning and purpose as friends of Jesus. God healed us by loving us. Now, with Jesus, we're highly valued and have everything to look forward to.

Yes, you've been healed, by putting your trust in the loving goodness of God. You did nothing to deserve it. It was God's gift. If we could bring about our own healing by performing a series of tasks, we would be sure to get bigheaded. We are what we are today because of God. We are designed to be helpful people, like Jesus. That has always been God's idea for us.

(11) By accident of birth some of you were regarded as "outsiders" by those who think of themselves as "insiders." You remember how painful it is to be looked on in that way. You were thought incapable of a relationship with God's Chosen. You were considered something alien, not included in God's promises or plans. You were shunned as hopeless and Godless. Jesus has changed all that. By dying for you he moved you from far outside into

the middle. Jesus makes peace between different types of people. He's broken down the barriers and made enemies into friends. We're all one family now. He scrapped the Rule Book with all its do's and don'ts, and turned a divided humanity into a united one. Peace has become a reality. As people become friends with one another, so together they are friends with God. The death of Jesus was the signal for all fighting to come to an end. Jesus came on a peace mission. He spoke to insiders and outsiders. Now we can all come close to the Loving God through the same Spirit. None of you should think of yourselves as outsiders, excluded, or banned. You're citizens of God's New World like the rest of God's people. You're all members of God's family. You're helping to build a community on the same basis as the very first Christians. Jesus is our basis. He's our model and example. The work continues from the start he made. Since Jesus is in charge of operations, it's going to be a very exciting venture. You're going to be a community of fine people with God at your heart.

3 This is a testimony from Paul himself, in prison for being a friend of Jesus, and for taking a stand against prejudice.

God gave me a special care for those excluded on racial grounds. How that came about is well known and I've written about it before. If you've read my letters, you'll know about my insight into the mind of Jesus. In the past, people were not aware of the truth that God's Spirit has recently made known to Christian leaders. The truth is quite simply this: God's promises are for every race; all are members of God's family; all can share God's gifts. That's the Good News of Jesus! I've passed it on with the help of God.

I may not be much of a Christian, but God has chosen me to tell people of all races the wonderful things Jesus has on offer. I have to explain to everyone the long-term plans of God, the one who brought everything into being. We're forming a community to reflect the variety of thought and culture God has inspired. It will impress all those in authority. Jesus, God's Chosen, our Leader, has put God's ideas into operation. We can become friends of God by trusting Jesus. We've nothing to be afraid of. So don't be too upset because my work for you has got me into trouble. It's all in your best interests.

My experiences have brought me close to the Loving God, the Parent of every race. I share with God my ambition for you. Let yourselves be influenced by the rich variety of God's glorious creation, and you will develop true strength of character. God's Spirit will be your driving force. Trust in Jesus and he'll make your hearts his home. Love must shape your attitude to everything. Seek unity with all God's people, no matter what their culture. You'll find that the love of Jesus has no limits. You can't make that discovery by mouthing slick formulas, or by believing you're superior. To be full of God, you must be full of love.[3]

Being full of God means energy to do things beyond our wildest dreams. Let's work together to make God famous. Let's advertise the name of Jesus from one age to another, non-stop, forever.

4 This is what Paul, a prisoner for Jesus, wants to impress upon you. Behave like Christians every moment of your lives, always modest, always kind and always patient. Love means trying to understand other people's point of view. Stay together, despite your differences. Be led by the Spirit. She creates harmony from variety. We all belong to one community; we rely on the same Spirit; we share a hope that gives us courage to go forward. We have one Leader; he alone has our trust. All in the community have equal status. The one and only God cares for every living being like a parent. God is distinct from anything else, and involved with everything at the same time.

(7) Jesus, God's Chosen, has shared out among us different aspects of his loving goodness. It's like the song about the victorious king returning to his capital city.

> "To loudest cheers
> He freedom brings;
> Scattering gifts,
> Kindest of kings."

---

[3] 3:18. Traditional translation "... the love of God which passes knowledge." Knowledge (Greek, *gnosis*) does not just stand for "knowing things," but for the philosophy of "gnosticism," the idea that you can know God by possession of insider knowledge.

(This song is about a dramatic reversal of fortunes. The king's triumph is all the more striking because it follows his humiliation. This reminds us of what happened to Jesus on earth and his appointment afterwards to the highest position in the universe.)

So the different parts each of us play in our Christian community are gifts from Jesus. He gave his first friends the task of handing on his message; then came other people able to speak for him; some travel from place to place taking the Good News; others use their talents as leaders and trainers in local groups. They're all working to the same end. They want to see every Christian engaged in work that will benefit the whole community. We need that sense of moving forward together, discovering together more about God's True Likeness, growing together to become completely like Jesus. We need to grow up, or we'll get thrown off course by those who employ techniques to control our minds and confuse us with false ideas. By cultivating the honesty that springs from love, we mature to become like Jesus, our model. Love produces unity where all talents are fully used in the service of all.

(17) Here is some strong advice from the Leader. Now that you are Christians, you must not live like those whose manner of life is un-Christian, without any guiding principle. Such people have no idea where they're going, and because they don't want to know, they don't give God a chance to change their lives. They have no feelings, do whatever they fancy from moment to moment, and engage in every kind of shady practice. You know very well, that's not the way Jesus lived. Remember the things you were told about him? You were taught to look to him as your example. That means a complete change of lifestyle. You must get rid of your old selfish habits. No more letting your cravings get the better of you. There must be a fresh way of looking at things. Put on the new suit of clothes God has made for you, then you'll stand out as people of character. You must be those whose words can be trusted by everyone, and you need to have a social conscience. It may be right to be angry on behalf of others. But make sure your anger doesn't turn to bitterness. Calm down before you go to bed at night. Don't be caught off guard. No more thieving. Do a decent job of work, and use some of your earnings to care for those less fortunate. If you can't say anything helpful, keep your mouth shut. What you have to say

should always make people feel better. Learn to appreciate what's good and beautiful. God's Spirit is opening a new world for you. Don't make her sad by showing no interest. Get rid of all your negative feelings. Don't set out to cause an argument, and don't gossip or run other people down. Be kind and sympathetic. Jesus has shown how God accepts us despite our faults. We should display the same generosity to one another.

5 Just as children copy their parents, you must copy God. That means living a life of love, like Jesus. He put our needs before his own. His life was beautiful in our eyes and in God's. It should be far from your thoughts to grab all you can, hatch plots, or indulge in frivolous relationships. That's not how God's people behave. You must watch your language and not say anything offensive or thoughtless. Use your mouths to pay compliments. No one who behaves irresponsibly, no one who is downright dishonest or hooked on material things, has any place in the New World that belongs to Jesus and God.

Don't get caught by clever sales talk. God doesn't tolerate those who engage in deliberate wickedness. Make sure you don't help such people. There was a time when you didn't know any better, but now the Leader has made everything clear. Let your principles control your behavior. You should be marked out as people who are good, dependable, and honest. Use your imagination to work out what the Leader would want you to do. Don't have anything to do with doubtful practices. Some things that go on behind closed doors are too bad even to mention. Those who think no one can see what they're up to will get a shock when the lights come on. Think of the words of the song we sing,

> "*Wake up time!*
> *Rise and shine!*
> *Jesus, like the sun, has risen!*"

So keep your wits about you. Make good use of your time. These are not the best days to be alive. Don't act the fool. Follow the Leader. Watch the drink, it can destroy. God's Spirit is all you need by way of stimulation. When you sing your hymns, songs, and choruses for the Leader, put your hearts into it. Make every occasion the chance to say "thank you" to God for everything we have by means of Jesus, our Leader, God's Chosen.

(21) Giving way to the Leader means giving way to one another. This includes those in committed relationships. Your consideration for your partner should reflect your consideration for the Leader. Because they have a physical relationship, husband and wife should act together as one person, just as the Christian community acts together because it represents the body of Jesus, the source of our life and health. Just as the Christian community consults Jesus, so you should consult your partner before deciding anything. Partners should love one another in the same way that Jesus loves all his friends. Jesus gave his life for those he loved, to make them into a special community, bright and clean, the bearer of a vital message. Jesus is out to make beautiful people with no unpleasant side to them. By loving one another as much as they love themselves, partners will encourage each other to be attractive. Loving your partner is a way of loving yourself. We should never hate our own bodies. We should look after them and see they're well fed. Jesus looks after *us*. We're his body. When someone leaves their parents for a relationship with someone else, they form a new bond. It's as if they become one body. No one quite knows how it happens. It's the same with Jesus and his friends. So partners should love and respect one another as much as they love and respect their own self.

6 Young people, you should follow the advice given you by your parents, based on the teachings of the Leader. Don't forget, the first rule in the old books that comes with a promise, is the one that asks you to respect those who look after you. If you keep that rule, you're promised a long and happy life.

Parents, you should be careful not to irritate your children. You should hand on to them the teachings of the Leader by word, and by example.

Those of you who work for other people should be respectful to your employers and carry out their instructions. You should work with enthusiasm, as if you were working for Jesus. Don't just do a good job when you're being watched, so as to create a good impression. Friends of Jesus do their best for God whether anyone is looking or not. Put your back into whatever you do. It's the Leader you have to answer to, not anyone else. At the end of the day it's the Leader who'll pay your wages, whether you're a worker or on the board of directors.

If you have people working for you, make sure they feel happy and secure. We all have the same boss, one who doesn't recognize rank or class.

(10) Stay close to the Leader and he'll restore your energies again and again. Let God equip you for life's adventure. Then you'll stand up to everything that gets thrown at you. You're going to meet challenges that need more than human resources. With God's survival kit you'll pull through however tough the conditions.

At the ready then! Honesty is your belt, good relations your weatherproofs, peace your hiking boots. Trust is your first-aid pack in case of accidents. The Spirit will provide a protective hard hat, a handy knife, and a map with God's directions.

Whenever you talk with God, seek the help of the Spirit. Be bold, and use your imagination. Keep your mind fresh, and always have a list of all those Christians needing special mention. I hope you'll mention my name to God. When I pass on the Good News, I need to find the right words and overcome my nerves. I'm doing time in prison right now for telling people the Good News. But it's got to be done. Ask God to give me the guts.

(21) Lucky will give you all the latest news about me. He's a dear friend and works hard for the Leader. I'm sending him specially, to tell you how we all are. I'm sure he'll cheer you up.

Be at ease with one another. Trust to the life of love, with the help of the Loving God and the Leader, Jesus, God's Chosen. As long as your love for Jesus lasts, you'll experience what love can do.

PART THREE

THE FOUR CALLS

The Call to Action

A message from James

1 From James, one of God's helpers and a friend of Jesus. Jesus is God's Chosen and our Leader. Greetings to God's people all over the world.

Friends, when you find yourselves in any kind of trouble, look on the bright side. You should realize your trust in God is being tried out, to see if it works. The experience will make you more stable, help you to develop your personalities, and get rid of your weaknesses.

So if you don't know what to do for the best, ask God for advice. God loves to help and doesn't make you feel bad about yourself. When you ask, *trust*. Don't give in to your doubts. Those who doubt are like waves of the sea, driven to and fro by the wind. If you have no strong convictions and can never make up your mind, you can't expect God to help you.

(9) Those Christians who are not thought of as being very important should be pleased God thinks highly of them. Prosperous Christians should be pleased when they lose their advantages because there's no more future in being wealthy than in being a wild flower. The strong rays of the sun shrivel the plant, the flower falls off, and that's the end of its beauty. It's going to be the same with the rich. At the height of their success, they'll suddenly find themselves stony broke.

Well done, those who come through their troubles with a smile on their faces! They'll be rewarded with life to the full, promised to those who love God. No one having bad times should say, "God's putting me through all this." God never has any thought of doing harm and isn't responsible for our difficulties. It's our own desires that get us into trouble. We let bad thoughts give birth to bad actions which then grow and multiply until they completely destroy us. It's time to face realities, dear friends!

(17) Everything good in our lives, every kind and generous act, bears the mark of God's influence. God made light itself and has no dark or changeable side. It was God's idea to make us what we are by speaking the truth to us. We're meant to be the pointers to what the rest of God's creation will be like.

Remember this, dear friends. Everyone should be eager to listen but careful about what they say, and slow to be angry. Anger is not what God wants from us. So get rid of all greed and selfishness, and be willing to let the truth God has planted in you grow, until your whole personality is changed for the good.

Don't just listen to God; do what God says. Otherwise you're only playing games. People who listen to God and do nothing are like those who notice the bags under their eyes when they look in the mirror, then carry on with the lifestyle which makes them look so tired. But those who are aware of what's best for them, the way of freedom, and keep on reminding themselves so they do something about it, are the ones who'll get happiness out of life.

(26) Do you think you're religious? If you don't know when to shut up, you're fooling yourself. Your religion's a fake. True religion, what the Loving God recognizes as the genuine article, involves caring for all who are suffering hardship, and not falling for popular prejudices.

2 My friends, those who are true followers of our great hearted Leader, Jesus the Chosen One, don't display snobbery. Suppose someone wearing expensive jewelry and clothes comes into your meeting, and someone poor, wearing dirty clothes, comes in at the same time. If you pay special attention to the one who's well-dressed and say, "Please take a seat" and then say to the one who looks down and out, "Stand over there" or "You can sit on the floor," you're being snobbish and judging on the basis of prejudice. Let's get this clear, my dear friends. God has chosen poor people from society to serve as the best examples of what it means to be a Christian, and to be the leading citizens in God's New World. The poor are the ones who really love God. So why do you look down on them? It's the rich who oppress you! They're the people who have you up

in court! They're the ones who give you a bad name!

If you keep to the high principle found in the old books, "Love other people as you love yourself," you'll do alright. But if you pick and choose who to be nice to, you've gone against that principle and put yourself completely in the wrong. Either you live your life according to God's rules or you don't. You can't pick and choose which rules you're going to keep. The one who said, "Don't entice somebody else's partner away from them" also said, "You must not kill." You get no credit for keeping one rule if you break the other. Instead of thinking about rules like this, it's better to model your life in such a way that will give freedom to everyone. God will have no compassion for those who haven't shown any. Compassion must take the place of judgment!

(14) What's the use, my friends, if you say you trust in God and it makes no difference to the way you behave? Can trust make you a better person? If there are people you know about who haven't enough food or clothes, do you think it will do any good if you say to them, "Have a nice day! Keep warm and make sure you have enough to eat!" unless you give them what they need? Trust without action is useless!

Someone will probably argue, "We're all different. You're a practical person, I'm a thinker." I say your thinking is shallow if it has no practical outcome. I'll show you the depth of my thinking by the way I act. So you think there's only one God? Well done – so do God's worst enemies. They tremble at the thought. It should be obvious, there's no point in trusting God if you don't put your trust to good effect.

It was your ancestor Abraham's willingness to offer his son as a gift to God that brought about his good relationship with God, wasn't it? His trust and his actions went hand in hand. His actions demonstrated his trust to perfection. That's why the old books say, "Abraham put his trust in God and God recognized him as a good person." And that's why Abraham was called "God's Friend." So you see, we get on good terms with God by what we do, and not just by the way we think.

I'll give you another example. Do you remember Barbara the prostitute? Barbara pleased God by what she did when she sheltered some spies in her house and helped them escape. Just as a body isn't alive if it's not breathing, so trust in God is dead without anything to show for it!

3 Friends, my advice to most of you is not to try to be teachers. It's difficult to keep up the standards expected of a teacher. All of us make lots of mistakes. You've got to be perfectly in control of yourself to be able to say the right thing every time. Think of the way a bit is put into a horse's mouth to get it to obey us, or the way a very large ship, needing strong winds to drive it along, is steered by a very small rudder wherever the pilot wants to go. The tongue is only a small part of the body, but it's got a lot of power. A big forest can be set on fire by a tiny spark. That's what the tongue can do. It can affect your whole personality with its evil influence, and ruin your life with its destructive force. It's possible to tame every kind of animal – birds, snakes, dolphins – it's been done! The tongue is a different matter. It's evil; it won't be controlled; its poison is deadly. We use our tongues to say "thank you" to the Loving God, and then we use them to be nasty to other people who've been made in God's likeness. We shout praise and abuse in the same breath! Friends, this won't do! Can you get clean and dirty water from the same tap? Have you ever seen olives growing on fig trees? Or figs on a grapevine? You can't get drinking water from the sea!

(13) Anyone who wants to be known as wise and understanding should lead a life worthy of respect, with the marks of gentleness and good sense. If you're full of bitter feelings or out to get your own way, don't make things worse by pretending to be a saint. That's the sort of cleverness really wicked people get up to. God doesn't think it clever! Wherever people are selfish and spiteful, there'll be quarrelling and all sorts of bad behavior. The wisdom that comes from God has no unpleasant side to it. It's peaceful, kind, and friendly; it takes account of the feelings of others and does lovely things; it's free from prejudice and humbug. A land needs peace if crops are to be sown and harvested successfully. Peace-lovers are the ones who bring true prosperity.

4 Why are you always squabbling and falling out among yourselves? It's because you're frustrated! You want something you can't have, and that makes you aggressive. You're even ready to kill to get your hands on something you fancy, but you still aren't satisfied. You have an empty feeling because you don't ask God to supply your needs. Even when you do ask God, you don't get anything because your motives are selfish. You're out to have a good time! You want to have it both ways! It's time you realized you can't be God's friends if you flirt with God's enemies. Anyone just trying to be popular is going against God. The old books warn us that the personalities God gave us have been twisted by our jealous desires. But we can get strength from God to put things right. The old books also say, "God has no time for those who are out for themselves. God's help is for those who recognize their need."

Allow God to help you. Don't give in to evil and it will soon lose its attraction. Step closer to God and God will step closer to you. If you've been playing with dirt, it's time to wash your hands! If you've been acting a part, it's time to be honest! Facing up to what you are should bring you to tears. It will be a change from your careless laughter. You've got nothing to laugh about! Allow God to take control of you and put you on a firmer footing.

Friends, don't say nasty things about one another. Anyone who runs somebody else down or recites the rules to another is not really a champion of good behavior. Good behavior means doing the right thing yourself, not criticizing other people. There's only one who has the right to tell us what to do and to criticize us – the one who can bring us to life or bring us to our knees! So stop playing God by telling other people what they're doing wrong!

(13) Now I want a word with those of you who say, "Today or tomorrow I'm off to the city. I'll spend a year there expanding my business and increasing my profits." How can you be so sure about what's going to happen tomorrow? Your life only lasts as long as a puff of smoke. If you had more sense you'd say, "If it's what God wants I'll live to do this or that." You're wrong to be so self-confident! It's especially wrong to know what's right and not to do it.

5 It's time for the wealthy to take the smile off their faces! I say to them: the value of your shares is falling fast; your smart clothes are wearing out; your precious possessions have turned out to be cheap imitations, and you're beginning to look foolish. You've been trying to make sure you'll be comfortable in your old age. But you'd better start listening to the complaints of the workers you underpaid. God knows their grievances! You've been having fun and living it up. But you've been responsible for the death of innocent people who weren't able to stand up for themselves.

Be patient, dear friends. The Leader is coming! Farmers have to be patient while they wait for their crops to grow. There has to be enough rain before anything comes up. Wait patiently and keep your spirits high. The Leader is near!

Dear friends, don't try to put the blame on someone else, or the blame will be put on you! It will all be sorted out, the moment Jesus comes.

If you want a good example of patience in the face of difficulties, remember the people in times gone by who spoke for God. We think of them as happy people because they kept going. You've heard about Job and how God made things come right for him after he'd come through his trials. God is compassionate and understanding.

(12) My friends, more than anything else, don't make rash promises. Calling heaven and earth to witness, or any other form of words, will make no difference. What's important is that your word can be relied on. Otherwise you'll put yourselves in the wrong.

Is there anybody with a problem? They should talk with God about it. Anybody feeling especially happy? They should sing. Anybody unwell? They should ask some friends of Jesus to visit them. They will speak with God on their behalf and bring some token as an expression of God's care. If this is done in a spirit of trust, those who are unwell will be made better, and God will put new heart into them. Anything they've done wrong will be forgiven.

Admit your faults to one another and together ask God to make you better people. If a good person seeks God's help, things quickly start to happen. Elijah was human like us. He asked God to stop the rain and there was a drought for three and a half years. Then he talked with God again. The drought ended and there was a good harvest.

My friends, if someone takes a wrong turning, and you are the friend who helps them find their way back, it's like giving the kiss of life. Your loving action will make up for many faults, theirs and yours!

The Call to Hope

A message from Rocky

1 This letter comes to you from Rocky, one of the very first friends of Jesus, God's Chosen. It's for those people who've been forced to seek asylum in countries far from home.[1] They're very special to the Loving God. They've been trained by God's Spirit to be loyal followers of Jesus, and to share his new life. May your lives be full of God's beauty and peace!

(3) What a wonderful God we have in the Parent of our Leader, Jesus, the Chosen! This God has shown us great understanding and given us a second chance. There's a bright future ahead because Jesus, who died, has come back to life. You have the firm guarantee of a life that nothing can destroy or spoil, in God's New World. In return for your trust, God is looking after you. One day, when history comes to an end, you'll be the complete people God intends you to be. So you can be happy, despite the various hardships you're having to put up with for a short while. It's as if your sincerity is being put to the test, in the same way as gold is tested in a furnace. You're worth more than gold, and there'll be a lot to be proud about and to celebrate when you see Jesus. You've not seen him yet, but you love him all the same. You've put your trust in him, and you're amazingly happy. You're feeling more confident and at ease with yourselves every day.

(10) God's speakers in olden times spoke of the new prospects for humanity. They thought hard and long about the way God would act on your behalf. As they tried to imagine how it would all happen, they foresaw the sufferings God's Chosen would have to go through and the rejoicing

---

[1] 1:1. "refugees." The Greek locates them in areas now in Turkey.

that would follow the completion of his work. They realized they were saying things that applied, not to their own situation, but to yours. Now that messengers, inspired by God's Spirit, have brought the Good News to you, it all makes sense. Those in the close presence of God are watching with keen interest as the story unfolds.

(13) So keep your heads clear and stick to a healthy routine; center your hope on that great present of love Jesus will have for you when you see him. Be like children who are grown up enough to guard their emotions, not like babies who can't control what they do. Just as God is not to be compared with anybody else, so you should develop a distinctive lifestyle others can look up to. According to the old books, God says, "I'm different, so you must be different too."[2]

You've given your loyalty to the God who appreciates people for what they do, not for what race they belong to. So respect the people you live among as refugees. Remember how you've been made free from the hangups and prejudices of your ancestors. A big price was paid for your freedom. No amount of money could buy it. The payment was made in blood, the blood of Jesus, a wonderful person, all goodness through and through. He was God's ideal, in God's mind and heart even before this world came into existence. You were the lucky ones, living at the time Jesus came. It's only because of him you've come to trust God. God brought Jesus to life again after he had died, and made him famous. That's why you trust God and are full of hope.

You are changed people since you accepted the truth. You're learning the true meaning of love. Now you must love one another with honesty and enthusiasm. You've begun a new life. You no longer have the personality you inherited from your natural parents. You now have the new personality you've been given by God, your eternal Parent. As one of the old books tells us,

> "Our human flesh is as the grass
> Which withers and grows pale;

---

[2] 1:16. This translation may come as a surprise to those not aware of the basic meaning of holy (*hagios*) – different.

> *Unlike the loveliest flowers on earth,*
> *God's words will never fail."*

The "words" referred to in those verses is the "Good News" which has been given to you.

2 So get rid of all evil plans, every intention to play dirty tricks or deceive, the desire to out-bid others or bring them down by talking behind their backs. You must be like babies who've just been born. Like babies who feed naturally from their mother's breast, you must think of God as your mother and seek God's nourishment. Then you'll grow to a full and complete life. Have you tasted how good God is?

Make Jesus the foundation of your lives. He was like the first brick to be laid in a building. Although rejected as a misfit by the people of his day, God thought him ideal for the job! Model yourselves on him. Come alive! Be part of the new movement. Together with Jesus you can be the sign of God's presence, the meeting point where people encounter God. Remember what God says in the old books?

> *"With skill I fit a cornerstone,*
> *A feature for all time;*
> *Whoever trusts my expertise,*
> *Will like that marble shine!"*

For those of you who trust God's skill, Jesus is the base on which to build. But for those who don't trust God, I would quote some other words:

> *"The stone the builders think quite useless*
> *Is God's choice to take the stress.*
> *They leave it lying in the way*
> *To cause an accident someday!"*

Those who don't follow the architect's plans are sure to come to grief!

But you are God's hand-picked team, expert and fully qualified. You can tell people about the splendid work God has been doing and how you came

THE CALL TO HOPE

to see it. There was a time when you were nobody special, but now you're God's friends. In those days you were no-hopers, but now that God's befriended you, you've got a reason for living.

(11) My dear friends, you must adopt a different lifestyle from those around you. Because they are so selfish, they cannot live God's way. If you treat people who differ from you with tolerance and consideration, they'll notice the good things you do, instead of pointing the finger at your shortcomings. Then they may be prepared to welcome the God they have seen shining through you.

You'll be a good advert for God if you obey the law and respect local customs. Respect the head of state and the government's representatives in your district. Their job is to restrain those who do wrong and commend those who do right. God wants you to be good citizens in order to correct the wrong ideas some people have about you. Because you're members of God's team, you're free to make your own choices. But your freedom must not be an excuse for bad behavior. Treat everybody with respect. Show special love to your Christian sisters and brothers. Worship God and honor the head of state.

(18) Those of you who work for others should recognize what you owe to them. Be respectful, not just to those who treat you well, but also to those who make life difficult for you. It shows you are friends of God if you put up with hardship and unfair treatment without complaining. If you accept a telling off when you've done something wrong, what's so special about that? If you don't deserve the criticism but take it without moaning, God is pleased with you. You can show your difference from other people in that way. Remember that Jesus, God's Chosen, suffered for your sake. He's your example. Try to be like him. He did things God's way and always told the truth. When people shouted abuse at Jesus he didn't shout back; when he received rough treatment he didn't threaten to get his revenge. Instead Jesus put himself in God's hands. Only God is in a position to judge fairly. Jesus took the weight of our wrongdoing on his own mind and heart when he was hung up to die. He longed for us to live a new and unselfish life. Through his suffering you've been given a fresh start. You'd completely lost your way, just like sheep, but now you've come back to the shepherd, the one who knows what's best for you.

3 You must treat your life-partners with honor and dignity. Then, even if they don't share your beliefs, they may be won over by the way you put your beliefs into practice, and be impressed by your sincerity and respect for others. Your partner will be influenced more by your good nature than by smart clothes or the latest hairstyle. That's what counts with God, too! Some of our ancestors long ago behaved with grace and beauty in their relationship with their partners. Sarah, for example, treated her husband, Abraham, like somebody special. We are Sarah's descendants as long as we stick to what's right and don't give in to intimidation.

You men should be particularly sensitive and understanding of your women, especially during their monthly periods and before and after giving birth. They are on an equal footing with you, since only together with them can you receive God's gift of children. You can't talk freely with God unless you talk freely with one another. Work toward a common mind; think and feel together – that's the mark of true love. Always be kind, and don't try to be the one in control. Don't return a wrong with a wrong; avoid shouting matches. Try answering a hurt with a loving gesture. Your task is to make the world a better place. That way, life will be better for you as well. What does our old song say?

> *"If you want a happy life,*
> *Keep your tongue from words of strife;*
> *Thought of evil deeds must cease;*
> *Set your mind on seeking peace.*
> *Such are those our God will hear*
> *When they bring their needs in prayer."*

(13) No harm is likely to come to you if it's obvious your intentions are good. But if you do get into trouble for doing the right thing, it's to your credit. Don't give in to bullies – they're just very insecure people. Keep uppermost in your minds the truth that Jesus is your Leader. Always be ready to explain to anyone why you have such a positive view of life. But you mustn't be pushy in the way you do it. You must respect the other person's right to their opinion. Don't have any secret vices, so there'll be

nothing your critics can bring against you when they seek to rubbish your good work for God's Chosen. Yes, it's much better to suffer for doing the right thing, when God's plan presents no other option, than to suffer for doing the wrong thing. Wrongdoing caused the suffering of Jesus. He was a good person, suffering for the benefit of bad people. His aim was to make you God's friends. Although his body died, his spirit still lives.

(19) Do you remember the story of Enoch, one of our ancestors? He went to preach to the people who'd been drowned in the Great Flood. Those people had refused to listen to the voice of God, despite the fact that, while Noah was building his big boat, God waited patiently for them to see reason. Noah's boat enabled eight people to survive the flood.[3]

That old story has a meaning for us. You are going to be dipped today. Like God's people of long ago, you're going to come through a watery experience to a new life. It's not the water that gets rid of your dirt, but the promise you make to God in sincerity of heart. You're going to come to life again with Jesus. Jesus is now in the presence of God and has the place of highest honor. All God's agents and key-workers have had to give way to him.[4]

4 Jesus had to put up with physical violence, so you should be ready for it. It's a good treatment for selfishness. When your selfish motives are under control, you'll be free to live the rest of your life on earth in the way God wants. You've had a great time living it up. You've tried it all – one big round of self-indulgence. Your former companions are surprised you no longer want to go to their wild parties, and now make you the target of their foul language. One day they'll have to give an account of their behavior. They will stand before the judge of those whose lives are worthwhile and those whose lives are destructive. The Good News is for all.

---

[3] 3:19. We follow the view of Moffatt, Rendell Harris, Barclay, and others, that the Greek of v. 19, *en ho kai*, traditionally translated "in the which," should read "Enoch." (There were no capital letters or spacings in the original Greek text.) There was a belief that Enoch did not die but went to preach to the victims of Noah's flood. Rocky uses the story as a picture of baptism to make the point that an awakened conscience is the central element in the rite. This translation makes more sense than the notion that Jesus went to preach to those in hell but is unpalatable for those who rely on the traditional translation to provide a scriptural basis for the so-called "Apostle's Creed."

[4] 3:21. Here we have the evidence that this letter was possibly based on a sermon intended for baptismal candidates. It is also appropriate for Easter, a period when baptisms often took place in the early Church.

This means that those who lead a selfish life get a chance to realize where they've been going wrong, and may choose to live God's life instead.

(7) There's not much time left, so put to best use what time you have. Make sure you set aside enough time to talk with God. Most of all, pile on the love for one another. Love makes up for many shortcomings. Don't just open your homes to one another, but make sure whoever comes in feels at home. God has given you what you have for a purpose, so use your talents and possessions for the benefit of one another. Are you a good communicator? Use your charm to get God's message across. Are you gifted with your hands? Use the abilities God has given you, in all your tasks, to give God a good name. Jesus was a skilled worker – he'll inspire you! His skill and artistry will last forever!

(12) My very dear friends, you shouldn't be surprised at the hard time you're going through as if it were the last thing you expected to happen. Be happy at the thought that you're suffering just like Jesus. One day when you get to meet him, you'll experience a happiness you've never known before. If people call you names because you're friends of Jesus, count it a big plus. God's Spirit is in charge of your reputation and she'll be especially close to you at such times. But she cannot guard your reputation if you get into trouble because you've broken the law, whether with a serious offense such as murder or stealing, or a minor offense such as being a nuisance. There's no disgrace in suffering as a Christian. You should be proud of the title and thank God for the opportunity to say who you belong to. It looks very much as if God is sorting out us Christians first. If God's judgment is hard for us, what will it be like for those who reject the Good News? As the old books say, "If it's a struggle for good people to achieve the full life God intends for us, how much harder it must be for those who refuse God's help because they don't want to be good." So then, those of you who are suffering must put yourselves completely into God's hands and be determined to do what's right. God has made us and can be trusted to see us through.

5 I want to say something to those who have special responsibilities within your group. I speak as a leader myself, one who was there when Jesus was being tortured. I share with you the bright hopes

we have for the future. Look after the people God has put into your care. Think of it as a privilege, not a chore. Don't do it for a reward: do it eagerly, out of love! Don't be a control freak – lead by example! Jesus is our Leader. You'll meet him one day and he'll congratulate you on your work. That will be enough reward to last all eternity! Those of you who've only recently joined the community should allow those with more experience to guide you. All of you should give way to one another. Remember the words we sing about God upsetting the plans of the arrogant and giving honor to the modest?[5] So have a modest opinion of yourself. You're nothing compared with God. God will give you the honor right for you at the proper time. Let slip all those worries from off your shoulders and allow God to carry them. God cares about you every moment of the day. Make careful use of your time and energy, and be aware of what's going on around you. Evil is a powerful enemy and often gets the better of us when we least expect it. Stand firm; hold on to your trust. Remember your Christian sisters and brothers all over the world are having a bad time too. It's not going to last long. God will bring your suffering to an end, give you new strength, and help you build on the experience. God is in charge now and for always. That's a fact!

(12) Silas has been helping me write all this down. He's a reliable friend. I hope my words will encourage you and that you'll realize they bear the true mark of God. Keep a tight grip on reality! Your Christian friends in the big city send their kind regards. Mark also sends his greetings. He's a like a son to me. Give one another a big kiss every time you meet! I send my own best wishes for the peace and happiness of all friends of Jesus.[6]

---

[5] 5:5. It's interesting that Rocky (or Silas) seems to know the song Mary sang for her cousin Lisa. Mary's song was based on the song of Hannah, but this quote is closer to Mary's variation.

[6] 5:13. "big city," literally "Babylon," probably a euphemism for Rome. It is a device for maintaining secrecy or a description of Rome as a center of evil, or both.

The Call to Love

A letter from a loving friend. (1 John)

1 The one who spoke when time began, the one who brought life into being, we have heard, seen, touched, and known as a living person. We want to share with you the experiences we've had. The life that flows from the very heart of God, we have known as a close companion and friend. We want you to be our friends, so that, like us, you can be friends with God and friends of Jesus, God's True Likeness. Listen to what we have to tell you. We want to share our joy.

This is what we've learnt from our experience and would like to pass on to you. God is pure light and has no dark features. If we say we're in touch with God, while all the time we're walking around with our eyes shut, we're living a lie. But if we open our minds and share God's clear view of everything, we can have honest relationships with one another. Jesus clears away everything that blocks our path to God. If we think there's nothing wrong with us, and that we've nothing to learn, we're fooling ourselves. If we own up to our faults, God is fair and without fail will accept us and show us the way to put things right. If we think we're perfect, we're saying that God is wrong. Or we haven't been listening to God's voice inside us.

2 My friends, you are in my care. I think of you as my children. I'm writing this letter to stop you going wrong. But no matter how far wrong any of us goes, our good friend Jesus will always stand up for us and restore our relationship with the Loving God. Jesus gave his life for others without any thought of self. What he did makes up for our badness, and promises a new and better world.

But do we really know Jesus? Here's a simple test. Are we doing what

Jesus asked of us? Anyone who says, "I know Jesus very well," but doesn't do what Jesus wants, is a fraud. They're either trying to fool you or they're fooling themselves. Whoever puts the words of Jesus into practice will live a life based on love. This is the easiest way to identify the true friends of Jesus. Anyone who says, "I'm a friend of Jesus," should model their life on his.

(7) Dear friends, I'm not telling you to do anything new. It's what you've been told from the start; it should be familiar to you by this time. Perhaps now you've had some experience I can shed new light on it. Anyone who says, "I see it all – it's as clear as day," while hating someone else, can't see a thing. They're still completely in the dark! Those who love other people are the ones who truly understand. They can't go wrong. Anyone who hates somebody has blocked the light from their minds and has no idea of right or wrong.

(12) I hope you'll all read this letter, however young or old you are; whether you have the responsibility of being parents or whether you're young and full of energy. You've come to know God, the one who was before time, as a loving parent; Jesus has made sure your wrongdoings are forgiven; your minds are free to receive what God has to say to you, and you're equipped to overcome evil.[1]

(15) Don't be like those who get hooked on the latest craze. Those desperate to be in fashion have no love for God. They're attracted by things they can see and by things that money can buy. Fashions change and what seems valuable today becomes worthless tomorrow. Those who live God's way will never be "out of date."

(18) My own dear people, history is speeding toward a climax. Someone may have told you that a great enemy of Jesus will appear on the world stage. Judging by the number of enemies Jesus has already, it's not going to be long. Some of Jesus' enemies used to be members of our community, but they were not truly committed, otherwise they would have stayed. They showed where their loyalties were by walking out on us! But you have been touched by God's Spirit and she's given you a special understanding of life. It's not my task to put you right because you're on the right track already. You're capable of seeing the difference between what's true and what's false.

---

[1] 2:12-14. The verses in the Greek are a sort of poem in prose, the effect of which is very difficult to convey in translation without being wordy and tedious. Our solution is to provide a précis.

(22) Those who say that Jesus is not God's Chosen are spreading a lie. Those who don't believe that Jesus is the True Likeness of the Loving God are out to do damage. If you have no regard for Jesus, you have no regard for God, his Parent. Everyone who accepts who Jesus is will be right about God too. Stick to what you were told when you joined the community. Then you'll keep close to God and to God's True Likeness. God has promised us life to the full.

(26) I'm sorry I've had to say so much about those who are out to confuse you. I would sooner talk about *you*. I'm so pleased that God's Spirit is still with you. As long as she's your guide, you don't need anybody to put you right. She gives you fresh insights into everything, and her view of life can be trusted. Stay close to her.

Also, dear friends, stay close to Jesus, so that when we meet him there won't be anything to feel nervous or ashamed about. If you've experienced his goodness, you'll be able to recognize his true friends by the way they display the same good qualities.

3 God's love for us is amazing! God looks on us as sons and daughters. People don't recognize the relationship because they don't recognize God. Dear friends, we are children of God already! We have no idea as yet about our future existence. We know that when we meet Jesus face to face, we'll have the form of existence he has now. That's how we'll be able to see him. Everyone who's looking forward to that day wants to be at their best. Nothing less will do for him!

People who have no regard for others behave badly. They don't let anything or anybody get in the way of what they want. Jesus came to do away with such selfishness. He was completely unselfish. His friends must be unselfish too. Selfish people have not got to know him or been influenced by him. I'm anxious for you, dear friends. Don't allow yourselves to be conned. Good people do what is good, just like Jesus. Troublemakers are evil. There's no other word for them. Evil has been around a long time. "God's Likeness" has been put on display for this very purpose – to rid the world of evil. Members of God's family don't cause harm. You can always spot the members of God's family. Those who don't love other people don't belong to God.

(11) When you became members of our community, you were told to love one another. Do you remember the story of Cain? He's an example of how not to behave. He murdered his brother Abel. Why did he do it? He was jealous because his brother was a better person than he was! Don't be surprised, my friends, that bad people hate you. We know we're living a new quality of life because we love one another. To have no love in your heart is deadly. Anyone who hates someone else has the character of a murderer. Murderers destroy life, including their own in the long run. Jesus has shown what true love is. He gave his life for us. We should give our lives for one another. How can someone love the way God loves if they're well off but refuse to help someone in need?

(18) Friends, let's not just talk about love. Let's get on with it. But make sure it's the real thing! If our words are matched by deeds, we'll have the confidence that comes from being genuine. We won't be afraid for God to look right into our hearts. If we feel we haven't kept up to the mark, don't forget God has a better opinion of us than we have of ourselves. That's because God can see everything, including our self-doubt. So long as our hearts are in the right place, we can approach God without fear. We'll get whatever we ask from God, because we're walking in step with God, and what pleases God pleases us.

This is what we have to do to please God. We must trust that Jesus is God's Chosen and God's True Likeness, and we must love one another, as Jesus told us. Then we're his friends and have his company all the time. That's the same as saying we have God's Spirit, the gift Jesus gave us.

4 Dear friends, don't accept every religious idea put before you. Think carefully whether it comes from God or not. Lots of people who claim to be God's speakers are nothing of the kind. This is how you know God's Spirit is speaking. If someone describes Jesus as being the most human of all humans as well as being God's Chosen, that is God's truth. Those who describe Jesus as if he were not a real person, don't speak on behalf of God. You've been warned to look out for troublemakers. Well, they've arrived! Well done, my own dear people, for dealing with them so effectively! You've proved you belong to God's family. Since Jesus has become part of your thinking and feeling, you speak with more

understanding than those who go along with popular prejudices. Because they say what people want to hear, people listen to them. We're God's people. Those who are used to listening for the true voice of God, recognize God's voice when we speak. They help to assure us that we are saying the right things.

(7) Dear friends, let's love one another, because love is a present from God. Everyone who loves shares a family likeness with God and has a relationship with God. Anyone who doesn't love doesn't have a relationship with God, because GOD IS LOVE. We've seen God's love in action. We know what God is like, because we've been shown God's character in the form of a human person. God wants us to have life to the full by means of Jesus. It's a great love story. We didn't fall in love with God. God fell in love with us. God sent Jesus to get rid of everything that comes between us and God. Dear friends, since God has shown us so much love, the least we can do is to love one another. No one has ever penetrated the mystery of God's being. But if we love one another, God is part of us. God's loving nature can be seen in our loving. Then there is the Spirit. She too is a present to convince us we're God's friends.

(14) We were there to witness the great event. The Loving God sent a true likeness to save the world from its misery. That's the news God's friends want to pass on! We trust God's love because we've experienced it first hand. GOD IS LOVE, and those who love are God's friends, and God is their friend. Love has become the basis of our lives. Sharing God's loving feelings for the world gives us confidence to face whatever the future may bring. There is nothing to fear in love. Lovers overcome their shyness and nerves. Fear has to do with feelings of guilt. You don't really love until all those feelings have gone. We love because God loved us first. Those who say, "I love God" while hating other people, are liars. If they don't love someone they've seen, how can they love God, who they've never seen? God has made quite clear what is expected of us. Those who love God must love all members of the human family.

5 Those who believe that Jesus is God's Chosen are members of God's family. They each love the other members of the family for the sake of God, the parent they have in common. This love binds

us together and inspires us to do what God wants. That's how we show our love for God. God doesn't ask us to do what's too hard for us. As members of God's family we can cope with whatever comes our way. Our confidence in God sees us through. We'll change the world with our belief that Jesus is God's Chosen!

(6) Jesus was a real human being. His body was made of the same elements as ours. He breathed the same air we breathe. He bled like us, he passed water like us, his lungs worked just like ours – that's enough proof! Those who knew Jesus well will tell you this. God also stands witness to the human form of the True Likeness. Those who accept Jesus as God's True Likeness are quite sure about it. Those who have other ideas make God out to be a liar. They don't accept God's evidence! What is God's evidence? God's present of life to the full, which came with Jesus. Those who have Jesus for a friend know what it is to be alive in every sense of the word. It's those who don't know Jesus who aren't really alive.

You already believe that Jesus is God's True Likeness. I'm writing this letter to make sure you have life to the full.

Our relationship with Jesus gives us such confidence! When we think like him, we can ask him to help us. We know he hears us. What we've asked from him is already on the way.

(16) If you notice a Christian doing something wrong, nothing too serious, ask for God's help and God will bring that person back to a healthy life again. Sometimes people go so far wrong, there's nothing that can be done. It may be better for you not to waste your energies.

Members of God's family don't make wrongdoing the pattern of their lives. The presence of Jesus prevents that from happening. They can resist the power of evil. We know we belong to God, though there's a lot of evil in the world today. God's True Likeness has come among us and opened our minds. He's shown us what God is really like. Now we have a good relationship with God and with Jesus, God's Chosen. We know what God is like, and we know what it means to live.

My very dear friends, I care so much for you. Don't allow anything or anybody to take the place of God in your lives.

The Call to Trust

Letter to those who want to go back to the old days. (Hebrews)

1 Up to now, God has always spoken to our people by means of special agents, each with their own way of putting things. But recently God has spoken to us by means of a human personality, someone so close to God as to share responsibility for everything, including the physical universe. This person is like a picture of God thrown in bright lights on a screen, or a lifelike sculpture, and speaks the words the world needs to stay in existence. I am talking about someone who gave the world a new beginning, free from the faults of the past, who is now part of everything we understand when we use the word God; someone who is much more significant than God's other agents and plays a much bigger part in the scheme of things.

God never said to any other agent, "You're my child; from now on I'm your parent." Or, "We're like mother and daughter or father and son!" Introducing this new wonder to the world, God says, "All my agents will realize they're in the presence of someone unique!" God describes the other agents as "wind" and "fire." But this is what's said about God's own likeness,

> *"Like God you last forever,*
> *Your New World just and fair;*
> *You love all good and loathe the bad –*
> *God's happy choice for heir!"*

And this,

> *"You stuck the world together,*

> *Space is your work of art;*
> *You will remain forever,*
> *The day things come apart;*
> *Like clothes no more in fashion,*
> *You put them by and change,*
> *But you stay in position,*
> *Never out of range."*

Which one of God's agents got this invitation from God – "Sit down beside me and together we'll put the world right"?

God's agents are only helpers, sent out on God's business to get people ready for life to the full.

2 So we need to keep aware of this new way God is speaking to us, otherwise we will lose all sense of direction. People always get into trouble when they ignore what God's agents tell them. If we take no notice of this new venture on our behalf, we're asking for big trouble. The Leader announced a fresh start for the world. Those who got the message passed it on to us. God has backed up their report by being active in events, helping us to do amazing things and discover new talents from God's Spirit. God hasn't put any special class of people in charge of the New World we're talking about. Somewhere in the old books this is made clear:

> *"Why care so much for common folk?*
> *They're only human and no more.*
> *You've given them such enormous powers –*
> *Control of land and sea and air!"*

God's plan is for humankind to be in charge of everything, without exception. But obviously God's plan hasn't worked yet. This is where Jesus comes in. During his brief lifetime, Jesus was on the same level as every other human being. But now he has the highest position in God's order of things. That's because he was willing to die a special death as part of God's plan to benefit everyone.

(10) Everything that exists is God's idea and has no point without God.

What happened in Jesus falls in line perfectly with God's long-term plan. In order to produce a large family living the ideal life, there had first to be one to show the way, and that could only come about through pain and hardship. God is the inventor of the prototype and all the models that conform to it. That's why Jesus is happy to accept us as his brothers and sisters. These words from the old song sound like Jesus talking to God,

> "I'll pass it on to the family –
> The news of what you've done for me."

God's speakers remind us of Jesus when they say things like,

> "God gets my vote every time!"

and,

> "I'm for you,
> And my children too!"

Children from the same family have genes in common. Jesus shared our genes. When he died, he cleared from our common bloodline those negative things that lead to our death. Anxiety about death inhibits personal growth. Jesus freed us from that. It's obvious Jesus didn't come to help super-human people, but people who have someone like Abraham, an ordinary person, as their ancestor. This is an important point. Jesus had to be like us, his brothers and sisters, in every way. Only then could he be our representative to God, someone who understands why we're like we are. He is best placed to get rid of those things that stand between us and God. Because he has come through so much trouble himself, he can help those who are going through it now.

3 So my friends, God has given us a job to do! If you think about Jesus, you'll know how to go about it. Jesus is the Company Director, the vital link between us and God. Jesus was loyal to the one who gave him his position, just as Moses before him was loyal in the

same firm. But someone who sets a company up has a higher status than someone who just works for the company. That's why Jesus has a higher status than Moses. Of course, there has to be someone in overall charge, and that's God. God has final responsibility for everything. Moses was a loyal employee and anticipated God's future instructions. But Jesus, God's Chosen, was loyal as a family partner in the firm. We too have a stake in the firm if we have the courage of our convictions. God's Spirit is saying something to us in the words of the old song:

> *"Today, if you hear,*
> *Don't plug up your ear;*
> *You did, once and more,*
> *In desert days before.*
> *Though helped for generations,*
> *You people tried my patience.*
> *I swore to every one,*
> *'You'll miss out on the fun!'"*

Watch your feelings carefully, friends. Make sure they're not taking you away from God, who is alive to all that's going on. Help one another day by day not to get in a rut or be sidetracked. Keep thinking about that word *"today"* in the song. We're business partners of God's Chosen, but only provided we have the same confidence in the firm at the end as when we joined! When the song condemns those who were deaf in olden times, who do you think it refers to? It must have been God's former partners from Egypt. Moses was in charge of them. After forty years, God was fed up to the teeth with them. Because of the things they did wrong, they never got out of the desert alive.

4 The holiday God promised is still on offer. Make sure you don't miss it! We've had the same good offer as others before us. They didn't take it up because they didn't think it genuine. The holiday is for those who've accepted the offer. Think again about God's words.

> *"I swore to every one,*

You'll miss out on the fun."

According to the old books, God had a holiday after making the world. The old books also say that some people aren't going to have a holiday. The holiday is now an option again, despite the fact that some didn't take it up in the past. God has set a new deadline for the offer to be accepted. That deadline is "TODAY." Listen to the words of the old song, believed to be by David. They were written a long time after the first holiday offer had been turned down.

> *"If you hear God's voice today,*
> *Don't lock your hearts away!"*

We must not confuse all this with the entry of the Jews into the Promised Land under Joshua. That was no holiday! God's latest promise of a holiday comes from after that time. That holiday is still on offer for God's people. It will be like God's own holiday, a well-earned break after a period of hard work. Let's make sure of it. Let's not miss out by being suspicious of the offer, like the people in times past.

When God speaks, things happen. God's words are like a surgeon's knife, cutting deep to the root of what's going on inside us. God knows all our thoughts and feelings. Nothing can be hidden from God. Everything that exists is completely open to God's inspection. It's to God we'll have to answer.

(14) Jesus, God's Likeness, is our go-between between this world and the world beyond time and space. So let's hold on to our trust in him. We have someone to represent us who can sympathize with our weaknesses. He has been through everything we have been through, without doing anything wrong. So let's boldly get close to God and experience God's love first hand. We will be accepted in spite of our faults, and get all the help we need.

5 The people who act as links between this world and God are human like the rest of us. They deal with things to do with God; they are in charge of religious ceremonies; they arrange forms of worship for those who want to express sorrow for their wrongdoings. They

can be kind to people who don't know what they're doing and who make mistakes, because they too have their weak spots. That's why they have to say sorry to God for their own faults as well as for the people they represent. This is a responsible task and no one can just take it on. You have to be asked by God, just like Ron, the brother of Moses. It was the same with Jesus. He didn't appoint himself to high office. God appointed him by saying, "You're my child; from now on I'm your parent." God also said that Jesus would always be a go-between, like the one called "Righteous Ruler" in Jerusalem in older times.

When Jesus lived here in a human body, he screamed and cried for God's help. He knew God could rescue him from death. He was heard because of his humble attitude. Although he was God's child, he went through the school of suffering and learnt to give way to another's wishes. When he had completed his lessons, he was able to give full life and health to those willing to let him show the way. God gave him the role of "Righteous Ruler." Jesus is the go-between between this world and God.

There is much more to be said about this. It's not easy to understand, and you are slow learners. By now you ought to be passing on the message to other people. But you still need someone to help you grasp the simplest ideas from God. You're still being breast fed and not ready for solids. Milk is for babies. Babies can't know what is right or wrong. Solids are for those who are learning to cope in the adult world and make decisions for themselves.

6 It's time to grow up. We should by now have gone beyond the lessons for beginners. We should stop trying to pull ourselves up by our shoelaces and trust God instead. We shouldn't have to learn again about ceremonies, or whether there is life after death, and how good and evil people are dealt with then. If God thinks we're ready to move on, let's go! You cannot go back to square one after you have been through the course! You've started a new life, adopted a new way of thinking, and experienced the thrill of being a Christian. You have shared God's Spirit, learnt the value of God's words, and the inner strength that comes from seeing God's New World on its way. Those who go backwards go back to the time before God's Likeness was put on the cross and made fun of. They make it happen all over again.

God is pleased with ground which, when it has soaked up rain for a long period, produces a worthwhile crop for the farmers. If that ground only produces stubborn weeds, the effort spent on it has been wasted and it has to be set on fire.

Perhaps I'm putting it too strongly, dear friends. I'm sure you're not as bad as that. You're on the way to becoming healthy and happy Christians. God is fair-minded, and won't forget your love and hard work in the cause. You've been of help to many other Christians and still are. I just want everyone to work as hard as you do, and for you to keep going, so that you achieve your highest hopes. Don't fall into lazy habits, but copy those whose patience and trust have seen God's promises coming true.

When God made a promise to Abraham, there was no one greater than God to make sure the promise would be kept. So Abraham was asked to trust in God's reputation as God. God said, "You have my word. I will bring happiness to you, and you will have a large family." Abraham had to wait patiently for a long time, but the promise was kept. When people make promises, they ask someone better known than they are to back them up. Then they give their solemn word. God wanted to show that a promise from God was just as binding, and could be trusted by those who received it. Those of us who have gone to God for help can confidently depend on two things – God's reliability and God's word. Hope is like an anchor. It keeps our lives steady. Our hope is secure in the center of God's being. That's where Jesus is now. He's gone where we will go one day. He's our vital link, our very own "Righteous Ruler."

7 There is a story in the old books about a mysterious character called "Righteous Ruler." He was the go-between with God for the people of Jerusalem. He met Abraham after Abraham had won a battle against an alliance of four local leaders. He wished Abraham well on behalf of God, and Abraham gave him ten per cent of the takings from the battle. He was the political leader as well as the religious leader of Jerusalem. "Salem" means "peace." So he was both "Righteous Ruler" and "Ruler in Peace." We don't know who his father or mother was or any of his ancestors, nor when he was born or died. That gives him a timeless quality. The same can be said about Jesus, God's Likeness. There's no time limit to

his role as the go-between with God.

Righteous Ruler must have been very important. Even Abraham, the ancestor we all claim, paid a tax to him from the profits of war. The people who are links with God because they are descendants of Levi also have a right by law to collect a percentage of the people's earnings. But this right only applies to their kith and kin – those who have Abraham as a common ancestor. Righteous Ruler was not related in any way to Abraham. Abraham was the one God made promises to. But Righteous Ruler collected tax from Abraham and was in a position to pass on God's best wishes to him. This means he was more important than Abraham. When taxes are paid to members of Levi's family, the money goes to people who only have a limited life span. But the tax paid to Righteous Ruler was paid to one who is timeless. We could stretch a point by saying that when Abraham met Righteous Ruler, Levi, Abraham's great-grandson, paid tax through Abraham, because he existed in Abraham's sperm.

The family of Levi were responsible for giving the Jewish people their book of rules. If rules had been able to make people good, there would have been no need for another link with God on the pattern of Righteous Ruler. Ron would have been good enough! When there is a new link with God, there is a new set of rules. Everything said about Righteous Ruler applies to Jesus. He belonged to a different family from that of Levi. No one from the family of Jesus ever conducted services of worship. Jesus belonged to the family of Judah, and Moses never said anything about that family acting as God's representatives. Everything is made very clear when a new representative arrives, someone who has more in common with Righteous Ruler. He's our new link with God. He isn't qualified by the book of rules, or by family connections, but by the impact of his life and its timeless quality. These words fit Jesus, "You'll always be my go-between, just like Righteous Ruler."

(18) The old rules have been scrapped because they were useless and made nobody any better. We now have much better prospects of getting close to God. This is underlined by a promise. Previous representatives of God promised nothing. God's new representative comes with God's own promise, "God has made a promise and will not go back on it: 'You'll always be my go-between.' " With this promise, Jesus guarantees a better

relationship with God.

There have been lots of people in times past acting as links with God, but in every case death brought their period of service to an end. Jesus is a permanent link because he is alive forever. So he is able to give full life and health to those who come to God through him. He is always there to make sure God knows what we need.

We need someone like this to help us relate to God. Jesus was a good man, his motives were pure, nobody could fault him. He stood out from among all the bad people around him. He has a special place in God's New World. He's not like God's other representatives. He doesn't have to make gifts to God over and over again to say sorry for his wrongdoings and the wrongdoings of his people. Jesus did this all in one go when he gave himself. The people appointed by the book of rules as links with God have failed because of their weaknesses. But on the basis of God's promise, which outdates the book of rules, God's Likeness is our link. He will always be up to the job.

8 We now have a go-between with God who is as close to God as it's possible to be. Jesus is to be found in the true place of worship, which God and not human builders set up. Everyone who acts as a link with God, has the task of leading worship. Worship is a means of giving presents to God. It's essential for a go-between to have something to give. If Jesus were here on earth, there would be rules to stop him being a link with God. Only properly qualified people can make gifts to God. But they lead worship in a place that cannot match the presence of God. When Moses made a tent to worship God in, he had to work from a flimsy pattern he was shown when he went up the mountain. Jesus can do better than that. He brings about a new relationship with God, with much better prospects. If the old relationship with God had been satisfactory, there would have been no need for another one. God says,

> *"I'm going to have a new relationship with my people. It will be quite different from the relationship I had with their ancestors, when I led them like children out of Egypt. They didn't behave like friends to me, so I didn't waste my time*

*with them! I'm going to make a new relationship with my
people one day. They'll know what I want from them without
being told. They'll really be my friends. They won't ram
religion down one another's throats. They'll all know me, no
matter who or what they are. I'll accept them and forget their
past record."*

By talking about a "new relationship," God has made the previous
relationship out of date.

9 The former relationship between God and God's people included
arrangements for worship and a place of worship here on earth.
The first place of worship was a tent. It was fitted with a lamp
stand, a table and some special bread. It was regarded as a special place set
apart for God. Behind a curtain in the tent was the most special place of all.
There was a table overlaid with gold, where the sweet-smelling crystals were
burnt. There was a box, also overlaid with gold, which contained some
relics, including a pot of the mysterious food God's people ate in the desert,
Ron's stick, which once budded into flower, and the stones on which the
Ten Rules were written. They thought this was the place where God sat to
accept the worshipers. It would take too long to describe it all.

When everything was ready, the people appointed as links with God
would go into the first part of the tent and busy themselves with various
duties. Only the chief of their number would enter the inside room and
only once a year, taking some blood as a gift to God. This was the way of
saying sorry for anything the people or their representatives had done to
displease God without knowing it. God's Spirit is teaching us something
about all this. She is saying there is no way through to God for ordinary
people while barriers like that old tent exist. She is also making it clear now
that gifts of animals made to God cannot give anyone peace of mind. The
same applies to rules about food and drink and washing. They are just
empty formalities, which belong to a time before God's new arrangements.

(10) When God's Chosen came, he became the go-between with God
under the new and improved arrangements. The tent Jesus has gone into is
not a physical tent like the old one. He has not taken with him the life-

blood of goats or calves, but his own life, his humanity of flesh and blood. He has only had to do this once to bring freedom for everybody forever. Under the old system, blood and ashes from goats and cattle were sprinkled over those who felt bad about themselves. But it only touched them on the outside. The life of Jesus pleased God in everything. His humanity is presented by the Spirit as a gift to God. This means we can come off the guilt trip caused by those deadly old arrangements and discover the God who enjoys life.

Jesus brings about a new relationship with God. Now God's people can have all the good things God has promised. The death of Jesus has set us free from the defects of the old relationship. When a will is read out, the death of the person who made the will has to be established. The former relationship with God always involved something dying. When Moses told the people all the rules they would have to keep, he took some blood from cattle and goats, mixed it with water, and using a sprinkler made of red wool and reeds, sprinkled some on the book of rules and some on the people. Then he said, "This blood marks the relationship God wants to have with you." Then Moses sprinkled the tent and the cups used in worship. The rules of that old relationship meant that practically everything had to be sprinkled with blood to make it all right. It was thought that only when blood was shed could wrongs be put right.

(23) These were not the best arrangements, though they seemed okay at the time. God has come up with a better idea. God's Chosen did not enter a place of worship built by human beings, a poor attempt to represent what cannot be imagined. Jesus went into the realm beyond time and space, into the very presence of God. He is our representative there. He doesn't have to go over things again and again, like the old links with God had to, year by year in the secret place, with blood taken from another living thing. Jesus does not go through this endless punishing ritual. He has achieved what is necessary all at once, in our own day and age. He's put paid to everything wrong, by giving *himself*. We all have to die. Then our lives are examined by God. God's Chosen also died. His life was acceptable to God, a gift which, at a stroke, made up for the bad behavior of many. Jesus will reappear, not to deal with wrongdoing this time, but to give full life and health to those who are looking forward to seeing him.

10

Life based on rules and regulations is poor by comparison with the life now taking its place. The new life is based on enjoying good things. The old life cannot even be thought of as second best. Those gifts made to God, the same year after year, cannot do anything for those seeking to make something of their lives. If that form of worship worked, why do the worshipers still feel guilty? If they felt forgiven and accepted for all time, they wouldn't have to go on making the same old gifts to God! All that happens, every year, is that they are reminded of their failings. How can blood from animals get rid of your faults? When Jesus lived in our world, he used the words of this old song,

> *"The guilt-filled heart brings you distress;*
> *Unsmiling are your lips;*
> *You're not amused by smoking flesh;*
> *It's me you want, not gifts.*
> *So here I am to do your work,*
> *Just like it says in the wise old book."*

Jesus realized that God does not enjoy the sight of someone feeling guilty, nor how they try to get rid of the feeling by making the gifts the rules demand. Jesus, by offering to work for God, got rid of the need for guilt or gifts. By working in partnership with God, Jesus made it possible for us to become God's people. His gift of himself to God is a gift for all of us forever.

It's sad to think there are still those appointed to be links with God, conducting the same old round of worship day after day. They don't ease anyone's conscience. Jesus offered his life as the final way of tackling the problem of wrongdoing. He is God's champion. It's only a matter of time before evil is defeated. In one act of self-giving, Jesus has put a lasting value on God's people. God's Spirit helps to make all this clear. Remember she said, "I'm going to have a new relationship with my people one day. They'll know what I want from them without being told." Then she went on to say, "I'll forget their past misconduct."

If our faults have been overlooked, we do not need to go on making gifts to God to clear our guilty consciences.

(19) Friends, we should no longer feel nervous in the presence of God.

Jesus has given his life for us. He has torn down the old curtain. He has made a way through to a new and fresh experience of God. Jesus is now the vital link between God and God's people.

So let's go straight into the presence of God, happy and confident. We have nothing to be ashamed of. Our consciences are clear and our bodies are clean. Let's stick to our hope and not dither. God always keeps a promise. Let's help one another to new ways of loving and new ways of doing good. Don't be loners, like some. Keep in touch. We need one another if we are to stay in good heart, especially since we have so little time.

If we keep on going the wrong way after we have been told the right way, what else can be done? It's frightening to think what will become of us if we deliberately make ourselves into God's enemies. It will be hot, that's for sure! Under the old rules that Moses set out, anyone who did anything wrong was put to death, without being given another chance. It only needed two witnesses to give evidence against the offender. So what will it be like for those who have turned their backs on God's Likeness, and treated lightly the gift of life based on the new friendship with God? What happens when you spit on love? God says, "Righting wrongs is my concern. Leave it to me!" We also remember the words, "God knows how to deal with people." God's offer of friendship has a scary side to it.

(32) Remember when you first set out on God's adventure. You had to put up with a lot of trouble, but you came through. Sometimes you were attacked in the streets or had insults shouted at you. Sometimes you bore the pain of watching others being ill treated. You protested about those in prison and your property was confiscated as a result. You happily put up with that because you knew you possessed something better and longer-lasting. So don't throw away your optimism. It will soon be rewarded. Just keep going, in tune with God, and you will reap the benefit God has promised. One of God's speakers said,

> "In just a little while
> The Coming One appears;
> The good survive on trust,
> Though some give in to fears."

We're not going to be the people who disappoint God by giving in to our fears. We're going to be the ones who trust, and so receive God's gift of life.

11

"*Trust*" means putting your confidence where your hopes are; it means believing there is a reality to things beyond what you can see. It was trust that made our ancestors famous. The idea that the universe came about as a result of God's thinking and planning is a matter of trust. What we now see with our eyes, started out from something we can't even imagine.

Abel's gift of worship to God was better than his brother Cain's, because Abel trusted God. Trust made him a good man, and God was pleased with his gifts. Although he died, his trust still inspires us today.

Enoch had that same quality of trust. When his life came to an end, he didn't experience death like the rest of us. He just went to be with God. Before that happened, he was known as God's favorite. That must mean he trusted God. No one can please God otherwise. Anyone who wants to get to know God must trust that God exists, and that God is worth knowing.

Noah is another example of trust. God warned him about what was going to happen, although it didn't seem likely at the time. Noah built a boat to save his family from a flood. Everybody else was made to look foolish. Noah kept the idea alive that goodness has to do with trusting God.

Abraham trusted God too. He took God's advice and set out to find a permanent home for his family. He had no idea where he was going. He had to keep on trusting because, although he spent a long time in the land God had in mind for him, it didn't seem like home. He only had tents to live in. The same was true for Isaac his son, and Jacob his grandson. They shared Abraham's dream. He had a vision of a city built on firm foundations. God would be the architect and the builder.

Sarah, Abraham's wife, was able to have a baby, even though she was past the normal age of having children. That was because she trusted God to keep a promise. Although Sarah and Abraham were coming to the end of their lives, they had as many descendants as there are stars in the sky or pebbles on the beach.

All these people trusted to the last moment of their lives. They didn't see their dreams fulfilled. Just the thought of what would come about one day made them happy. They looked on themselves as refugees. Earth was a foreign land to them. People who have this way of thinking about life are living proof there is another world to discover. The land they left behind was not home for them. They could have gone back any time, if they had wanted to. These were people with a longing for a better home, beyond time and space. God is proud to be linked with them and is getting a place ready for them.

(17) God set a test for Abraham, to see how much he trusted. Abraham offered Isaac's life as a gift to God. Abraham's hope for the future depended on his only son. He had been told, "Isaac will carry on the family name." Abraham trusted that God could make the dead come alive again. In a sort of way, that's what happened.

Isaac trusted by asking God's help in the future for his sons Jacob and Esau. Then Jacob did the same for his grandsons, the sons of Joseph, just before he died. He lent on his stick and bowed down to show his respect for God. When it was Joseph's turn to die, he showed his trust in God by talking about the future escape of his people from Egypt. He even made arrangements so that his remains would not be left behind when it happened.

The parents of Moses had trust in God. They hid Moses for three months after he was born. Their little boy was so beautiful, they lost all fear of the ruler of Egypt and his orders for all male children to be killed.

Moses was a man of trust. When he became an adult, he gave up his privileges as the adopted son of Pharaoh's daughter. He chose to share the persecution God's people were suffering, rather than indulging in selfish pleasures, which soon become boring. He thought it better to anticipate the rough time God's future Chosen One would have, than be a member of Egypt's wealthy upper classes. He pinned his hopes on the future. In trust Moses left Egypt and didn't worry about getting on the wrong side of Pharaoh. Although God cannot be seen, Moses kept his eyes where he believed God to be. In trust, Moses established the festival that recalls his actions to prevent his people dying from a mysterious illness. In trust, God's people found a dry path across the Red Sea. When the Egyptians tried to follow, the tide cut them off. The trust of those who tramped around the walls of Jericho for seven days made the walls collapse.

Barbara was a prostitute whose trust was rewarded. She entertained spies from the Jewish camp and so didn't die with those who had not sided with God.

(32) I could go on and on. But I'm running out of paper. There's a long list of God's friends I'd like to tell you about. They are well-known names in the old books. In a spirit of trust they made conquests, sided with justice, saw their dreams coming true, tamed lions, put out fires, dodged the weapons aimed at them, counted weakness as their strength, triumphed mightily over their enemies. Women who thought their children dead had them back again, alive and well.

On the other hand, some were tortured to death, refusing to say the words that would set them free. They trusted that one day they would know a better kind of freedom. Some were made fools of and beaten up, handcuffed and sent to prison. Some died by having stones thrown at them, some by being mutilated or stabbed. They had no smart clothes to wear. They were among the deprived, the persecuted, the discriminated against. Society didn't deserve to have such fine people in it. Often indeed they were forced to take refuge in the mountains and desert, living in caves and dugouts.

These people were famous for their trust. Yet they didn't see their dreams come true in their lifetime. God has kept the best things for later, so that when we are all ready, we can enjoy them together.

12 Since there are so many spectators watching us from the terraces, let's get our tracksuits off! (Our selfish ways which stick so closely to us.) Let's put all our energy into the race we've been entered for. Let's keep our eyes on Jesus our coach. He knows the course from experience. He was so looking forward to winning the prize, he put up with the pain of the cross and the jeers of the onlookers. Now he has the best seat in the grandstand, next to God.

Think of the example Jesus set you. He took so much spite from bad people. He's an inspiration to you not to get tired or depressed. In your efforts to defeat what's wrong, you've not yet gone so far as to get killed. I wonder if you remember the wise words to children in the old books?

> "Girls and boys, don't get uptight
> When God tries to put you right;

Words and deeds to right your wrong
Show you that God's love is strong,
Mark you as a daughter, son."

Try and cope with difficulties as part of your training. God is treating you like daughters and sons. All good parents train their children. If you can't accept the challenges children have to face in growing up, you aren't God's children but somebody else's. If we respected our parents when they took us to task, shouldn't we respect out spiritual Parent even more? God wants us to have life to the full! Our human parents guided us for a short period of time as best they could. God's guidance is more skillful and puts us on the road to being Godlike. Training is often hard and painful. We don't like it at the time. It's later on we get the reward of being people who are nice to know.

So get on with your exercises – arms up, knees bend! Keep your movements well balanced, so those weak muscles develop their full strength.

Try to get on well with everybody. Only by imitating God will you one day see God. Make sure none of you take lightly what God has done for us all. Make sure you're not the weed that prevents other plants from growing strong. Don't be careless and irresponsible, like Esau who sold his prospects for a bowl of soup. He was sorry for what he'd done afterwards and wanted to put matters right. He cried his eyes out, but it was too late.

(18) There's no mountain for you, like there was for the people of God in olden times. There's nothing obvious to your senses. No erupting volcano, no trumpet sounding, no voice booming out! Those who were there at the time wanted to escape from the experience. Everyone was ordered to keep their distance, including animals, on pain of death. The sight was so terrible that even Moses said, "I'm so afraid, I can't stop shaking."

But you have come to the spiritual mountaintop, the place where God is always present, the God who enjoys life. You've arrived at the permanent home of God's people, the Jerusalem beyond time and space. God's friends are having a party. There are lots of people here, all God's new children, and good people from times past, who now have reached their goal. You have come to God, the one who knows what's right for everybody. Jesus is here, the one who's made possible a new relationship with God. The death of good people like Abel is an inspiration; but the death of Jesus has changed things.

You'd better listen to God this time! If people got into trouble when they refused to listen to the voice speaking from a place on earth, it's even more dangerous to ignore the voice coming from beyond time and space. Last time, the voice caused an earthquake. Now God has said, "Next time I won't just shake the physical world. I'll shake the spiritual world as well."

This "next time" will be a period when everything is challenged. Only what stands the test will survive. Since we've become citizens of a state that cannot be undermined, let's be thankful and give of our very best to God.

Hold your breath. God does everything on a grand scale!

13 Keep on loving one another. Open your homes to the sort of people you wouldn't normally mix with. Some who did that in the past gave shelter to God's agents without realizing it. Care for those in prison. Imagine what it would be like to be in prison yourself. In the same way, share the feelings of those who are in pain.

You must all respect a committed relationship. Partners must be loyal to one another. When they're making love they should be gentle. Anyone breaking up someone else's relationship will have to answer to God.

Don't keep wanting more money. Manage on what you've got. God has said, "I will never go away; I will never let you down." So let's be brave and take these words as our motto:

> "God is my helper;
> I won't be scared;
> How can anyone do me harm?"

Remember the people who showed you the way, those who gave you the Christian message. Think how it made them into really good people. Try to copy them. Jesus can be relied on today and in the future, just as in the past. Don't fall for silly ideas. God's the one who gives us good health. There's no need to go on a special diet. We can eat a wider variety of food than the old religion allowed its followers.

The leaders of the old religion burn the meat they're not allowed to eat, well away from their place of worship. They treated Jesus in the same way, killing him outside the city. His death made us God's people. So let's join Jesus in that place of rejection. We're outcasts from society, like him. We belong to the world's homeless. But we'll have a home one day. Let's join in the new way of worshiping God, by naming Jesus as our Leader. Don't forget to help those in need, and share what you have with others. That's the worship God appreciates.

Follow the advice of those appointed to help you, and show them respect, because they're looking after your long-term welfare and must report to God on your progress. Make sure they have cause to smile and not groan. They can't help you if they're unhappy.

(18) Mention us when you talk with God. We've nothing to hide. We always try to do the right thing. Please ask God to make it possible for me to see you again soon.

The peace-loving God has made possible a lasting relationship with us by bringing Jesus, our Leader, back to life. So I'm asking you to become the complete people who do God's work and do it well. May God also be pleased with the work we are doing. We look to Jesus, God's Chosen One, for help. His fame will last forever!

Friends, I hope you'll read this letter through carefully and find it helpful. It's not very long.

The latest news is that our friend Timothy has been let out of prison. If he gets to me in time, I'll bring him with me when I come to see you.

Give everybody our best wishes. The Christians in Italy send their greetings. God bless you all!